T0373271

MURTY CLASSICAL
LIBRARY OF INDIA

Sheldon Pollock, General Editor

MAGHA

THE KILLING OF SHISHUPALA

MCLI 11

MURTY CLASSICAL LIBRARY OF INDIA

Sheldon Pollock, General Editor

Editorial Board
Monika Horstmann
Sheldon Pollock
Sunil Sharma
David Shulman

MAGHA

माघ

THE KILLING OF SHISHUPALA

Edited and translated by
PAUL DUNDAS

MURTY CLASSICAL LIBRARY OF INDIA

HARVARD UNIVERSITY PRESS

Cambridge, Massachusetts

London, England

2017

Copyright © 2017 by the President and Fellows of Harvard College
All rights reserved
Printed in the United States of America

SERIES DESIGN BY M9DESIGN

Library of Congress Cataloging-in-Publication Data

Names: Māgha, author. | Dundas, Paul, 1952– editor, translator. |
Container of (expression): Māgha. Śiśupālavadha. |
Container of (expression): Māgha. Śiśupālavadha. English.
Title: The killing of Shishupala / Magha ; edited and translated
by Paul Dundas.
Other titles: Murty classical library of India ; 11.
Description: Cambridge, Massachusetts : Harvard University Press, 2017. |
Series: Murty classical library of India ; 11 |
This is a facing-page volume in English and Sanskrit. |
Includes bibliographical references and index.
Identifiers: LCCN 2016015542 | ISBN 978-0-674-66039-7 (cloth)
Subjects: LCSH: Death—Poetry—Early works to 1800. | Krishna (Hindu
deity)—Poetry—Early works to 1800.
Classification: LCC PK3798.M215 S513 2017 | DDC 891/.21—dc23
LC record available at https://lccn.loc.gov/2016015542

CONTENTS

INTRODUCTION

Magha's *mahākāvya,* or "great poem," *The Killing of Shish-upala* has been long acclaimed as one of the most distinguished and elaborate works within the canon of Sanskrit literature. Unfortunately, as with most early Sanskrit poets, virtually nothing can be said with confidence about Magha, and even the century in which he flourished has not been securely established. The brief *praśasti,* or encomiastic description, of Magha's immediate ancestry appended to the conclusion of *The Killing of Shishupala* names the poet's father as Dattaka and describes his grandfather Suprabhadeva as having been a minister in the service of a ruler called Varmala. If this individual is identical with the king named Varmalata mentioned in an inscription from Sirohi dated to 625 C.E., then it is possible to judge Magha to have lived in the second half of the seventh century in what is today the far south of Rajasthan. However, the spelling of the king's name differs in several versions of the *praśasti,* and other evidence could support the conclusion that Magha might possibly be dated around the middle of the eighth century.[1]

There is also uncertainty about Magha's social status and background. Clearly steeped in traditional Sanskrit learning and poetic technique, he may have been a court functionary or a professional poet dependent on patronage, but no reference is made in the *praśasti* to any sort of aristocratic patron or a specific courtly connection. While it is possible that he was an independent man of letters, there is no significant evidence for such an authorial type in early medieval India.[2]

The Narrative of The Killing of Shishupala

Magha's only known work is *The Killing of Shishupala*.[3] In common with the authors of the other early *mahākāvyas*, he uses a well-known plot, transmuting an episode in the great Sanskrit epic the Mahabharata, which in its barest terms depicts a dispute between the five Pandava brothers and their ally Krishna and the latter's kinsman Shishupala.[4] However, as Vallabhadeva states at the outset of his commentary on *The Killing of Shishupala,* the action of the poem takes place at the junction of two world ages, the Dvapara and Kali Yugas, when the universe goes through a jarring period of transition, and the real issues at stake in both Magha's poem and its source are ultimately cosmic in nature, confirming the triumph over demonic power of the deity Vishnu, incarnated as Krishna, and the continuity of the world.[5] The Mahabharata version of the story of the killing of Shishupala is as follows.

Shishupala, king of the Chedis, while present at the sacrifice being performed to confirm the regal authority of Yudhishthira, the eldest of the five Pandava brothers, aggressively refuses to accept the decision that Krishna, their ally, should receive the gift of honor that concludes the ritual. He derides Krishna and the Pandava counselor Bhishma, and the latter responds by praising Krishna's divinity. The tension increases as Shishupala incites the other kings present to disrupt the sacrifice, pointing out the various offenses of Krishna and the Pandavas, including the killing of Jarasandha, the king of Magadha, Shishupala's confederate and patron.

Bhishma then describes Shishupala's monstrous birth as a three-eyed, four-armed freak who, according to a prophecy, would gain normal human form only after having sat in the lap of his eventual killer. This had duly occurred when Shishupala was placed by his mother, the sister of Krishna's father, Vasudeva, in the lap of her nephew. As a boon, Krishna promised his aunt that he would tolerate a hundred crimes perpetrated by her son. Bhishma asserts that Shishupala represents a fragment of the divine Krishna, who must have willed him to endanger his life by boastfulness so he could recover his pristine status.

Shishupala responds by calling on Bhishma to honor appropriately the other kings present at the sacrifice, but Bhishma expresses contempt for them and invites Shishupala to challenge Krishna to a duel, in which he will be killed and thus enter Krishna's body. Shishupala accordingly issues a formal challenge, whereupon Krishna enumerates his manifold misdemeanors, including his futile attempt to marry Rukmini, who had become Krishna's wife, and declares that the permissible number of one hundred crimes has been reached. After listening to further insults, Krishna summarily beheads Shishupala with his discus, and the audience of kings watches as, to heavenly acclamation, his foe's life energy transfers itself into Krishna's body. The funeral rituals are performed for Shishupala, and his son is appointed his successor as king of the Chedis.

In *The Killing of Shishupala* Magha pares down the

Mahabharata's narrative of an attempted disruption of ritual order, while clearly emphasizing at the outset Shishupala's earlier demonic incarnations as Hiranyakashipu and Ravana, which had been described for the first time in the *Viṣṇupurāṇa* (c. fifth century C.E.), the earliest textual description of the developed mythology of the god Vishnu.[6] *The Killing of Shishupala* alludes only in passing to the young Shishupala's encounter with Krishna, his mother's plea, and his subsequent acts of delinquency, and Bhishma's contemptuous appraisal of Shishupala's royal followers is omitted or partially transposed.[7] As well as deploying numerous descriptive set pieces characteristic of the *mahākāvya* genre, Magha introduces other episodes to amplify the Mahabharata's emplotment, most notably the lengthy advice proffered to Krishna by his half brother Balarama and his councillor Uddhava about the appropriate political reaction to Shishupala, the duplicitous speech by a Chedi emissary, the great battle between the Pandava and Chedi armies, and the culminating duel between Krishna and Shishupala. All these narrative events reflect the preoccupations of the highly militarized Hindu aristocracy which most likely represented a substantial part of the original audience for this *mahākāvya*.

The main action of *The Killing of Shishupala* involves only male protagonists—warriors, kings, and a semidivine sage. The lengthy descriptions of the erotic adventures of the anonymous Yadava women in the first half of the poem serve to create a generalized sensual ambience rather than to define characters, providing a counterpart to the second half, in which a narrative of increasing tension relates to ritual, politics, and preparation for war. There the roles of women are purely incidental: as enthusiastic spectators of Krishna's procession through the streets of Indraprastha (13.30–48), a version of a standard trope of the *mahākāvya* genre, or as apprehensive harbingers of the death in battle of their husbands, Shishupala's followers (15.79–95).

The Mahākāvya *Genre*

By the early centuries of the second millennium C.E., *The Killing of Shishupala* was numbered among a group of five *mahākāvyas* that had come to be regarded as the prime representatives of this prestigious mode of poetic composition.[8] Irrespective of exactly when Magha wrote his poem, the *mahākāvya* genre itself had become well established by the seventh century C.E., with its beginnings coinciding with the acceptance (at least in the north of the subcontinent) of Sanskrit in the form codified by the grammarian Panini (c. fourth century B.C.E.) as an elite linguistic vehicle for poetry, drama, philosophy, and a range of intellectual and technical disciplines. The earliest author of what can be recognized as *mahākāvyas* in nascent form was Ashvaghosha (c. second century C.E.) who composed two poems respectively describing the life of the Buddha and the conversion of his half brother Nanda. This writer by his own account employed a stylized poetic idiom with the aim of promoting the Buddhist worldview, and while his works undoubtedly had some influence on his immediate successors, they were to fall out of circulation and be excluded from the wider Sanskrit literary canon.

It is with Kalidasa (c. fifth century C.E.) and Bharavi (c. sixth century C.E.), who both drew on Hindu narrative subjects, that the *mahākāvya* displays most of the generic traits that were to characterize it as a specific literary form for more than a millennium. These two poets deployed, and sometimes devised, an extensive repertoire of thematic conventions and figurative topoi that expanded the stylistic range of preexisting literary sources, most significantly inscriptional royal panegyric, the two great Sanskrit epics, the Mahabharata and the Ramayana, and individual, often anonymously composed stanzaic verses, which may have emerged in a vernacular context.[9] Furthermore, Kalidasa and Bharavi displayed a markedly novel poetic sensibility in their depictions of, for example, emotions and the pleasures of the natural world. Magha can be regarded as consolidating this foundational phase of the *mahākāvya* by fully defining its rhetorical landscape, and *The Killing of Shishupala* came to be a representative model of the genre's possibilities with which later generations of Sanskrit poets were repeatedly to engage, both in reworkings of traditional epic and mythological narratives and in more innovative modes, such as biography and dynastic history.

The Sanskrit *mahākāvya* unquestionably presents problems for modern readers unfamiliar with the genre's background, tone, and conventions, but attempts to define it as analogous to more familiar literary forms are misplaced. In particular, the lazy if common assessment of the *mahākāvya* as representing a variety of epic poetry will immediately frustrate expectations. Leaving aside the question of the transcultural viability of the Western genre category of "epic," a cursory inspection will reveal that the *mahākāvya* typically embodies a narrative logic, linguistic and metrical ingenuity, and sophisticated figurative patterning largely at variance with virtually all types of ancient epic poetry. Furthermore, although the *mahākāvya* is often concerned with the standard epic subjects of kingship and conflict, its royal and warrior protagonists are not depicted in any particularly nuanced fashion, and they generally lack the moral ambivalence and flawed personality verging on the tragic that regularly characterize the heroes of works like the Mahabharata or, in the Western canon, Homer's *Iliad*.[10] Nor is there any preoccupation with the narrative theme of grief and lamentation, whether male or female, that animates so many ancient epic poems.[11]

However, most *mahākāvyas* do undoubtedly possess an epic-like capaciousness. The two earliest Sanskrit literary critics, Bhamaha and Dandin, who may have been nearly contemporary with Magha, provide prescriptive accounts of the ideal *mahākāvya,* in which they identify an array of possible topics and scenarios, apparently reflecting their familiarity with lost as well as extant examples of the genre. In his *Ornament of Poetry* Bhamaha defines a *mahākāvya* as a work composed in *sargas* (loosely, chapters; also often, and rather unhelpfully, called cantos), with its designation as "great" (*mahā*) deriving from its length and its having mighty protagonists and deeds as its subject matter. Typically, Bhamaha asserts, a *mahākāvya* contains descriptions of councils, embassies, expeditions, war, and the good fortune of the poem's hero. Such a poem should be structured around five major plot transitions in the same manner as a drama, should not require much explication, and should conclude auspiciously with the triumph of its protagonist. The plot of a *mahākāvya* must relate to the four traditional aims of man (gain, pleasure, dutiful action, and liberation), conform to the way of the world, and deploy the various aesthetic flavors (*rasa*).[12]

According to Dandin's *Mirror for Poetry*, the subject matter of a *mahākāvya* should be derivative, being taken from epic narrative or some equivalent source, and should describe the virtuous, with its hero being both ingenious and elevated of temperament. Dandin's enumeration of a *mahākāvya's* set pieces is more extensive than Bhamaha's, and includes accounts of cities, oceans, mountains, seasons, sunrise and moonrise, amorous encounters in gardens or by lakes, drinking parties, and passionate lovemaking. He also identifies additional themes, such as separated lovers, marriages, the birth and rise to glory of princes, discussions of matters of state, embassies, armies on the march, battles, and the hero's final triumph.[13]

Bhamaha and Dandin are frustratingly unhelpful about the environment in which an audience would have engaged with an elaborate literary work of the sort they describe. The conventional rendering of *mahākāvya* as "court poem" is hardly precise, since connections between any of the early *mahākāvyas* and specific courtly locations can be made only in approximate terms.[14] Nonetheless, it can be conjectured with reasonable confidence that one of the main functions of a *mahākāvya* such as Magha's was to mirror the cultural ambience and concerns of a royal court and to depict the idealized actions of mythical protagonists in light of the various emotional and social codes that governed the behavior of the aristocrats and courtiers who peopled such surroundings. The early medieval Indian courtly world was one of substantial material splendor in which a highly cultivated aesthetic and intellectual sensibility, intense sensuality, and profound esteem of martial valor were enmeshed with a religiosity attuned to the lively and colorful narratives of the *purāṇas,* the compendia of Hindu mythology that were codified from around the fourth and fifth centuries C.E.[15] Apparently mirroring the opulence and brilliance on the surface of this sophisticated environment, the linguistic contours of the *mahākāvya,* of which *The Killing of Shishupala* is the near-archetypal exemplar, are markedly characterized by the manipulation of outward form embodied in a wide range of elaborate figures of speech and recherché grammatical and lexical usage.

As for the medium through which an audience experienced a *mahākāvya* such as *The Killing of Shishupala,* the absence of manuscripts dating from before the second millennium precludes any clear conclusions about the extent of such poems' early circulation in written form, although it seems clear that a complex genre such as the *mahākāvya* presupposes writing rather than orality as the means and context of poetic composition. However, it is possible that, at the outset and by way of experiment, the author of a *mahākāvya* declaimed or, more likely, sang each verse of his poem in a quasi-performative manner in front of an assembly of *sahṛdayas,* or cultivated aficionados, possibly presided over by a courtier or king versed in the techniques of Sanskrit poetry, pausing for acclamation or critical adjudication before moving on to the next verse.[16] This speculative scenario might explain the presence in *The Killing of Shishupala* of extended episodes dealing with a single narrowly focused and reiterated theme, such as the descriptions of the dust enveloping rival armies on the battlefield, of a sort already found in Kalidasa's *The Dynasty of Raghu* (*Raghuvaṃśa* 7.39–43) and Pravarasena's *The Building of the Causeway* (*Setubandha* 13.49–61) and exploited to striking and lengthier effect by Magha (17.52–69).[17] Rather than viewing such a set piece as involving a miscalculated repetition of subject matter, one might envisage the poet here as similar to a connoisseur of precious stones, inspecting a fine jewel from a variety of perspectives in the presence of like-minded experts, meticulously turning it around to comment on its differing facets before moving on to admire another choice gem from his collection.

The Title of Magha's Mahākāvya

The Sanskrit title of Magha's poem, *Śiśupālavadha,* is encoded, along with the name of its author, in the concluding verse of chapter 19. The critic Kuntaka (c. eleventh century) was to stigmatize this title as prosaic and not conducive to the enhancement of the overall beauty of the *mahākāvya.*[18] While this criticism may be as true for the other early *mahākāvyas* as it is for Magha's poem, it is in fact not entirely certain how best to translate the title *Śiśupālavadha.* The Sanskrit word *vadha* usually denotes "killing," and as the action of the poem appears to climax in the penultimate verse, when Krishna strikes off his foe Shishupala's head with his discus, the title *The Killing of Shishupala* (or some version thereof) has become nearly standard and is accordingly adopted here. However, *vadha* can also mean "death," and given that the very last verse of the poem describes the beheaded Shishupala's life energy merging into Krishna, a culminating moment of transfiguration for an erstwhile demonic career, the alternative translation "The Death of Shishupala" undoubtedly has some merit.

The Killing of Shishupala *as a* Mahākāvya

An often cited Sanskrit verse, of no clear provenance, describes Magha's poetic skills as encompassing and surpassing the attainments of three of his most illustrious predecessors: "Kalidasa is famous for use of simile, Bharavi for gravity, and Dandin for verbal grace; but Magha is master of all three of these qualities."[19]

Leaving aside the merits of Dandin, whose surviving narrative writings represent a form of nonmetrical poeticized prose, there can be no doubt that Magha's poetic style and imagery are frequently more complex than those of the *mahākāvyas* of Kalidasa and Bharavi. Furthermore, Magha employs a range of vocabulary (it is tempting to call it lexical overload) that became near proverbial. However, while *The Killing of Shishupala* is undoubtedly somewhat less accessible than the earlier *mahākāvyas,* this does not imply, as some modern commentators would have it, that Magha is therefore a more "artificial" poet than his celebrated predecessors, since the corollary, a "natural" poet, lacks any serious interpretative value in Sanskrit poetic literature, which consistently privileges the ornate.

The Killing of Shishupala is a poem of twenty chapters consisting (in the edition offered here) of 1,638 verses composed in forty-one different meters. Some of these meters are only used once by Magha and can be viewed as variants of more common metrical structures. While no single meter predominates, the *anuṣṭubh,* a highly flexible verse form consisting of four quarters of eight syllables each, which is standard in the Mahabharata, is used throughout virtually the entirety of chapter 2 and the bulk of chapter 19, the two longest chapters of the poem, where the subject matter evokes the atmosphere of the great epic.[20] The individual verses of Magha's poem can generally stand as self-contained poetic utterances encapsulating one particular moment or observation, but they are also sometimes grouped in extended cumulative series as vehicles for elaborate scenic description or forceful statement, or, less commonly, organized in syntactically linked clusters.[21]

In common with the other authors of *mahākavyas,* Magha deploys an elaborate array of figurative devices (*alaṃkāra*) intended to ornament and enhance language and thus, as the early Sanskrit literary theorists understood it, to represent a heightened, specifically poetic mode of diction. These figures of speech were classified under the generic categories "ornaments of meaning" (*arthālaṃkāra*) and "ornaments of sound" (*śabdālaṃkāra*). The former includes the ubiquitous tropes of simile (*upamā*) and metaphor (*rūpaka*) and others more specific to ancient Indian rhetoric, such as "substantiation" (*arthāntaranyāsa*) in which a specific example is supported by a general observation.[22] Most noteworthy among the ornaments of meaning, and a source of some difficulty for modern readers, is *śleṣa*, literally "embrace (of two meanings)," a form of wordplay going far beyond the implications of the conventional renderings of the term as "paronomasia" or "punning." This "extreme poetry," as it has been styled, is intended to subvert the reader's or listener's expectations, sometimes amplifying and reinforcing the primary denotation of a verse, sometimes destabilizing and reversing it, and sometimes yielding a totally variant register of meaning, as in chapter 16 of *The Killing of Shishupala*, where a devious ambassador conveys simultaneously an emollient and a hostile message.[23]

While ornaments of sound occur relatively infrequently in the poems of Ashvaghosha and Kalidasa, from Bharavi's time they came to occupy an increasingly prominent formal position in the *mahākāvya*, and Magha skillfully exploits the Sanskrit language's rich phonetic texture to produce aesthetic effects that defy adequate translation. For example, in every third verse of the fourth chapter of *The Killing of Shishupala* (and randomly elsewhere in the poem) he employs intricate rhyming effects called "twinning" (*yamaka*), based on Sanskrit's easy susceptibility to resegmentation and regrouping of clusters of words and their constituent phonetic elements in order to generate alternative meaning.[24] One straightforward example may suffice to convey how this figure functions. The first line of 4.3 (a description of Mount Raivataka) contains a *yamaka* that can be identified by underlining: *krāntaṃ rucā kāñca-*_navaprabhājā_ _navaprabhājā_labhṛtāṃ maṇīnām. Here the identical groups of phonemes are to be respectively grouped as *kāñcana-vapra-bhājā,* "(possessed by the luster) pervading its golden slopes" and *nava-prabhā-jālabhṛtām,* "(of jewels) endowed with a mass of fresh brilliance."

A more marked example of this formalism occurs throughout chapter 19, where Magha, expanding Bharavi's techniques, deploys what poetic theoreticians came to call "brilliant poetry" (*citrakāvya*), as a linguistic echoing of the organized chaos of battle. A range of verses in this chapter are made up of words with a highly restricted range of phonemes, often producing a staccato or drumming-like rhythm, or they are structured across lines in conformity to predetermined patterns, such as the wrap-around "binding of a drum" (*murajabandha*) or the zigzag "urinating of a grazing cow" (*gomūtrikā*).[25]

The Killing of Shishupala contains a substantial number of the themes and settings prescribed for a *mahākāvya* by the critics Bhamaha and Dandin. Indeed Magha structures his poem around a series of such kaleidoscopically vivid representations of urban, natural, erotic, and martial scenes that the central narrative of Shishupala's enmity toward Krishna and the Pandava brothers is at times totally occluded. Although the principal theme of the poem ensures that it is not lacking in solemnity at significant moments in the plot, perhaps the most striking feature of *The Killing of Shishupala* is a pervasive playfulness and lightheartedness. These qualities can be found even in the culminating bloody battlefield scenes that are described with an exuberant gusto, but they are most evident in chapters 7 to 10, which elaborately depict the highly charged erotic interaction of the Yadava men and women within the setting of Mount Raivataka, whose terrain is envisaged by Magha as a type of fantasy pleasure park. The outing to a lake by the Yadavas, the subject of chapter 8, is like a choreographed scene from a Bollywood extravaganza, involving sly glances, voyeuristic gazing by men, rivalry between cowives, splashing water, and revealingly wet garments, while the drinking party elaborately described in chapter 10 takes place in a realm of languid sensuality, artfulness, and wit.[26]

Numerous allusions to traditional branches of learning, such as grammar, the ancient Indian intellectual discipline par excellence, occur throughout *The Killing of Shishupala* and might strike some modern readers as intrusively incongruous.[27] However, these learned references would most likely have been viewed by Magha's immediate audience as further examples of poetic playfulness, redolent of the all-embracing nature of the *mahākāvya* genre and the common intellectual culture linking poet and connoisseurs. A less obvious example of Magha's learning worthy of mention is his frequent reference to elephants and their behavior.[28] Although elephants had no doubt been employed by rulers for ceremonial and military purposes long before the beginning of the Common Era, by the time of Kautilya's *Arthaśāstra* (c. second–third century C.E.) identifying characteristics of these animals, training them, ensuring their health, and understanding how to deploy them in battle had become an important branch of practical knowledge.[29] While clearly familiar with the technical vocabulary of "elephant science" (*gajaśāstra*), Magha can also sympathetically convey the varying experiences of elephants, whether casually destroying the jungle while on the march, playing in rivers, wistfully recalling life in the forest before they were captured, or experiencing the horror of mutilation and slaughter on the battlefield. *The Killing of Shishupala* is perhaps the first extended Sanskrit literary work to highlight not just the military importance of the war elephant in ancient India but also the animal's personality, prowess, and frequent suffering.

Krishna in The Killing of Shishupala

The immediate literary influence on *The Killing of Shishupala* can be judged to have been the *mahākāvya* by Bharavi, *Arjuna and the Hunter* (*Kirātārjunīya*).[30] That poem describes how the Pandava hero Arjuna attempts to win divine weapons from the god Shiva, who has disguised himself as a fierce hill tribesman, and culminates in a description of a great duel, at the conclusion of which the deity reveals himself in his true form to grant his opponent the boon he seeks. *The Killing of Shishupala,* which also has a duel at its climax but instead exalts Krishna, the incarnation of the god Vishnu, might be regarded as a deliberate counterpart to *Arjuna and the Hunter* and its lauding of Shiva.[31]

Like *Arjuna and the Hunter, The Killing of Shishupala* commences with the auspicious word *śrī,* and the final verse of every chapter of the poem also incorporates this as a kind of signature.[32] The eleventh-century scholar-king Bhoja claimed that *The Killing of Shishupala* was in essence about counsel, and the poem does undoubtedly exemplify the nature of good and bad policy as represented, respectively, by Krishna and Shishupala.[33] However, it is the concept of *śrī* that provides a particularly apt master theme for Magha's *mahākāvya*. As an abstract noun, *śrī* embodies a nexus of notions that pertain to majesty, prosperity, and auspiciousness. Every early Indian ruler was perceived ideally as being intimately connected with *śrī*, which both served as a necessary underpinning of his regal behavior and was itself the product of dutiful kingship.[34] Prominent manifestations of *śrī*, such as political acumen, orderly governance of the capital city and its populace, due attention to the requirements of sacrificial ritual, disbursement of wealth to Brahmans, and honorable martial endeavor, are accordingly foregrounded throughout *The Killing of Shishupala*, serving a literary function as much didactic as aesthetic.

Unlike Yudhishthira, the eldest of the Pandava brothers, whose sacrifice to confirm his royal status is the flashpoint for the climactic battle in the poem, Krishna, a prince of the Yadava clan, is not actually a fully consecrated king, as his adversary Shishupala, king of the Chedis, sarcastically points out in order to justify his own inimical stance toward him (15.15, 20–22, and 27). Nonetheless, Krishna is closely associated with *śrī* in a very specific manner. In many early iconic representations of Vishnu, of whom Krishna is an earthly manifestation, the god's chest is adorned with the diamond-shaped hair-whorl of the *śrīvatsa*, or "mark of *śrī*," which is indicative of his divine majesty. As Vaishnava Hinduism took shape in the first millennium C.E., *śrī* became deified as the goddess Shri, who has the role of Vishnu's consort. So Magha refers to Krishna as husband of Shri, who clings to his chest in a wifely embrace (2.118 and 3.12, and 13.11), thus establishing his continuing identity as Vishnu, the divine creator and protector.

Krishna is more broadly portrayed throughout *The Killing of Shishupala* as representing the two main manifestations of Vishnu found in the *purāṇas:* a transcendent yogic god envisaged as the primal being overseeing the universe, and an interventionist deity who saves the world through a series of "descents" (*avatāra*), or incarnations.[35] At the same time, Magha alludes on several occasions to what was to become an increasingly significant aspect of Krishna, adumbrated for the first time in the Mahabharata and greatly expanded in the *Harivaṃśa* (a kind of narrative supplement to the great epic), as a pastoral figure who engages in love affairs with cowherd girls, miraculously protects the cattle he is guarding by holding a mountain above them, and is, above all, the youthful slayer of demons and Kamsa, the evil king of Mathura.[36] However, as opposed to his depiction in the Mahabharata, Krishna is given very little to say in the course of *The Killing of Shishupala,* actually speaking only in chapters 1, 2, and 13, and he is barely present at all as an agent in many chapters of the poem. Prior to the full manifestation of his divine heroism in chapters 19 and 20, his character and nature are largely defined by other protagonists in eulogistic terms, or by misguided abuse, as when Shishupala and subsequently his emissary denounce him in chapters 15 and 16. Throughout the poem a controlled reticence and restraint characterize Krishna, most strikingly in the course of his final violent encounter with Shishupala.[37] While occasional references are made to Krishna's amorous activity with court ladies (for example, at 3.13), and his sexual allure brings the women of Indraprastha flocking to ogle him (13.30–48), it is his Yadava followers who engage in the uninhibited pleasures of lovemaking and wine drinking.

By contrast with Krishna, Shishupala's demonic nature ensures that he is conspicuously lacking in both self-control and self-knowledge. Balarama points out in passing (2.38; see also 20.6) that Shishupala may have been harboring a genuine grievance because Krishna had taken Rukmini to wife, despite the fact she had been promised to Shishupala. However, Shishupala himself does not dwell on this in his diatribe in chapter 15; instead he scorns Krishna as a confidence trickster who refuses to acknowledge the claims of his betters. *The Killing of Shishupala* frequently evinces a strong devotional tenor, but it is not a "religious" poem as such. Significantly, Magha does not introduce a significant theological theme found in the *purāṇas*' treatment of the narrative that would interpret Shishupala's obsessive antagonism toward Krishna as being in reality a form of piety, informed by his intense preoccupation with the god, which ultimately brings deliverance.[38] However, the mingling of the beheaded Shishupala's life energy with Krishna at the very end of *The Killing of Shishupala* signifies not just the victory of the hero over his foe, the sole appropriate ending for a *mahākāvya* as stipulated by the early Indian poetic theorists. Shishupala's death is itself also a kind of triumph, for his beginningless round of rebirths has come to an end, and the cosmic disruption he represented has been demonstrated to have no absolute or continuing status.

By reconfiguring the mythology of Krishna, first established by the epic and puranic tradition, within the ornate poetic conventions of the elite genre of the Sanskrit *mahā-kāvya,* Magha definitively confirmed the centrality of this divine figure in Vaishnava Hinduism in the concluding centuries of the first millennium C.E. At the same time, *The Killing of Shishupala* is a unique literary work of elaborate and coruscating imagination, dealing with universally engrossing cultural themes such as sex, war, and the natural world, that deserves to be encountered purely on its own aesthetic terms. At a time when there is increasing openness to premodern India's artistic achievement and the manifold literary modes couched in Sanskrit and other Indian languages, it is appropriate to offer the first complete English rendering of Magha's celebrated *mahākāvya.*

Acknowledgments

I must thank Sheldon Pollock for inviting me to contribute this volume to the Murty Classical Library of India and for giving me a great deal of profitable advice about how best to produce it. Seldom can anyone have had such an encouraging, good-humored, and scholarly editor. Dàniel Balogh was an exemplary proofreader of the Sanskrit text who saved me from many slips. I would like to record my gratitude to two former Edinburgh Sanskritists, Peter Bisschop and John Brockington, for having provided an enriching collegial atmosphere, alas, no longer accessible to me.

This volume is for Rowan Flett; her love and support have been essential ingredients in bringing it to completion.

NOTES

1   See Kielhorn 1908 and Lienhard 1984: 187–188. It is uncertain whether the *praśasti* was composed by Magha himself. Of the two most important commentators on *Shishupala*, Vallabhadeva and Mallinatha, only the former comments on the *praśasti*.

2   Indian scholars sometimes invoke a Jain tradition recorded by the fourteenth-century chronicler Merutunga that claims Magha was a scholar who died in poverty owing to his excessive generosity, but there is no corroborative evidence for this. See Merutuṅga 1901: 48–52.

3   Fourteen verses attributed to Magha are found in various anthologies of Sanskrit poetry compiled in the medieval period. These may be judged to be variants or supplementary verses associated with *The Killing of Shishupala* that have not been included in currently accessible recensions. See Trynkowska 2007.

4   *Mahābhārata* 2.33–42. See *Mahābhārata* 1975: 97–104. The centuries-long development of the Mahabharata can be regarded as effectively concluded by the fifth century C.E. See Couture and Chojnacki 2014: 45–48 for a portion of the Mahabharata vulgate version of the Shishupala episode. The wider epic context of Shishupala's alliance with Jarasandha, king of Magadha, his sins, his disruption of Yudhishthira's sacrifice, and his death are discussed in Brockington 2002 and 2010, Dumézil 1983: 51–69, and Minkowski 2001.

5   Magha refers throughout his poem to the cataclysmic tempest and conflagration that arise as the universe enters the final phase of this particular epoch.

6   *Viṣṇupurāṇa* 4.15.1–8.

7   For example, at *Mahābhārata* 2.41.25 Bhishma states that he does not count Shishupala's followers as worth a straw, while at *The Killing of Shishupala* 15.61 these followers are portrayed as deriding Krishna in the same terms. See *Mahābhārata* 1975: 103.

8   On the five "canonical" *mahākāvyas*—Kalidasa's *The Birth of the Prince* (*Kumārasaṃbhava*) and *The Dynasty of Raghu* (*Raghuvaṃśa*), Bharavi's *Arjuna and the Hunter* (*Kirātārjunīya*), Magha's *The Killing of Shishupala*, and, Shriharsha's *The Adventures of Nala* (*Naiṣadhīyacarita*)—see Patel 2014: 59. These *mahākāvyas* may have been grouped together because of a commentarial tradition that facilitated understanding of their difficulties. See

Hahn 2013: i. The group is sometimes increased to six poems with the addition of Bhaṭṭi's *The Killing of Ravana* (*Rāvaṇavadha*), c. seventh century, a work famous for its systematic deployment of a wide range of grammatical forms but stylistically very close to the Mahabharata and Ramayana. See Bronner, Shulman, and Tubb 2014: parts II and III; Lienhard 1984: 161–196; and Smith 1985 on the *mahākāvya* genre in general, and Patel 2014 and Peterson 2003 for studies of two major examples. The Polish study by Trynkowska (2004b) is the only recent full-length discussion of the literary context of *The Killing of Shishupala*. Tenshe 1972 examines Magha's *mahākāvya* from a largely linguistic perspective.

9   See Ali 2004: 78–85. Scholarship has yet to assess adequately the role played in the establishment of the *mahākāvya* genre and its conventions by extended, linguistically complex poems from the first half of the common millennium in Prakrit, an alternative literary language to Sanskrit that eventually lost its prestige as a poetic medium. The earliest of these Prakrit poems to survive in complete form is *The Building of the Causeway* (*Setubandha*) by Pravarasena (fifth century C.E.), who seems to have been a contemporary of Kalidasa. For Kalidasa's literary connection to the Buddhist poet Ashvaghosha, see Tubb 2014a: 75–80.

10   For all Shishupala's quasi-heroic bravado displayed in chapters 15, 19, and 20 of *The Killing of Shishupala*, his character is depicted by Magha in unambiguously negative terms.

11   The distress of the wives of Shishupala's followers is presented at 15.79–95 in the form of a series of ill omens predictive of imminent disaster, rather than as a reaction to the deaths of their husbands.

12   Bhamaha, *Kāvyālaṅkāra* 1.19–23.

13   Dandin, *Kāvyādarśa* 1.14–18.

14   Kalidasa's generally accepted connection with the Gupta court is based as much on inference and tradition as actual historical evidence. Bharavi is usually regarded as having flourished in south India, but there is uncertainty about which royal house provided this poet with employment. See Bharavi 2016: ix. His patron may in fact have been Yashodharman (also known as Vishnuvardhana), the Aulikara king whose capital was Dashapura in the region of Malwa in western India. See Bakker 2014: 35–37. For the connections between the Sanskrit language, literary culture, and political power in ancient India, see Pollock 2006.

15 See Ali 2004.

16 The Sanskrit term for such a poet is *kavi*. The verses ushering in the morning that constitute chapter 11 of *The Killing of Shishupala* are intoned by *vaitālikas*, approximately "bards," responsible for punctuating the salient moments of the royal day and eulogizing their lord. See also 5.67.

17 Magha is able to draw on the extensive resources of the Sanskrit lexicon, which has several words for "dust," such as *pāṃsu, rajas,* and *reṇu,* along with poetic kennings like *maruddhvaja,* literally "wind's banner." Further semantic depth is provided by *rajas* that can polyvalently signify "pollen," "passion," and "menstruation." See Lienhard 2007: 392–395.

18 Kuntaka, *Vakroktijīvita* 4.24 autocommentary, p. 281.

19 See Patel 2014: 94–95.

20 The second most common meter is *upajāti,* a hybrid metrical form that is used throughout chapters 3 and 12, with the exception of their concluding verses. See the Hindi introduction to the edition of Musalgāonkara 2006: 71–72 for a conspectus of the meters employed in *The Killing of Shishupala,* and Cappeller 1915: 182–185 for a description of twenty-six of these. Morgan 2011: 74–189 analyzes the formal structure of many of the meters employed by Magha. Velankar 1948–49 places Magha's metrical usage in the context of that of other major Sanskrit poets.

21 See, for example, 7.7–11 and 53–56 for series of verses depicting miniscenes, or 7.62–68, and 19.26–29 and 83–87 for verses grouped together in extended descriptions. Magha also regularly deploys repetitions of vocabulary or synonyms to bind groups of verses together. See Trynkowska 2004b: 188.

22 See 1.67 for an example of this type of figure of speech, which occurs throughout *The Killing of Shishupala.* Cappeller 1915: 186 identifies the figures of speech used most commonly by Magha, while Gerow 1971 provides descriptions of them.

23 On "extreme poetry," see Bronner 2010. For a survey of varieties of *śleṣa,* see Gerow 1971: 288–306; for a study of an extended Sanskrit narrative poem with simultaneous meanings throughout, see Brocquet 2010. See also Note on the Text and Translation.

24 See Tubb 2014b: 173–189, 190–192 for Magha's use of *yamaka* in chapters 4 and 19. Magha also employs *yamaka* in chapter 6. For a survey of varieties of *yamaka,* see Gerow 1971: 223–238.

25 See Hahn 2007 and Lienhard 2007: 133–157 and 173–189 for detailed descriptions and positive assessments of *citrakāvya*.

26 Magha compares the Yadava women to actresses at 8.63 and 9.79.

27 See, for example, 2.112, 10.15, 14.66, 16.80, and 19.75.

28 Most notably at 5.30–52, 12.45–50 and 58–62, 17.35–39, 18.26–51 and 56–58.

29 See Edgerton 1985 and Trautmann 2015: 50–215.

30 Magha appears to assert his superiority to Bharavi by playing on his own and his predecessor's names; see 6.62. For *The Killing of Shishupala's* extensive intertextual engagement with Bharavi's *mahākāvya* in terms of narrative structure, episodic detail, and figurative usage, see Jacobi 1970 and Tubb 2014b: 171–176 and 190–193. Bharavi 2016 is a complete English translation of *Arjuna and the Hunter*.

31 Shishupala's original manifestation as described in the Mahabharata can be regarded as a version of Shiva.

32 The Prakrit poets Sarvasena (fourth century C.E.) and Pravarasena (fifth century C.E.) seem to have inaugurated the practice of signing the end of each chapter with an emblematic word. Bharavi employs the word *lakṣmī*, synonymous with *śrī*, in the concluding verse of every chapter of *Arjuna*.

33 See Sudyka 2002–2003: 536.

34 See Hara 1996–1997.

35 For the initial phase of the evolution of the mythology of Krishna, see Schmid 2010, and for the early textual articulation of three incarnations of Vishnu (the Boar, the Man-Lion, and the Dwarf) mentioned in *The Killing of Shishupala*, see Saindon 2009. For the development of the relationship between Vishnu and Krishna in the *Harivaṃśa* and the *Viṣṇupurāṇa*, central works of Vaishnava mythology and theology that inform Magha's treatment of the two deities throughout his *mahākāvya*, see Matchett 2001: 23–106.

36 See Couture 1991 and 2015: 163–313, Couture and Chojnacki 2014: 21–76, and Matchett 2001: 44–64.

37 McCrea 2014 proposes a reading of *The Killing of Shishupala* in terms of the tension embodied in Krishna as a self-conscious divine figure who is essentially inactive and as a human incarnation temporarily obliged to follow a course of political and martial action. See also Trynkowska 2002–2003.

38 See Sheth 1999.

NOTE ON THE TEXT
AND TRANSLATION

No critical edition of the Sanskrit text of *The Killing of Shishupala* has as yet been produced, and the multitude of manuscripts available would undoubtedly make the production of such an edition a difficult undertaking. The text I have prepared for this volume is based on the recension transmitted by the tenth-century Kashmiri commentator Vallabhadeva rather than the better known version from the fourteenth century by Mallinatha, the most celebrated commentator on the canonical *mahākāvyas*.[1]

Vallabhadeva's commentary on *The Killing of Shishupala* is the oldest available, although he makes clear that he was familiar with earlier, now lost commentaries on the poem whose authors he refers to by name and whose readings he occasionally adduces (for example, at 10.20 and 20.54). My reliance on Vallabhadeva's version of the text rather than Mallinatha's does not derive simply from his chronological priority, for it is questionable whether he invariably provides direct access to Magha's poem in its most pristine form. However, investigations into the textual tradition of Kalidasa's *mahākāvya, The Dynasty of Raghu* (*Raghuvaṃśa*), have demonstrated that in at least one significant case Mallinatha most likely reworked or edited portions of the text on which he was commenting to smooth over perceived infelicities.[2] The nature of many of the frequent discrepancies between Vallabhadeva's recension and that of Mallinatha suggests that the latter may have refashioned the text of the *The Killing of Shishupala* in a similar manner. I have deemed it judicious on several occasions to follow Mallinatha's version of the text, but when a discrepancy with Vallabhadeva's recension does arise, it is impossible to guarantee that Mallinatha transmitted a genuinely valid reading as opposed to an "improvement" of his own devising. The small number of variants signaled in the notes to the text have been selected on the basis of their perceived merit or interest rather than the weight of manuscript testimony.[3]

The one major divergence between the recensions of Vallabhadeva and Mallinatha requires comment. In chapter 15 of Vallabhadeva's recension there occurs a lengthy speech by Shishupala in which an ostensible message of insult to Krishna is subverted, through wordplay, by an encomium couched in the vocabulary of the dualist Samkhya philosophical system (which by Magha's time had assumed a theistic dimension), in which the speaker simultaneously but unknowingly reveals himself as a devotee of Vishnu-Krishna. Mallinatha's recension contains at the same point in the poem a speech by Shishupala that is equally mordant in its mockery of Krishna's status and deeds, but slightly shorter and without any extensive wordplay (15.14–39).[4] On the basis of manuscript and stylistic evidence, a good case can be made for Mallinatha's version being the original, or at least near to it, and it has accordingly been adopted here.[5]

The earliest translation of any portion of *The Killing of Shishupala* was Sutherland's English version of the opening twenty verses of the first chapter, published in 1839. The first complete translation attempted in a European language seems to have been that published in French in 1863 by Hippolyte Fauche, who, at the beginning of his introduction, characterized the poem as "fort difficile à comprender, fort difficile à traduire" (very difficult to understand, very difficult to translate), a judgment few would deny. Fauche's pioneering effort was undoubtedly heroic, but it was produced at a time when critical understanding and appreciation of the Sanskrit *mahākāvya* and its conventions were in their infancy, and as a result of its many misapprehensions of the poem this rendering now has little more than antiquarian interest. Carl Cappeller's German version of 1915, while containing some useful annotation, restricts itself to excerpts from only twelve of the poem's twenty chapters. A complete German translation, published by Eugen Hultzsch in 1926, provides much help in understanding the complexities of Magha's diction, but it has remained little known even to scholarly specialists.

The Killing of Shishupala has not fared well in English since Sutherland's rendering of a tiny portion of the poem, and what translations there are have been confined to very literal versions of the opening chapters, produced for the aid of Indian university students studying Sanskrit literature.[6] The version offered here is in straightforward prose, through which I hope readers will gain some appreciation of the color and imaginative brilliance of Magha's recreation of the story of Krishna and Shishupala.

One significant problem for the translator of *The Killing of Shishupala* must be acknowledged, namely Magha's regular use of *śleṣa*, "polysemy", as a form of wordplay.[7] This can range from individual words that have more than one sense to entire verses that generate an elaborate alternative meaning, sometimes markedly at variance with their *prakṛtārtha,* or "primary meaning." I have tried to signal in the notes where wordplay takes place, while in the translation I have taken a pragmatic approach to the more complex examples, judging each on its merits.[8] So, for example, at 2.74 the *aprakṛtārtha,* or "secondary meaning," amplifies the primary meaning and has been integrated into the translation, whereas at 2.86 the secondary sense does not fully mesh with the primary meaning, at least so far as the translation is concerned, and locating it in the supporting note serves the purposes of the reader better.

NOTES

1   For Vallabhadeva's recension and commentary I use the 1990 printing of the 1935 edition by Ram Candra Kak and Harabhatt Shastri. Hultzsch (1926: 226–241) identifies discrepancies between Mallinatha's recension and a Kashmiri *śāradā*-script manuscript of Vallabhadeva's recension. Rau 2012 discusses the textual tradition of Vallabhadeva's recension in some detail; see also Zadoo 1947. For Vallabhadeva's background and significance as a commentator, see Goodall and Isaacson 2003: xv–xxi. For Mallinatha's recension and commentary I use the ninth edition by Durgaprasad and Shivadatta (1927), revised by Wasudev Laxman Shastri Panshikar. The most commonly used edition of Mallinatha's recension in India today is that of Gajananshastri Musalgaonkara (1998), published by Chaukhamba Sanskrit Bhawan, of which I have used the second printing from 2006. For details of other Indian editions and a selection of manuscripts, see Bronner and McCrea 2012: 452–453.

2   See Goodall 2001.

3   I have silently corrected obvious misprints in Kak and Shastri's (1990) text. Mallinatha's recension provides on two occasions (3.22 and 30) readings which appear to adjust, without altering

meaning, metrically incorrect forms in V's recension. The first of these may be an editorial error (Dániel Balogh, personal communication).

4   The version with wordplay occurs at 15.13–55 of Vallabhadeva's recension as edited by Kak and Shastri, with a commentary that appears to be inauthentic. The non-Kashmiri manuscript tradition of Vallabhadeva's recension contains both versions of Shishupala's diatribe.

5   See Bronner and McCrea 2012 and Salomon 2014. The reason Shishupala's unambiguous denigration of Krishna is replaced in Vallabhadeva's recension of the poem need not be ascribed to misgivings about possible blasphemy, a concept that had no obvious linguistic or cultural correlate in early India. Certainly the abuse of Krishna found in the Mahabharata's version of this episode seems never to have been expunged from transmitted versions of that epic. However, it may be relevant that mockery of Hindu deities, of a style similar to that in Vallabhadeva's version of Shishupala's diatribe, was a staple of Jain sectarian satire. The most celebrated example of this type of polemic was the *Dhuttakkhāṇa* (Lowlife Tales) by the c. eighth century C.E. Jain monk Haribhadrasuri, who came from the same region of southern Rajasthan with which Magha can plausibly be associated. See Krümpelmann 2000. Even before Haribhadrasuri's time, Krishna had been absorbed into Jain mythology in the role of a morally flawed layman who is eventually reborn in hell, a destiny that may be alluded to in *The Killing of Shishupala,* 15.31 and 16.8. See Dundas 2000: 95–97. Indeed a tradition, chronologically unsustainable but reflecting later uncertainty about Magha's date and social identity, came to circulate among the Jains that the author of *The Killing of Shishupala* was a cousin of another celebrated Jain monk who flourished in southern Rajasthan, the allegorical novelist Siddharshi (tenth century). See Klatt 1890 and 14.63 note.

Whether Magha was connected by Vallabhadeva and other commentators with the Jain style of satirizing Hindu divinities cannot be established decisively. However, it may well have seemed to some later Vaishnava readers of *The Killing of Shishupala,* whether in Kashmir or elsewhere, that the unambiguous insults directed at aspects of Krishna's divinity in chapter 15 were a little too close to Jain sectarian satire for comfort. An appropriate strategy may then have been to replace this passage of the poem with another version in which Krishna's divine status could be confirmed through wordplay, with the alteration being effected in a changed theological environment in which the malignity of Shishupala's disposition had come to represent a form of unwitting devotion. By contrast, while chapter 16 also contains fierce denunciation of Krishna and his activities, on this occasion by Shishupala's emissary, such a lengthy and fully integrated episode could hardly have been altered without extensive reconfiguration of this section of the poem.

6   See Bhandare 2010.
7   See Introduction.
8   I base my renderings of wordplay on the interpretations of Vallabhadeva and Mallinatha.

CHAPTER 1

Narada's Message

श्रियः पतिः श्रीमति शासितुं जग-
ज्जगन्निवासो वसुदेवसद्मनि ।
वसन्ददर्शावतरन्तमम्बरा-
द्धिरण्यगर्भाङ्गभुवं मुनिं हरिः ॥

गतं तिरश्चीनमनूरुसारथे:
प्रसिद्धमूर्ध्वं ज्वलनं हविर्भुज: ।
पतत्यधो धाम विसारि सर्वतः
किमेतदित्याकुलमीक्षितं जनैः ॥

चयस्त्विषामित्यवधारितं पुर-
स्ततः शरीरीति विभाविताकृतिम् ।
विभुर्विभक्तावयवं पुमानिति
क्रमादमुं नारद इत्यबोधि सः ॥

नवानधो ऽधो बृहतः पयोधरा-
न्समूढकर्पूरपरागपाण्डुरम् ।
क्षणं क्षणोत्क्षिप्तगजेन्द्रकृत्तिना
स्फुटोपमं भूतिसितेन शम्भुना ॥

Majesty's lord, Vishnu, containing the whole world
    within himself, had taken up residence as Krishna
    in Vasudeva's* majestic palace to rule that world in
    person.[1] There he saw the son of Golden Embryo,† the
    sage Narada,‡ descending from the sky.

"The sun journeys across the heavens, while all know
    that the flame of fire the offering-eater races upward.
    But here is light streaming down, diffusing itself
    everywhere. What can it be?" None could make sense
    of this apparition.

As for Krishna, first he reckoned the brilliance to be
    clustering sunbeams, then realized that it was taking
    physical shape, until finally, as separate limbs became
    discernible, he grasped that it was actually a man. So
    he recognized by degrees that Narada had come.

Narada, pale as fine camphor powder, was approaching
    beneath looming banks of storm clouds; for an instant
    he seemed to be Shiva, all silvery with funeral-ground
    ashes after throwing off his elephant-skin cape in his
    wild dance.[2]

---

* Krishna's father.
† Brahma, the god of creation.
‡ An intermediary between the divine and human worlds and
  inventor of the vina or lute.

५ दधानमम्भोरुहकेसरद्युती-
जटाः शरच्चन्द्रमरीचिरोचिषम् ।
विपाकपिङ्गास्तुहिनस्थलीरुहो
धराधरेन्द्रं व्रततीततीरिव ॥

पिशङ्गमौञ्जीयुजमर्जुनच्छविं
वसानमेणाजिनमञ्जनद्युति ।
सुवर्णसूत्राकलिताधराम्बरां
विडम्बयन्तं शितिवाससस्तनुम् ॥

विहङ्गराजाङ्घ्रुहैरिवाततै-
र्हिरण्यमयोर्वीरुहवल्लितन्तुभिः ।
कृतोपवीतं हिमशुभ्रमुच्चकै-
र्घनं घनान्ते तडितां गुणैरिव ॥

निसर्गचित्रोज्ज्वलसूक्ष्मपक्ष्मणा
लसद्विसच्छेदसिताङ्गसङ्गिना ।
चकासतं चारुचमूरुचर्मणा
कुथेन नागेन्द्रमिवेन्द्रवाहनम् ॥

अजस्रमास्फालितवल्लकीगुण-
क्षतोज्ज्वलाङ्गुष्ठनखांशुभिन्नया ।
पुरः प्रवालैरिव पूरितार्धया
विभान्तमच्छस्फटिकाक्षमालया ॥

His matted ascetic's hair gray as lotus filaments, his body   5
    white as autumnal moonbeams, he seemed just like
    the Himalaya mountain, its snowy slopes festooned
    with age-hoared creeper strands.

His belt of tawny *muñja* grass, his complexion pallid as an
    arjuna flower, and his kohl-black antelope-skin cloak
    all made Narada appear to be dark-clad Balarama[3]
    wearing a gold cord knotted around his robe.

He bore a sacred thread[4] of tendrils culled from a golden
    tree, like the outstretched wings of Garuda, king of
    birds; dazzling as a snowdrift, he seemed like a cloud
    on high flecked by flashing lightning at the rainy
    season's end.

He was draped in a handsome deer pelt, fine-haired,
    dappled, and light-colored; it clung close to his body,
    pale as fronds of white lotus fiber, so that he seemed
    to be the mighty elephant mount of Indra, lord of the
    gods, swathed in its ornamental blanket.

Narada carried a bright crystal rosary that made him
    gleam; its upper portion appeared half set with coral,
    for it was shot through by glinting rays refracted from
    his thumbnail, reddened by continually plucking his
    lute.

१० रणद्भिराघट्टनया नभस्वतः
पृथग्विभिन्नश्रुतिमण्डलैः स्वरैः ।
स्फुटीभवद्ग्रामविशेषमूर्च्छना-
मवेक्षमाणं महतीं मुहुर्मुहुः ॥

निवर्त्य सो ऽनुव्रजतः कृतानती-
नतीन्द्रियज्ञाननिधिर्नभःसदः ।
समासदत्सादितदैत्यसंपदः
पदं महेन्द्रालयचारु चक्रिणः ॥

पतन्पतङ्गप्रतिमस्तपोनिधिः १
पुरो ऽस्य यावान्न भुवि व्यलीयत ।
गिरेस्तडित्वानिव तावदुच्चकै-
र्जवेन पीठादुदतिष्ठदच्युतः ॥

अथ प्रयत्नोन्नमितानमत्फणै-
र्धृते कथंचित्फणिनां गणैरधः ।
न्यधायिषातामभिदेवकीसुतं
सुतेन धातुश्चरणौ भुवस्तले ॥

तमर्घ्यमर्घ्यादिकयादिपूरुषः
सपर्यया साधु स पर्यपूपुजत् ।
गृहानुपैतुं प्रणयादभीप्सवो
भवन्ति नापुण्यकृतां मनीषिणः ॥

This lute was called Mahati, and Narada was gazing at it 10
intently. When it was caressed by the breeze, there
swelled forth modulations of various scales rich in
cascading notes wherein all the quarter tones could
still be heard individually even as they resonated
together.

Narada dismissed his retinue of deities after they had
paid homage to him. Then that treasure-house of
transcendent knowledge proceeded toward the
palace, fair as Indra's heaven, of the discus bearer,[5]
destroyer of demons' ease.

But before the descending ascetic, blazing like the sun,
could enter his presence, Krishna had already risen
swiftly from his high throne, like a thundercloud from
a mountain peak.

The serpents in the underworld struggled bravely to
stiffen their hoods; bending under the weight, they
could scarcely support the earth once the son of the
creator had alighted before Devaki's* offspring.

Then Krishna, the primal being, respectfully welcomed
his guest with a hospitable offering of water and other
refreshments. The prudent are not overeager to visit
those negligent about proper procedures.

———

* Krishna's mother.

7

१५ न यावदेतावुदपश्यदुत्थितौ
जनस्तुषाराञ्जनपर्वताविव ।
स्वहस्तदत्ते मुनिमासने मुनि-
श्चिरंतनस्तावदभिन्यवीविशत् ॥

महामहानीलशिलारुचः पुरो
निषेदिवान्कंसकृषः स विष्टरे ।
श्रितोदयाद्रेरभिसायमुच्चकै-
रचूचुरच्चन्द्रमसो ऽभिरामताम् ॥

विधाय तस्यापचितिं प्रसेदुषः
प्रकाममप्रीयत यज्वनां प्रियः ।
ग्रहीतुमार्यान्परिचर्यया मुहु-
र्महानुभावा हि नितान्तमर्थिनः ॥

अशेषतीर्थोपहृताः कमण्डलो-
निर्धाय पाणावृषिणाभ्युदीरिताः ।
अघौघविध्वंसविधौ पटीयसी-
र्नतेन मूर्ध्ना हरिरग्रहीदपः ॥

स काञ्चने यत्र मुनेरनुज्ञया
नवाम्बुदश्यामवपुर्न्यविक्षत ।
जिगाय² जम्बूजनितश्रियः श्रियं
सुमेरुशृङ्गस्य तदा तदासनम् ॥

Krishna, long ago an ascetic himself,[6] had already shown   15
  the ascetic Narada to a seat, offered so quickly that
  nobody could have marked the two of them standing
  together like the snowy Himalaya and dark Anjana*
  mountains.

Seated on this throne in front of Kamsa's[7] slayer, dark blue
  as a great slab of sapphire, Narada robbed the evening
  moon of its beauty as it rises high above the eastern
  mountain peak.

Krishna, friend of sacrificers, was delighted to welcome
  his guest, and Narada himself was no less pleased. The
  illustrious are always eager to show courtesy to the
  noble.

From a pot Narada poured into his hand water collected
  from all the holy places. He sprinkled this upon
  Krishna, who received it with bowed head, for such
  water will swiftly stem sin's flow.

With the sage's leave Krishna, dark as a fresh rain cloud,
  then took his seat on his golden throne, which thereby
  surpassed the magnificent peak of Mount Meru, its
  splendor enhanced by the black plum tree growing
  beside it.[8]

---

* Literally, "Collyrium."

२० स तप्तकार्तस्वरभास्वराम्बरः
कठोरताराधिपलाञ्छनच्छविः ।
विदिद्युते वाडवजातवेदसः
शिखाभिराश्लिष्ट इवाम्भसां निधिः ॥

रथाङ्गपाणेः पटलेन रोचिषा-
मृषित्विषः संवलिता विरेजिरे ।
चलत्पलाशान्तरगोचरास्तरो-
स्तुषारमूर्तेरिव नक्तमंशवः ॥

प्रफुल्लतापिच्छनिभैरभीशुभिः
शुभैश्च सप्तच्छदपांसुपाण्डुभिः ।
परस्परेण च्छुरितामलच्छवी
तदैकवर्णाविव तौ बभूवतुः ॥

युगान्तकालप्रतिसंहृतात्मनो
जगन्ति यस्यां सविकासमासत ।
तनौ ममुस्तत्र न कैटभद्विष-
स्तपोधनाभ्यागमसंभवा मुदः ॥

निदाघधामानमिवाधिदीधितिं
मुदा विकासं यतिमभ्युपेयुषी ।
विलोचने बिभ्रदधिश्रितश्रिणी
स पुण्डरीकाक्ष इति स्फुटो ऽभवत् ॥

Krishna's garment gleamed like molten gold, his skin was   20
    dark as the full moon's mark,[9] and he blazed like the
    ocean aflame with underwater fire.[10]

The brilliance radiating from the sage blended with the
    luster flowing from the discus bearer so that it glowed
    like moonbeams settling at night among the rustling
    leaves of a tree.

Narada and Krishna appeared to share the same
    complexion; their flawless skins, fused by bright
    streams of light, had become at once as dark blue as
    opening *tamāla* blossoms and as pale as pollen from a
    saptacchada* flower.

Even though his body encompassed the whole universe
    absorbed at the end of the previous world age, the foe
    of the demon Kaitabha[11] could not contain his joy at
    Narada's arrival.

As lotuses expand to the blazing sun, so, on seeing the
    lustrous sage, Krishna's bright eyes widened in
    delight—he was now truly lotus-eyed.[12]

---

* "Seven-leafed." The tree of this name, also known as *saptaparṇa*,
typically bears clusters of seven leaves.

२५ सितं सितिम्ना सुतरां मुनेर्वपु-
र्विसारिभिः सौधमिवाथ लम्भयन् ।
द्विजावलिव्याजनिशाकरांशुभिः
शुचिस्मितां वाचमवोचदच्युतः ॥

हरत्ययं संप्रति हेतुरेष्यतः
शुभस्य पूर्वाचरितैः कृतं शुभैः ।
शरीरभाजां भवदीयदर्शनं
व्यनक्ति कालत्रितये ऽपि योग्यताम् ॥

जगत्यपर्याप्तसहस्रभानुना
न यत्रियन्तुं समभावि भानुना ।
प्रसह्य तेजोभिरसंख्यातां गतै-
रदस्त्वया नुत्तमनुत्तमं तमः ॥

कृतः प्रजाक्षेमकृता प्रजासृजा
सुपात्रनिक्षेपनिराकुलात्मना ।
सदोपयोगे ऽपि गुरुस्त्वमक्षति-
र्निधिः श्रुतीनां धनसंपदामिव ॥

विलोकनेनैव तवामुना मुने
कृतः कृतार्थो ऽस्मि निबृंहितांहसा३ ।
तथापि शुश्रूषुरहं गरीयसी-
र्गिरो ऽथ वा श्रेयसि केन तृप्यते ॥

Then he addressed his guest with a broad smile; his   25
    flashing teeth seemed to diffuse moonbeams, further
    saturating with radiance Narada's body, already like a
    white stuccoed mansion.

"Your arrival shows how worthy living creatures must
    surely be at all three times, for it removes present sin,
    effects future good, and is clearly the result of pious
    actions performed long ago.

A profound darkness afflicts the world, against which
    even the sun's infinite rays are powerless. It is now
    completely dispelled by the limitless splendor
    emanating from you.

The creator effects well-being for his mortal offspring
    and is not disquieted at bestowing bounty on the
    deserving. Therefore he has made you a teacher
    and an unfailing treasure-house of scripture,[13]
    to be consulted eternally; you are like a deposit
    of money constantly drawn upon but remaining
    undiminished.[14]

The mere sight of you, sage, removes sin and I have been
    fulfilled by it. At the same time, I am eager to hear
    your weighty words, for no one can have enough of
    good fortune.

३० गतस्पृहो ऽप्यागमनप्रयोजनं
वदेति वक्तुं व्यवसीयते यया ।
तनोति नस्तामुदितात्मगौरवो
गुरुस्तवैवागम एष धृष्टताम् ॥

इति ब्रुवन्तं तमुवाच स व्रती
न वाच्यमित्थं पुरुषोत्तम त्वया ।
त्वमेव साक्षात्करणीय इत्यतः
किमस्ति कार्यं गुरु योगिनामपि ॥

उदीर्णरागप्रतिरोधकं जनै-
रभीक्ष्णमक्षुण्णतयातिदुर्गमम् ।
उपेयुषो मोक्षपथं मनस्विन-
स्त्वमग्रभूमिर्निरपायसंश्रया ॥

उदासितारं निगृहीतमानसै-
र्गृहीतमध्यात्मदृशा कथंचन ।
बहिर्विकारं प्रकृतेः पृथग्विदुः
पुरातनं त्वां पुरुषं पुराविदः ॥

निवेशयामासिथ हेलयोद्धृतं४
फणाभृतां छादनमेकमोकसः ।
जगत्त्रयैकस्थपतिस्त्वमुच्चकै-
रहीश्वरस्तम्भशिरःसु भूतलम् ॥

Your momentous arrival has given me self-esteem and   30
    increases my confidence; so I am emboldened to ask
    the purpose of your visit, since you are detached from
    all concerns."

Narada the ascetic replied, "You should not speak in this
    way, supreme being. What greater goal can there be,
    even for yogis, beyond seeing you at close hand?

The road to deliverance is menaced by that brigand,
    passion, and the other perils besetting it ensure that
    few journey there. You are the final destination on that
    path, a safe haven for any intrepid traveler.

Sages of old have recognized you as the primal person,
    barely glimpsed with the inner eye by those
    disciplined of mind, since you are beyond worldly
    action, immune to phenomenal change, and wholly
    different from material nature.[15]

At the same time, you alone are the architect of the three
    worlds. And when you were incarnated as the Boar,
    you easily lifted up the earth and placed it on the
    pillar-like heads of Vasuki the snake king[16] to serve as
    a roof over the serpents' subterranean realm.

३५ अनन्यगुर्व्यास्तव केन केवलः
पुराणमूर्तेर्महिमावगम्यते ।
मनुष्यजन्मापि सुरासुरानुणै-
र्भवान्भवच्छेदकरैः करोत्यधः ॥

लघूकरिष्यन्नतिभारभङ्गुरा-
मम्मूं किल त्वं त्रिदिवादवातरः ।
उदूढलोकत्रितयेन सांप्रतं
गुरुर्धरित्री क्रियतेतरां त्वया ॥

निजौजसोज्जासयितुं जगद्द्रुहा-
मुपाजिहीथा न महीतलं यदि ।
समाहितैरप्यनिरूपितस्ततः
पदं दृशः स्याः कथमीश माद्दृशाम् ॥

उपप्लुतं पातुमदो मदोद्धतै-
स्त्वमेव विश्वंभर विश्वमीशिषे ।
ऋते रवेः क्षालयितुं क्षमेत कः
क्षपातमस्काण्डमलीमसं नभः ॥

करोति कंसादिमहीभृतां वधा-
ज्जनो मृगाणामिव यत्तव स्तवम् ।
हरेर्हिरण्याक्षपुरःसरासुर-
द्विपद्द्विषः प्रत्युत सा तिरस्क्रिया ॥

Who can fully appreciate the magnitude of your unique   35
    primordial manifestation? Even when born as a
    mortal you surpass the gods and demons by your
    virtues that end rebirth.

All know you descended from heaven to lighten the earth
    as it buckled under oppression's burden, but now it
    is heavier still through bearing you, container of all
    three realms.

If you had not actually come down to this world to put its
    enemies to flight, then how, lord, could you become
    visible to one such as me? Even those sunk deep in
    meditation have not witnessed you directly.

It is you who support the entire universe and you alone
    have the capacity to protect it, overwhelmed as it is
    by those swollen with pride. Can anything but the sun
    wipe away the foul stain of night's murk?

You are everywhere praised for killing Kamsa and others
    like him, although these enemies were as feeble as
    deer; but that can only detract from Vishnu, who once
    overcame mighty demons such as Hiranyakashipu, as
    the lion does elephants.[17]

४० प्रवृत्त एव स्वयमुज्झितश्रमः
क्रमेण पेष्टुं भुवनद्विषामसि ।
तथापि वाचालतया युनक्ति मां
मिथस्त्वदाभाषणलोलुभं मनः ॥

तदिन्द्रसंदिष्टमुपेन्द्र यद्वचः
क्षणं मया विश्वजनीनमुच्यते ।
समस्तकार्येषु गतेन धुर्यता-
महिद्विषस्तद्द्रवता निशाम्यताम् ॥

अभूदभूमिः प्रतिपक्षजन्मनां
भियां तनूजस्तपनद्युतिर्दितेः ।
यमिन्द्रशब्दार्थनिसूदनं हरे-
र्हिरण्यपूर्वं कशिपुं प्रचक्षते ॥

समत्सरेणासुर इत्युपेयुषा
चिराय नाम्नः प्रथमाभिधेयताम् ।
भयस्य पूर्वावतरस्तरस्विना
मनःसु येन द्युसदां व्यधीयत ॥

दिशामधीशांश्चतुरो यतः सुरा-
नपास्य तं रागहृताः सिषेविरे ।
अवापुरारभ्य ततश्चला इति
प्रवादमुच्चैरयशस्करं श्रियः ॥

Of your own free will you have undertaken tirelessly to   40
    extirpate those hostile to the world. However,
    I should pause—eagerness to converse with you makes
    me garrulous!

Brother of Indra,[18] I must at once deliver a message of
    universal concern entrusted to me by that same god.
    Listen attentively, for you have become preeminent in
    all the plans of Vritra's* foe.

The demon Diti had a son called Hiranyakashipu, brilliant
    as the sun, unperturbed by any enemy, negating the
    mighty implications of the name of Indra, lord of the
    gods.[19]

Through his strength and ill intent he eventually came to
    embody all the malice in the word 'demon,' and it was
    because of him that fear entered the gods' minds for
    the very first time.

Royal Fortune herself became infatuated, abandoned
    the four deities of the directions, and entered his
    service. From that moment she gained the inglorious
    reputation of being fickle.

---

* In the *Ṛg Veda,* a dragon-like being conquered by Indra, later
  envisaged as a demon.

४५ पुराणि दुर्गाणि निशातमायुधं
बलानि शूराणि घनाश्च कञ्चुकाः ।
स्वरूपशोभैकगुणानि नाकिनां
गणैस्तमाशङ्क्य तदादि चक्रिरे ॥

स संचरिष्णुर्भुवनान्तराणि यां
यदृच्छयाशिश्रियदाश्रयः श्रियः ।
अकारि तस्यै मुकुटोपलस्खल-
त्करैस्त्रिसंध्यं त्रिदशैर्दिशे नमः ॥

सटच्छटाभिन्नघनेन बिभ्रता
नृसिंह सैंहीमतनुं तनुं त्वया ।
सा मुग्धकान्तास्तनसङ्गभङ्गुरै-
रुरोविदारं प्रतिचस्करे नखैः ॥

विनोदमिच्छन्नथ दर्पजन्मनो
रणेन कण्ड्वास्त्रिदशैः समं पुनः ।
स रावणो नाम निकामभीषणं
बभूव रक्षः क्षतरक्षणं दिवः ॥

प्रभुर्बुभूषुर्भुवनत्रयस्य यः
शिरो ऽतिरागाद्दृशमं चिकर्तिषुः ।
अतर्कयद्द्विघ्नमिवेष्टसाहसः
प्रसादमिच्छासदृशं पिनाकिनः ॥

Then, in terror of that demon, all the gods ensured that   45
    their fortresses were secure, their weapons sharp,
    their armies valiant, and their armor strong; until then
    the qualities of these had served simply to enhance
    divine splendor.

So he traversed the universe, Royal Fortune in his wake,
    while the gods uneasily fingered the jewels in their
    diadems as they bent in homage at morning, noon,
    and night toward whatever region he had happened to
    reach.

Then you, lord, assumed the vast body of a lion, piercing
    the clouds with the tips of your mane, and became the
    Man-Lion. With your claws, full-curved by cupping
    your lovers' voluptuous breasts, you ripped open the
    demon's belly and killed him.

But he still wished to ease the itch of his arrogance
    through further conflict with the gods, so he took
    birth as another terrible demon called Ravana and
    proceeded to destroy heaven's defenses.

Aspiring to rule the universe, his ambition was so
    unbridled that he was willing even to cut off his tenth
    and last head as an offering to Shiva; later, with a
    rashness become habitual, he was to conclude that the
    goodwill of that god, by then sympathetic to him, was
    simply impeding his progress.[20]

५० समुत्क्षिपन्यः पृथिवीभृतां वरं
वरप्रदानस्य चकार शूलिनः ।
त्रसत्तुषाराद्रिसुताससंभ्रम-
स्वयंग्रहाश्लेषमुखेन निष्क्रयाम् ॥

पुरीमवस्कन्द लुनीहि नन्दनं
मुषाण रत्नानि हरामराङ्गनाः ।
विगृह्य चक्रे नमुचिद्विषा वशी
य इत्थमस्वास्थ्यमहर्दिवं दिवः ॥

सलीलयातानि न भर्तुरभ्रमो-
र्न चित्रमुच्चैःश्रवसः पदक्रमम् ।
अनुद्रुतः संयति येन केवलं
वलस्य शत्रुः प्रशशंस शीघ्रताम् ॥

अशक्नुवन्सोढुमधीरलोचनः
सहस्ररश्मेरिव यस्य दर्शनम् ।
प्रविश्य हेमाद्रिगुहागृहान्तरं
निनाय बिभ्यद्दिवसानि कौशिकः ॥

बृहच्छिलानिष्ठुरकण्ठघट्टना
विकीर्णलोलाग्निकणं सुरद्विषाम् ।
जगत्प्रभोरप्रसहिष्णु वैष्णवं
न चक्रमस्याक्रमताधिकन्धरम् ॥

22

Still, by lifting up Kailasa, the mightiest of mountains, he   50
    repaid Shiva's granting of the boon he had sought,
    when the frightened Parvati, daughter of Himalaya,
    suddenly clung to her husband in a spontaneous
    embrace.

After dueling with Indra, he launched a violent assault on
    his capital city; he cut down the Nandana* pleasure
    garden there, looted the god's treasury, and carried off
    his divine women, bringing about lasting disquiet in
    heaven.

Pursued by Ravana in battle, Indra extolled neither the
    graceful gait of his elephant Airavata nor the varied
    pace of his steed Ucchaihshravas,[21] only the speed of
    these mounts in retreat.

Indra was no more capable of enduring direct sight of the
    sun than of his foe; withdrawing, bedazzled, deep into
    his palace, by then just a cave in the Meru mountain,
    he spent his days there like an owl,[22] cowering in fear.

Vishnu's discus was showered with sparks of fire flying up
    on impact with Ravana's throat, hard as a great rock;
    it could gain no purchase on the neck of the gods'
    enemy, now the overlord of the world.

---

* Literally, "Delighting."

५५ विभिन्नशङ्कुः कलुषीभवन्मुहु-
र्मदेन दन्तीव मनुष्यधर्मणः ।
निरस्तगाम्भीर्यमपास्तपुष्पकः
प्रकम्पयामास न मानसं न सः ॥

रणेषु तस्य प्रहिताः प्रचेतसा
सरोषहुंकारपराङ्कुखीकृताः ।
प्रहर्तुरेवोरगराजरज्जवो
जवेन कण्ठं सभयं प्रपेदिरे ॥

परेतभर्तुर्महिषो ऽमुना धनु-
र्विधातुमुत्खातविषाणमण्डलः ।
कृते ऽपि भारे महतस्त्रपाभरा-
दुवाह दुःखेन भृशानतं शिरः ॥

स्पृशन्सशङ्कुः समये शुचावपि
स्थितः कराग्रैरसमग्रपातिभिः ।
अघर्मघर्मोदकबिन्दुमौक्तिकै-
रलंचकारास्य वधूरहस्करः ॥

कलासमग्रेण गृहानमुञ्चता
मनस्विनीरुत्कयितुं पटीयसा ।
विलासिनस्तस्य वितन्वता रतिं
न नर्मसाचिव्यमकारि नेन्दुना ॥

Darkening in his pride, Ravana destroyed the precious   55
    conch shell of Kubera, the god of wealth, then
    overturned his chariot Pushpaka* and repeatedly
    menaced him, robbing him of his composure. So
    Indra's elephant, temples streaming with ichor,[23]
    thrashes the Manasa lake† in a frenzy and scatters the
    lotuses floating in its shallows.[24]

When Ravana roared with rage, the mighty serpents
    hurled by Varuna‡ as rope-snares in battle turned tail
    and fled back in terror to the god's neck.

To fashion a bow, Ravana dug out the curved horn of the
    buffalo mount of Yama, lord of the dead. Although
    that weight had been removed, the creature still had
    to strain to support its head, pressed down by the
    heavy burden of shame.

Even in summer the sun caressed Ravana's wives quite
    timidly with only a few rays, ornamenting them with
    pearls, the cool drops of their perspiration.

The moon was adept at artfully softening the love-anger
    of these women with all its light, and without leaving
    his palace it gratified Ravana, always eager for
    lovemaking, by ministering to his lust.[25]

———

* Literally, "Flowery."
† Located beside Mount Kailasa in the Himalaya range.
‡ The guardian of the western quarter of the sky who wears a noose
  made of snakes.

६० विदग्धलीलोचितदन्तपत्रिका-
चिकीर्षया नूनमनेन मानिना ।
न जातु वैनायकमेकमुद्धृतं
विषाणमद्यापि पुनः प्ररोहति ॥

निशान्तनारीपरिधानधूनन-
स्फुटागसाप्यूरुषु लोलचक्षुषः ।
प्रियेण तस्यानपराधबाधिताः
प्रकम्पनेनानुचकम्पिरे सुराः ॥

तिरस्कृतस्तस्य जनाभिभाविना
मुहुर्महिम्ना महसां महीयसाम् ।
बभार बाष्पैर्द्विगुणीकृतं तनु-
स्तनूनपाद्धूमवितानमाधिजैः ॥

तदीयमातङ्गघटाविघट्टितैः
कटस्थलप्रोषितदानवारिभिः ।
गृहीतदिक्कैरपुनर्निवर्तिभि-
श्चिरस्य याथार्थ्यमलम्भि दिग्गजैः ५ ॥

परस्य मर्माविधमुज्झतां निजं
द्विजिह्वतादोषमजिह्मगामिभिः ।
तमिद्धमाराधयितुं सकर्णकैः
कुलैर्न भेजे फणिनां भुजङ्गता ॥

Once he tore out one of Ganesha's* tusks with the   60
    intention of making ivory earrings suitable for the
    debonair gallant he arrogantly fancied himself to be—
    to this day it has not grown back.

The gods, punished despite their innocence, were pitied
    by the wind; clearly guilty of disheveling the palace
    women's underskirts, it had still gained Ravana's
    goodwill as he eagerly ogled their thighs.

Agni, the god of fire, became dim, obscured by the luster
    of Ravana's overwhelming might; his smoke canopy
    doubled in size through the vapor rising from his tears
    of grief.

The elephants of the celestial directions[26] at last became
    appropriately titled; as the ichor dried on their
    temples butted by Ravana's war elephants, they fled
    to their various quarters in the heavens, never again to
    stir from there.

In order to serve that ferocious demon, snakes no longer
    deployed their natural serpentine traits; they stopped
    piercing creatures' vitals with their malign forked
    tongues, ceased moving deviously, and grew ears to
    hear with.[27]

---

* The elephant-headed, single-tusked son of Shiva.

६५ तपेन वर्षाः शरदा हिमागमो
वसन्तलक्ष्या शिशिरः समेत्य च ।
प्रसूनकूर्मं ददतः सदर्तवः
पुरे ऽस्य वास्तव्यकुटुम्बितां दधुः ॥

अभीक्ष्णमुष्णैरपि तस्य सोष्मणः
सुरेन्द्रवन्दीश्वसितानिलैर्यथा ।
सचन्दनाम्भःकणकोमलैस्तथा
वपुर्जलार्द्रापवनैर्न निर्ववौ ॥

अमानवं जातमजं कुले मनोः
प्रभाविनं भाविनमन्तमात्मनः ।
मुमोच जानन्नपि जानकीं न यः
सदाभिमानैकधना हि मानिनः ॥

स्मरस्यदो दाशरथिर्भवन्भवा-
नमुं वनान्ताद्रनितापहारिणम् ।
पयोधिमाविद्धचलज्जलाविलं६
विलङ्घ्य लङ्कां निकषा हनिष्यति ॥

अथोपपत्तिं छलनापरो ऽपरा-
मवाप्य शैलूष इवैष भूमिकाम् ।
तिरोहितात्मा शिशुपालसंज्ञया
प्रतीयते संप्रति सो ऽप्यसः परैः ॥

The monsoon united with summer, early winter with   65
    autumn, and the cold period with spring's abundance;
    the seasons continually gave birth to floral offspring
    and maintained settled households in Ravana's
    capital.

Burning with passion as it was, his body was not cooled
    by the breeze from moist fans softened by sprinkled
    sandalwood water, but only by the sirocco of sighing
    of the women captured from the king of the gods.

Ravana was aware that a hero, no mortal but yet born in
    the lineage of the first man, Manu—in reality, the
    eternal god Vishnu—was to bring about his death.[28]
    However, he still did not release Sita.* The arrogant
    persist in clinging to pride as their one precious
    resource.

Krishna, do you recall how in your birth as Rama you
    bridged the turbulent, murky ocean washing the
    island of Lanka and killed that demon who had
    abducted your wife from the Dandaka forest?

Bent on further deception, he has now entered upon
    another existence, like an actor assuming a new role,
    and concealed himself behind the name of Shishupala,
    unrecognized for who he is, but in reality the very
    same demon.

* The wife of Rama.

७० स बाल आसीद्द्रुपषा चतुर्भुजो
मुखेन पूर्णेन्दुरुचिस्त्रिलोचनः ।
युवा कराक्रान्तमहीभृदुच्चकै-
रसंशयं संप्रति तेजसा रविः ॥

स्वयं विधाता सुरदैत्यरक्षसा-
मनुग्रहापग्रहयोर्यदृच्छया ।
दशाननादीनभिराद्धदेवता-
वितीर्णवीर्यातिशयान्हसत्यसौ ॥

बलावलेपादधुनापि पूर्वव-
त्प्रबाध्यते तेन जगज्जिगीषुणा ।
सतीव योषित्प्रकृतिः सुनिश्चिता७
पुमांसमन्वेति भवान्तरेष्वपि ॥

तदेनमुल्लङ्घितशासनं विधे-
र्विधेहि कीनाशनिवेशनातिथिम् ।
शुभेतराचारविपक्रिमापदो
विपादनीया हि सतामसाधवः ॥

हृदयमरिवधोदयादुपोढ-
द्रढिम दधातु पुनः पुरन्दरस्य ।
घनपुलकपुलोमजाकुचाग्र-
द्रुतपरिरम्भनिपीडनक्षमत्वम् ॥

As a boy his body was four-armed like Vishnu's, and his   70
    face, bright as the full moon, was three-eyed like
    Shiva's.[29] When no more than a youthful prince, he
    cruelly oppressed vassals by raising punitive levies;
    now through his brilliance he has become as taxing
    to men as the very sun on high, suffusing mountains
    with its rays.[30]

Capriciously displaying goodwill and contempt to
    gods, demons, and ogres alike, Shishupala sneers
    at those such as Ravana who in their time accepted
    their mighty valor as a boon from the deities they
    propitiated.

At this very moment, in the arrogance of his strength, he
    belligerently threatens the world once again. A fixed
    disposition follows a man through each existence
    like a faithful wife.

Shishupala has transgressed the command of the
    creator, so make him a guest in the palace of the
    lord of the dead. The evil inevitably experience
    retribution for their immorality, but the virtuous
    must still destroy them first.

Indra's heart will grow young again when his enemy has
    been slain. Let him once again feel his wife Shachi's
    nipples tight with desire in a passionately eager
    embrace."

७५ ओमित्युक्तवतो ऽथ शार्ङ्गिण इति व्याहृत्य वाचं नभ-
स्तस्मिन्नुत्पितिते पुरः सुरमुनाविन्दोः श्रियं बिभ्रति ।
शत्रूणामनिशं विनाशपिशुनः कर्तुर्मतिं संयति
व्योम्नीव भृकुटिच्छलेन वदने केतुश्चकारास्पदम् ॥

No sooner had the divine sage Narada, pale as the moon,   75
    finished speaking, than he disappeared into the sky.
    Krishna commended his words and then turned his
    mind to battle; and on his face in the guise of a frown
    there appeared a heavenly comet presaging the
    relentless destruction of foes.

CHAPTER 2

The Discussion in the Council Chamber

यियक्षमाणेनाहूतः पार्थेनाथ मुरं द्विषन् ।
चैद्यं प्रति प्रतिष्ठासुरासीत्कार्यद्वयाकुलः ॥

गुरुकाव्यानुगां बिभ्रच्चान्द्रीमभिनभः श्रियम् ।
सार्धमुद्धवसीरिभ्यामथासावासदत्सदः ॥

जाज्वल्यमाना जगतः शान्तये समुपेयुषी ।
व्यद्योतिष्ट सभावेद्यामसौ नरशिखित्रयी ॥

रत्नस्तम्भेषु संक्रान्तप्रतिमास्ते चकाशिरे ।
एकाकिनो ऽपि परितः पौरुषेयवृता इव ॥

५ अध्यासामासुरुत्तुङ्गहेमपीठानि यान्यमी ।
तैरूहे केसरिक्रान्तत्रिकूटशिखरोपमा ॥

गुरूभयस्मै गुरुणोरुभयोरथ कार्ययोः ।
हरिर्विप्रतिषेधं तमाचचक्षे विचक्षणः ॥

Krishna wanted to act against Shishupala, but he had
     already been summoned by Yudhishthira,* who
     intended to perform a sacrifice; so he was caught
     between two obligations.

Accordingly he entered his council chamber in the
     company of his adviser Uddhava† and his brother
     Balarama, glowing like the moon in the heavens with
     Mercury and Venus in attendance.

These three, meeting together in the assembly hall to
     alleviate disharmony in the world, blazed forth in
     their splendor, like fires burning on an altar.

As their images were reflected on the hall's jeweled
     pillars, each appeared to be surrounded by thronging
     servants.

The high gold thrones they occupied were like the lion-   5
     haunted triple peak of Mount Trikuta.‡

Then Krishna proceeded to give his relatives a shrewd
     account of his dilemma concerning his pressing
     commitments.

---

* The eldest of the Pandava brothers.
† Sometimes said to be the cousin of Krishna's father, Vasudeva.
‡ The mountain of gold, also known as Suvela, located on the island
   of Lanka.

द्योतितान्तःसभैः कुन्दकुड्मलाग्रदतः स्मितैः ।
स्नपितेवाभवत्तस्य शुद्धवर्णा सरस्वती ॥

भवद्विरामवसरप्रदानाय वचांसि नः ।
पूर्वरङ्गः प्रसङ्गाय नाटकीयस्य वस्तुनः ॥

करदीकृतभूपालो भ्रातृभिर्जित्वरैर्दिशाम् ।
विनाप्यस्मदलंभूष्णुरिज्यायै तपसः सुतः ॥

१० उत्तिष्ठमानस्तु परो नोपेक्ष्यः पथ्यमिच्छता ।
समौ हि शिष्टैराम्रातौ वर्त्स्यन्तावामयः स च ॥

न दूये सात्वतीसूनुर्यन्मह्यमपराध्यति ।
यत्तु दंदह्यते लोकमतो दुःखाकरोति माम् ॥

मम तावन्मतमदः श्रूयतामङ्ग वामपि ।
ज्ञातसारे ऽपि खल्वेकः संदिग्धे कार्यवस्तुनि ॥

यावदर्थपदां वाचमेवमादाय माधवः ।
विरराम महीयांसः प्रकृत्या मितभाषिणः ॥

His speech was flawless, as if cleansed by his smiles,
    revealing teeth like jasmine buds, illuminating the
    council hall's furthest corners.

"I will speak merely to give you an opportunity to reply. A
    play's prologue serves only to introduce the plot to be
    enacted.

Yudhishthira, the son of austerity,[1] is fully capable of
    performing his sacrifice without me, for his brothers,
    conquerors of the earth's four quarters, have already
    made a vassal of every ruler.[2]

But a potential foe should not be overlooked if one wishes   10
    to flourish. The wise have always viewed an enemy
    and a disease in their incipient stages as equivalent.

I am not troubled that Shishupala, my aunt Satvati's son,
    is wronging me; what concerns me much more is the
    fact that he is menacing the world.

This is my opinion for the moment; now by all means let
    me hear yours. Even when the substance of a problem
    has been grasped, it is possible to remain uncertain
    how to react."

Krishna spoke just as much as his purpose required and
    ceased, for the great are naturally economical with
    words.

39

ततः सपत्नापनयस्मरणानुशयस्फुरा ।
ओष्ठेन रामो रामौष्ठबिम्बचुम्बनचुञ्चुना ॥

१५ विवक्षितामर्थविदस्तत्क्षणं प्रतिसंहृताम् ।
प्रापयन्पवनव्याधेर्गिरमुत्तरपक्षताम् ॥

घूर्णयन्मदिरास्वादमदपाटलितद्युती ।
रेवतीदशनोच्छिष्टपरिपूतपुटे दृशौ ॥

आश्लेषलोलुपवधूस्तनकार्कश्यसाक्षिणीम् ।
म्लापयन्नभिमानोष्णैर्वनमालां मुखानिलैः ॥

दधत्संध्यारुणव्योमस्फुरत्तारानुकारिणीः ।
द्विषद्द्वेषोपरक्ताङ्गसङ्गिनीः स्वेदविप्रुषः ॥

प्रोल्लसत्कुण्डलप्रोतपद्मरागदलत्विषा ।
कृष्णोत्तरासङ्गरुचिं विदधच्छौतपल्लवीम् ॥

२० ककुद्मिकन्यावक्रान्तर्वासलब्धाधिवासया ।
मुखामोदं मदिरया कृतानुव्याधमुद्वमन् ॥

जगाद वदनच्छद्मपद्मपर्यन्तपातिनः ।
नयन्मधुलिहः श्रैत्यमुदंशुदशनांशुभिः ॥

Then Balarama replied, his lower lip trembling, not just
  from his habitual eagerness to kiss the luscious mouth
  of his adored wife Revati, but from indignation as he
  reflected on their enemy's crimes.

Uddhava, well versed in strategy as he was, had intended   15
  to speak before him. However, he kept his silence
  at that moment, for Balarama had ensured that his
  speech would conclude the discussion.

By now Balarama was rolling his eyes; they were tinged
  with red from his drunken delight in wine, while their
  lids had been laved by Revati's moist kisses.

His panting, hot with excitement, withered his garland
  of forest flowers already crushed by his wife's firm
  breasts in her eagerness for an embrace.

As he flushed with hatred toward his foe, drops of sweat
  broke out upon him, like glinting stars in the rosy
  evening sky.

The glow from the sparkling ruby shards set in his earrings
  turned his dark cloak the deep red of mango shoots.

His breath was saturated with the aroma of wine, fragrant   20
  from being held in Revati's mouth as they kissed.

When he spoke, the bees circling his lotus-like face were
  whitened by the bright rays from his teeth.[3]

यद्वासुदेवेनादीनमनादीनवमीरितम् ।
वचसस्तस्य सपदि क्रिया केवलमुत्तरम् ॥

नैतलृघ्वपि भूयस्या वचो वाचातिशय्यते ।
इन्धनौघधगप्यग्निस्त्विषा नात्येति पूषणम् ॥

विरोधिवचसो मूकान्वागीशानपि कुर्वते ।
जडानप्यनुलोमार्थप्रवाचः कृतिनां गिरः१ ॥

२५ संक्षिप्तस्याप्यतो ऽस्यैव वाक्यस्यार्थगरीयसः ।
सुविस्तरतरा वाचो भाष्यभूता भवन्तु मे ॥

सर्वकार्यशरीरेषु मुक्त्वाङ्गस्कन्धपञ्चकम् ।
सौगतानामिवात्मान्यो नास्ति मन्त्रो महीभृताम् ॥

षड्गुणाः शक्तयस्तिस्रः सिद्धयश्चोदयास्त्रयाः ।
ग्रन्थानधीत्य व्याकर्तुमिति दुर्मेधसो ऽप्यलम् ॥

अनिर्लोठितकार्यस्य वाग्जालं वाग्मिनो वृथा ।
निमित्तादपराद्धेषोर्धानुष्कस्येव वल्गितम् ॥

"Krishna's words are resolute and without defect; the
　　simple response to them must be immediate action.

He may have spoken briefly, but there is no real need for
　　more. Fire does not surpass the sun in brilliance after
　　consuming heaps of fuel.

An able person's speech can reduce even articulate
　　opponents to silence and compel fools to speak to the
　　point.

So my remarks, even if slightly drawn out, can serve as　　25
　　commentary on Krishna's statement; for however
　　succinct it may have been, its import is great.

In every pressing situation rulers should not be counseled
　　to follow any stratagem beyond the five principles of
　　statecraft,[4] just as the Buddhists do not accept that
　　living creatures can possess a self beyond the five
　　psychophysical constituents.[5]

Even dullards can study books and then expound the six
　　modes of strategy, the three types of power, the three
　　successes, and the three phases of action.[6]

But vain is the web of words of an orator who fails in his
　　purpose; it is like boastful posturing on the part of an
　　archer after his arrow has missed its target.

मन्त्रो योध इवाधीरः सर्वाङ्गैः कल्पितैरपि२ ।
चिरं न सहते स्थातुं परेभ्यो भेदशङ्कया ॥

३० आत्मोदयः परज्यानिर्द्वयं नीतिरितीयती ।
तदूरीकृत्य कृतिभिर्वाचस्पत्यं प्रतायते ॥

तृप्तियोगः परेणापि न महिम्ना महात्मनाम् ।
पूर्णश्चन्द्रोदयाकाङ्क्षी दृष्टान्तो ऽत्र महार्णवः ॥

संपदा सुस्थितंमन्यो भवति स्वल्पयापि यः ।
कृतकृत्यो विधिर्मन्ये न वर्धयति तस्य ताम् ॥

समूलघातमघ्नन्तः परान्नोद्यन्ति मानिनः ।
प्रध्वंसितान्धतमसस्तत्रोदाहरणं रविः ॥

विपक्षमखिलीकृत्य प्रतिष्ठा खलु दुर्लभा ।
अनीत्वा पङ्क्तां धूलिमुदकं नावतिष्ठते ॥

While counsel may be offered taking account of every
possible expedient, its enactment cannot be delayed
for any length of time in case it is revealed to others;
it is like a timid warrior—even when fully armored he
hesitates to stand his ground, lest he be struck by the
enemy.[7]

Promotion of one's own interests and a rival's undoing   30
go hand in hand. Politics is no more than that insight,
although experts continue to devote much verbiage to
confirming it.

The mighty do not feel sated even when their power is at
its height; just think of the vast ocean, always yearning
for the moonrise so it can swell still further.

Fate does what it must, but in my view it cannot increase
the sense of well-being of someone satisfied with just
a little.

Those already held in esteem cannot rise any further
unless they totally extirpate their enemies. The sun,
destroyer of pitch darkness, exemplifies this principle.

It is certainly difficult to win renown without crushing
one's foes. Water does not cease flowing until it has
turned dust into mud.

३५ ध्रियते यावदेको ऽपि रिपुस्तावत्कुतः शिवम् ।
पुरः क्लिश्नाति सोमं हि सैंहिकेयो ऽसुरद्रुहाम् ॥

सखा गरीयान्शत्रुश्च कृत्रिमस्तौ हि कार्यतः ।
स्यातामिमित्रौ मित्रे च सहजप्राकृतावपि ॥

उपकर्त्रारिणा संधिर्न मित्रेणापकारिणा ।
उपकारापकारौ हि लक्ष्यं लक्षणमेतयोः ॥

त्वया विप्रकृतश्चैद्यो रुक्मिणीं हरता हरे ।
बद्धमूलस्य मूलं हि महद्वैरतरोः स्त्रियः ॥

त्वयि भौमं गते जेतुमरौत्सीत्स पुरीमिमाम् ।
प्रोषितार्यमणं मेरोरन्धकारस्तटीमिव ॥

४० आलप्यालमिदं बभ्रोर्यत्स दारानपाहरत् ।
कथापि खलु पापानामलमश्रेयसे यतः ॥

So long as a single enemy survives, how can there be   35
    success? Rahu, the eclipse demon, still torments the
    moon, while the gods can only look on.

A friend or a foe can be acquired through the course of
    events and must be treated with due gravity. Equally,
    an ally by family connection may turn into a foe as
    a result of circumstance, while a natural enemy can
    become a friend.[8]

Peace can be made with a foe if he has provided assistance,
    not with an ally who has done a disservice. Their
    capacity to help and to harm should be regarded as the
    characteristics defining the status of each.

Now, Krishna, you have injured Shishupala in taking
    Rukmini, his betrothed, as a wife.[9] If the manifold
    roots of the tree of enmity all run deep, then surely
    woman is its main root.

While you went off to conquer the demon Naraka, he
    besieged this city of Dvaraka,* like deep gloom
    shrouding Mount Meru's slopes after sunset.

Do not reply that Shishupala abducted Babhru's† wife   40
    from here—the mere mention of evil is enough to
    bring about misfortune!

───────

* Krishna's capital.
† A kinsman of Krishna, also known as Akrura.

विराद्ध एवं भवता विराद्धा बहुधा च नः ।
निर्वर्त्यते ऽरिः क्रियया स श्रुतश्रवसः सुतः ॥

विधाय वैरं सामर्षे नरो ऽरौ य उदासते ।
प्रक्षिप्योदर्चिषं कक्षे शेरते ते ऽभिमारुतम् ॥

मनागनभ्यावृत्त्या वा कामं क्षाम्यतु यः क्षमी ।
क्रियासमभिहारेण विराध्यन्तं क्षमेत कः ॥

अन्यदा भूषणं पुंसः शमो लज्जेव योषितः ।
पराक्रमः परिभवे वैयात्यं सुरतेष्विव ॥

४५ मा जीवन्यः परावज्ञादुःखदग्धो ऽपि जीवति ।
तस्याजननिरेवास्तु जननीक्लेशकारिणः ॥

पादाहतं यदुत्थाय मूर्धानमधिरोहति ।
स्वस्थादेवापमाने ऽपि देहिनस्तद्द्वरं रजः ॥

He has been wronged by you and has consequently gone
 on to injure us in many ways. Shishupala, the son of
 Shrutashravas, has been turned into an enemy by your
 actions.

The man who starts a quarrel with an irascible foe and
 then does nothing is effectively setting brushwood on
 fire and lying down to sleep in the face of the wind.

Granted an indulgent person may forgive some slight or
 fleeting injury, but who can pardon one who offends
 by repeated misdeeds?

As a rule, patient restraint enhances an individual's
 character, as modesty does a woman's. But when an
 insult has been delivered, a spirited response from a
 man is a virtue, as is enthusiasm in a woman making
 love.

To hell with the man who lives on as the object of   45
 another's withering contempt! May he die without
 being reborn, for he will only cause pain to his mother!

The dust kicked up into the air and settling on the head
 is far superior to one who remains passive when
 insulted.

असंपादयतः कश्चिदर्थं जातिक्रियागुणैः ।
यदृच्छाशब्दवत्पुंसः संज्ञायै जन्म केवलम् ॥

तुङ्गत्वमितरा नाद्रौ नेदं सिन्धावगाधता ।
अलङ्घनीयताहेतुरुभयं तन्मनस्विनि ॥

तुल्ये ऽपराधे स्वर्भानुर्भानुमन्तं चिरेण यत् ।
हिमांशुमाशु ग्रसते तन्नदिम्नः स्फुटं फलम् ॥

५० स्वयं प्रणमते ऽल्पे ऽपि परवायावुपेयुषि ।
निदर्शनमसाराणां लघुर्बहुतृणं नरः ॥

तेजस्विमध्ये तेजस्वी दवीयानपि गण्यते ।
पञ्चमः पञ्चतपसस्तपनो जातवेदसाम् ॥

What is more, for the man failing to attain any success in
　　life through social station, actions, or talents, birth
　　has no purpose other than simply to assign a label; he
　　is like a nonce word which, as the grammarians teach,
　　cannot communicate any meaning through signifying
　　class membership, agency, or attribute.[10]

A mountain is lofty but has no profound depth, while the
　　ocean plumbs depths while lacking any height. Their
　　respective loftiness and profundity are the reasons
　　why neither should be treated lightly; both of these
　　attributes are found in the man of acumen.

Though Rahu's deed is equally cruel in each case, he
　　consumes the blazing sun slowly but the cool-rayed
　　moon swiftly;[11] that can only be the result of the
　　latter's weak disposition.

The feeble man of straw inadvertently bends when even　　50
　　an insignificant enemy approaches or only a gentle
　　breeze blows; he epitomizes everything inferior.

On the other hand, any truly vigorous man, no matter how
　　far removed he may be, will still be judged energetic.
　　For one performing the austerity of the five fires, the
　　fifth will always be the blazing sun, however high in
　　the sky.[12]

अकृत्वा हेलया पादमुच्चैर्मूर्धसु विद्विषाम् ।
कथंकारमनालम्बा कीर्तिर्द्यामधिरोहति ॥

अङ्काधिरोपितमृगश्चन्द्रमा मृगलाञ्छनः ।
केसरी निष्ठुरक्षुण्णमृगपूगो मृगाधिपः ॥

चतुर्थोपायसाध्ये ऽपि रिपौ सान्त्वमपक्रिया ।
स्वेद्यमामज्वरं प्राज्ञः को ऽम्भसा परिषिञ्चति ॥

५५   सामवादाः सकोपस्य तस्य प्रत्युत दीपकाः ।
प्रतप्तस्येव सहसा सर्पिषस्तोयबिन्दवः ॥

गुणानामायथातथ्यादर्थं विस्नावयन्ति ये ।
अमात्यव्यञ्जना राज्ञां दूष्यास्ते शत्रुसंहिताः ॥

स्वशक्त्युपचये केचित्परस्य व्यसने ऽपरे ।
यात्रामाहुरुदासीनं त्वामुत्थापयति द्वयम् ॥

52

How can fame, ill-defined in its beginnings, eventually
   ascend to heaven, if it does not disdainfully place its
   foot on foes' lofty heads?

Because the moon has benignly sheltered a deer in its lap,
   it is disparagingly called "deer-marked";[13] the lion
   ruthlessly slaughters herds of deer and is known as
   "king of the beasts."

Appeasing a foe who can be subdued only by the fourth
   expedient, force,[14] is bad strategy. Who with any
   intelligence bathes an invalid racked by a burning
   fever? An illness of that kind must be sweated out.

On the contrary, conciliatory words will only provoke an   55
   enraged enemy, just as drops of water immediately
   cause heated ghee to spatter.

Those who ruin their rulers' policy because their abilities
   do not match requirements are not counselors but
   imposters; they should be condemned as no different
   from enemies.

Some advocate conducting aggressive war from a position
   of strength; others, when the foe is at a disadvantage.
   Both situations now pertain and impel you to move
   from neutrality to action.

लिलङ्घयिषतो लोकानलङ्घ्यानलघीयसः ।
यादवाम्भोनिधीन्रुन्धे वेलेव भवतः क्षमा ॥

विजयस्त्वयि सेनायाः साक्षिमात्रे ऽपदिश्यताम् ।
फलभाजि समीक्षोक्ते बुद्धेर्भोग इवात्मनि ॥

६० हते हिडिम्बरिपुणा राज्ञि द्वैमातुरे युधि ।
चिरस्य मित्रव्यसनी सुदमो दमघोषजः ॥

नीतिरापदि यद्द्रुम्यः परस्तन्मानिनो हिये ।
विधुर्विधुंतुदस्येव पूर्णस्तस्योत्सवाय सः ॥

अन्यदुच्छृङ्खलं सत्त्वमन्यच्छास्त्रनियन्त्रितम् ।
सामानाधिकरण्यं हि तेजस्तिमिरयोः कुतः ॥

Your patience alone holds back the vast, invincible
    Yadava* hosts from sweeping over the earth, as only
    the shore prevents the mighty, boundless ocean from
    inundating everything.

In that light let your army's victory be credited to you.
    Relish the outcome without actually participating
    in the battle. In the same way, so the followers of
    Samkhya philosophy claim, what is apprehended
    by consciousness is attributed to the self, neutral in
    essence yet still experiencing the results of physical
    actions.[15]

Now that King Jarasandha, son of two mothers,[16] has been   60
    killed in battle by the Pandava Bhima, enemy of the
    demon Hidimba, Shishupala, son of Damaghosha,
    is left without his close associate and will be easy to
    tame.

Attacking an enemy in difficulties is a policy shameful
    to the proud. It is when the foe is at the height of his
    power that the joy of battle arises, just as only the full
    moon really pleases Rahu the eclipse demon.

Completely unfettered strength is one thing, power
    inhibited by technical niceties quite another. How can
    light and darkness coexist and interact?

———

* Krishna's clan, also known as the Vrishnis.

इन्द्रप्रस्थगमस्तावत्कारि मा सन्तु चेदयः ।
आस्माकदन्तिसांनिध्यवामनीभूतभूरुहः ॥

निरुद्धवीवधासारप्रसारां गा इव व्रजम् ।
उपरुन्धन्तु दाशार्हाः पुरीं माहिष्मतीं द्विषः ॥

६५ यजतां पाण्डवः स्वर्गमवत्विन्द्रस्तपत्विनः ।
वयं हनाम द्विषतः सर्वः स्वार्थं प्रतीहते ॥

प्राप्यतां विद्युतः संपत्संपर्कादर्ककरोचिषाम् ।
शस्त्रैर्द्विषच्छिरश्छेदप्रोच्छलच्छोणितोक्षितैः ॥

इति संरम्भिणो वाणीर्बलस्यालेख्यदेवताः ।
सभाभित्तिप्रतिध्वानैर्भयादन्ववदन्निव ॥

निशम्य ताः शेषगवीरभिधातुमधोक्षजः ।
शिष्याय बृहतां पत्युः प्रस्तावमदिशद्दृशा ॥

So do not go to Indraprastha* for the sacrifice. Instead let
the trees of the Chedi† land be dwarfed by our war
elephants as they march past.

Let the Yadavas block off provisions, reinforcements, and
materials and then besiege Mahishmati, the enemy's
capital, in the same way that cattle penned in a stall
are denied grazing and freedom of movement.[17]

Let Yudhishthira perform his sacrifice, Indra protect   65
heaven, and the sun shine! For our part, we will kill
our enemies. All seek to pursue their own aims.

Let our swords be washed with the blood streaming from
our decapitated foes! May they flash like lightning
when the sun's rays glint upon them!"

So excited was Balarama that the deities painted on the
council chamber's walls seemed to echo his words
nervously.

Krishna listened to what he had to say and signaled with
a glance that it was the turn of Uddhava, pupil of
Brihaspati,‡ to speak.

---

* Yudhishthira's capital.
† Shishupala's clan.
‡ The priest and teacher of the gods.

भारतीमाहितभरामथानुद्धतमुद्धवः ।
तथ्यामुतथ्यानुजवज्जगादाग्रे गदाग्रजम् ॥

७० संप्रत्यसांप्रतं वक्तुमुक्ते मुसलपाणिना ।
निर्धारिते ऽर्थे लेखेन खलूक्त्वा खलु वाचिकम् ॥

तथापि यन्मय्यपि ते गुरुरित्येव गौरवम् ।
तत्प्रयोजककर्तृत्वमुपैति मम जल्पतः ॥

वर्णैः कतिपयैरेव ग्रथितस्य स्वैरिव ।
अनन्ता वाङ्मयस्याहो गेयस्येव विचित्रता ॥

बह्वपि स्वेच्छया कामं प्रकीर्णमभिधीयते ।
अनुज्झिताभिसंबन्धः प्रबन्धो दुरुदाहरः ॥

म्रदीयसीमपि घनामनल्पगुणकल्पिताम् ।
प्रसारयन्ति कुशलाश्चित्रां वाचं पटीमिव ॥

Uddhava then modestly delivered a sober but
    straightforward speech, worthy of his teacher himself,
    to Krishna, elder brother of Gada.

"Since Balarama has spoken, I have no need to say more.   70
    A subject definitively inscribed requires no verbal
    padding.

Still, the respect that you as elder show to me is motivation
    to speak further.

How endlessly varied is speech if only of a few finite
    syllables! It is like a song composed with no more than
    the seven main notes of the scale.

No doubt it is possible to speak at length spontaneously
    and without focus, but a developed and fully coherent
    argument is more difficult to present.

Nonetheless, the eloquent can formulate a complex
    and substantial statement even when speaking
    quite calmly, embellishing it with numerous verbal
    qualities. It is like skillfully woven cloth, of diverse
    colors and created out of many strands of thread,
    which may be thickly textured but still soft to the
    touch.[18]

७५ विशेषविदुषः शास्त्रं यत्तवोद्वाह्यते पुरः ।
हेतुः परिचयस्थैर्ये वक्तुर्गुणनिकैव सा ॥

प्रज्ञोत्साहावतः स्वामी यतेताधातुमात्मनि ।
तौ हि मूलमुदेष्यन्त्या जिगीषोरात्मसंपदः ॥

सोपधानां धियं धीराः स्थेयसीं खट्वयन्ति ये ।
तत्रानिशं निषण्णास्ते जानते जातु न श्रमम् ॥

स्पृशन्ति शरवत्तीक्ष्णाः स्तोकमन्तर्विशन्ति च ।
बहुस्पृशापि स्थूलेन स्थीयते बहिरश्मवत् ॥

आरभन्ते ऽल्पमेवाज्ञाः कामं व्यग्रा भवन्ति च ।
महारम्भाः कृतधियस्तिष्ठन्ति च निराकुलाः ॥

८० उपायमास्थितस्यापि नश्यत्यर्थः प्रमाद्यतः ।
हन्ति नोपशयस्थो ऽपि शयालुर्मृगयुर्मृगान् ॥

I intend now to rehearse the science of polity in your 75
presence, although you are an expert, since repetition
can serve to consolidate the speaker's understanding
of a subject.

A king should strive to instill in himself both intellect and
energy, the twin foundation of imminent power for
any ruler ambitious to expand his kingdom.

Determined men make intelligence and reason their
secure bed and headrest; reclining on these, they can
never flag.

The opinions of the quick-witted are light of touch but
deep-penetrating, like a sharp arrow. Although the
naively outspoken man may hit a larger target, his
impetus is dissipated, like a spent slingshot.

Fools engaging in a trifling enterprise become obsessed
with it, whereas the intelligent are able to remain
impassive while performing much.

As for the careless man, even when initiating an 80
appropriate plan he still misses his goal. The hunter
who dozes off does not kill his prey, although he may
be well concealed in a covert.

उदेतुमत्यजन्नीहां राजसु द्वादशस्वपि ।
जिगीषुरेको दिनकृदादित्येष्विव कल्पते ॥

तन्त्रावापविदा योगैर्मण्डलान्यधितिष्ठता ।
सुनिग्रहा नरेन्द्रेण फणीन्द्रा इव शत्रवः³ ॥

करप्रचेयामुत्तुङ्गः प्रभुशक्तिं प्रथीयसीम् ।
प्रज्ञाबलबृहन्मूलः फलत्युत्साहपादपः ॥

बुद्धिशस्त्रः प्रकृत्यङ्गो घनसंवृतिकञ्चुकः ।
चारेक्षणो दूतमुखः पुरुषः को ऽपि पार्थिवः ॥

८५ तेजः क्षमा वा नैकान्तः कालज्ञस्य महीपतेः ।
नैकमोजः प्रसादो वा रसभागविदः कवेः ॥

Alone among the twelve types of ruler,[19] the aggressive
    king of unflagging ambition is fit to gain ascendancy,
    like the sun among the Adityas.*

Opponents are easily controlled by a king if he is familiar
    with the affairs of both his own and his neighbors'
    domains and can manipulate political events with
    solid stratagems. In the same way, deadly serpents
    can be tamed by a snake charmer well versed in spells
    and potions who focuses his mental powers while
    protected within a magic circle.[20]

Firmness of purpose is a lofty tree; its sturdy roots are
    forceful intelligence, and it readily brings forth, as an
    abundant yield of fruit, extensive royal power, which
    can be further augmented by tribute.

A king is no ordinary man; his sword is his intellect, his
    limbs are his subjects, his armor is his tight security,
    his eyes are his spies, and his mouth his emissaries.

The ruler who grasps what the moment demands cannot   85
    be exclusively aggressive or defensive. A poet capable
    of manipulating the various moods does not restrict
    himself to either an elaborate or a simple style.

---

* A class of deity, sometimes enumerated as twelve, connected with
natural and social phenomena.

कृतापचारो ऽपि परैरनाविष्कृतविक्रियः ।
असाध्यः कुरुते कोपं प्राप्ते काले गदो यथा ॥

मृदुव्यवहितं तेजो भोक्तुमर्थान्प्रकल्पते ।
प्रदीपः स्नेहमादत्ते दशया ह्यन्तरस्थया ॥

नालम्बते दैष्टिकतां न निषीदति पौरुषे ।
शब्दार्थौ सत्कविरिव द्वयं विद्वानपेक्षते ॥

स्थायिनो ऽर्थे प्रवर्तन्ते भावाः संचारिणो यथा ।
रसस्यैकस्य भूयांसस्तथा नेतुर्महीभृतः ॥

९० अनल्पत्वात्प्रधानत्वादंशस्यैवेतरे स्वराः ।
विजिगीषोर्नृपतयः प्रयान्ति परिवारताम् ॥

अप्यनारभमाणस्य विभोरुत्पादिताः परैः ।
व्रजन्ति गुणतामर्थाः शब्दा इव विहायसः ॥

यातव्यपार्ष्णिग्राहादिमालायामधिकद्युतिः ।
एकार्थतन्तुप्रोतायां नायको नायकायते ॥

Such a king does not show any uncertainty in the face of
enemy attack, but only reveals his full wrath at the
appropriate time, when he has become unassailable.[21]

Vigor tempered by an underlying emollience can bring
policy to a suitable conclusion. A lamp draws up oil by
a wick hidden within.

The wise ruler does not rely exclusively on destiny or
depend on effort alone; rather, he takes both into
account, as a skilled poet deploys word and meaning
in equal measure.

According to dramatic theory, the transient mental states
evinced in a play function to enhance the stable
emotion underlying each aesthetic flavor.[22] So do
many vassals work to support a supreme ruler.

In music the main tone is regular and dominant and other   90
notes enhance it; in the same way princes become
vassals of an ambitious monarch.

Even when he does not actually exert himself, results
effected by others are still attributed to his qualities,
as sounds derive from inert ether.

Through his brilliance such a monarch becomes the
central jewel in a necklace whose other gems include
his enemies located to his front and rear; all are
threaded on the string of the single goal of victory.

षाड्गुण्यमुपयुञ्जीत शक्त्यपेक्षं रसायनम् ।
भवन्त्यस्यैवमज्ञानि स्थास्नूनि बलवन्ति च ॥

स्थाने शमवतां शक्त्या व्यायामे वृद्धिरङ्गिनाम् ।
अयथाबलमारम्भो निदानं क्षयसंपदः ॥

९५ तदीशितारं चेदीनां भवांस्तमवमंस्त मा ।
निहन्त्यरीनेकपदे स उदात्तः स्वरानिव ॥

मा वेदि यदसावेको जेतव्यश्चेदिराडिति ।
राजयक्ष्मेव रोगाणां समूहः स महीभृताम् ॥

संपादितफलस्तेन सपक्षः परभेदतः ।
कार्मुकेणेव गुणिना बाणः संधानमेष्यति ॥

A king should consume the elixir of the six modes of
strategy[23] in accordance with his capacity. In this way
his limbs and all the elements that make him a ruler
become firm and sturdy.

Rulers, holding back when it is appropriate, become all the
stronger when they eventually exert themselves, while
an enterprise unsupported by appropriate force ends
in disaster.

So do not underestimate Shishupala, the lord of the   95
Chedis. He is powerful and can get the better of his
enemies in an instant, as within one and the same
word the high-pitched accent supersedes and elides
other tones.[24]

You should not conclude that the Chedi ruler is isolated
and so will be easily conquered, for he is equivalent
to a host of kings, just as consumption involves a
combination of ailments.

The demon Bana* has received favors from him and when
leagued with his own followers is fully capable of
destroying any enemies. No doubt he will ally himself
with Shishupala, who is, when all is said and done, a
gifted man; he will be like an arrow nocked on a bow,
piercing any target it is aimed at.[25]

---

* Literally, "Arrow"; the son of the demon Bali, bested by Vishnu in
his Dwarf incarnation.

ये चान्ये कालयवनसाल्वरुक्मिद्रुमादयः ।
तमःस्वभावास्ते ऽप्येनं प्रदोषमनुयायिनः ॥

उपजापः कृतस्तेन तानाकोपवतस्त्वयि ।
आशु दीपयितात्पो ऽपि साग्रीनेधानिवानिलः ॥

१०० बृहत्सहायः कार्यान्तं क्षोदीयानपि गच्छति ।
संभूयाम्भोधिमभ्येति महानद्या नगापगा ॥

तस्य मित्राण्यमित्रास्ते ये च ये चोभये नृपाः ।
अभियुक्तं त्वयैनं ते गन्तारस्त्वामतः परे ॥

मखविघ्नाय सकलमित्थमुत्थाप्य राजकम् ।
हन्त जातमजातारेः प्रथमेन त्वयारिणा ॥

संभाव्य त्वामतिभरक्षमस्कन्धं सुबान्धवः ।
सहायमध्वरधुरां धर्मराजो विवक्षते ॥

And there are other kings with darkness in their hearts—
    Kalayavana, Salva, Rukmin, and Druma—who will
    join forces with Shishupala, for with his many faults
    he has something of the night about him.[26]

The dissension stirred up by Shishupala is for the moment
    insignificant, but it will soon enflame those already
    angry with you. Just a slight gust of wind can quickly
    cause smoldering fuel to blaze.

When allied with the powerful, even the weakest can   100
    achieve their goal. A stream with its source in the
    mountains will eventually reach the ocean after
    merging with a great river.

Those kings who are his friends, those who are your
    enemies, and those who are in both camps will flock
    to Shishupala when you have attacked him, while only
    the residue will ally themselves with you.

In rousing all the kings to hinder his sacrifice in this way,
    you would then unfortunately also become the main
    foe of Yudhishthira, who otherwise feels no enmity
    toward anyone.

Yudhishthira is your relative, after all, reckoning you to be
    an ally whose shoulders are equal to any great burden;
    he himself intends to bear the yoke of performing the
    sacrifice.

महात्मानो ऽनुगृह्णन्ति भजमानान्त्रिपूनपि ।
सपत्नीः प्रापयन्त्यब्धिं सिन्धवो नगनिम्नगाः ॥

१०५ चिरादपि बलात्कारो बलिनः सिद्ध्ये ऽरिषु ।
छन्दानुवृत्तिदुःसाधाः सुहृदो विमनीकृताः ॥

मन्यसे ऽरिवधः श्रेयान्प्रीतये नाकिनामिति ।
पुरोडाशभुजामिष्टमिष्टं कर्तुमलन्तराम् ॥

अमृतं नाम यत्सन्तो मन्त्रजिह्वेषु जुह्वति ।
शोभैव मन्दरक्षुब्धक्षुभिताम्भोधिवर्णना ॥

प्रतीक्ष्यं च प्रतीक्ष्यायै पितृष्वस्रे सुतस्य ते ।
सहिष्ये शतमागांसि प्रत्यश्रौषीः किलेति यत्⁴ ॥

तीक्ष्णा नारुन्तुदा बुद्धिः कर्म शान्तं प्रतापवत् ।
नोपतापि मनः सोष्म वागेका वाग्मिनः सतः ॥

The illustrious will assist even rivals if they are suppliants.
    Rivers always ensure that mountain rivulets, their
    cowives, gain access to their husband, the ocean.

An aggressive stance toward foes will eventually lead to   105
    the triumph of the powerful, but allies when offended
    are difficult to win back by simply indulging their
    whims.

You may reckon that killing enemies is the best way of
    pleasing the gods. However, what they truly relish
    is the cakes offered up in the ritual, so performing
    the sacrifice anticipated by them will be very much
    preferable.

The substance known everywhere as ambrosia is actually
    the oblation dedicated to the gods in the sacrificial
    fires by expert priests. The traditional account of how
    it was extracted from the ocean churned relentlessly
    by Mount Mandara is no more than a piece of literary
    flummery![27]

As is well known, you promised your father's sister
    that you would tolerate as many as a hundred sins
    committed by her son Shishupala.[28] She deserves
    respect, so you must uphold that commitment.

The wits of a man of truth are sharp but not wounding, his
    deeds are forceful but calm, his heart is warm but not
    fiery, and while eloquent, his speech is consistent.

71

११० स्वयंकृतप्रसादस्य तस्याह्लो भानुमानिव ।
समयावधिमप्राप्य नान्तायालं भवानपि ॥

कृत्वा कृत्यविदस्तीर्थेरतः ५ प्रणिधयः पदम् ।
विदांकुर्वन्तु महतस्तलं विद्विषदम्भसः ॥

अनुत्सूत्रपदन्यासा सद्वृत्तिः सन्निबन्धना ।
शब्दविद्यैव नाभाति राजनीतिरपस्पशा ॥

अज्ञातदोषैर्दोषज्ञैरुद्दूष्योभयवेतनैः ।
भेद्याः शत्रोरभिव्यक्तशासनैः सामवायिकाः ॥

उपेयिवांसि कर्तारः पुरीमाजातशात्रवीम् ।
राजन्यकान्युपायज्ञैरेकार्थानि चरैस्तव ॥

११५ सविशेषं सुते पाण्डोर्भक्तिं भवति तन्वति ।
वैरायितारस्तरलाः स्वयं मत्सरिणः परे ॥

You have freely shown goodwill to Shishupala and cannot   110
    kill him without breaking your word. In this respect
    you are like the sun, bestowing light but unable to end
    the day without reaching the dusk of evening.

So let experienced agents craftily insinuate themselves
    and take the measure of your mighty foe. The depth of
    a river is ascertained by testing its fords.[29]

The course of a king's strategy may well not deviate from
    accepted practice and be sensibly conducted with a
    firm foundation; however, it is worthless if spies are
    not first dispatched. Although the science of grammar
    deploys various layers of exegesis to analyze words in
    a rigorous fashion, it would lack full intellectual force
    without its introductory commentary.[30]

Wily double agents working undercover should isolate the
    enemy's confidants by means of forged documents
    alleging their treason and thus alienate them from
    Shishupala.

Meanwhile, your crafty spies should persuade the kings
    already gone to Yudhishthira's capital to share a
    common purpose with you.

When Yudhishthira, son of Pandu, pays you particular   115
    honor, your enemies, headstrong and jealous, will
    start a quarrel of their own making.

य इहात्मविदो विपक्षमध्ये
सहसंवृद्धियुजो ऽपि भूभुजः स्युः ।
बलिपुष्टकुलादिवान्यपुष्टैः
पृथगस्मादचिरेण भाविता तैः ॥

सहजचापलदोषसमुद्धत-
श्र्वलितदुर्बलपक्षपरिग्रहः ।
तव दुरासदवीर्यविभावसौ
शलभतां लभतामसुहृद्गणः ॥

इति विशकलितार्थामौद्धवीं वाचमेना-
मनुगतनयमार्गामर्गलां दुर्नयस्य ।
जनितमुदमुदस्थादुच्चकैरुच्छ्रितोरः-
स्थलनियतनिषण्णश्रीश्रुतां शुश्रुवान्सः ॥

Then, as this dispute gains momentum, any self-
respecting princes in the enemy party will quickly
detach themselves from Shishupala like cuckoos from
a nest of crows, even if their fortunes are linked to his.

Your foes are a swarm of moths, borne aloft by their innate
capricious folly and drawn to dangerous objects by
their fluttering wings. May they then plunge into the
fire of your invincible heroism."

The substance of this speech of Uddhava's, carefully
sifted and politically sound, offered no scope for any
ill-judged enterprise. It had been so discreet that the
only other person to hear it was the goddess Shri,
as always clinging to her husband's broad chest.[31]
Krishna listened with pleasure and drew himself up to
his full height.

CHAPTER 3

Departure for Indraprastha

कौबीरदिग्भागमपास्य मार्ग-
मागस्त्यमुष्णांशुरिवावतीर्णः ।
अपेतयुद्धाभिनिवेशसौम्यो
हरिर्हरिप्रस्थमथ प्रतस्थे ॥

जगत्पवित्रैरपि तं न पादैः
स्प्रष्टुं जगत्पूज्यमयुज्यतार्कः ।
यतो बृहत्पार्वणचन्द्रचारु
तस्यातपत्रं बिभरांबभूवे ॥

मृणालसूत्रामलमन्तरेण
स्थितश्चलच्चामरयोर्द्वयं सः ।
भेजे ऽभितः पातुकसिद्धसिन्धो-
रभूतपूर्वां श्रियमम्बुराशेः ॥

चित्राभिरस्योपरि मौलिभाजां
भाभिर्मणीनामनणीयसीभिः ।
अनेकधातुच्छुरिताश्मराशे-
र्गोवर्धनस्याकृतिरन्वकारि ॥

५ तस्योल्लसत्काञ्चनकुण्डलाग्र-
प्रत्युप्तगारुत्मतरत्नभासा ।
अवाप बाल्योचितनीलकण्ठ-
पिच्छावचूडाकलनामिवोरः ॥

Krishna was calm, since for the moment he had lost his
   appetite for war. Now he set off for Indraprastha,
   Yudhishthira's capital, like the sun leaving the
   northern sky and descending southward.

The sun's rays might purify the world, but they were unfit
   to touch the one revered by all; so a huge parasol, fair
   as the new moon, was carried over Krishna.

Standing between two fluttering yak-tail whisks white as
   lotus fiber, dark Krishna looked like the ocean with
   the celestial Ganga[1] cascading on both sides—an
   unprecedented marvel.

The jewels in his diadem blazed with a deep and many-
   colored glow so that he took on the look of Mount
   Govardhana,* its rocky crags richly studded with
   precious minerals.

Radiance poured from the emeralds set on the tips of   5
   Krishna's flashing gold earrings; they made his breast
   seem once again wreathed in the peacock feathers he
   had worn as a child.

---

* A hill lifted up by the youthful Krishna.

तमङ्गदे मन्दरकूटकोटि-
व्याघट्टनोत्तेजनया मणीनाम् ।
बंहीयसा दीप्तिवितानकेन
चकासयामासतुरुल्लसन्ती ॥

निसर्गरक्तैर्वलयावबद्ध-
ताम्राश्मरश्मिच्छुरितैर्नखाग्रैः ।
व्यद्योतताद्यापि सुरारिवक्षो-
विक्षोभजासृक्स्नपितैरिवासौ ॥

उभौ यदि व्योम्नि पृथक्प्रवाहा-
वाकाशगङ्गापयसः पतेताम् ।
तेनोपमीयेत तमालनील-
मामुक्तमुक्तालतमस्य वक्षः ॥

तेनाम्भसां सारमयः पयोधे-
र्दध्रे मणिर्दीधितिदीपिताशः ।
अन्तर्वसन्निम्बगतस्तदङ्घ्रे
साक्षादिवालक्ष्यत यत्र लोकः ॥

१० मुक्तामयं सारसनावलम्बि
भाति स्म दामाप्रपदीनमस्य ।
अङ्गुष्ठनिष्च्यूतमिवोर्ध्वमुच्चै-
स्त्रिस्रोतसः सन्ततधारमम्भः ॥

The gems in his armlets illuminated him within a canopy
of light; their brilliance was all the more intense from
being scoured and polished by Mount Mandara's peak
when Vishnu churned the ocean.

His fingernails, already red, were further saturated by the
rays of light seeping from the rubies in his bracelet;
they seemed still soaked with the blood from the
demon Hiranyakashipu's breast, ripped open by the
Man-Lion.[2]

If you can imagine two white streams of the celestial
Ganga flowing separately in the heavens, then
Krishna's chest, dark as a *tamāla* tree and draped with
a pearl necklace, could be compared with the sky.

He wore the Kaustubha jewel containing the essence of
the ocean from which it had been churned; it lit up
all the directions with its radiance and the entire
world was reflected within, appearing to be visibly
encompassed within Krishna's body.

A pearl rosary hung from his belt down to his feet; it   10
seemed to be the stream of the Ganga flowing steadily
up from his toe.[3]

स इन्द्रनीलस्थलनीलमूर्ती
रराज कर्चूरिपिशङ्गवासाः[१] ।
विसृत्वरैरम्बुरुहां रजोभि-
र्यमस्वसुश्चित्र इवोदभारः ॥

प्रसाधितस्याथ मुरद्विषो ऽभू-
दन्यैव लक्ष्मीरिति युक्तमेतत् ।
वपुष्यशेषे ऽखिललोककान्ता
सानन्यकाम्या ह्युरसीतरा तु[२] ॥

दैत्याधिपप्राणमुषां नखाना-
मुपेयुषां भूषणतां क्षतेन ।
प्रकाशकार्कश्यगुणौ दधानाः
स्तनौ तरुण्यः परिवव्रुरेनम् ॥

आकर्षतेवोर्ध्वमपि क्रशीया-
नत्युन्नतत्वात्कुचमण्डलेन ।
ननाम मध्यो ऽतिगुरुत्वभाजा
नितान्तमाक्रान्त इवाङ्गनानाम् ॥

१५ यां यां प्रियः प्रैक्षत कातराक्षीं
सा सा हिया नम्रमुखी बभूव ।
निःशङ्कमन्याः सममाहितेर्ष्यै-
स्तत्रान्तरे जघ्नुरमुं कटाक्षैः ॥

82

With a body dark as a sapphire-inlaid pavement and
    his clothes yellow as camphor, he looked like the
    Yamuna's watery flood[4] tinctured with drifting lotus
    pollen.

It could well be claimed that with all his finery the demon
    Mura's enemy possessed a remarkable double mode
    of beauty—one aspect, adored by the world, pervaded
    his entire body, while the other, his faithful consort
    Shri, could be found only on his chest.[5]

Young women crowded around Krishna, their breasts
    rough-skinned for all to see from lovemaking's
    scratches. Claws that had once torn out the life of the
    demons' king now bestowed decorative nail markings.

The women's heavy breasts seemed to overpower their
    slender waists and force them to bend, yet they jutted
    out so prominently that they also appeared to be
    pulling them up.[6]

When Krishna looked at any one of the women, she   15
    shyly dropped her timid gaze, whereupon the others
    brazenly flashed annoyed glances at him.

तस्यातसीसूनसमानभासो
भ्राम्यन्मयूखावलिमण्डलेन ।
चक्रेण रेजे यमुनाजलौघः
स्फुरन्महावर्त इवैकबाहुः ॥

विरोधिनां विग्रहभेददक्षा
मूर्तेव शक्तिः क्वचिदस्खलन्ती ।
नित्यं हरेः संनिहिता निकामं
कौमोदकी मोदयति स्म चेतः ॥

न केवलं यः स्वतया मुरारे-
रनन्यसाधारणतां दधानः ।
अत्यर्थमुद्वेजयिता परेषां
नाम्नापि तस्यैव स नन्दको ऽभूत् ॥

न नीतमन्येन नतिं कदाचि-
त्कर्णान्तिकप्राप्तगुणं क्रियासु ।
विधेयमस्याभवदन्तिकस्थं
शार्ङ्गं धनुर्मित्रमिव द्रढीयः ॥

२० प्रबद्धमन्द्राम्बुदनादधीरं
कृष्णार्णवाभ्यर्णचरैकहंसः ।
मन्दानिलापूरकृतं दधानो
निध्वानमश्रूयत पाञ्चजन्यः ॥

The discus of indigo-dark Krishna was a shimmering
    circle of light; as he held it, his forearm looked like the
    Yamuna in spate with a great whirlpool swirling on its
    surface.

His club Kaumodaki, always to hand, which unfailingly
    wreaked destruction on enemies, was like Krishna's
    energy personified, a joy to his mind.

His sword Nandaka* lived up to its name; it did not give
    pleasure to Krishna simply because it was his exclusive
    weapon, to be wielded by no one else—he also
    delighted in it as a continual source of terror to his
    enemies.[7]

Nearby was his trusty bow Sharnga,† which only Krishna
    could draw and employ to full effect in battle. It was
    as good as a loyal friend, never cowed by another, its
    constant reliability well established.[8]

His conch-shell trumpet Panchajanya‡ was a solitary swan   20
    gliding on a dark ocean. When filled by the breeze,
    it could be heard sounding loud as the deep rolling
    thunder of rainclouds.

---

* Literally, "Delighter."
† Literally, "Made of Horn."
‡ Taken by Vishnu from the demon Panchajana.

रराज संपादकमिष्टसिद्धेः
सर्वासु दिक्ष्वप्रतिषिद्धमार्गम् ।
महारथः पुष्यरथं स शार्ङ्गी
क्षिप्रं क्षपानाथ इवाधिरूढः ॥

ध्वजाग्रधामा दद‍ृशे ऽथ शौरेः
संक्रान्तमूर्तिर्मणिमेदिनीषु ।
फणावतस्त्रासयितुं रसाया-
स्तलं विविक्षन्निव³ पन्नगारिः ॥

यियासतस्तस्य महीधरन्ध्र-
भिदा पटीयान्पटहप्रणादः ।
जलान्तराणीव महार्णवौघः
शब्दान्तराण्यन्तरयांचकार ॥

यतः स धर्ता जगतां जगाम
धर्त्री धरित्र्याः फणिना ततो ऽधः ।
महाभराभुग्नशिरःसहस्र-
साहायकव्यग्रभुजं प्रसस्ने ॥

२५ अथोच्चकैस्तोरणसङ्गभङ्ग-
भयावनम्रीकृतकेतनानि ।
क्रियाफलानीव सुनीतिभाजं
सैन्यानि सोमान्वयमन्वयुस्तम् ॥

Like the moon ascending into the constellation of Pushya,
the great warrior Krishna quickly mounted his
splendid chariot, which responded to everything
demanded of it and moved with complete freedom.[9]

Garuda could be seen perched atop his banner; reflected
on the jeweled pavements, he appeared ready to
invade the underworld to terrorize the serpents
dwelling there.[10]

As Krishna was about to set out, the thunder of drums,
redoubled by the echo from mountain caverns,
muffled every sound, as the ocean's mighty roar
drowns out the noise of other waters.

Wherever the god who bore all worlds set foot, Shesha,
the serpent who supported the all-bearing earth,
extended himself beneath, all the while stiffening his
coils to bear his thousand heads, pressed down by the
massive weight upon them.

Dipping their banners to avoid breaking them on the lofty   25
gateways, divisions of troops followed Krishna. In
the same manner, success ensues for a ruler adopting
sound policy.

श्यामारुणैर्वारणदानतोयै-
रालोडिताः काञ्चनभूपरागाः ।
आनेमिमग्रैः शितिकण्ठपक्ष-
क्षोदद्युतश्चुक्षुभिरे रथौघैः ॥

न लङ्घयामास महाजनानां
शिरांसि नैवोद्धतिमाजगाम ।
अचेष्टताष्टापदभूमिरेणुः
खुराहतो यत्सदृशं गरिम्णः ॥

निरुध्यमाना यदुभिः कथंचि-
न्मुहुर्यदुच्चिक्षिपुरग्रपादौ ।
ध्रुवं गुरून्मार्गरुधः करीन्द्रा-
नुलङ्घ्य गन्तुं तुरगास्तदीषुः ॥

अवेक्षितानायतवल्गमग्रे
तुरङ्गिभिर्यल्ननिरुद्धवाहैः ।
प्रक्रीडितात्रेणुभिरेत्य तूर्णं
निन्युर्जनन्यः पृथुकान्पथिभ्यः ॥

३० दिदृक्षमाणाः प्रतिरथ्यमीयु-⁴
र्मुरारिमारादनघं जनौघाः ।
अनेकशः संस्तुतमप्यनल्पा⁵
नवं नवं प्रीतिरहो करोति ॥

As the chariots sank up to their axles, golden dust mingled
with dark-red elephant ichor was flung into the air like
pulverized peacocks' wings.

That dust had been vigorously kicked up by the horses'
hooves, but it was so thick that it neither settled upon
the watching crowds nor floated above them.[11]

The horses, barely reined in by the Yadavas, reared up
time and again, for they were eager to overtake the
mighty elephants blocking the road with their bulk
and proceed on their way.

Mothers rushed to snatch their children from the highway
as they played in the dust; spying them ahead, the
cavalrymen had already reined in their steeds in the
nick of time.

Crowds of people came from afar in their desire to see   30
the faultless Krishna on the march. Sincere affection
completely refreshes even one accustomed to praise.

उपेयुषो वर्त्म निरन्तराभि-
रसौ निरुच्छ्वासमनीकिनीभिः ।
रथस्य तस्यां पुरि दत्तचक्षु-
र्विद्वान्विदामास शनैर्न यातम् ॥

मध्येसमुद्रं ककुभः पिशङ्गी-
र्या कुर्वती काञ्चनवप्रभासा६ ।
तुरङ्गकान्ताननहव्यवाह-
ज्वालेव भित्त्वा जलमुल्ललास ॥

कृतास्पदा भूमिभृतां सहस्रै-
रुदन्वदम्भःपरिवीतमूर्तिः ।
अनिर्विदा या विदधे विधात्रा
पृथ्वी पृथिव्याः प्रतियातनेव ॥

त्वष्टुः सदाभ्यासगृहीतशिल्प-
विज्ञानसंपत्प्रसरस्य सीमा ।
अट्टद्दश्यतादर्शतलामलेषु
च्छायेव या स्वर्जलधेर्जलेषु ॥

३५ रथाङ्गभर्त्रे ऽभिनवं वराय
यस्याः पितेव प्रतिपादितायाः ।
प्रेम्णोपकण्ठं मुहुरङ्कभाजो
रत्नावलीरम्बुधिराबबन्ध ॥

Krishna was aware of everything, but as he glimpsed his
capital Dvaraka, he did not notice the slow progress of
his chariot—no breathing space could be found on the
road, owing to the packed soldiery.

Yellowing the horizons with the glow from its golden
ramparts, Krishna's sea-girt capital blazed like the
flame of underwater fire bursting above the surface.[12]

That vast ocean-encompassed city, the abode of thousands
of kings, had been constructed by the unwearied
creator as a replica of the earth.[13]

Dvaraka was the consummation of Tvashtri's* sublime
knowledge of architectural craft, mastered through
eternal practice; it appeared mirrored in the ocean's
pellucid waters like heaven's reflection.

In affection, the sea continually lavished heaps of jewels   35
on the shores of that city bestowed on the peerless
Krishna as his capital during that era, just as a father
lovingly fastens a necklace on his daughter clinging to
him after being given to her new husband.[14]

---

* Literally, "Fashioner", the divine craftsman.

यस्याश्चलद्वारिधिवारिवीचि-
च्छटोच्छलच्छङ्खकुलाकुलेन ।
वप्रेण पर्यन्तचरोडुचक्रः
सुमेरुवप्रो ऽन्वहमन्वकारि ॥

वणिक्पथे पूगकृतानि यत्र
भ्रमागतैरम्बुभिरम्बुराशिः ।
लोलैरलोलद्युतिभाञ्जि मुष्ण-
न्रत्नानि रत्नाकरतामवाप ॥

अम्भश्च्युतः कोमलरत्नराशी-
नपांपतिः फेनपिनद्धभासः ।
यत्रातपं दातुमिवोपतल्पं
विसारयामास तुरङ्गहस्तैः ॥

यत्सालमुत्तुङ्गतया विजेतुं
दूरादुदस्थीयत सागरस्य ।
महोर्मिभिर्व्याहतवाञ्छितार्थै-
र्व्रीडादिवाभ्याशगतैर्विलिल्ये ॥

४० कुतूहलेनेव जवादुपेत्य
प्राकारभित्त्या सहसा निषिद्धः ।
रसन्नरोदीद्धृशमम्बुवर्ष-
व्याजेन यस्या⁷ बहिरम्बुवाहः ॥

The city ramparts, carpeted with heaps of conch shells
    thrown up by a relentless surge of waves, daily
    imitated the heights of Mount Meru encircled by
    constellations of stars.

With the whirling ebb and flow of its waters the ocean
    stole away gems of unfading brilliance piled up for sale
    in the marketplace, becoming a true mine of precious
    stones.[15]

Then with hand-like waves it spread out in the market's
    lanes fresh heaps of jewels, dripping with brine, their
    brilliance masked by foam, as if to dry them in the
    heat.

Huge rolling breakers aspired to overtop the ramparts, but
    they could not reach quite high enough and sank back
    as if embarrassed.

A monsoon cloud floated along briskly, thundering as   40
    it went, as if curious to inspect the city. Lofty walls
    suddenly blocked its progress, and it was compelled to
    remain outside, weeping piteously under the guise of
    pouring down rain.

यदङ्गनारूपसरूपतायाः
किंचिदूनं भेदकमिच्छतीभिः ।
आराधितो ऽद्धा मनुरप्सरोभि-
श्चक्रे प्रजाः स्वाः सनिमेषचिह्नाः ॥

स्फुरत्तुषारांशुमरीचिजाल-
विनिहुताः स्फाटिकसौधपङ्क्तीः ।
आरुह्य नार्यः क्षणदासु यस्यां
नभोगता देव्य इव व्यराजन् ॥

कान्तेन्दुकान्तोपलकुट्टिमेषु
प्रतिक्षपं हर्म्यतलेषु यत्र ।
उच्चैरधःपातिपयोमुचो ऽपि
समूहमूहुः पयसां प्रणाल्यः ॥

रतौ ह्रिया यत्र निशम्य दीपा-
ञ्ज्वालागताभ्यो ऽधिगृहं गृहिण्यः ।
बिभ्युर्विडालेक्षणभीषणाभ्यो
वैदूर्यकुड्येषु शशिद्युतिभ्यः ॥

४५ यस्यामतिश्लक्ष्णतया गृहेषु
विधातुमालेख्यमशक्नुवन्तः ।
चक्रुर्युवानः प्रतिबिम्बिताङ्गाः
सजीवचित्रा इव रत्नभित्तीः ॥

The apsarases had longed to have some slight difference
   from the city women, whose beauty was no less than
   theirs. They begged Manu,* father of humanity,
   so intensely that he caused his progeny to be
   distinguished by their blinking of the eyes.[16]

At night the city's avenues of crystal mansions became
   invisible amid the dense rays of the glowing moon,
   and women ascending to their roofs seemed like
   goddesses floating in the sky.

Each night the conduits on the high palace terraces
   overflowed; although the rainclouds were far below,
   the moonstones inlaid on the walkways oozed streams
   of water when caressed by moonbeams.

In every residence women ready for lovemaking modestly
   doused the lamps, but then they took fright at the
   moonbeams, scary as yellow cats' eyes, streaming
   through the window-grills onto the beryl partitions.

The young men there could not paint murals on the   45
   mansions' jeweled walls; when reflections were cast on
   their surface, the brilliantly smooth sheen made them
   seem overlaid with living pictures.

---

* The first king and lawgiver.

सावर्ण्यभाजः प्रतिमागतायाः
लक्ष्यैः स्मरापाण्डुतया तरुण्याः^८ ।
यस्यां कपोलैः कलधौतधाम-
स्तम्भेषु भेजे मणिदर्पणश्रीः ॥

शुकाङ्गनीलोपलनिर्मितानां
लिम्पेषु भासा गृहदेहलीनाम् ।
यस्यामलिन्देषु न चक्रुरेव
मुग्धाङ्गना गोमयगोमुखानि ॥

गोपानसीषु क्षणमास्थिताना-
मालम्बिभिश्चन्द्रकिणां कलापैः ।
हरिन्मणिश्यामतृणाभिरामै-
र्गृहाणि नीध्रैरिव यत्र रेजुः ॥

बृहत्तुलैरप्यतुलैर्वितान-
मालावनद्धैरपि चावितानैः ।
रेजे विचित्रैरपि या सचित्रै-
र्गृहैर्विशालैरपि भूरिशालैः ॥

५० चिक्रंसया कृत्रिमपत्रिपङ्क्तेः
कपोतपालीषु निकेतनानाम् ।
मार्जारमप्यानतनिश्चलाङ्गं
यस्यां जनः कृत्रिममेव मेने ॥

96

In that city, women's cheeks, tinged with paleness from
love's passion, had the same hue as the silvery-gold
palace pillars on which they were reflected, gleaming
like bejeweled mirrors.

Housewives did not need to make auspicious designs of
cow dung on the terraces; they were already suffused
with the glow from domestic thresholds made of
emeralds green as a parrot's feathers.

The houses there were swathed in the hanging tail feathers
of peacocks momentarily roosting on their roofs, so
that the eaves seemed thatched with emerald-green
straw.

The city was packed with splendid mansions, unequaled in
their mighty roof beams; draped with heavy awnings
and stocked with luxurious furniture, they were
a wonder to the eye, crammed with fine pictures,
spacious, and many-chambered.

A cat arched its back, completely still, poised to pounce   50
on the rows of ornamental birds on the mansions'
dovecots—so motionless people took it for an
imitation.

क्षितिप्रतिष्ठो ऽपि मुखारविन्दै-
र्वधूजनश्चन्द्रमधश्चकार ।
अतीतनक्षत्रपथानि यत्र
प्रासादशृङ्गाणि मुधाध्यारोहत् ॥

रम्या इति प्राप्तवतीः पताका
रागं विविक्ता इति वर्धयन्तीः ।
यस्यामसेवन्त नमद्द्रुलीकाः
समं वधूभिर्वल्लभीर्युवानः ॥

सुगन्धितामप्रतियत्नपूर्वं
बिभ्रन्ति यत्र प्रमदाय पुंसाम् ।
मधूनि वक्त्राणि च कामिनीना-
मामोदकर्मव्यतिहारमीयुः ॥

रतान्तरे यत्र गृहान्तरेषु
वितर्दिनिर्यूहविटङ्कनीडः ।
रुतानि शृण्वन्वयसां गणो ऽन्ते-
वासित्वमाप स्फुटमङ्गनानाम् ॥

५५ छन्नेष्वपि स्पष्टतरेषु यत्र
स्वच्छानि नारीकुचमण्डलेषु ।
आकाशसाम्यं दधुरम्बराणि
न नामतः केवलमर्थतो ऽपि ॥

Young women, firmly earthbound, had already conveyed
    the moon down to that city through the beauty of
    their lotus-like faces. No need for them to climb to
    palace turrets higher than the stars' pathways in order
    to gaze upon it!

The roofs of the mansions, with their overhanging eaves
    bedecked with flags to enhance their charm, evoked
    an amorous atmosphere through intimate seclusion.
    Young men frequented them with their wives, women
    famed for their looks, enflaming lust with their
    flawless complexions, all with delightfully rippling
    folds on their stomachs.[17]

Wine and the mouths of beauties, each with their own
    naturally delicious scent, took turns delighting men
    by imparting a sweet fragrance.

Flocks of birds, nesting high on the balcony turrets, heard
    the billing and cooing of women making love indoors
    and became their pupils by immediate imitation.

Light gossamer, revealing ample breasts even as it covered   55
    them, was like air not just in name but in effect as
    well.[18]

यस्यामजिह्वा महतीमपङ्का:
सीमानमत्यायतयो ऽत्यजन्त: ।
जनैरजातस्खलनैर्न जातु
द्वये ऽप्यमुच्यन्त विनीतमार्गा: ॥

परस्परस्पर्धिपरार्ध्यरूपा:
पौरस्त्रियो यत्र विधाय वेधा: ।
श्रीनिर्मितिप्राप्तघुणक्षतैक-
वर्णोपमावाच्यमलं ममार्ज ॥

क्षुण्णं यदन्त:करणेन वृक्षा:
फलन्ति कल्पोपपदास्तदेव ।
अध्यूषुषस्तामभवन्जनस्य
या: संपदस्ता मनसो ऽप्यभूमि: ॥

कला दधान: सकला: स्वभाभि-
रुद्भासयन्सौधसिताभिराशा: ।
यां रेवतीजानिरियेष हातुं
न रौहिणेयो न च रोहिणीश: ॥

Citizens traveled without mishap on two kinds of road—
    Dvaraka's well-constructed highways: straight, clean,
    and although very long, never diverging from major
    boundary markers—and the paths of good conduct:
    undeviating, free from sin, never transgressing moral
    limits, requiring great restraint, followed by those
    who cannot err.[19]

In creating the city women, vying with each other in
    sublime good looks, Brahma* dispelled the calumny
    that his creation of the goddess of beauty was a mere
    accident.

Wishing trees in heaven deliver as their fruit whatever
    the mind conceives of, but the prosperity attained by
    the city's inhabitants was beyond even the power of
    imagination.

Balarama, the son of Rohini and husband of Revati,
    was master of every art, while the moon, lord of
    the constellations Rohini and Revati,† possessed a
    full sixteen phases.[20] Both in their radiance could
    illuminate every direction as they gleamed like
    whitened palaces, but neither wished to leave that
    city.

---

* The creator god.
† Respectively, the fourth and twenty-seventh asterisms through
  which the moon moves.

६० बाणाहवव्याहतशाम्भुशक्ते-
रासत्तिमासद्य जनार्दनस्य ।
शरीरिणा जैत्रशरेण यत्र
निःशङ्कमूषे मकरध्वजेन ॥

निषेव्यमाणेन शिवैर्मरुद्धि-
रध्यास्यमाना हरिणा चिराय ।
उद्रश्मिरत्नाङ्कुरधाम्नि सिन्धा-
वाह्लास्त मेरावमरावतीं या ॥

स्निग्धाञ्जनश्यामरुचिः सुवृत्तो
वध्वा इवाध्वंसितवर्णकान्तेः ।
विशेषको वा विशिशेष यस्याः
श्रियं त्रिलोकीतिलकः स एव ॥

तामीक्षमाणः स पुरीं पुरस्ता-
त्प्रापत्प्रतोलीमतुलप्रतापः ।
वज्रप्रभाक्रान्तसुरायुधश्री-
र्या देवसेनेव परैरलङ्घ्या ॥

There the god of love with his all-conquering arrows lived 60
  securely, now in embodied guise; he had been reborn
  as Pradyumna, Krishna's son, who had battled with
  the demon Bana and so destroyed Shiva's power.[21]

Dvaraka had now been Krishna's capital for some time.
  Situated by the pearl-filled sea, its soft breezes
  continuously caressed him; it rivaled Amaravati on
  Mount Meru,[22] carpeted with precious stones, ever
  ruled by Indra, attended by Rudras and Maruts.*

But its beauty was surpassed by Krishna himself, dark as
  a smooth cream, the ornament of the universe, and
  virtuous maintainer of the integrity of society; he
  stood out like a collyrium mark on the forehead of a
  girl of flawless fair complexion.[23]

Viewing the city as he went, the unrivaled hero arrived
  at the thoroughfare leading to the eastern gateway.
  Hemmed in by bejeweled mansions, it glittered like a
  rainbow; immune from any attack, it was like the army
  of the gods whose divine weapons are surpassed in
  luster only by Indra's mace.[24]

---

* Subordinate warrior-like deities associated with the god Rudra and
 the storm wind.

प्रजा इवाङ्घ्रदरविन्दनाभेः
शाम्भोर्जटाजूटतटादिवापः ।
मुखादिवाथ श्रुतयो विधातुः
पुरान्त्रिरीयुर्मुरजिद्भुजिन्यः ॥

६५ श्लिष्यद्भिरन्योन्यमुखाग्रसङ्ग-
स्खलत्खलीनं हरिभिर्विलोलैः ।
परस्परोत्पीडितजानुभागा
यत्नेन निश्चक्रमुरश्ववाराः ॥

निरन्तराले ऽपि विमुच्यमाने
दूरं पथि प्राणभृतां गणेन ।
तेजोमहद्भिस्तमसेव दीपै-
र्द्विपैरसंबाधमयांबभूवे ॥

शनैरनीयन्त रयात्पतन्तो
रथाः क्षितिं हस्तिनखादखेदैः ।
सयत्नसूतायतरश्मिभुग्न-
ग्रीवान्तसंसक्तयुगैस्तुरङ्गैः ॥

बलोर्मिभिस्तत्क्षणहीयमान-
रथ्याभुजाया वलयैरिवास्याः ।
प्रायेण निष्क्रामति चक्रपाणौ
नेष्टं पुरो द्वारवतीत्वमासीत् ॥

At last Krishna's army emerged from the city, like
    humankind from Vishnu's body, or the Ganga from
    Shiva's piled hair,[25] or the Veda from the creator's
    mouth.

The cavalry rode out in some disarray, knee jammed   65
    against knee, the horses' bridle bits loosening as
    muzzles collided in the confusion.

The very moment the squadrons of chargers and their
    riders finally left the densely packed road, the mighty
    elephants entered, moving freely; it was like darkness
    fleeing from blazing lamps.

The chariots, built for speed, were slowly brought to level
    ground from the high turreted gateway. Their horses
    were on their mettle, and the charioteers had to haul
    on the reins so tightly that the neck yokes bent from
    the strain.

The floods of troops were now disappearing from the
    highway, like armlets sliding from a wasted arm.[26]
    As Krishna himself was about to leave, the city of
    Dvaraka regretted having gates.[27]

पारेजलं नीरनिधेरपश्य-
न्नुरारिरानीलपलाशराशीः ।
वनावलीरुत्कलिकासहस्र-
प्रतिक्षणोत्कूलितशैवलाभाः ॥

७० लक्ष्मीभृतो ऽम्मोधितटाधिवासा-
न्दूमानसौ नीरदनीलभासः ।
लतावधूसंप्रयुजो ऽधिवेलं
बहूकृतान्स्वानिव पश्यति स्म ॥

आश्लिष्टभूमिं रसितारमुच्चै-
र्लेलड्डुजाकारबृहत्तरङ्गम् ।
फेनायमानं पतिमापगाना-
मसावपस्मारिणमाशशङ्के ॥

पीत्वा जलानां निधिनातिगर्धा-
द्वृद्धिं गते ऽप्यात्मनि नैव मान्तीः ।
क्षिप्ता इवेन्दोः सरुचो ऽधिवेलं
मुक्तावलीराकलयांचकार ॥

साटोपमुर्वीमनिशं नदन्तो
यैः प्लावयिष्यन्ति समन्ततो ऽमी ।
तान्येकदेशान्निभृतं पयोधौ
सो ऽम्भांसि मेघान्पिबतो ददर्श ॥

Krishna now beheld beside the shore dense woodlands
    swathed in masses of dark green foliage, like seaweed
    incessantly washed up by thousands of waves.

The vast throngs of majestic trees, dark as storm clouds,   70
    Krishna saw growing on the shore were entwined with
    vines; they could be taken for himself in his wife's
    embrace—repeated over and over.[28]

He thought the ocean, lord of rivers, must have been
    possessed by a demon; it was hugging the earth and
    roaring out loud, while its huge breakers looked like
    waving arms as it foamed.

He fancied the pearls on the shore to be moonbeams,
    seemingly not remaining in the sea after it had
    greedily drunk them but instead being hurled back
    when the tide rolled in at moonrise.

Krishna saw the clouds silently drinking from one part
    of the ocean the water with which, amid thunder's
    incessant rumbling, they will eventually flood the
    entire earth on doomsday.

उद्धृत्य मेघैस्तत एव तोय-
मर्थं मुनीन्द्रैरिव संप्रणीताः ।
आलोकयामास हरिः पतन्ती-
र्नदीः स्मृतीर्वेदमिवाम्बुराशिम् ॥

७५ विक्रीय दिश्यानि धनान्युरूणि
द्वैप्यानसावुत्तमलाभभाजः ।
तरीषु तत्रत्यमफल्गु भाण्डं
सांयात्रिकानावपतो ऽभ्यनन्दत् ॥

उत्पित्सवो ऽन्तर्नदभर्तुरुच्चै-
र्गरीयसा निःश्वसितानिलेन ।
पयांसि भक्त्या गरुडध्वजस्य
ध्वजानिवोच्चिक्षिपिरे फणीन्द्राः ॥

तमागतं वीक्ष्य युगान्तबन्धु-
मुत्सङ्गशय्याशयमम्बुराशिः ।
प्रत्युज्जगामेव गुरुप्रमोद-
प्रसारितोत्तुङ्गतरङ्गबाहुः ॥

उत्सर्जिताम्भःकणिको नभस्वा-
नौदन्वतः स्वेदलवान्ममार्ज ।
तस्यानुवेलं व्रजतो ऽतिवेल-
मैलालतास्फालनलब्धगन्धः ॥

108

He next beheld the rivers flowing into the sea, brought
into being by clouds sucking up marine water. In
similar manner the texts on law had been collected by
mighty sages on the basis of the meaning of the Veda
and then became included within that very Veda.[29]

Krishna then greeted merchants, voyagers from across   75
the ocean. They had made a rich profit through
selling their cargo of foreign luxuries and were now
loading stores of local wares onto their ships for future
enterprises.

The serpent lords were near arising from the ocean's
depths. With the great gale of their hissing they
seemed to have piled up huge waves as banners of
fealty to Krishna, whose ensign is Garuda, enemy of
snakes.

The sea for its part saw Krishna had arrived, and in delight
stretched out its towering arm-like waves in apparent
welcome; for he had reclined there as its divine ally in
ending the world at the close of every world age.[30]

As Krishna proceeded beyond the shore, an ocean breeze,
trailing spray, fragrant from brushing against nearby
cardamom vines, diligently wiped away beads of
sweat.

उत्तालतालीवनसंप्रवृत्त-
समीरसीमन्तितकेतकीकाः ।
आसेदिरे लावणसैन्धवीनां
चमूचरैः कच्छभुवां प्रदेशाः ॥

८० लवङ्गमालाकलितावतंसा-
स्ते नारिकेलान्तरपः पिबन्तः ।
आस्वादितार्द्रक्रमुकाः समुद्रा-
दभ्यागतस्य प्रतिपत्तिमापुः ॥

तुरगशताकुलस्य परितः परमेकतुरङ्गजन्मनः
प्रमथितभूभृतः प्रतिपथं मथितस्य भृशं महीभृता ।
परिचलतो बलानुजबलस्य पुरः सततं धृतश्रिय-
श्चिरविगतश्रियो जलनिधेश्च तदाभवदन्तरं महत् ॥

Eventually the soldiers arrived at the marshy ground
    abutting onto the salt sea, where the *ketaki** creepers
    were parted by a wind flowing from lofty palm groves.

There, receiving the ocean's guest-welcome, they   80
    decorated themselves with garlands of cloves, drank
    coconut milk, and ate juicy betel nut.

How inferior the ocean seemed just then! When Krishna's
    army marched from the city, its squadrons of cavalry
    extended in their hundreds as far as the eye could
    see; it could destroy any enemy king in its path and
    always won the day. But the sea—only one horse,
    Ucchaihshravas, had ever emerged from it, while a
    mere mountain had violently churned it, and it had
    forever given up Shri, the goddess of royal fortune.[31]

---

* The screw pine, or umbrella tree.

CHAPTER 4

Mount Raivataka

विश्वासधूमं सह रत्नभाभि-
र्भित्त्वोत्थितं भूमिमिवोरगाणाम् ।
नीलोपलस्यूतविचित्रधातु-
मसौ गिरिं रैवतकं ददर्श ॥

गुर्वीरजस्त्रं दृषदः समन्ता-
दुपर्युपर्यम्बुमुचां वितानैः ।
विन्ध्यायमानं दिवसस्य कर्तु-
र्मार्गं पुरो रोद्धुमिवोन्नमद्भिः ॥

क्रान्तं रुचा काञ्चनवप्रभाजा
नवप्रभाजालभृतां मणीनाम् ।
श्रितं शिलाश्यामलताभिरामं
लताभिरामन्त्रितषड्पदाभिः ॥९

सहस्रसंख्यैर्गगनं शिरोभिः
पादैर्भुवं व्याप्य वितिष्ठमानम् ।
विलोचनस्थानगतोष्णरश्मि-
निशाकरं साधु हिरण्यगर्भम् ॥

Krishna now beheld Mount Raivataka* overlaid with
    every kind of mineral intermingled with sapphires. It
    looked like a column of steam, tinted with the gleam
    of jewels, from the hissing of serpents splitting the
    earth's surface.

Raivataka seemed like another Vindhya† mountain; its
    high crags were shrouded with cloud canopies rising
    ever upward in all directions as if to block the path of
    the sun in the east.

It was suffused with the brilliance of glistening gems
    strewn over its golden slopes, a source of delight from
    the dark glow of its sapphires, wreathed with vine
    tendrils summoning bees with their fragrance.

This mountain was firmly planted, a repository of finest
    gold, its thousand peaks spreading over the sky and its
    foothills stretching over the earth, with the sun and
    moon doing duty for its eyes. Raivataka was truly like
    the god Golden Germ,[1] all-encompassing foundation
    of the universe, with his myriad heads and feet.[2]

---

* Literally, "Opulence"; Mount Girnar in what is now the Saurashtra
  region of Gujarat.
† The mountain range traditionally regarded as marking the
  boundary between northern and southern India.

५ क्वचिज्जलापायविपाण्डुराणि
धौतोत्तरीयप्रतिमच्छवीनि ।
अभ्राणि बिभ्राणमुमाङ्गसङ्ग-
विभक्तभस्मानमिव स्मरारिम् ॥

छायां निजस्त्रीचटुलालसानां
मदेन किञ्चिच्चटुलालसानाम् ।
कुर्वाणमुत्पिञ्जलजातपत्रै-
र्विहङ्गमानां जलजातपत्रैः ॥

स्कन्धाधिरूढोज्ज्वलनीलकण्ठा-
नुर्वीरुहः श्लिष्टतनूनहीन्द्रैः ।
प्रनर्तितानेकलताभुजाग्रा-
न्रुद्राननन्तानिव धारयन्तम् ॥

विलम्बिनीलोत्पलकर्णपूराः
कपोलभित्तीरिव रोध्रगौरीः ।
नवोलपालंकृतसैकताभाः
शुचीरपः शेवलिनीर्दधानम् ॥

राजीवराजीवशलोलभृङ्गं
मुष्णन्तमुष्णं ततिभिस्तरूणाम् ।
कान्तालकान्ता ललनाः सुराणां
रक्षोभिरक्षोभितमुद्वहन्तम् ॥

116

On one side the clouds above Raivataka were white after   5
    releasing their rain and now looked like a freshly
    washed garment. The mountain itself resembled
    Shiva's body only half-covered with ash after his wife
    Uma's embrace.

It seemed to be casting a shadow with full-opened lotus
    parasols—but these were the outstretched wings of
    birds hovering listlessly as they pined for their mates'
    endearments.

Raivataka was thick with trees, glossy peacocks roosting
    on their branches, huge snakes coiled around their
    trunks, arm-like vines set quivering by the wind; they
    were like countless Shivas, throats stained dark by the
    fierce poison,[3] belted with Vasuki, king of serpents,
    slender arms gesturing in the dance.[4]

Its pellucid pools blanketed with duckweed were radiant
    with white sand banks adorned with fresh grass, like
    a girl's high cheeks pale as *lodhra* blossoms, dark lily-
    earrings hanging beside them.

Bees swarmed everywhere, meandering through the
    mountain's lotus clumps; as stands of trees kept heat
    at bay, divine women, elegantly coiffed, haunted its
    slopes, now secure from demons.

१० मुदे मुरारेरमरैः सुमेरो-
रानीय यस्योपचितस्य शृङ्गैः ।
भवन्ति नोद्दामगिरां कवीना-
मुच्छ्रायसौन्दर्यगुणा मृषोद्याः ॥

यतो महार्घाणि भृतान्यनूनैः
प्रस्थैर्मुहुर्भूरिभिरुच्छिखानि ।
आढ्यादिव प्रापणिकादजस्रं
जग्राह रत्नान्यमितानि लोकः ॥

अखिद्यतासन्नमुदग्रतापं
रविं दधाने ऽप्यरविन्दधाने ।
भृङ्गावलिर्यस्य तटे निपीत-
रसा नमत्तामरसा न मत्ता ॥

यत्राधिरूढेन महीरुहोच्चै-
रुन्निद्रपुष्पाक्षिसहस्रभाजा ।
सुराधिपाधिष्ठितहस्तिमल्ल-
लीलां दधौ राजतगण्डशैलः ॥

विभिन्नवर्णा गरुडाग्रजेन
सूर्यस्य रथ्याः परितः स्फुरन्त्या ।
रत्नैः पुनर्यत्र रुचं रुचा स्वा-
मानिन्यिरे वंशकरीरनीलैः ॥

To Krishna's delight, Raivataka had been augmented by   10
    other peaks brought by the gods from Mount Meru.
    Inspired poets have not exaggerated in describing its
    striking loftiness and beauty.[5]

Blazing heaps of fabulous jewels could be unceasingly
    garnered from its many broad slopes as if from a
    wealthy merchant.

These slopes were rich in lotuses, and even when exposed
    to the blazing sun, intoxicated bees, which had drunk
    their honey and bent the blooms with their weight,
    swarmed there unwearyingly.

One especially fine tree festooned with myriad open-eyed
    blossoms grew tall on Raivataka's great silver crag; it
    looked like the elephant Airavata mounted by Indra,
    king of the gods.[6]

There the horses of the sun's chariot changed color in the
    face of dawn's pink glow and were restored to their
    normal hue by the emeralds, dark-green as bamboo
    shoots, gleaming everywhere.[7]

१५ यत्रोज्झिताभिर्मुहुरम्बुवाहैः
समुन्नमद्भिर्न समुन्नमद्भिः ।
वनं बबाधे विषपावकोत्था
विपन्नगानामविपन्नगानाम् ॥

वमद्भिरुष्णांशुकरावमर्शा-
त्कार्षाणवं धाम पतङ्गकान्तैः ।
शशंस यः पात्रगुणादुणानां
संक्रान्तिराक्रान्तगुणान्तरेति२ ॥

दृष्टो ऽपि शैलः स मुहुर्मुरारे-
रपूर्ववद्विस्मयमातताान ।
क्षणे क्षणे यन्नवतामुपैति
तदेव रूपं रमणीयतायाः ॥

उच्चारणज्ञो ऽथ गिरां दधान-
मुच्चा रणत्पक्षिगणास्तटीस्तम् ।
उत्कन्धरं द्रष्टुमवेक्ष्य शौरि-
मुत्कं धरं दारुक इत्युवाच ॥

आच्छादितायतदिगम्बरमुच्चकैर्गा-
माक्रम्य च स्थितमुदग्रविशालशृङ्गम् ।
मूर्ध्नि स्खलत्तुहिनदीधितिकोटिमेन-
मुद्वीक्ष्य को न भुवि विस्मयते नगेशम् ॥

No threat from the fiery venom of lurking snakes   15
     disturbed its forest trees, for lowering clouds
     continuously salved them with rain.

Sunstones poured forth a fierce radiance when touched
     by the sun's rays. Raivataka affirmed a general
     principle—attributes, when transferred, are altered in
     conformity to their recipient's caliber.[8]

Although Krishna had already gazed intently at that
     mountain, it still astonished him as if he was seeing it
     for the very first time. It is characteristic of beauty to
     renew itself continually.

He went on craning his neck in his eagerness to inspect
     Raivataka, its slopes thronged with choruses of birds.
     Krishna's charioteer, Daruka, a man eloquent of
     speech,[9] looked at him and then spoke.

"Who on earth is not amazed on seeing this towering
     mountain? It obscures the broad horizon and bears
     down on the earth with the mighty ranges of its peaks,
     while the lunar horn brushes against its summit.
     Raivataka is as astonishing as Shiva, lord of Kailasa*—
     naked, he wears only air for clothing, sitting upright
     on a bull with sharp, long horns as the crescent moon
     glints upon his head.[10]

———

* Shiva's mountain home in the Himalayas.

२० उदयति विततोर्ध्वरश्मिरज्जा-
वहिमरुचौ हिमधाम्नि याति चास्तम् ।
वहति गिरिरियं विलम्बिघण्टा-
द्वयपरिवारितवारणेन्द्रलीलाम् ॥

वहति च परितः कनकस्थलीः
सहरिता लसमाननवांशुकः ।
अचल एष भवानिव राजते
सहरितालसमाननवांशुकः ॥

पाश्चात्यभागमिह सानुषु सन्निषण्णाः
पश्यन्ति शान्तमलसान्द्रतरांशुजालम् ।
संपूर्णलब्धललनालपनोपमान-
मुत्सङ्गसङ्गिहरिणस्य हिमांशुमूर्तेः ॥

कृत्वा पुंवत्पातमुच्चैर्भृगुभ्यो
मूर्ध्नि ग्रावणां जर्जरा निर्झरौघाः ।
कुर्वन्ति द्यामुत्पतन्तः स्मरार्त-
स्वर्लोकस्त्रीगात्रनिर्वाणमत्र ॥

स्थगयन्त्यमूः शमितचातकार्तस्वरा
जलदास्तडित्तुलितकान्तकार्तस्वराः ।
जगतीरिह स्फुरितचारुचामीकराः
सवितुः क्वचित्कपिशयन्ति चामी कराः ॥

When the sun rises and the moon sets, each extending   20
    upward slender ropes of rays, this mountain appears
    as graceful as a mighty elephant with a bell hanging
    down each side.[11]

Early morning sunlight plays everywhere on its golden
    meadows, dark green with grass. Raivataka is as fair as
    you, Krishna, when clad in your fresh turmeric-yellow
    robe.

These slopes are so lofty that those seated atop can view
    the far side of the deer-marked moon.[12] Totally
    without blemish, the brightness it emits is all the more
    intense—it now looks like the perfectly oval face of a
    pretty girl.

Here waterfalls cascade in torrents from high precipices
    onto the rocks below, like suicides dashing themselves
    to pieces; their spray flies into the sky to cool the
    bodies of heavenly women tormented by passion.

On this side of the mountain, rain clouds, calming the
    yearning cries of *cātaka* birds,[13] rivaling blazing gold
    with their lightning, conceal its expanses; elsewhere
    sunrays, likewise flashing like bright gold, turn them
    yellow.

२५ उत्क्षिप्तमुच्छितसितांशुकरावलम्बै-
रुत्तम्भितोडुभिरतीवतरां शिरोभिः ।
श्रद्धेयनिर्झरजलव्यपदेशमस्य
विष्वक्तटेषु पतति स्फुटमन्तरिक्षम् ॥

एकत्र स्फटिकतटांशुभिन्ननीरा
नीलाश्मद्युतिभिदुराम्भसो ऽपरत्र ।
कालिन्दीजलजनितश्रियः श्रयन्ते
वैदग्धीमिह सरितः सुरापगायाः ॥

इतस्ततो ऽस्मिन्विलसन्ति मेरोः
समानवप्रे मणिसानुरागाः ।
स्त्रियश्च पत्यौ सुरसुन्दरीभिः
समा नवप्रेमणि सानुरागाः ॥

उच्चैर्महारजतराजिविराजितासौ
दुर्वर्णभित्तिरिह सान्द्रसुधासवर्णा ।
अभ्येति भस्मपरिपाण्डुरितं स्मरारे-
रुद्द्विलोचनललामललाटलीलाम् ॥

अयमतिजरढाः प्रकामगुर्वी-
रलघुविलम्बिपयोधरोपरुद्धाः ।
सततमसुमतामगम्यरूपाः
परिणतदिक्करिकास्तटीर्बिभर्ति ॥

124

Raivataka's peaks, propped up by the stars resting on   25
     moonbeam hands reaching up from below, provide a
     firm support for the sky. It has the totally convincing
     look of a waterfall tumbling down over the mountain
     slopes.

The waters of its streams are pierced on one side by bright
     rays flowing from their crystalline banks, while on the
     other they are dappled by the dark light of sapphires;
     they resemble the Ganga, its loveliness heightened on
     mingling with the black waters of the Yamuna.

Raivataka's craggy escarpments rival those of Meru. As
     the brilliant light from its bejeweled ridges flickers all
     around, women dance there like heavenly nymphs,
     enraptured with their adoring husbands.

That silver cliff alight with seams of gold on its heights
     shares the rich hue of ambrosia; it is as striking as
     Shiva's forehead, ornamented with his blazing third
     eye, whitened with funeral-ground ashes.

This mountain is crowned with beetling rock crags; when
     overcast by lowering rain-filled clouds, they remain
     inaccessible to mortals, and such is their eminence
     that they are actually struck by the tusks of the
     elephants of the celestial quarters.[14]

३० धूमाकारं दधति पुरः सौवर्णे
वर्णेनाग्रेः सदृशि तटे पश्यामी ।
श्यामीभूताः कुसुमसमूहे ऽलीनां
लीनां श्रेणीमिह तरवो बिभ्राणाः ॥

व्योमस्पृशः प्रथयता कलधौतभित्ती-
रुन्निद्रपुष्पचणचम्पकतुल्यभासः ।
सौमेरवीमधिगतेन नितम्बशोभा-³
मेतेन भारतमिलावृतवद्विभाति ॥

रुचिरचित्रतनूरुहशालिभिः
प्रचलितैः परितः प्रियकव्रजैः ।
विविधरत्नमयैरभिभात्यसा-
ववयवैरिव जङ्गमतां गतैः ॥

कुशेशयैरत्र जलाशयोषिता
मुदा रमन्ते कलभा विकस्वरैः ।
प्रगीयते सिद्धगणैश्च योषिता-
मुदारमन्ते कलभाविकस्वरैः ॥

आसादितस्य तमसा नियतेर्नियोगा-
दाकाङ्क्षतः पुनरुपक्रमणेन कालम् ।
पत्युस्त्विषामिह महौषधयः कलत्र-
स्थानं परैरपरिभूतममूर्भजन्ते ॥

126

Look, here before you on this fire-gold slope, these trees   30
    harboring swarms of bees within their luxuriant
    blossoms have now darkened, almost turning into
    smoke.

Displaying its gilded cliffs reaching the sky, yellow as
    the *champak* tree with blossoms in full display, the
    mountain emulates the beauty of Meru's slopes, and
    so Bharata, the continent of mortals, takes on the look
    of the golden wonderworld.*

Herds of deer, dappled pelts glistening, roam everywhere
    on the mountain, seeming to endow it with jeweled
    limbs in continual motion.

Here young elephants pass the day in pools, playing
    happily with the blossoming lotuses, while choirs of
    celestial sages serenade their wives in sweet tones
    redolent of deep emotion.

Here nocturnal luminescent plants assume the role of the
    sun's wives, unchallenged by any other light. As fate
    decrees, their lord has once more been assailed by
    darkness and now awaits reunion with his rays when
    morning comes.

---

* Ilavrita, a region near Mount Meru where the span of life is twelve
  thousand years.

३५ पुरः पतिस्कन्धनिषण्णबाल-
प्रवालहस्ताः प्रमदा इवात्र ।
पुष्पेक्षनैलम्बितलोचकैर्वा
मधुव्रतव्रातवृतैर्व्रतत्यः ॥

विहगाः कदम्बसुरभाविह गाः
कलयन्त्यनुक्षणमनेकलयम् ।
भ्रमयन्नुपैति मुहुरभ्रमयं
पवनश्च धूतनवनीपवनः ॥

विद्वद्द्विरागमपरैर्विवृतं कथंचि-
च्छुत्वापि दुर्ग्रहमनिश्चितधीभिरन्यैः ।
श्रेयान्द्विजातिरिव हन्तुमघानि दक्षं
गूढार्थमेष निधिमन्त्रगणं बिभर्ति ॥

बिम्बोष्ठं बहु मनुते तुरङ्गवक्र-
श्शुम्बन्तं मुखमिह किंनरं प्रियायाः ।
श्लिष्यन्तं मुहुरितरो ऽपि तं निजस्त्री-
मुत्तुङ्गस्तनभरभङ्गभीरुमध्याम् ॥

यदेतदस्यानुतटं विभाति
वनं ततानेकतमालतालम् ।
न पुष्पितात्र स्थगितार्करश्मा-
वनन्तताने कतमा लतालम् ॥

Here you can see vines imitating young women, for their   35
    fresh shoots entwine the tree trunks as if they were
    embracing their husbands; their blossoms, seething
    with bees, look like eyes made up with black mascara.

On the mountain fragrant with orange flowers, birds sing
    incessantly as their melody takes them, while the
    breeze you now feel stirs the young *kadamba* clusters
    and constantly whirls the clouds in circles.

This wondrous mountain, like a Brahman who has
    mastered the scriptures, hides within itself riches
    sufficient to alleviate all distress. But such wealth can
    be discovered only with effort by experienced treasure
    hunters—amateurs, however well informed, cannot
    get hold of it.[15]

Over here a horse-headed creature can be seen admiring
    a centaur kissing the luscious lips of his beloved;
    over there another centaur gazes wistfully at a horse-
    headed creature as he passionately embraces his
    girl, her jutting breasts so heavy that her waist fears
    breaking.[16]

The luxuriant forest on this mountain's slopes harbors a
    mass of *tamāla* and palm trees stretching far into the
    distance. What vine has not blossomed fully beneath
    this endless canopy immune to the sun's burning rays?

४० दन्तोज्ज्वलासु विमलोपलमेखलान्ताः
सद्रत्नचित्रकटकासु बृहन्नितम्बाः ।
अस्मिन्भजन्ति घनकोमलगण्डशैला
नार्यो ऽनुरूपमधिवासमधित्यकासु ॥

अनतिचिरोज्झितस्य जलदेन चिर-
स्थितबहुबुद्बुदस्य पयसो ऽनुकृतिम् ।
विरलविकीर्णवज्रशकला सकला-
मिह विदधाति धौतकलधौतमही ॥

वर्जयन्त्या जनैः सङ्गमेकान्तत-
स्तर्कयन्त्या सुखं सङ्गमे कान्ततः ।
योषयैष स्मरासन्तापाङ्गया
सेव्यते ऽनेकया सन्नतापाङ्गया ॥

संकीर्णकीचकवनस्खलितैकवाल-
विच्छेदकातरधियश्चलितुं चमर्यः ।
अस्मिन्मृदुश्वसनगर्भतदीयरन्ध्र-
निर्यत्स्वरश्रुतिसुखादिव नोत्सहन्ते ॥

मुक्तं मुक्तागौरमिह क्षीरमिवाभ्रै-
र्वापीष्वन्तर्लीनमहानीलदलासु ।
शस्त्रीश्यामैरंशुभिराशु द्रुतमम्भ-
श्छायामच्छामृच्छति नीलीसलिलस्य ॥

130

Raivataka's lofty plateaus offer a fine place for young   40
     women to frolic, as the attractions of each manifest
     themselves identically—verdant foliage and bright
     smiles, ridges and peaks studded with brilliant
     gems and gorgeously bejeweled belts and bracelets,
     imposing slopes and broad buttocks, prominent
     gleaming rocks and full delicate cheeks.[17]

Here the silvery earth sprinkled all over with diamond
     shards appears no different from fresh rainwater, foam
     bubbling on its surface.

This mountain is the haunt of many women; feverish with
     passion, slyly glancing, they are concerned only with
     the delights of intimate union with their lovers and
     show no interest in anyone else.

On this mountain female yaks take fright on losing just a
     single strand of hair entangled in the dense bamboo
     thickets; but they cannot bring themselves to move
     away, apparently enchanted by the fluting of hollow
     stems as the breeze blows softly through them.

Here clouds pour pearl-white rainwater like milk
     into pools whose beds are carpeted with sapphire
     fragments; it blends in an instant with their rays, dark
     as a polished knife, gaining the deep luster of indigo
     juice.

४५ या न ययौ प्रियमन्यवधूभ्यः
सारतरागमना यतमानम् ।
तेन सहेह बिभर्ति रहः स्त्री
सा रतरागमनायतमानम् ॥

भिन्नेषु रत्नकिरणैः किरणेष्विहेन्दो-
रुच्चावचैरुपगतेषु सहस्रसंख्याम् ।
दोषापि नूनमहिमांशुरसौ किलेति
व्याकोशकोकनदतां दधते नलिन्यः ॥

अपशङ्कमङ्कपरिवर्तनोचिता-
श्चलिताः पुरः पतिमुपैतुमात्मजाः ।
अनुरोदितीव करुणेन पत्रिणां
विरुतेन वत्सलतयैष निम्नगाः ॥

मधुकरविटपानमिता-
स्तरुपङ्क्तीर्बिभ्रतो ऽस्य विटपानमिताः ।
परिपाकपिशङ्गलतारजसा
रोधश्चकास्ति कपिशङ्गलता ॥

प्राग्भारतः पतदिहेदमुपत्यकासु
शृङ्गारितायतमहेभकराभमम्भः ।
संलक्ष्यते विविधरत्नकरानुविद्ध-
मूर्ध्वप्रसारितसुराधिपचापचारु ॥

A woman, skilled in bestowing passion's special delights 45
    during intercourse, had formerly spurned her lover
    when he implored her to grant her favors; now on this
    mountain she is no longer aloof and eagerly makes
    love with him in seclusion.

Here the lustrous rays of the moon, pierced by jewel-light,
    diffuse themselves a thousandfold; the day lotuses
    confuse this with the sun and open their red blossoms
    at evening time.

As birds plaintively cry, this mountain seems to be
    lamenting poignantly for its daughters, the rivers;
    previously they played happily at its feet, but now they
    have set out to join their husband, the ocean.

Avenues of trees flaunt themselves on the mountain
    slopes; kissed by lustful bees and bending under their
    branches' weight, they seem to be gilded with pollen
    drifting from vines, now tawny in their maturity.

Over here water cascading from the mountain heights
    onto the foothills is like a mighty elephant's trunk
    decked out along its full length with glittering
    ornaments; permeated by the rays from many-colored
    jewels, it is as fair as a rainbow arching across the sky.

५० दधति च विकसद्भिश्चित्रकल्पद्रुम-
कुसुमैरभिगुम्फितानिवैताः ।
क्षणमलघुविलम्बिपिञ्छदाम्नः
शिखरिशिखाः शिखिशेखरानमुष्य ॥

सवधूकाः सुखिनो ऽस्मि-
न्नवरतममन्दरागतामरसदृशः ।
नासेवन्ते रसवन्न
नवरतममन्दरागतामरसदृशः ॥

आच्छाद्य पुष्पपटमेष महान्तमन्त-
रावर्तिभिर्गृहकपोतशिरोधराभैः ।
स्वाङ्गानि धूमरुचिमागुर्वीं दधानै-
र्धूपायतीव पटलैर्नवनीरदानाम् ॥

अन्योन्यव्यतिकरचारुभिर्विचित्रै-
रत्रस्यन्नवमणिजन्मभिर्मयूखैः ।
विस्मेरानगगनसदः करोत्यमुष्मि-
न्नाकाशे रचितमभित्ति चित्रकर्म ॥

समीरशिशिरः शिरःसु वसतां
सतां जवनिका निकामसुखिनाम् ।
बिभर्ति जनयन्नयं मुदमपा-
मपायधवला बलाहकततीः ॥

134

These peaks are the mountain's coiffured hair! They sport   50
    peacock-crowns thickly garlanded with pendant
    tail feathers and seem to be plaited with many-hued
    flowers from blossoming wishing trees.

Fortunate men on this mountain, like gods come to earth,
    can unceasingly renew their ardent lovemaking with
    their wives, eyes like deep-colored lotuses.

This mountain, already swathed in a great robe of flowers,
    now seems to be perfuming itself with incense as
    clusters of fresh rain clouds swirl around, gray-white
    as aloe-wood smoke or the neck of a pet dove.

A picture without canvas, painted in the sky by the
    mountain's flawlessly gleaming jewels with
    coruscating rays of light, it astonishes the gods.

Cooled by the breeze, a joy to those dwelling on its heights
    in perfect content, Raivataka is curtained with cloud
    banks, now white after pouring down their rain.

५५ मैत्र्यादिचित्तपरिकर्मविदो विधाय
क्लेशप्रहाणमिह लब्धसबीजयोगाः ।
ख्यातिं च सत्त्वपुरुषान्यतयाधिगम्य
वाञ्छन्ति तामपि समाधिभृतो निरोद्धुम् ॥

मरकतमयमेदनीषु भानो-
स्तरुविटपान्तरपातिनो मयूखाः ।
अवततशितिकण्ठकण्ठलक्ष्मी-
मिह दधति स्फुरिताणुरेणुजालाः ॥

या बिभर्ति कलवल्लकीगुण-
स्वानमानमतिकालिमालया ।
नात्र कान्तमुपगीतया तया
स्वानमा४ नमति कालिमालया ॥

सायं शशाङ्ककिरणाहतचन्द्रकान्त-
निस्यन्दिनीरनिकरेषु५ कृताभिषेकाः ।
अर्कोपलोल्लसितवह्निभिरह्नि दीप्ता-
स्तीव्रं महाव्रतमिवात्र चरन्ति वप्राः ॥

एतस्मिन्नधिकपयःश्रियं वहन्त्यः
संक्षोभं पवनभुवा जवेन नीताः ।
वाल्मीकेररहितरामलक्ष्मणानां
साधर्म्यं दधति गिरां महासरस्यः ॥

Here can be found, sunk in profound contemplation,   55
    adepts who have mastered positive dispositions such
    as goodwill toward living creatures and eliminated
    mental afflictions; having gained advanced yogic
    attainment by focusing on the transcendent, they are
    now fully aware, directly experiencing the difference
    between evolved entities and the self. But they aspire
    to suppress even that and attain final deliverance.[18]

On this mountain's emerald slopes the sun's rays, brilliant
    as a peacock's outstretched neck, are flecked with
    motes of shimmering pollen as they pierce through
    gaps in the foliage.

What susceptible woman would not yield to her lover here
    when she hears the buzzing of dark-swarming bees,
    softly thrumming like lute strings?

At night Raivataka's slopes are anointed[19] by streams of
    water trickling from moonstones struck by lunar rays,
    while by day they are scorched by flames spreading
    from sunstones, as if following a sincere vow of
    penance.

The deep mountain lakes are like Valmiki's delightful
    poem; haunted by cranes and their mates, they are
    brimming with vast quantities of water, but can still be
    whipped up by the wind.[20]

६० इह मुहुर्मुदितैः कलभैरवः
प्रतिदिशं क्रियते कलभै रवः ।
स्फुरति चानुवनं चमरीचयः
कनकरत्नभुवां च मरीचयः ॥

त्वक्साररन्ध्रपरिपूरणरक्तगीति-
रस्मिन्नसौ मृदितपक्ष्मलरल्लकाङ्कः ।
कस्तूरिकामृगविमर्दसुगन्धिरेति
रागीव सक्तिमधिकां विषयेषु वायुः ॥

प्रीत्यै यूनां व्यवहिततपनं
प्रौढध्वान्तं दिनमिह जलदाः ।
दोषामन्यं विदधति सुरत-
क्रीडायासश्रमशमपटवः ॥

भग्नो निवासो ऽयमिहास्य पुष्पैः
सदा नतो येन विषाणिनागः ।
तीव्राणि तेनोज्झति कोपितो ऽसौ
सदानतोयेन विषाणि नागः ॥

प्रालेयशीतमचलेश्वरमीश्वरो ऽपि
सान्द्रेभचर्मवसनाभरणो ऽधिशेते ।
सर्वर्तुनिर्वृतिकरे निवसन्नुपैति
न द्वन्द्वदुःखमिह किञ्चिदकिञ्चनो ऽपि ॥

Everywhere young elephants relishing their freedom   60
    trumpet in a softly menacing manner, while
    throughout the forests yaks roam and a glittering light
    flows from the gold and jewels carpeting the ground.

The wind, as if totally given over to sensual delights, is
    deeply attached to every part of the mountain; it
    sings passionately as it blows through the holes in the
    bamboo, fondles the stags' thick pelts, and is made
    fragrant by intimate caressing of the musk deer.

Here, to the delight of young people, the rain clouds make
    the day think it is night; they blot out the sun with
    their murkiness and deftly soothe away lassitude after
    intense bouts of lovemaking.

Here a snake spits out its bitter venom in fury that the
    sandalwood tree, its home, ever bending with flowers,
    has been destroyed by a rutting elephant.

On Mount Kailasa, chilly and snowbound, Shiva must
    sleep clad in a thick elephant skin, but Raivataka is
    so benign all the year that even a poor man in no way
    suffers from cold or heat.

६५ नवनगवनलेखाश्याममध्याभिराभिः
स्फटिककटकभूभिर्नाटयत्येष शैलः ।
अहिपरिकरभाजो भास्मनैरङ्गरागै-
रधिगतधवलिम्नः शूलपाणेरिभर्व्याम् ॥

दधद्भिरभितस्तटौ विकचवारिजाम्बू नदै-
र्विनोदितदिनक्रमाः कृतरुचश्च जाम्बूनदैः ।
निषेव्य मधु माधवाः सरसमत्र कादम्बरं
हरन्ति रतये रहः प्रियतमाङ्गकादम्बरम् ॥

दर्पणनिर्मलासु पतिते घनतिमिरमुषि
ज्योतिषि रूप्यभित्तिषु पुरः प्रतिफलति मुहुः ।
व्रीडमसंमुखो ऽपि रमणैरपहृतवसनाः
काञ्चनकन्दरासु तरुणीरिह नयति रविः ॥

अनुकृतशिखरौघश्रीभिरभ्यागते ऽसौ
त्वयि सरभसमभ्युत्तिष्ठतीवाद्रिरुच्चैः ।
द्रुतमरुदुपनुन्नैरुन्नमद्भिः सहेलं
हलधरपरिधानश्यामलैरम्बुवाहैः ॥

140

With its crystal slopes, dark-girded with rows of saplings,   65
    this mountain actually imitates Shiva, snake-belted,
    all white-smeared with ash.

Here the Vrishnis,* resplendent with golden ornaments,
    shake off daytime listlessness by bathing in rivulets,
    blossoming lotuses bobbing beside their banks, then
    drink heady *kadamba* wine, and in seclusion remove
    their girls' clothes for lovemaking.

Even though invisible to them, the sun embarrasses the
    young women stripped of their garments by their
    lovers in the mountain's golden caverns; its rays,
    endlessly reflected off silvery cliffs, clear as mirrors,
    dispel the deep darkness within.

With your arrival, Krishna, the mountain seems to rise in
    eagerness to greet its guest, as its clouds, sped on by
    breezes, skittishly ascend the sky, like another range
    of majestic peaks, dark as Balarama's cloak."

---

* Krishna's clan.

CHAPTER 5

On the March

इत्थं गिरः प्रियतमा इव सो ऽव्यलीकाः
शुश्राव सूततनयस्य तदाव्यलीकाः ।
रन्तुं निरन्तरमियेष ततो ऽवसाने
तासां गिरौ च वनराजिपटं वसाने ॥

तं स द्विपेन्द्रतुलितातुलतुङ्गशृङ्ग-
मत्युल्लसत्कदलिकावनराजिरुच्चैः ।
विस्ताररूढवसुधो ऽन्वचलं चचाल
लक्ष्मीं दधत्प्रतिगिरेरलघुर्बलौघः ॥

भास्वत्करव्यतिकरोल्लसिताम्बरान्ताः
सापत्रपा इव महाजनदर्शनेन ।
संविव्युरम्बरविराजि चमूसमुत्थं
पृथिवीरजः करभकण्ठकडारमाशाः ॥

आवर्तिनः शुभफलप्रदशुक्तियुक्ताः
संपन्नदेवमणयो भृतरन्ध्रभागाः ।
अश्वाः प्यधुर्वसुमतीमतिरोचमाना-
स्तूर्णं पयोधय इवोर्मिभिरापतन्तः ॥

५ आरक्षमग्रमवमन्य सृणिं शिताग्र-
मेकः पलायत जवेन कृतार्तनादः ।
अन्यः पुनर्मुहुरुदप्लवतास्तभार-
मन्योन्यतः पथि बताबिभितामिभोष्ट्रौ ॥

The charioteer's description was precise in every respect
and captivating as a lovely woman. He had hardly
finished when Krishna set off to take his pleasure on
that densely forested mountain.

Its forest of banners fluttering on high, pressing down
heavily on the earth, Krishna's mighty army flowed
along with the appearance of Raivataka's rival. As it
marched alongside, its elephant battalions matched
the mountain's peaks, hitherto unequaled in loftiness.

The horizon, already tinged by the sunlight, now wrapped
itself in the army's dust floating everywhere, yellow
as a camel's neck. So a woman, embarrassed by men
gawking at her, fusses over the edge of her dress,
hands glinting with gold ornaments, before tugging it
around herself.[1]

Horses, sporting auspicious hair whorls on their necks and
bellies,[2] were galloping everywhere, like the ocean
swiftly inundating the world.[3]

On the highway an elephant and a camel took fright at   5
each other; the one, ignoring the sharp goad jabbing
its temples, gave a loud screech and took off at
speed, while the other repeatedly reared and bucked,
throwing off its load.

आयस्तमैक्षत जनश्चटुलाग्रपादं
गच्छन्तमुच्चलितचामरचारुमक्षम् ।
नागं पुनर्मृदुसलीलनिमीलिताक्षं
सर्वः प्रियः खलु भवत्यनुरूपचेष्टः ॥

त्रस्तः समस्तजनहासकरं करेणो-
स्तावत्त्वरः प्रखरमुल्लसयांचकार ।
यावच्चलासनविलोलनितम्बबिम्ब-
विस्रस्तवस्त्रमवरोधवधूः पपात ॥

शैलोपशल्यनिपतद्रथनेमिधारा-
निष्पिष्टनिष्ठुरशिलातलचूर्णगर्भाः ।
भूरेणवो नभसि बद्धपयोदचक्रा-
श्चक्रीवदङ्ग्रुहधूम्ररुचो विससुः ॥

उद्यत्कृशानुशकलेषु खुराभिघाता-
द्भूमीसमायतशिलाफलकाचितेषु ।
पर्यन्तवर्त्मसु विचक्रमिरे महाश्वाः
शैलस्य दर्दुरपुटानिव वादयन्तः ॥

१० तेजोनिरोधसमतावहितेन यन्त्रा
सम्यक्क्षात्रयविचारविदा नियुक्तः ।
आरट्यजश्चटुलनिष्ठुरपातमुच्चै-
श्चित्रं चकार पदमर्धपुलालयेन ॥

A stallion pranced along, resplendent with its fluttering
yak-tail pennants; meanwhile, an elephant plodded
stolidly on its way, eyes closed in calm contentment.
People stared at both alike—anything behaving as
anticipated is gratifying.

Alarmed by a cow elephant, an ass reared up so high that
its mount, a harem woman, fell off; everyone laughed
as her skirt rolled over her plump buttocks when she
slid from the loosened saddle.

As the highway was pounded by the wheels of the massed
chariots racing along beside the mountain, its
pulverized stone mingled with dust; rising into the
sky, it formed billowing clouds gray as an ass's pelt.

The road by the mountain was evenly paved with long
slabs of stone; sparks of fire flew up as they were
battered by the mighty chargers' galloping hooves
drumming out a rhythmic thundering.

A thoroughbred stallion was skillfully reined in by a rider   10
determined to restrain his steed's wild spirit and
compel it to proceed at a measured pace; as he was
well versed in subtly applying the whip, the horse
made steady progress at a graceful yet resolute canter.

नीहारजालमलिनः पुनरुक्तसान्द्राः
कुर्वन्वधूजनविलोचनपक्ष्ममालाः ।
क्षुण्णः क्षणं यदुबलैर्दिवमातितांसुः
पांसुर्दिशां मुखमतुत्थयदुत्थितो ऽद्रेः ॥

उच्छिद्य विद्विष इव प्रसभं मृगेन्द्रा-
निन्द्रानुजानुचरभूपतयो ऽध्यवात्सुः ।
वन्येभमस्तकनिखातनखाग्रमुक्त-
मुक्ताफलप्रकरभाञ्जि गुहागृहाणि ॥

बिभ्राणया बहुलजापकपङ्कपिङ्ग-
पिञ्छावचूलमनुमाधवधाम जग्मुः ।
चञ्चग्रदष्टचटुलाहिपताकयान्ये
स्वावासभागमुरगाशनकेतुयष्ट्या ॥

छायामपास्य महतीमपि वर्तमाना-
मागामिनीं जगृहिरे जनतास्तरुणाम् ।
सर्वो हि नोपनतमप्यपचीयमानं
वर्धिष्णुमाश्रयमनागतमभ्युपैति ॥

१५ अग्रेगतेन वसतिं परिगृह्य रम्या-
मापात्यसैनिकनिराकरणाकुलेन ।
यान्त्यो ऽन्यतः प्लुतकृतस्वरमाशु दूरा-
दुद्ग्राहुनाजुहुविरे मुहुरात्मवर्ग्याः ॥

148

Dark as a cloud of fog, doubling the thickness of women's
    long eyelashes, dust stirred up by the Yadava infantry
    rose from the mountain; aspiring to ascend to heaven,
    for an instant it smeared the face of the horizon.

Some of the kings accompanying Krishna aggressively
    drove away lions as if they were sworn rivals and took
    possession of their lairs, caves covered with pearl dust
    fallen from sharp claws sunk into the heads of wild
    elephants.[4]

The other kings understood where to stop for lodging by
    the lofty Garuda banner near Krishna's encampment;[5]
    its emblem was a wriggling snake skewered by a sharp
    beak, its pennant peacock plumage, gold-colored with
    thick turmeric paste.

Everyone ignored trees already casting a deep shade,
    no matter how cool, and moved on to arbors where
    shadow was yet to fall. Nobody seeks a patron waning
    in influence but looks for one on the ascendant.

An outrider claiming a comfortable lodging place was   15
    desperate to prevent soldiers in his wake from
    descending upon it. Waving his arms, he at once gave
    a long repeated cry to summon his companions from
    afar just as they were setting off in another direction.

सिक्ता इवामृतजलेन मुहुर्जनानां
क्लान्तिच्छिदो वनवनस्पतयस्तदानीम् ।
शाखावसक्तवसनाभरणाभिरामाः
कल्पद्रुमैः सह विचित्रफलैर्विरेजुः ॥

यानाञ्जनः परिजनैरवरोप्यमाना
राज्ञीर्निरापनयनाकुलसौविदल्लाः ।
स्रस्तावगुण्ठनपटक्षणलक्ष्यमाण-
वक्त्रश्रियः सभयकौतुकमीक्षते स्म ॥

कण्ठावसक्ततनुबाहुलतास्तुरङ्गा-
द्राजावरोधनवधूरवतारयन्त्यः ।
आलिङ्गनान्यधिकृताः स्फुटमापुरेव
गण्डस्थलं शुचितया न चुचुम्बुरासाम् ॥

दृष्ट्वैव निर्जितकलापभरामधस्ता-
द्व्याकीर्णमाल्यकवरां कवरीं तरुण्याः ।
प्रादुद्रुवत्सपदि चन्द्रकवान्द्रुमाग्रा-
त्संघर्षिणा सह गुणाभ्यधिकैर्दुरासम् ॥

२० रोचिष्णुकाञ्चनचयांशुपिशङ्गिताशा
वंशध्वजैर्जलदसंहतिमुल्लिखन्त्यः ।
भूभर्तुरायतनिरन्तरसन्निविष्टाः
पादा इवाभिबभुरावलयो रथानाम् ॥

The forest trees were dispelling weariness as if sprinkled
with ambrosia; resplendent with votive offerings of
cloth and jewelry, they looked like heavenly wishing
trees festooned with every type of fruit.

Royal consorts, helped from their palfreys, were stared at
with timidity and curiosity; while attendants sternly
drove away the crowd of onlookers, the ladies' lovely
faces could be momentarily glimpsed as their veils
slipped off.

The courtiers delegated to assist the harem women in
dismounting from their horses received an embrace
for all to see as slender arms were cast around their
necks, but their perfect manners ensured that they did
not snatch a kiss.

A peacock flew away quickly from a treetop, as if catching
sight below of a young woman's elaborate garland-
braided coiffure, thicker than its own feathered train.
The envious have difficulty enduring those better
endowed.

The columns of gold-inlaid chariots yellowed the sky with 20
gleaming shafts of light and scraped the cloud banks
with their regal pennants; extending far, yet jammed
close together, they were like Mount Raivataka's
foothills, bright seams of ore illuminating the heavens,
bamboo forests reaching banner-like to touch the sky.[6]

छायाविधायिभिरनुज्झितभूतिशोभै-
रुच्छायिभिर्बहुलपाटलधातुरागैः ।
दूष्यैरिव क्षितिभृतां द्विरदैरुदार-
तारावलीविरचनैर्व्यरुचन्निवासाः ॥

उत्क्षिप्तकाण्डपटकान्तरलीयमान-
मन्दानिलप्रशमितश्रमघर्मतोयैः ।
दूर्वाप्रवालसहजास्तरणेषु भेजे
निद्रासुखं वसनसद्मसु राजदारैः ॥

प्रस्वेदवारिसविशेषविषक्तमझे
कुर्पासकं क्षतनखक्षतमुत्क्षिपन्ती ।
आविर्भवद्घनपयोधरबाहुमूला
च्छातोदरी युवदृशां क्षणमुत्सवो ऽभूत् ॥

यावत्स एव समयः सममेव ताव-
दव्याकुलाः पटमयान्यभितो वितत्य ।
पर्यापतत्क्रयिकलोकमगण्यपण्य-
पूर्णापणं विपणिनो विपणिं विभेजुः ॥

२५ अल्पप्रयोजनकृतोरुतरप्रयासै-
रुद्दूर्णलोष्टलगुडैः परितो ऽनुबद्धम् ।
उद्घातमुद्धतमनौकहजालमध्या-
देकः शशं गुणमनल्पमवन्नवाप ॥

Majestically towering elephants, rubbed down with ashes
and thick-smeared with vermilion, thronged the
royal encampment, their decorations brilliant as star
clusters; they looked like luxuriously capacious tents
sewn with pearls, casting a shadow all around.

Within the tents themselves the kings' wives rested at
their ease on beds of fresh *dūrvā* grass, while a gentle
breeze blowing under the awning dispelled the
perspiration of travel weariness.

As a slim-waisted girl removed her bodice sticking tightly
to her with sweat, she revealed her heavy breasts and
upper arms all marked with love scratches, becoming
for a moment a feast for young men's eyes.

While the royal camp was being established, merchants
methodically erected pavilions nearby and set up a
market, its stalls packed with luxury goods, enticing
customers to crowd around.

One of them gained much applause by protecting a hare   25
fleeing in terror from a copse of trees after it had been
set upon from all sides with stones and sticks.[7] What a
lot of fuss for so little result!

153

त्रासाकुलः परिपतन्परितो निकेता-
न्पुंभिर्न कैश्चिदपि धन्विभिरन्वबन्धि ।
तस्थौ तथापि न मृगः क्वचिदङ्गनाभि-
राकर्णपूर्णनयनेषुहतेक्षणश्रीः ॥

स्वास्तीर्णतल्परचितावसथः क्षणेन
वेश्याजनः कृतनवप्रतिकर्मकाम्यः ।
खिन्नानखिन्नमतिरापततो मनुष्या-
न्प्रत्यग्रहीच्चिरनिविष्ट इवोपचारैः ॥

सस्नुः पयः पपुरनेनिजुरम्बराणि
जक्षुर्बिसं धृतविकासिबिसप्रसूनाः ।
सैन्याः श्रियामनुपभोगनिरर्थकत्व-
दोषप्रवादममृजन्नगनिम्नगानाम् ॥

नाभीह्रदैः परिगृहीतरयाणि निम्नैः
स्त्रीणां बृहज्जघनसेतुनिवारितानि ।
जग्मुर्जलानि जलमण्डुकवाद्यवल्गु-
वल्गद्धनस्तनतटस्खलितानि मन्दम् ॥

३० आलोलपुष्करमुखोल्ललितैरभीक्ष्ण-
मुक्षांबभूवुरभितो वपुरम्बुवर्षैः ।
खेदायतश्वसितवेगनिरस्तमुग्ध-
मूर्धन्यरत्ननिकरैरिव हास्तिकानि ॥

A terrified deer running around the tents had not been a
   target for archers but would not stand still anywhere;
   its beautiful eyes had already been struck by shafts—
   the arching glances of the kings' women.

Prostitutes, gorgeous in their fresh makeup,
   enthusiastically made space in a trice to spread out
   their beds, welcoming travel-weary passersby with
   refreshments as if they had been there for ages.

Soldiers bathed in the water of the mountain streams,
   they drank it and cleaned their clothes in it, they
   seized the lotuses floating on it and ate their fibers;
   they completely washed away the accusation that its
   delights were useless because nobody made use of
   them.

The water flowed gently; its current was checked by
   deep pools—the navels of bathing women—and held
   back by dams—their broad buttocks. It splashed on
   riverbanks—firm breasts swaying seductively to the
   rhythm of croaking frogs.[8]

Troops of elephants repeatedly sluiced their bodies with   30
   streams of water, which flowed from the nostrils of
   their waving trunks like strings of fine pearls expelled
   from their heads by their long weary moaning.[9]

ये पक्षिणः प्रथममम्बुनिधिं गतास्ते
ये ऽपीन्द्रपाणितुलितायुधलूनपक्षाः ।
ते जग्मुरद्रिपतयः सरसीं विगाढु-
माक्षिप्तकेतुकुथसैन्यगजच्छलेन ॥

आत्मानमेव जलधेः प्रतिबिम्बिताङ्ग-
मूर्मौ महत्यभिमुखापतितं जवेन⁹ ।
क्रोधादधावदपभीरितितूर्णमन्य-
नागाभियुक्त² इव युक्तमहो महेभः ॥

नादातुमन्यकरिमुक्तमदाम्बुतित्तं
धूताङ्कुशेन न विहातुमपीच्छताम्भः ।
रुद्धे गजेन सरुषा सरितो ऽवतारे
रिक्तोदपात्रकरमास्त चिरं जनौघः ॥

पन्थानमाशु विजहीहि पुरा स्तनौ ते
पश्यन्प्रतिद्विरदकुम्भविशङ्कितेताः ।
स्तम्बेरमः परिणिनंसुरसावुपैति
शिङ्खैरगद्यत ससंभ्रममेवमेका ॥

३५ कीर्णं शनैरनुकपोलमनेकपानां
हस्तैर्विगाढमदतापरुजः शमाय ।
आकर्णमुल्ललितमम्बु विकासिकाश-
नीकाशमाप समतां सितचामरस्य ॥

The mighty mountains originally had wings when they
    fled to the ocean, but these had been cut off by
    Indra.[10] Now they came to plunge into the river in the
    guise of army elephants divested of their banners and
    palanquins.

A huge elephant saw its reflection close up on the river's
    broad surface and, enraged and fearless—as you
    would expect—rushed at it as if menaced by a rival.

Another one angrily blocked the path down to the river,
    oblivious to its driver's goading, and a crowd of people
    had to stand for an age holding empty water pots.
    The beast was refusing to drink water pungent with
    another elephant's ichor, yet at the same time did not
    wish to leave it.

Cheeky young men were teasing a woman fetching
    water. "Quick! Get off the road!" they shouted at her
    excitedly. "An elephant has seen your jutting breasts
    and thinks they are a rival's forehead lobes—it's about
    to charge up on the attack!"

Yet other elephants contentedly poured water from their   35
    trunks over their temples to ease the increasingly
    feverish heat of rutting; it splashed around their ears
    like blossoming *kāśa* grass, taking on the appearance
    of a white chowrie.

गण्डूषमुज्झितवता पयसः सरोषं
नागेन लब्धपरवारणमारुतेन ।
अम्भोधिरोधसि पृथुप्रतिमानभाग-
रुद्धोरुदन्तमुसलप्रसरं निपेते ॥

दानं ददत्यपि जलैः सहसाधिरूढे
को विद्यमानगतिरासितुमुत्सहेत ।
यद्दन्तिनः कटकटाहतटान्निमग्नो-
र्मझ्झूदपाति परितः पटलैरलीनाम् ॥

अन्तर्जलौघमवगाढवतः कपोलौ
हित्वा क्षणं विततपक्षतिरन्तरिक्षे ।
द्रव्याश्रयेष्वपि गुणेषु रराज नीलो
वर्णः पृथग्गत इवालिगणो गजस्य ॥

संसर्पिभिः पयसि गैरिकरेणुरागै-
रम्भोजगर्भरजसाङ्गविषङ्गिणा च ।
क्रीडोपभोगमनुभूय सरिन्महेभा-
वन्योन्यवस्त्रपरिवर्तमिव व्यधाताम् ॥

४० यां चन्द्रकैर्मदजलस्य महानदीनां
नेत्रश्रियं विकसतो विदधुर्गजेन्द्राः ।
तां प्रत्यवापुरविलम्बितमुत्तरन्तो
धौताङ्गलग्ननवनीलपयोजपत्रैः ॥

One had picked up the scent of a rival and left off drinking
 to thrust down angrily at the riverbank with its thick
 club-like tusks, only its broad forehead checking their
 full impact.

What man with any alternative would bother to remain
 if his patron, however generous, suddenly became
 influenced by fools? When a rutting elephant, driven
 by desire for cool water, was about to plunge into the
 river, the clouds of bees buzzing around its broad
 temples quickly flew away.[11]

Swarming bees abandoned another's temples as it plunged
 into the flood, and hovered for an instant above it.
 Even though qualities normally inhere within physical
 objects, as philosophers argue, in this case blackness
 seemed to have become totally detached from the
 creature's hide.

Another elephant seemed to be playing with the river and
 affectionately exchanging clothes; the water mingled
 with its red coating of vermilion powder, while
 floating lotus pollen covered the tusker's body.

Bull elephants gave the great stream lovely eyes as ichor   40
 globules spread over its surface; clambering out of
 the water, they received in exchange fresh lotus leaves
 sticking to their wet bodies.

प्रत्यन्यदन्ति निशिताङ्कुशदूरभिन्न-
निर्याणनिर्यदसृजं चलितं निषादी ।
रोढुं महेभमपरिवृढिमानमागा-
दाक्रान्तितो न वशमेति महान्परस्य ॥

सेव्यो ऽपि सानुनयमाकलनाय यन्त्रा
नीतेन वन्यकरिदानकृताधिवासः ।
नाभाजि केवलमभाजि गजेन शाखी
नान्यस्य गन्धमपि मानभृतः सहन्ते ॥

अद्रीन्द्रकुञ्जचरकुञ्जरगण्डकाष-
संक्रान्तदानपयसो वनपादपस्य ।
सेनागजेन मथितस्य निजप्रसूनै-
र्मम्ले यथागतमगामि कुलैरलीनाम् ॥

नोच्चैर्यदा तरुतलेषु ममुस्तदानी-
माधोरणैरभिहिताः पृथुमूलशाखाः ।
बन्धाय चिच्छिदुरिभास्तरसात्मनैव
नैवात्मनीनमथ वा क्रियते मदान्धैः ॥

A mahout was powerless to restrain his powerful beast
  charging toward a rival, blood pouring from the
  corner of an eye split open by a blow from the sharp
  goad. The great cannot be subjugated through mere
  force.

Another mahout was coaxing his elephant to a tethering
  tree. At first the beast found it tempting, but smeared
  with traces of wild ichor it did not prove uplifting and
  was torn down.[12] The proud do not tolerate even the
  whiff of a rival.

A jungle tree, sticky with ichor rubbed from the temples
  of an elephant roaming free in Mount Raivataka's
  groves, had been smashed by an army elephant; its
  flowers withered and the hovering bees went off the
  way they had come.

Some elephants stood so high that there was no space for
  them beneath the trees. On their drivers' command
  they quickly cleared away swathes of roots and
  branches so they could be tethered. The contrary
  is normally the case: those blinded by pride—or by
  ichor—cannot do anything to their own advantage.[13]

४५ उष्णोष्णशीकरमुचः प्रबलोष्मणो ऽन्त-
रुत्फुल्लनीलनलिनोदरतुल्यभासः ।
एकान्विशालशिरसो हरिचन्दनेषु
नागान्बबन्धुरपरान्मनुजा निरासुः ॥

कण्डूयतः कटभुवं करिणो मदेन
स्कन्धं सुगन्धिमनुलीनवता नगस्य ।
स्थूलेन्द्रनीलशकलावलिकोमलेन
कण्ठेगुणत्वमलिनां वलयेन भेजे ॥

निर्धूतवीतमपि चालकमुल्लसन्तं
यन्ता क्रमेण परिसान्त्वनतर्जनाभिः ।
शिक्षावशेन शनकैर्वशमानिनाय
शास्त्रं सुनिश्चितधियां क्व न सिद्धिमेति ॥

स्तम्भं महान्तमुचितं सहसा मुमोच
दानं ददावतितरां सरसाग्रहस्तः ।
बद्धापराणि परितो निगडान्यलावी-
त्स्वातन्त्र्यमुज्ज्वलमवाप करेणुराजः ॥

जज्ञे जनैर्मुकुलिताक्षमनाददाने
संरब्धहस्तिपकनिष्ठुरचोदनाभिः ।
गम्भीरवेदिनि पुरः कवलं करीन्द्रे
मन्दो ऽपि नाम न महानवगृह्य साध्यः ॥

Mahouts tethered to yellow sandalwood trees their broad-   45
    templed elephants—emitting warm spray from their
    trunks, intensely energetic, so dark they resembled
    the calyx of a blue water lily in blossom. Then they
    drove away flat-headed snakes—spitting venom,
    consumed with burning heat, deep black.[14]

A tree trunk, richly fragrant from the ichor of an elephant
    scratching its temples, drew a swarm of bees that
    clung to it like a string of thick sapphire chunks,
    forming a necklace.

One rutting elephant was agitated and not responding
    to the goad, but by dint of familiarity with his craft a
    mahout gradually calmed it with a mixture of cajoling
    and threats. Specialized knowledge always brings
    success for experts.

Another mighty elephant displayed a glorious
    independence befitting a king. It rushed away from
    its familiar sturdy tethering post, pouring out so
    much ichor that its trunk was soaked to the very tip,
    and broke apart the chains on its hind feet.[15]

Yet another stately elephant, eyes closed in deep
    contemplation, would not accept the handful of
    fodder offered to it, although coaxed by irritated
    mahouts—confirmation that the mighty, however
    slow to react, cannot be compelled against their will.

५० क्षिप्रं पुरो न जगृहे मुहुरिक्षुकाण्डं
नापेक्षते स्म निकटोपगतां करेणुं ।
सस्मार वारणपतिः परिमीलिताक्षं
स्वेच्छाविहारवनवासमहोत्सवानाम् ॥

कृच्छ्रेण भोजयितुमाशयिता शशाक
तुङ्गाग्रकायमनमन्तमनादरेण ।
उत्क्षिप्तहस्ततलदत्तविधानपिण्ड-३
स्नेहस्नुतिस्नपितबाहुरिभाधिराजम् ॥

शुक्लांशुकोपरचितानि निरन्तराभि-
र्वेश्मानि रश्मिविततानि नराधिपानाम् ।
चन्द्राकृतीनि गजमण्डलिकाभिरुच्चै-
र्नीलाभ्रपङ्क्तिपरिवेशमिवाधिजग्मुः ॥

गत्यूनमार्गगतयो ऽपि गतोरुमार्गाः
स्वैरं समाचकृषिरे भुवि वेल्हनाय ।
दर्पोदयोल्लसितफेनजलानुसार-
संलक्ष्यपल्ययनवध्रपदास्तुरङ्गाः ॥

आजिघ्रति प्रणतमूर्धनि वाहिजे ऽश्वे
तस्याङ्गसंगमसुखानुभवोत्सुकायाः ।
नासानिरोकपवनोल्ललितं तनीयो
रोमाञ्चतामिव जगाम रजः पृथिव्याः ॥

164

One lordly elephant did not take the piece of sugar   50
    cane repeatedly placed before it and ignored the
    female alongside. Eyes squeezed shut, the beast was
    dreaming of the many delights of life in the forest
    when it once roamed free.

The keeper's arms were sticky wet from the food morsels
    lifted as offering to his mighty elephant; he only just
    contrived to get it to eat, as it reared up playfully and
    refused to lower its head.

The kings' white cloth tents tied down with ropes looked
    like moons diffusing beams of light, while the packed
    troops of towering elephants clustering around
    seemed to wreathe them in dark clouds.

After a long journey at a steady pace, the horses were
    gradually reined in and made to turn on the spot; the
    contours of their saddle straps were visible against the
    flecks of lather worked up in their fierce exertion.

As a Balkhi[16] steed lowered its head to sniff the ground,
    the film of dust stirred up by its breath seemed to be
    the earth's hair amorously stirring in eagerness for the
    delights of intercourse.

५५ हेम्नः स्थलीषु परितः परिवृत्य वाजी
धुन्वन्वपुर्नतनिरायतकेशपङ्क्तिः ।
ज्वालाकणारुणरुचा निकरेण रेणोः
शेषेण तेजस इवोल्लसता रराज ॥

दन्तालिकाधरणनिश्चलपाणियुग्म-
मर्धोदितो हरिरिवोदयशैलमूर्ध्नः ।
स्तोकेन नाक्रमत वल्लभपालमुच्चैः
श्रीवृक्षकी पुरुषकोन्नमिताग्रकायः ॥

रेजे जनैः स्नपनसान्द्रतरार्द्रमूर्ति-
र्देवैरिवानिमिषदृष्टिभिरीक्ष्यमाणः ।
श्रीसंनिधानरमणीयतरो ऽश्व उच्चै-
रुच्चैःश्रवा जलनिधेरिव जातमात्रः ॥

अश्रावि भूमिपतिभिः क्षणवीतनिद्रै-
रश्वन्पुरो हरितकं मुदमादधानः ।
ग्रीवाग्रलोलकलकिङ्किणिकानिनाद-
मिश्रं दधद्द्विशानबर्बुरशब्दमश्वः ॥

उत्खाय दर्पचलितेन सहैव रज्ज्वा
कीलं प्रयत्नपरमानवदुर्ग्रहेण ।
आकुल्यकारि कटकस्तुरगेण तूर्ण-
मश्वेति विद्रुतमनुद्रवतान्यमश्वम् ॥

166

A stallion, its long mane tumbling down, spun around on   55
     the golden earth and shook itself; it glowed as if with
     an excess of fiery energy amid the mass of floating
     dust, tawny as flecks of flame.

An elegant steed reared up to a man's full height, looking
     like the sun half-risen above the eastern mountain's
     peak, but it did not kick out in the slightest at the
     groom holding its bridle with steady hands.

A magnificent tall stallion, wet from being washed down,
     now had a sheen on its coat. Bystanders stared at
     it, just as the gods gazed unblinkingly at the divine
     horse Ucchaihshravas newly churned from the ocean,
     its beauty enhanced by the presence of the goddess
     Shri.[17]

Dozing kings stirred for an instant as they heard the sound
     of a horse contentedly champing its fodder to the
     accompaniment of the soft tinkling of ornamental
     bells moving up and down on its neck.

Elsewhere, the camp was thrown into turmoil by a stallion
     escaping the control of its groom, no matter how he
     struggled with it. Tearing up rope and tethering peg,
     the beast excitedly galloped off full tilt after another
     fleeing horse, taking it to be a mare.

६० अव्याकुलं प्रकृतमुत्तरधेयकर्म-
धाराः प्रसाधयितुमव्यतिकीर्णरूपाः ।
सिद्धं मुखे नवसु वीथिषु कश्चिदश्वं
वल्गाविभागकुशलो गमयांबभूव ॥

मुक्तास्तृणानि परितः कटकं चरन्त-
स्तुट्यद्द्वितानतनिकाव्यतिषङ्गभाजः ।
सस्रुः सरोषपरिचारकवार्यमाणा
दामाञ्छनस्खलितलोलपदं तुरङ्गाः ॥

उत्तीर्णभारलघुनाप्यलघूलपौघ-
सौहित्यनिःसहतरेण तरोरधस्तात् ।
रोमन्थमन्थरचलद्गुरुसास्नमासां-
चक्रे निमीलदलसेक्षणमौक्षकेण ॥

मृत्पिण्डशेखरितकोटिभिरर्धचन्द्रं
शृङ्गैः शिखाग्रगतलक्ष्ममलं हसद्भिः ।
उच्छृङ्गितान्यवृषभाः सरितां नदन्तो
रोधांसि धीरमपचस्करिरे महोक्षाः ॥

मेदस्विनः सरभसोपगतानभीकं
भङ्क्त्वा परानन्दुहो मुहुराहवेन ।
ऊर्जस्वलेन सुरभिमनु निःसपत्नं
जग्मे जयोद्धुरविशालविषाणमुक्ष्णा ॥

A rider skilled with the reins was putting his mount   60
     through its paces; it was confident, alert, and familiar
     with how to turn in the various directions. He rode
     the horse over the nine types of terrain so that it could
     practice each of the galloping styles occasion might
     require.

Stallions untethered for grazing cantered friskily all round
     the camp, stumbling over tent ropes and getting
     tangled in the broken cords of the awnings, while
     infuriated servants tried to control them.

A herd of oxen rested beneath a tree, heavy dewlaps
     moving slowly as they chewed the cud, eyes closing
     listlessly. Although lightened of their loads, they
     were now quite overcome with lassitude after filling
     themselves with thick clumps of grass.

Powerful bulls, who had broken the horns of rivals, were
     tearing up riverbanks, deeply bellowing; the tips of
     their own horns were now crowned with lumps of
     clay—comically like the half moon dark-marked on its
     crescent point.

One lusty bull pursued a cow without interference from
     rivals; it held its mighty horns erect in triumph,
     having fearlessly and repeatedly vanquished hefty
     rivals.

169

६५ बिभ्राणमायतिमतीमवृथा शिरोधिं
प्रत्यग्रतामधिरसामधिकं दधन्ति ।
लोलौष्ठमौष्ट्रकमुदग्रमुखं तरूणा-
मभ्रंलिहानि लिलिहे नवपल्लवानि ॥

साकं कथंचिदुचितैः पिचुमन्दपत्रै-
रास्यान्तरालगतमाम्रदलं म्रदीयः ।
दाशेरकः सपदि संवलितं निषादै-
र्विघ्रं पुरः पतगराडिव निर्जगार ॥

स्पष्टं बहिःस्थितवते ऽपि निवेदयन्त-
श्रेष्ठविशेषमनुजीविजनाय राज्ञाम् ।
वैतालिकाः स्फुटपदप्रकटार्थमुच्चै-
र्भोगावलिं कलगिरो ऽवसरेषु पेठुः ॥

उन्नम्रताम्रपटमण्डपमण्डितं त-
दानीलनागकुलसंकुलमाबभासे ।
संध्यांशुभिन्नघनकर्बुरितान्तरिक्ष-
लक्ष्मीविडम्बि शिविरं शिवकीर्तनस्य ॥

धरस्य प्रोद्धर्ता त्वमिति ननु सर्वत्र जगति
प्रतीतिस्तत्किं मामतिभरमधः प्रापिपयिषुः ।
उपालब्धेवोच्चैर्गिरिपतिरिति श्रीपतिमसौ
बलाक्रान्तः क्रीडद्विरदमथितोर्वीरुहरवैः ॥

A herd of camels lifted their muzzles and stretched their   65
    necks to good effect; their busy lips could lick, at the
    trees' topmost point, green leaves of surpassingly
    fresh savor.

One of them suddenly spat out an unusually soft
    mango leaf that it had gobbled up with the bitter
    nimba leaves, its normal fodder. So, once upon a
    time, Garuda, king of the birds, had expectorated
    a Brahman mixed in with the barbarians he was
    devouring.[18]

At intervals, sweet-voiced bards recited praise poems clear
    of diction and transparent of meaning. They so loudly
    described the distinguished deeds of the kings that
    even servants standing outside the tents could hear.

Krishna's encampment was embellished with lofty
    red tents and thronged with troops of pitch-dark
    elephants, seeming to imitate the beauty of the sky
    when flecked with rain clouds pierced by evening
    sunshine.

"The entire world accepts without argument that you are
    the one who once lifted up a mountain.[19] So why must
    you now try to drag me down with all my weight?"
    Mount Raivataka, harassed by the army, thus seemed
    to rebuke Krishna noisily as its trees groaned when
    idly felled by his rutting elephants.

CHAPTER 6

The Seasons on Mount Raivataka

अथ रिरंसुममुं युगपद्विरौ
कृतयथास्वतरुप्रसवश्रिया ।
ऋतुगणेन निषेवितुमादधे
भुवि पदं विपदन्तकरं सताम् ॥

नवपलाशपलाशवनं पुरः
स्फुटपरागपरागतपङ्कजम् ।
मृदुलतान्तलतान्तमरूपय-
त्स सुरभिं सुरभिं सुमनोभरैः ॥

विलुलितालकसंहतिरामृष-
न्मृगदृशां क्रमवारि ललाटजम् ।
तनुतरङ्गततीः सरसां दल-
त्कुवलयं वलयन्मरुदाववौ ॥

तुलयति स्म विलोचनतारकाः
कुरबकस्तबकव्यतिषङ्गिणि ।
गुणवदाश्रयलब्धगुणोदये
मलिनिमालिनि माधवयोषिताम् ॥

५ स्फुटमिवोज्ज्वलकाञ्चनकान्तिभि-
र्युतमशोकमशोभत चम्पकैः ।
विरहिणां हृदयस्य भिदाभृतः
कपिशितं पिशितं मदनाग्निना ॥

174

Then all at once the seasons beautified the trees with
    appropriate flowers and set foot on earth to attend
    Krishna, destroyer of the good's misfortune; for he
    was about to devote time to pleasure upon Mount
    Raivataka.[1]

Krishna witnessed spring appearing before his eyes,
    fragrant with blossom clusters, graced with thickets
    of scarlet-flowering flame trees.[2] The lotuses, now
    opening wide, were full of pollen, and delicate vines
    drooped in the sunlight.

A breeze disheveled the hairdos of doe-eyed girls and
    brushed away the sweat from their foreheads; it
    stirred up little billows on ponds where blossoming
    lilies floated.

A bee clinging to a clump of white *kurabaka* flowers[3]
    could in its dark color easily bear comparison with the
    pupils in the eyes of Krishna's womenfolk. After all, a
    quality only appears at its best when juxtaposed with
    an object endowed with some other attribute.[4]

An *aśoka* tree was blooming amid *champak* flowers bright   5
    as blazing gold; it looked like the flesh, scorched red
    by passion's flame, of the breaking hearts of men
    bereft of their mistresses.

स्मरहुताशनमुर्मुरचूर्णतां
दधुरिवाम्रवणस्य रजःकणाः ।
निपतिताः परितः पथिकव्रजा-
नुपरि ते परितेपुरतो भृशम् ॥

रतिपतिप्रहितेव कृतक्रुधः
प्रियतमेषु वधूरनुनायिका ।
बकुलपुष्परसासवपेशल-
ध्वनिरगान्निरगान्मधुपावलिः ॥

प्रियसखीसदृशं प्रतिबोधिताः
किमपि काम्यगिरा परपुष्टया ।
प्रियतमाय वपुर्गुरुमत्सर-
च्छिदुरयादुरयाचितमङ्गनाः ॥

मधुकरैरववादकरैरिव⁹
स्मृतिभुवः पथिका हरिणा इव ।
कलतया वचसः परिवादिनी-
स्वरजिता रजिता वशमाययुः ॥

१० समभिसृत्य रसादवलम्बितः
प्रमदया कुसुमावचिचीषया ।
अविनमन्न रराज वृथोच्चकै-
रनृतया नृतया वनपादपः ॥

Pollen flecks drifting from a mango thicket seemed to
 be ashes from the dying embers of love's fire; they
 showered down upon travelers far from home and
 burned them painfully.[5]

A swarm of bees sped from a tree, humming softly after
 drinking the nectar of *bakula* flowers, as if dispatched
 by the god of love to placate women angry with their
 partners.

Unasked, ladies gave themselves to their lovers, discreetly
 advised, as if by a girlfriend, by the cuckoo dispelling
 with its seductive tones all their jealous feelings.

As the sound of hunters' lures entraps deer, so love
 overpowered travelers with the bees' soft song,
 sweeter than a lute's thrumming.

A woman ran up to a forest tree and grasped it   10
 passionately, intending—to pick its flowers. It did
 not bend in acknowledgment, so its superficial
 resemblance to a tall handsome man could not alter
 the fact of its insentience.[6]

इदमपास्य विरागि परागिणी-
रलिकदम्बकमम्बुरुहां ततीः ।
स्तनभरेण जितस्तबकानम्-
न्नवलते वलते ऽभिमुखं तव ॥

सुरभिणि श्वसिते दधतस्तृषं
नवसुधामधुरे च तवाधरे ।
अलमलेरिव गन्धरसावमू
मम न सौमनसौ मनसो मुदे ॥

इति वदन्तमनन्तरमञ्जना
भुजयुगोन्नमनोच्छतरस्तनी ।
प्रणयिनं रभसादुदरश्रिया
वलिभयालिभयादभिषस्वजे ॥

वदनसौरभलोभपरिभ्रम-²
द्भ्रमरसंभ्रमसंभृतशोभया ।
वलितया विदधे कलमेखला-
कलकलो ऽलकलोलदृशान्यया ॥

१५ अजगणन्गणशः प्रियमग्रतः
प्रणतमप्यतिमानितया न याः ।
सति मधावभवन्मदनव्यथा-
विधुरिता धुरि ताः कुकुरस्त्रियः ॥

178

"You gorgeous girl, your full breasts so surpass the young
    vine bending under its flower cluster that a swarm of
    bees has abandoned the pollen-rich lotuses in distaste
    and is now heading toward you.

The scent and honey of those flowers give me no real
    pleasure; instead I too have become like a bee, craving
    your fragrant breath and your lips sweet as fresh
    nectar."

When her lover murmured these words, the girl's breasts
    heaved and the three folds rippled on her stomach.
    Then she raised her arms and threw herself into his
    embrace—as if in fear of bees!

Another girl was quite delightful in her agitation at the
    bees circling greedily around her fragrant mouth; her
    hairdo came undone, falling over her eyes, and her
    belt rustled softly as she shied away.

The Yadava women were so haughty that they frequently   15
    paid no regard to their lovers even when prostrate at
    their feet; but with spring under way they were the
    first to be tormented by pangs of love.

कुसुमकार्मुककार्मुकसंहित-
द्रुतशिलीमुखखण्डितविग्रहाः ।
मरणमप्यपराः प्रतिपेदिरे
किमु मुहुर्मुमुहुर्गतभर्तृकाः ॥

रुरुदिषा वदनाम्बुरुहश्रियः
सुतनु सत्यमलंकरणाय ते ।
तदपि संप्रति सन्निहिते मधा-
वधिगमं धिगमङ्गलमसृणः ॥

त्यजति कष्टमसावचिरादसू-
न्विरहवेदनयेत्यघशङ्किभिः ।
प्रियतया गदितास्त्वयि बान्धवै-
रवितथा वितथा सखि मा गिरः ॥

न खलु दूरगतो ऽप्यतिवर्तते
महमसाविति बन्धुतयोदितैः ।
प्रणयिनो निशमय्य वधूर्बहिः
स्वरमृतैरमृतैरिव निर्ववौ ॥

२० मधुरया मधुबोधितमाधवी-
मधुसमृद्धिसमेधितमेधया ।
मधुकराङ्गनया मुहुरुन्मद-
ध्वनिभृता निभृताक्षरमुज्जगे ॥

Those women separated from their husbands were
　　wounded by the swift arrows nocked on the bow of
　　love, the flowery archer, and prepared as they were
　　to accept even death, what wonder that they fainted
　　dead away.

"My lovely, your fair lotus-like face is still more beautiful
　　on the verge of tears, but now that spring is at hand,
　　please don't cry—it's unlucky.

Those who care for you are concerned you might soon die
　　from the pain of separation. Dear friend, don't make
　　affectionate exaggerations about you come true."

Her friends assured the young woman that although
　　her lover might be far away on his travels, he
　　would certainly not miss the spring festival. She
　　was overjoyed at their words as if through tasting
　　ambrosia, and they were true—she had just heard his
　　voice outside the house!

A bee quietly hummed on and on, delightful in her　　　20
　　intoxicated song, with inspiration stimulated by the
　　abundant honey of vines blossoming in the vernal
　　season.

अरुनिताखिलशैलवना मुहु-
र्विदधती पथिकान्परितापिनः ।
विकचकिंशुकसंहतिरुच्चकै-
रुदवहद्द्वहव्यभुजः श्रियम् ॥

रवितुरङ्गतनूरुहतुल्यतां
दधति यत्र शिरीषरजोरुचः ।
उपययौ विदधन्नवमल्लिकाः
शुचिरसौ चिरसौरभसंपदः ॥

दलितकोमलकुड्डलपाटले
निजवधूश्चसितानुविधायिनि ।
मरुति वाति विलासिभिरन्वित-
भ्रमदलौ मदलौल्यमुपाददे ॥

निदधिरे दयितोरसि तत्क्षण-
स्नपनवारितुषारभृतः स्तनाः ।
सरसचन्दनरेणुरनुक्षणं
विचकरे च करेण वरोरुभिः ॥

२५ स्फुरदधीरतडिन्नयना मुहुः
प्रियमिवागलितोरुपयोधरा ।
जलधरावलिरप्रतिपालित-
स्वसमया समयाज्जगतीधरम् ॥

Blossoming flame-tree flowers reddened every grove on
    the mountain heights with the splendor of a forest
    fire, incessantly tormenting travelers.

Summer now came forth, imbuing the jasmine with a
    rich and lasting fragrance. It was the time when the
    bright acacia pollen looked like the coats of the sun's
    stallions.

The breeze blew, opening the soft trumpet-flower buds;
    it made lovers giddy with excitement, mimicking their
    girls' breath as it whirled the intoxicated bees.

Sleek-thighed young women, breasts studded with
    waterdrops from recent bathing, pressed their bodies
    tight against their partners' chests; they sprinkled
    damp sandalwood pollen to cool them still further.

Then an unseasonal bank of clouds, like a daring woman   25
    resolutely advancing toward her lover, moved
    relentlessly toward the mountain with flashing,
    flickering eye-like lightning, but held back any heavy
    downpour.[7]

गजकदम्बकमेचकमुच्चकै-
र्नभसि वीक्ष्य नवाम्बुदमम्बरे ।
अभिससार न वल्लभमङ्गना
न चकमे च कमेकरसं रहः ॥

अनुययौ विविधोपलकुण्डल-
द्युतिवितानकसंवलितांशुकम् ।
धृतधनुर्वलयस्य पयोमुचः
शवलिमा बलिमानमुषो वपुः ॥

द्रुतसमीरचलैः क्षणलक्षित-
व्यवहिता विटपैरिव मञ्जरी ।
नवतमालनिभस्य नभस्तरो-
रचिररोचिररोचत वारिदैः ॥

पटलमम्बुमुचां पथिकाङ्गना
सपदि जीवितसंशयमेष्यती ।
सनयनाम्बुसखीजनसंभ्रमा-
द्विधुरबन्धुरबन्धुरमैक्षत ॥

३० प्रवसतः सुतरामुदकम्पय-
द्विदलकन्दलकम्पनलालितः ।
नमयति स्म वनानि मनस्विनी-
जनमनोनमनो घनमारुतः ॥

184

No sooner did they see in the rainy month of Shravana*
    a cloud high above gray as an elephant herd, than
    women went secretly to their sweethearts and made
    love with passionate commitment.

A cloud entwined with a rainbow imitated in its ever-
    changing colors the dark body of Krishna, destroyer
    of the demon Bali's† pride, when wrapped in his robe
    dappled by light glinting from jewel-studded earrings.

Lightning flashed in a sky dark as a fresh *tamāla* blossom
    momentarily revealed and then hidden by clouds
    scudding in the wind. So a cluster of flowers is
    partially obscured by branches when a breeze blows
    through a tree.

A woman whose husband was far from home was on the
    verge of death. She stared in misery at the clustering
    storm clouds, while her girlfriends' distraught
    weeping distressed her relatives still further.

A wind from the clouds shook the flowering banana vines,   30
    subduing the hearts of haughty women and making
    travelers shudder and forests bend.

---

* The equivalent of August–September.
† Bali was overcome by Vishnu's Dwarf incarnation.

जलदपङ्क्तिरनर्तयदुन्मदं
कलविलापि कलापिकदम्बकम् ।
कृतसमार्जनमर्दलमण्डल-
ध्वनिजया निजया स्वनसंपदा ॥

नवकदम्बरजो ऽरुणिताम्बरै-
रधिपुरन्ध्रि सिलिन्ध्रसुगन्धिभिः ।
मनसि रागवतामनुरागिता
नवनवा वनवायुभिरादधे ॥

शमिततापमपोढमहीरजः
प्रथमबिन्दुभिरम्बुमुचो ऽम्भसाम् ।
प्रविरलैरचलाङ्गनमङ्गना-
जनसुगं न सुगन्धि न चक्रिरे ॥

द्विरददन्तवलक्षमलक्ष्यत
स्फुरितभृङ्गमृगच्छवि केतकम् ।
घनघनौघविघट्टनया दिवः
कृशशिखं शशिखण्डमिव च्युतम् ॥

३५ दलितमौक्तिकचूर्णविपाण्डवः
स्फुटितनिर्झरशीकरचारवः ।
कुटजपुष्पपरागकणाः स्फुटं
विदधिरे दधिरेणुविडम्बनाम् ॥

The deep rumbling of the rain clouds outdid a thundering
orchestra of taut drums, urging on the soft-wailing
peacocks to an excited dance.[8]

Forest breezes, reddening the air with fresh pollen,
fragrant with plantain flowers, awoke in lovers' minds
as never before an infatuation with their girls.

Clouds calmed the heat and settled the dust with their
first hesitant raindrops; they made the mountain
promenade most fragrant, a favorite spot for women.

The narrow-tipped *ketaki* flower, white as an elephant's
tusk, had been visited by a black bee; it looked like
the crescent moon fallen from the sky after colliding
with the massed clouds, its dark deer-mark intact[9] but
emitting a feeble light.

Flecks of pollen from *kuṭaja* flowers, pale as crushed pearl   35
powder, delightful as spray from a cascading waterfall,
seemed like bubbles of milk.

नवपयःकणकोमलमालती-
कुसुमसंततिसंततसङ्गिभिः ।
प्रचलितोडुनिभैः परिपाण्डिमा
शुभरजोभरजो ऽलिभिराददे ॥

निजरजः पटवासमिवाकिर-
द्धृतपटोपमवारिमुचां दिशाम् ।
प्रियविमुक्तवधूजनचेतसा-
मनवनी नवनीपवनावलिः ॥

प्रणयकोपभृतो ऽपि पराङ्मुखाः
सपदि वारिधरारवभीरवः ।
प्रणयिनः परिरब्धुमनन्तरं
ववलिरे वलिरेचितमध्यमाः ॥

विगतरागगुणो ऽपि नरो न क-
श्चलति वाति पयोदनभस्वति ।
अभिहिते ऽलिभिरेवमिवोच्चकै-
रननृते ननृते नवपल्लवैः ॥

४० अरमयन्भवनादचिरद्युतः
किल भयादपयातुमनिच्छवः ।
यदुनरेन्द्रगणं तरुणीगणा-
स्तमथ मन्मथमन्मनभाषिणः ॥

Bees, swarming among the rows of jasmine flowers soft
   as fresh raindrops, had been turned quite pale by a
   coating of thick pollen and now looked like flickering
   stars.

A grove of *kadamba* saplings, no friends to the hearts of
   women abandoned by their lovers, scattered pollen
   like a cloak over a sky already hung with cloudy
   picture cloths.[10]

Although they had teasingly feigned annoyance with their
   lovers and averted their gaze, girls at once took fright
   at the roaring downpour and quickly turned around,
   seeking an embrace in alarm.

"What man, however lacking in passion, is not disturbed
   when the monsoon wind blows?" The bees buzzed out
   this truth and the young saplings danced.

Groups of young women, feigning reluctance to leave   40
   the tent for fear of the monsoon thunder, delighted
   the Yadava king's party with their soft seductive
   whispering.

ददतमन्तरिताहिमदीधितिं
खगकुलाय कुलायनिलायिताम् ।
जलदकालमबोधकृतं निशा-
मपरथाप रथावयवायुधः ॥

सविकचोत्पलचक्षुषमैक्षत
क्षितिभृतो ऽङ्गगतां³ दयितामिव ।
शरदमच्छगलद्द्रसनोपमा-
क्षमघनामघनाशनकीर्तनः ॥

जगति नैशमशीतकरः करै-
र्वियति वारिदवृन्दमयं तमः ।
जलजराशिषु नैद्रमदिद्रव-
न्न महतामहताः क्व च नारयः ॥

समय एव करोति बलाबलं
प्रणिगदन्त इतीव शरीरिणाम् ।
शरदि हंसरवाः परुषीकृत-
स्वरमयूरमयू रमणीयताम् ॥

४५   तनुरुहाणि पुरो विजितध्वने-
रमलपक्षविहङ्गमकूजितैः ।
जगलुरक्षमयेव शिखण्डिनः
परिभवो ऽरिभवो हि सुदुःसहः ॥

Their lord, Krishna, apprehended the monsoon time as
night in another guise; it obscured the sun, made birds
take refuge in their nests, and brought about slumber.

Then Krishna—mention of whose name destroys sin—
beheld autumn as if it were a lovely woman seated on
the mountain's lap, the opening lotuses her eyes, the
clouds her white dress slipping down.

With its rays the sun put to flight nocturnal darkness
throughout the world, the gloom of rainclouds in the
sky, and the dark sleep of the closed lotuses. The foes
of the mighty are nowhere secure.

As if announcing that the same season can have good or
bad effects on living creatures, the cries of the geese in
autumn sounded sweet and the tones of the peacocks
harsh.

The peacock's call was drowned out by the white-
feathered goose crying loudly nearby and its fine
plumage disappeared, as if in a jealous pique. Defeat
by a rival is difficult to endure.

45

अनुवनं वनराजिवधूमुखे
बहलरागजपाधरचारुणि ।
विकचबाणदलावलयो ऽधिकं
रुरुचिरे रुचिरेक्षणविभ्रमाः ॥

कनकभङ्गपिशङ्गदलैर्दधे
सरजसारुणकेसरचारुभिः ।
प्रियविमानितमानवतीरुषां
निरसनैरसनैरवृथार्थता ॥

मुखसरोजरुचं मदपाटल-
मनुचकार चकोरदृशां यतः ।
धृतनवातपमुत्सुकतां ततो
न कमलं कमलम्भयदम्भसि ॥

विगतसस्यजिघत्समघट्टय-
त्कलमगोपवधूर्न मृगव्रजम् ।
श्रुततदीरितकोमलगीतक-
ध्वनिमिषे ऽनिमेषेक्षणमग्रतः ॥

५० कृतमदं निगदन्त इवाकुली-
कृतजगत्त्रयमूर्जमतङ्गजम् ।
ववुरयुच्छदगुच्छसुगन्धयः
सततगास्ततगानगिरो ऽलिभिः ॥

192

Throughout the forest rows of blossoming *bāṇa* flowers
  glinted at the threshold of every grove where exquisite
  roses of a deep scarlet flowered—glossy red lips, they
  seemed, on the face of a girl with flashing flirtatious
  eyes.

The full-blown *asana* flowers, petals yellow as gold
  pieces, enchanting with tawny pollen-covered
  filaments, had a fitting name—they really did blow
  away the annoyance of ladies sulking at their lovers'
  indiscretion.[11]

Who would not succumb to desire as the lotus was
  suffused with the early morning light? It was pretty as
  a woman's flower-like face, flushed with intoxication,
  eyes as sparkling as those of tawny partridges.

The girl guarding the rice crop in the month of Ashvin* did
  not need to shoo away the deer in front of her; their
  hunger disappeared as they listened unblinking to the
  sound of her soft song.

Breezes were blowing, fragrant with thick *saptaparṇa*   50
  blossoms, singing with bees' humming; they seemed
  to announce the month of Karttika,† a rutting
  elephant which enflames lust[12] and disturbs all the
  world.

---

* The equivalent of October–November.
† The equivalent of November–December.

विगतवारिधरावरणाः क्वचि-
द्दृशुरुल्लसितासिलतासिताः ।
क्वचिदिवेन्द्रगजाजिनकञ्चुकाः
शरदि नीरदिनीर्यदवो दिशः ॥

विलुलितामनिलैः शरदङ्गना
नवसरोरुहकेसरसंभवाम् ।
विकिरितुं परिहासविधित्सया
हरिवधूरिव धूलिमुदक्षिपत् ॥

हरितपत्रमयीव मरुद्द्रणैः
स्रगवबद्धमनोरमपल्लवा ।
मधुरिपोरतिताम्रमुखी मुदं
दिवि तता विततान शुकावलिः ॥

स्मितसरोरुहनेत्रसरोजला-
मतिसिताङ्गविहङ्गहसद्द्विवम् ।
अकलयन्मुदितामिव सर्वतः
स शरदं शरदन्तुरदिङ्मुखाम् ॥

५५ गजपतिद्वयसीरपि हैमन-
स्तुहिनयन्सरितः पृषतां पतिः ।
सलिलसन्ततिमध्वगयोषिता-
मतनुतातनुतापभृतां दृशोः ॥

In autumn as the rains were ending, the Yadavas beheld
   one quarter of the sky stripped of its cloudy blanket
   and bright as a flashing sword blade; elsewhere, it was
   covered with white clouds, clad in a corselet, it seemed,
   of the hide of Indra's elephant.

Lady Autumn gathered pollen from lotus filaments stirred
   by the breeze and threw it as if in fun upon Krishna's
   wives.

Krishna himself was enchanted by a flock of green-winged
   parrots, their beaks deep red, spread over the sky by
   the winds as if they were a garland of shiny leaves
   bedecked with dainty buds.

He imagined the autumn to be everywhere manifesting
   joy—the ponds had cheerful lotus eyes, the sky
   laughed with birds of the most brilliant white, while
   the horizons smilingly displayed their teeth, the
   blossoming cane reeds.

Even though the rivers would normally swell to the height   55
   of a mighty elephant, the wintry wind froze them
   solid, but to the eyes of women whose husbands were
   far from home it brought a flood of burning tears.

इदमयुक्तमहो महदेव य-
द्वरतनोः स्मरयत्यनिलो ऽन्यदा ।
स्मृतसयौवनसोष्मपयोधरा-
न्सतुहिनस्तु हिनस्तु वियोगिनः ॥

प्रियतमेन यया सरुषा स्थितं
न सह सा सहसा परिरभ्य तम् ।
श्लथयितुं क्षणमक्षमताङ्गना
न सहसा सहसा कृतवेपथुः ॥

भृशमदूयत चाधरपल्लव-
क्षतिरनावरणा हिममारुतैः ।
दशनरश्मिपटेन च सीत्कृतै-
र्निवसितेव सितेन सुनिर्वबौ⁴ ॥

धृततुषारकणस्य नभस्वत-
स्तरुलताङ्गुलितर्जनविभ्रमाः ।
पृथु निरन्तरमिष्टभुजान्तरं
वनितयानितया न विषेहिरे ॥

६० हिमऋतावपि ताः स्म भृशस्विदो
युवतयः सुतरामुपकारिणि ।
प्रकटयत्यनुरागमकृत्रिमं
स्मरमयं रमयन्ति विलासिनः ॥

How unfair! In any other season the wind just rouses a
memory for those separated from their beloveds; but
when full of snow it can kill men as they recall their
wives' warm youthful breasts.

One woman angered by her lover could not tolerate his
presence; then she suddenly started to tremble—it
was winter, after all—and she embraced him with a
smile, not intending to loosen her grasp for even an
instant.[13]

The very moment the raw bite wound on a woman's full
lip was assailed by the wintry gale, her discomfort was
relieved; for as she moaned passionately, the gleam
from her dazzling teeth appeared to apply a white
dressing.

Tree branches seemed to rebuke the snow-filled wind
with wagging fingers; no woman who had not pressed
herself tightly against her lover's broad chest could
endure its blast.

But winter is most benign in revealing the true passion   60
awoken by love, since even in that season young
women's sweat runs hot as they fill their lovers with
ecstasy.

कुसुमयन्फलिनीरलिनीरवै-
र्मदविकासिभिराहितहुंकृतिः ।
उपवने निरभर्त्सयत प्रिया-
न्वियुवतीर्युवतीः शिशिरानिलः ॥

उपचितेषु परेष्वसमर्थतां
व्रजति कालवशाद्बलवानपि ।
तपसि मन्दगभस्तिरभीशुमा-
न्न हि महाहिमहानिकरो ऽभवत् ॥

अभिषिषेणयिषुं भुवनानि यः
स्मरमिवाख्यत रोधरजश्रयः ।
क्षुभितसैन्यपरागविपाण्डुर-
द्युतिरियं तिरयन्नुदभूद्दिशः ॥

शिशिरमासमपास्य गुणो ऽस्य नः
क इव शीतहरस्य कुचोष्मणः ।
इति धियास्तरुषः परिरेभिरे
घनमतो नमतो ऽनुमतान्प्रियाः ॥

६५ अधिलवङ्गममी रजसाधिकं
मलिनिताः सुमनोदलतालिनः ।
स्फुटमिति प्रसवेण पुरो ऽहस-
त्सपदि कुन्दलता दलतालिनः ॥

The late winter breeze brought to flower the *priyaṅgu*
shrubs in the bowers; with the humming of bees rising
in a crescendo of intoxicated excitement, it sighed in
reproach of young women separated from their lovers.

If enemies thrive, even a powerful man becomes impotent
in the course of time. When the sun's rays weaken
in the month of Magha,* it is powerless to melt the
snowdrifts.[14]

A cloud of *lodhra* pollen, white as the dust thrown up by
an army, floated into the air and hid the sky; it seemed
to summon the god of love, eager to march against the
universe.

"Is there any point in having warm breasts except in late
winter when they take away the cold?" That's what
women thought, and so they stopped being angry
with their lovers, embracing them tightly as they
apologized.

"Those bees clinging to the clove tree buds have been   65
darkened all over by pollen." The jasmine creeper
laughed aloud at them as its white flowers suddenly
opened.[15]

---

* The equivalent of February–March.

अतिसुरभिरभाजि पुष्पश्रिया
मतनुतरतयेव सन्तानकः ।
तरुणपरभृतः स्वनं रागिणा-
मतनुत रतये वसन्तानकः ॥

नोज्झितुं युवतिमाननिरासे
दक्षमिष्टमधुवासरसारम् ।
चूतमालिरलिनामतिरागा-
दक्षमिष्ट मधुवासरसारम् ॥

जगद्वशीकर्तुमिमाः स्मरस्य
प्रभावनीके तनवै जयन्तीः ।
इत्यस्य तेने कदलीर्मधुश्रीः
प्रभावनी केतनवैजयन्तीः ॥

स्मररागमयी वपुस्तमिस्रा
परितस्तार रवेरसत्यवश्यम् ।
प्रियमाप दिवापि कोकिले स्त्री
परितस्ताररवे रसत्यवश्यम् ॥

७० वपुरम्बुविहारहिमं शुचिना
रुचिरं कमनीयतरा गमिता ।
रमणेन रमण्यचिरांशुलता-
रुचिरङ्कमनीयत रागमिता ॥

A wealth of blossoms clung to the fragrant *santānaka*
　　tree[16] like a woman bent on passionate lovemaking.
　　The young cuckoo, spring's celebratory tabor,
　　sounded forth to the delight of lovers.

The mango tree, at its best in the vernal days, was expert
　　in dispelling young women's aloof reserve. The
　　swarming bees could not bear to leave it, for they were
　　addicted to passing time amid the honey they loved so
　　much.

Divine spring, the creator, unfolded banana leaves to
　　fashion victory banners for love's army bent on
　　subduing the world.

It seemed that a malign darkness engendered by amorous
　　passion had obscured the sun's disc; even as the
　　cuckoo was sounding its shrill note in every direction,
　　a woman went unthinkingly to a daytime assignation
　　with her beloved.[17]

A most seductive young woman was drawn to her　　　　70
　　lover's lap; her body, cool from bathing, had been
　　given a lustrous sheen by the springtime, and in its
　　impassioned state it glowed like a shaft of lightning.

201

मुदमब्दभुवामपां मयूराः
सहसायन्त नदी पपाट लाभे ।
अलिनार मतालिनी सिलिन्ध्रे
सह सायन्तनदीपपाटलाभे ॥

कुटजानि वीक्ष्य शिखिभिः शिखरीन्द्रं
समयावनौ घनमदभ्रमराणि ।
गगनं च गीतनिनदस्य गिरोच्चैः
समया वनौघनमदभ्रमराणि ॥

अभीष्टमासाद्य चिराय काले
समुद्धृताशं कमनी चकाशे ।
योषिन्मनोजन्मसुखोदयेषु
समुद्धृताशङ्कमनीचकाशे ॥

स्तनयोः समयेन याङ्ग्नाना-
मभिनद्धारसमा न सा रसेन ।
परिरम्भरुचिं ततिर्जलाना-
मभिनद्धा रसमानसारसेन ॥

७५ जातप्रीतिर्या मधुरेणानुवनान्तं
कामे कान्ते सारसिकाकाकुरुतेन ।
तत्संपर्कं प्राप्य पुरा मोहनलीलां
कामेकान्ते सा रसिका का कुरुते न ॥

On feeling a shower fall from the clouds, the peacocks
    immediately rejoiced, the river flowed in spate, while
    the bee made love with her partner in the plantain
    tree, red as evening lamplight.

The white *kuṭaja* flowers on the mighty mountain's
    flanks were alive with drunken bees, and the sky was
    carpeted with clouds lowering with the weight of rain.
    Seeing this, the peacocks shrieked out with a cry like
    the note of a song.[18]

In the autumn season, the time when the *kāśa* grass grows
    high, delight filled any woman surrendering to passion
    and finally uniting with her man, the object of her
    desire. Eager for love's intimacies, he dispelled any
    fear they might be separated again.

The heat of autumn, the season when the cranes cry,
    produced a streak of perspiration like a necklace on
    the breasts of women, but in no way diminished their
    need for a passionate embrace.

At the sound of the female cranes' sweetly plaintive cry   75
    at the forest's edge, every amorous woman yearned
    for her man, now become like the god of love to her.
    Each would go to him before he even suggested it and
    intimately engage in all the delights of intercourse.

रामाजनेन रहसि प्रसभं गृहीत-
केशे रते स्मरसहासवतोषितेन ।
प्रेम्णा मनःसु रजनीष्वपि हैमनीषु
के शेरते स्म रसहासवतोषितेन ॥

गतवतामिव विस्मयमुच्चकै-
रसकलामलपल्लवलीलया ।
मधुकृतामसकृद्दिरमावली
रसकलामलपल्लवलीलया ॥

कुर्वन्तमित्यतिभरेण नगानवाचः
पुष्पैर्विराममलिनां न च गानवाचः ।
श्रीमान्समस्तमनुसानु गिराविहर्तुं
बिभ्रत्यचोदि स मयूरगिरा विहर्तुम् ॥

During wintry nights, when love's exchanges are under
   way, women take delight in the lust-awakening wine
   and tug on their lovers' hair with a lascivious smile.
   At that time who can sleep as passion takes possession
   of their minds?

The bees pressing round the *lavalī* flowers, as if bemused
   by the gentle swaying of their fresh leaves, did not
   cease their deliciously noisy buzzing.

In this way all the seasons were experienced at once on the
   slopes of Raivataka; they made the trees bow down
   with the weight of blossoms and never put an end to
   the humming of bees. Krishna, the husband of Shri,
   was urged by the peacocks' song to pass the time
   there.

CHAPTER 7

Forest Flirtations

अनुगिरमृतुभिर्विततायमाना-
मथ स विलोकयितुं वनान्तलक्ष्मीम् ।
निरगमदभिराद्रुमाहतानां
भवति महत्सु न निष्फलः प्रयासः ॥

दधति सुमनसो वनानि बह्वी-
र्युवतियुता यदवः प्रयातुमीषुः ।
मनसिशयमहास्त्रमन्यथामी
न कुसुमपञ्चकमप्यलं विसोढुम् ॥

अवसरमधिगम्य तं हरन्त्यो
हृदयमयत्नकृतोज्ज्वलस्वरूपाः ।
अवनिषु पदमञ्जनास्तदानीं
न्यदधत विभ्रमसंपदो ऽङ्गनासु ॥

नखरुचिरचितेन्द्रचापलेखं
ललितगतेषु गतागतं दधाना ।
मुखरितवलयं पृथौ नितम्बे
भुजलतिका मुहुरस्खलत्तरुण्याः ॥

५ अतिशयपरिणाहवान्वितेने
बहुतरमापितरत्नकिङ्किणीकः ।
अलघुनि जघनस्थले ऽपरस्या
ध्वनिमधिकं कलमेखलाकलापः ॥

Then Krishna came out to observe the woodland's
    beauties unfolded by the seasons on the mountain.
    Effort expended on honoring the great is never
    unrewarded.

The Yadavas intended to visit the forests with their wealth
    of blossoms only in the company of their young
    women. Otherwise they could not have endured
    unaided a mere five flowers, the mighty arrows of the
    love god.[1]

These girls, captivating, artlessly delightful to the eye,
    understood that this was their opportunity; so the
    moment they took their first step to set off on the
    outing, flirtatiousness of every sort set its foot upon
    them.

One young woman sashayed along gracefully to the sound
    of jingling bracelets; her bright fingernails traced out
    rainbows as her slender arms swung back and forth,
    only to be repeatedly obstructed by her broad hips.

A wide ornamental belt, studded all over with jeweled   5
    bells, tinkled noisily on the swelling hips of another
    girl.

गुरुनिबिडनितम्बबिम्बभारा-
क्रमणनिपीडितमङ्गनागणस्य ।
चरणयुगमसुसुवत्पदेषु
स्वरसमसक्तमलक्तकच्छलेन ॥

तव सपदि समीपमानये ता-
महमिति तस्य मयाग्रतो ऽभ्यधायि ।
अतिरभसकृतालघुप्रतिज्ञा-
मनृतगिरं गुणगौरि मा कृथा माम् ॥

न च सुतनु न वेद्मि यन्महीया-
नसुनिरसस्तव निश्चयः परेण ।
वितथयति न जातु मद्वचो ऽसा-
विति च तथापि सखीषु मे ऽभिमानः ॥

सततमनभिभाषणं मया ते
परिपणितं भवतीमनानयन्त्या ।
त्वयि तदिति विरोधनिश्चितायां
भवतुˮ भवत्वसुहृज्जनः सकामः ॥

१० गतधृतिरवलम्बितुं बतासू-
ननलमनालपनादहं भवत्याः ।
प्रणयिनि यदि न प्रसादबुद्धि-
र्भव मम मानिनि जीविते दयालुः ॥

210

Their plump round buttocks pressed down so heavily on
these young women's feet that with each step their
passionate essence oozed out in the guise of red lac.[2]

"I promised him to his face that I would bring you at once.
You may well possess all the powers of a goddess;[3]
still, you shouldn't transform me into a liar after I've
made a sincere pledge, however rash.

Just you listen to me, good-looking! I'm well aware that
no one can change your mind when you're set on
something, but my friends respect me because I never
twist their words.

I swore not to speak to you again if I didn't bring you.
Since you are content with that and determined to
quarrel with him, then well and good—may your
rivals' wishes come true!

But oh dear! If we don't remain close friends, I will simply   10
lose all my will to live and I'll not be able to go on.
You may not want to show any goodwill toward your
lover, but at least have some consideration for me, you
haughty young lady."

प्रियमिति वनिता नितान्तमागः-
स्मरणसरोषकषायितायताक्षी ।
चरणगतसखीवचो ऽनुरोधा-
त्किल कथमप्यनुकूलयांचकार ॥

द्रुतपदमिति मा वयस्य यासी-
र्ननु सुतनूमनुपालयानुयान्तीम् ।
न हि न विदितखेदमेतदीय-
स्तनजघनोद्वहने तवापि चेतः ॥

इति वदति सखीजने ऽनुरागा-
द्दयिततमामपरश्चिरं प्रतीक्ष्य ।
तदनुगमवशादनायतानि
न्यधित मिमान इवावनिं पदानि ॥

यदि मयि लघिमानमागतायां
तव धृतिरस्तु गतास्मि संप्रतीयम् ।
अनिभृतपदपातमापपात
प्रियमिति कोपपदेन कापि सख्याः ॥

१५ अविरलपुलकः सह व्रजन्त्याः
प्रतिपदमेकतरः स्तनस्तरुण्याः ।
घटितविघटितः प्रियस्य वक्षः-
स्थलभुवि कन्दुकविभ्रमं बभार ॥

The girl's long eyes were tinged red with anger as she
    called to mind her lover's indiscretion; but, apparently
    responding to the pleading of her friend, now fallen at
    her feet, she contrived to be reconciled toward him.

"Don't hurry off like that, dear! Won't you wait for that
    gorgeous girl following you? Even you must realize
    how exhausting it is to carry such heavy breasts and
    buttocks."

As the girl's friends called out to him, her lover
    affectionately tarried a little, walking with deliberate
    steps; he appeared to be measuring out the ground so
    that she could follow him more easily.

"If you're happy for me to look foolish and flighty, then
    here I am on my way now." Feigning annoyance, she
    ran all the more quickly after her man.

Then, while she clung to him as she went along, one of her   15
    breasts, covered in goose bumps, rolled up and down
    like a ball on his chest at each step she took.

अशिथिलमपरावसज्य कण्ठे
दृढपरिरब्धबृहद्द्विहिःस्तनेन ।
हृषिततनुरुहो भुजेन भर्तुृ-
मृदुममृदु व्यतिविद्धमेकबाहुम् ॥

मुहुरसुसममाघ्नती नितान्त-
प्रणदितकाञ्चि नितम्बमण्डलेन ।
विषमितपृथुहारयष्टि तिर्य-
क्कुचमितरं तदुरःस्थले निपीड्य ॥

गुरुतरकलनूपुरानुनादं
सललितनर्तितबाह्यपादपद्मा ।
इतरदनतिलोलमादधाना
पदमथ मन्मथमन्थरं जगाम ॥

लघुललितपदं तदंसपीठ-
द्व्यनिहितोभयपाणिपल्लवान्या ।
सकठिनकुचचूचुकप्रणोदं
प्रियमबला सविलासमन्वियाय ॥

२० जघनमलसपीवरोरु कृच्छ्रा-
दुरुनिबिरीसनितम्बभारखेदि ।
दयिततमशिरोधरावलम्बि-
स्वभुजलताविभवेन काचिदूहे ॥

214

Another girl passionately gripped her lover, tightly
　　entwining her slender right arm with his left, the
　　down thrilling with excitement as he ardently
　　uncovered her ample breast and fondled it.

She repeatedly pressed against him with her round
　　buttocks, her belt jingling loudly, and rubbed her
　　right breast sideways on his chest, pushing her heavy
　　necklace over to the other side of her body.

Then, elegantly disposing her lotus-like left foot to the
　　accompaniment of the soft ringing of her anklets, she
　　planted her right foot more carefully, walking beside
　　her man with the slow preoccupation of love.

One woman playfully followed her lover with swift,
　　graceful paces, placing her hands on his broad
　　shoulders and pressing her hard nipples against him.

Another girl bore her hips and heavy, sumptuous thighs　　20
　　only with difficulty; they labored so much under the
　　weight of her broad, firm buttocks that she had to
　　throw her slender arms around her partner just to
　　support herself.

अनुवपुरपरेण बाहुमूल-
प्रहितभुजाकलितस्तनेन निन्ये ।
निमितदशनवाससा कपोले
विषमवितीर्णपदं बलादिवान्या ॥

अनुवनमसितभ्रुवः सखीभिः
सह पदवीमपरः पुरोगतायाः ।
उरसि सरसरागपादलेखा-
प्रतिमतयानुययावसंशयानः ॥

मदनरसमहौघपूर्णनाभी-
ह्रदपरिवाहितरोमराजयस्ताः ।
सरित इव सविभ्रमप्रयात-
प्रणदितहंसकभूषणा विरेजुः ॥

श्रुतपथमधुराणि सारसाना-
मनुनदि शुश्रुविरे चिरं रुतानि ।
विदधति जनतामनःशरव्य-
व्यधपटुमन्मथचापनादशङ्काम् ॥

२५ मधुमथनवधूरिवाह्वयन्ति
भ्रमरकुलानि जगुर्यदुत्सुकानि ।
तदभिनयमिवावलिर्वनाना-
मतनुत नूतनपल्लवाङ्गुलीभिः ॥

Yet another woman was also walking unsteadily. She was
almost forcibly carried from behind by her lover who
put his hands under her armpits and took hold of her
breasts, nuzzling her cheek.

Meanwhile, a man was confidently following the path of
a dark-browed girl as she went ahead with her friends
to the forest; the damp tracks of her lac-reddened
feet were the same as the marks left on his chest in
lovemaking.

These women were like rivers: the thin lines of hair on
their stomachs were channels flowing from the lake of
their navels, and these brimmed over with the flood of
love's passion. Like geese calling out as they played on
the water, their anklets rang in time to their seductive
movements.

The cries of cranes, sweet to the ears, could be heard for a
long while along the river—the singing of the bow of
the love god, it almost seemed, the master at hitting
his target, mortals' hearts.

The song of excited swarms of bees seemed to summon   25
Krishna's wives; the avenues of trees appeared to act
out an invitation with gestures of their fresh leaves.

217

असकलकलिकाकुलीकृतालि-
स्खलनविकीर्णविकासिकेसराणाम् ।
मरुदवनिरुहां रजो वधूभ्यः
समुपहरन्विचकार कोरकाणि ॥

उपवनपवनानुपातदक्षै-
रलिभिरलाभि यदङ्गनागणस्य ।
परिमलविषयस्तदुन्नताना-
मनुगमने खलु संपदो ऽग्रतःस्थाः ॥

रथचरणधराङ्गनाकराब्ज-
व्यतिकरसंपदुपात्तसौमनस्याः ।
जगति सुमनसस्तदादि नूनं
दधति परिस्फुटमर्थतो ऽभिधानम् ॥

अभिमुखपतितैर्गुणप्रकर्षा-
दवजितमुद्धतिमुज्ज्वलं दधानैः ।
तरुकिसलयजालमग्रहस्तैः
प्रसभमनीयत भङ्गमङ्गनानाम् ॥

३० मुदितमधुभुजो भुजेन शाखा-
श्चलितविश्रृङ्खलशङ्कुकं धुवत्याः ।
तरुरतिशयितापराङ्गनायाः
शिरसि मुदेव मुमोच पुष्पवर्षम् ॥

As it blew open the buds on the trees, the breeze offered
pollen to the girls; the unfolding filaments were
dispersed by the nudging of bees agitated by yet
unopened blossoms.

The bees were adept at following the wind in the forest
groves and so could catch the women's scent. Good
fortune awaits those in the train of the mighty.

The flowers had bloomed delightfully through contact
with the lotus-like hands of Krishna's women; only
from that moment did the world employ the term
"blossom" in conformity to its real meaning.[4]

The girls were now plucking clusters of shoots from trees,
but these were surpassed in beauty by the fingers
stretching far up in the air toward them.

As if in ecstasy a tree rained flowers upon the head of   30
a supremely beautiful girl; all the while her loose
armlets were jingling as she shook branches teeming
with drunken bees.

अनवरतरसेन रागभाजा
करजपरिक्षतिलब्धसंस्तवेन ।
सपदि तरुणपल्लवेन वध्वा
विगतदयं खलु खण्डितेन मम्ले ॥

प्रियमभि कुसुमोद्धतस्य बाहो-
र्नवनखमण्डलचारु मूलमन्या ।
मुहुरितरकराहितेन पीन-
स्तनतटरोधि तिरोदधेंऽशुकेन ॥

विततवलिविभाव्यपाण्डुलेखा-
कृतपरभागविनीलरोमराजिः ।
कृशमपि कृशतां पुनर्नयन्ती
विपुलतरोन्मुखलोचनावलग्नम् ॥

प्रसकलकुचबन्धुरोद्धुरोरः-
प्रसभविभिन्नतनूत्तरीयबन्धा ।
अवनमदुदरोच्छ्वसद्दुकूल-
स्फुटतरलक्ष्यगभीरनाभिमूला ॥

३५ व्यवहितमविजानती किलान्त-
र्वणभुवि वल्लभमाभिमुख्यभाजम् ।
अधिविटपि सलीलमग्रपुष्प-
ग्रहणपदेन चिरं विलम्ब्य काचित् ॥

A fresh young shoot, bright red and full of sap, was severed
    by a girl's nails and, mercilessly plucked, immediately
    dried up.[5]

As a girl raised her arm to pick a flower under the gaze of
    her lover, she used her other hand to tug her bodice
    over her shoulder, fetchingly decorated with fresh love
    scratches, and cover her firm jutting breasts.

When she looked up with wide-open eyes, her slim waist
    tautened further; the dark line of hair above her navel
    was enhanced by the pale nail-marks now discernible
    between the fleshy folds of her midriff.

The thin knot on her bodice had come undone as her chest
    heaved under the weight of her heavy breasts; her
    deep cleft was clearly exposed by her dress slipping
    from her waist as she bent.

She made a pretty fuss about lingering by a tree on the   35
    pretext of plucking a flower from its topmost branch,
    while apparently not realizing that her lover was
    concealed in the undergrowth before her.

अथ किल कथिते सखीभिरत्र
क्षणमपरेव ससंभ्रमा भवन्ती ।
शिथिलितकुसुमाकुलाग्रपाणिः
प्रतिपदसंयमितांशुकावृताङ्गी ॥

कृतभयपरितोषसंनिपातं
सचकितसस्मितवक्रवारिजश्रीः ।
मनसिजगुरुतत्क्षणोपदिष्टं
किमपि रसेन रसान्तरं भजन्ती ॥

अवनतवदनेन्दुरिच्छतीव
व्यवधिमधीरतया यदस्थितास्मै ।
अहरत सुतरामतो ऽस्य चेतः
स्फुटमभिभूषयति स्त्रियस्त्रपैव ॥

किसलयशकलेष्ववाचनीयाः
पुलकिनि केवलमङ्के निधेयाः ।
नखपदलिपयो ऽपि दापितार्थाः
प्रणिदधिरे दयितैरनङ्गलेखाः ॥

४० कृतकृतकरुषा सखीमपास्य
त्वमकुशलेति कयाचिदात्मनैव ।
अभिमतमभि साभिलाषमावि-
ष्कृतभुजमूलमबन्धि मूर्ध्नि माला ॥

When told about this by her friends, she became confused
for a moment just as any woman would, and put a stop
to her busy gathering of flowers, pulling her bodice
around herself at every step.

There was a timid smile, redolent of apprehension and
happiness, on her delightful lotus-like face; but
her deeper emotion was reaching another level of
intensity thanks to her teacher, love, tutoring her that
very moment.

Finally she modestly lowered her face, oval as the moon,
seemingly so shy that she wanted to disappear; when
she displayed herself to her man in this way, she
completely captured his heart. Embarrassment really
does enhance women's allure.

Couples exchanged love letters on leaf fragments;
although incised with nail marks and not to be read,
they were explicit and had simply to be placed on a
slender body thrilling with emotion.[6]

One woman feigned annoyance and rebuffed her friend's   40
attempts to tie a garland in her hair, accusing her of
clumsiness. Then, lusting after the man she fancied,
she did the job herself so that she could flaunt her
upper arms in front of him.

अभिमुखमुपयाति मा स्म किंचि-
त्त्वमभिदधाः पटले मधुव्रतानाम् ।
मधुसुरभिमुखाब्जगन्धलब्धे-
रधिकमधित्वदनेन मा निपाति ॥

सरजसमकरन्दनिर्भरासु
प्रसवविभूतिषु वीरुधां विरक्तः ।
ध्रुवममृतपनामवाञ्छया ऽसा-
वधरममुं मधुपस्तवाजिहीते ॥

इति वदति सखीजनं निमील-
द्द्विगुणितसान्द्रतराक्षिपक्ष्ममाला ।
अपतदलिभयेन भर्तुरङ्कं
भवति हि विक्लवता गुणो ऽङ्गनानाम् ॥

मुखकमलकमुन्नमय्य यूना
यदभिनवोढवधूर्बलादचुम्बि ।
तदपि न किल बालपल्लवाग्र-
ग्रहपरया विविदे विदग्धसख्या ॥

४५ व्रततिविततिभिस्तिरोहितायां
प्रतियुवतौ वदनं प्रियः प्रियायाः ।
यददधदधरावलोपनृत्य-
त्करवलयस्वनितेन तद्विवव्रे ॥

224

"A swarm of bees is heading this way and your lovely
    mouth is fragrant with wine. Keep quiet, in case they
    pick up the scent of your breath and descend upon
    you.

One honey-drinking bee has lost its taste for the trees'
    flowery wealth of pollen and juice; now it craves
    the renown of an ambrosia-consuming god and is
    relentlessly bearing down on that sweet lower lip of
    yours."

As her friends were telling her this, she squeezed her long
    eyelashes together, doubling their thickness, and in
    terror of the bee, fled to her man's embrace. To be
    sure, timidity heightens a woman's appeal.

A young husband raised his new bride's exquisite face
    and kissed her passionately; her friend, discreetly
    preoccupied with picking a fresh bud, apparently
    noticed nothing.

When a man kissed his wife full on the mouth, her cowife,   45
    concealed amid the thick creeper fronds, found out
    from the jingling of her rival's armlets as her fingers
    played over the wound on her lip.[7]

विलसितमनुकुर्वती पुरस्ता-
द्वरणिरुहाधिरुहो वधूर्लतायाः ।
रमणमृजुतया पुरः सखीना-
मकलितचापलदोषमालिलिङ्ग ॥

सललितमवलम्ब्य पाणिनांसे
सहचरमुच्छ्रितगुच्छवाञ्छयान्या ।
सकलकलभकुम्भविभ्रमाभ्या-
मुरसि रसादवतस्तरे स्तनाभ्याम् ॥

मृदुचरणतलाग्रदुःस्थितत्वा-
दसहतरा कुचकुम्भयोर्भरस्य ।
उपरि निरवलम्बनं प्रियस्य
न्यपतदथोच्चतरूरुच्चिकीषयान्या ॥

उपरिजतरुजानि याचमानां
कुशलतया परिरम्भलोलुभो ऽन्यः ।
प्रथितपृथुपयोधरां गृहाण
स्वयमिति मुग्धवधूमुदास दोर्भ्याम् ॥

५० इदमिदमिति भूरुहां प्रसूनै-
र्मुहुरभिलोभयता पुरःपुरो ऽन्या ।
अनुरहसमनायि नायकेन
त्वरयति रन्तुमहो जनं मनोभूः ॥

Oblivious to accusations of silliness, a young girl imitated
    a sinuous vine twined around a nearby tree and
    innocently embraced her man in front of her friends.

Another woman, trying to pluck an elusive cluster of
    flowers, leaned gracefully on her lover's shoulder,
    passionately pressing against his chest with her
    breasts, round as an elephant's forehead lobes.

One woman wanted to pick a flower still higher up, but her
    breasts were so heavy she could not stand on tiptoe
    and tumbled helplessly upon her lover.

A pretty young wife pressed her bosom against her
    husband's chest as she reached for some flowers high
    in a tree. Eager for an embrace, he cleverly hoisted her
    up in the air—just so she could pluck them!

Another girl, hankering after every flower she saw on   50
    the trees ahead of her, was coaxed to a secluded spot
    by her husband repeating, "Take this one—and that
    one!" Lust can turn into lovemaking in a trice.

विजनमिति बलादमुं गृहीत्वा
क्षणमथ वीक्ष्य विपक्षमन्तिके ऽन्या ।
अभिपतितुमना लघुत्वभीते-
रभवदमुञ्चति वल्लभे ऽतिगुर्वी ॥

अधिरजनि जगाम धाम तस्याः
प्रियतमयेति रुषा स्रजावबद्धः ।
पदमपि चलितुं युवा न सेहे
किमिव न शक्तिहरं ससाध्वसानाम् ॥

न खलु वयममुष्य दानयोग्याः
पिबति च पाति च यासकौ रहस्त्वाम् ।
व्रज विटपममुं ददस्व तस्यै
भवतु यतः सदृशोश्चिराय योगः ॥

तव कितव किमाहृतैर्वृथा नः
क्षितिरुहपल्लवपुष्पकर्णपूरैः ।
ननु जनविहितैर्भवद्व्यलीकै-
श्चिरपरिपूरितमेव कर्णयुग्मम् ॥

५५ मुहुरुपहसितामिवालिनादै-
र्वितरसि नः कलिकां किमर्थमेताम् ।
वसतिमुपगतेन धाम्नि तस्याः
शठ कलिरेष महांस्त्वयाद्य दत्तः ॥

228

Yet another woman grabbed hold of her lover for an
   instant because nobody else was present, but then
   noticed her rival nearby. Scared of being thought
   undignified, she tried to disengage herself, becoming
   quite stern when her man did not release her at once.

A young man had been angrily tethered with a garland by
   his girl so that he could not take a single step. Why?
   Because he had gone to her cowife's apartment during
   the night. It takes little to unman the guilty.

"I don't deserve to receive this sapling branch you offer me
   in supplication. It's so fresh and immature—why don't
   you go and give it to that girl who has her fill of you in
   secret and wants you all to herself? Let two identical
   things be united for once and all![8]

You cheat, what do I want with leaves and flowers you strip
   from trees and give to me for ear ornaments? They are
   worthless! Don't you know that my ears have already
   been filled by your lies, recognized by everyone for
   what they are?

Why do you give me this little twig repeatedly mocked,   55
   it seems, by the bees buzzing around it? You went
   to pass the time in her company and cheated on me.
   What you have really given me today is a slice of bad
   luck."[9]

इति गदितवती रुषा जघान
स्फुरितमनोरमपक्ष्मकेसरेण ।
श्रवणनियमितेन कान्तमन्या
सममसिताम्बुरुहेण चक्षुषा च ॥

विनयति सुदृशो दृशोः परागं
प्रणयिनि कौसुममाननानिलेन ।
तदहितयुवतेरभीक्ष्णमक्ष्णो-
र्द्वयमपि रोषरजोभिरापुपूरे ॥

स्फुटमिदमभिचारमन्त्र एव
प्रतियुवतेरभिधानमञ्जनानाम् ।
वरतनुरमुनोपहूय पत्या
मृदुकुसुमेन यदाहताप्यमूर्च्छत् ॥

समदनमवतंसिते ऽधिकर्णं
प्रणयवता कुसुमे सुमध्यमायाः ।
व्रजदपि लघुतां बभूव भारः
सपदि हिरण्मयमण्डनं सपत्न्याः ॥

६० अविजतममुना तवाऽहमक्ष्णा
रुचिरतयेत्यवनम्य लज्जयेव ।
श्रवणकुवलयं विलासवत्या
भ्रमररुतैरुपकर्णमाचचक्षे ॥

With this, a woman angrily struck her beloved with the
dark lotus she wore behind her ear, its filaments like
charmingly fluttering eyelashes. Yet she also darted
a sidelong glance at him from eyes whose lashes were
like daintily flickering filaments.

While her lover was blowing away the flowery pollen from
his lovely girl's eye, anger's dust suddenly clogged her
rival's sight.

The mere name of a rival is clearly a magic spell with the
power to bewitch women; her husband inadvertently
used it to call over his wife, and she fainted away when
he did no more than gently tap her with a flower.

After the ear of one slender girl had been affectionately
decorated with a flower by her husband, her cowife's
gold ornament immediately became as nothing—yet it
burdened her grievously.[10]

The water lily on a young beauty's ear hung down, as   60
if shamefully admitting to being surpassed by the
brightness of her eyes, and whispered to her with
bees' humming.

अवचितकुसुमा विहाय वल्ली-
र्युवतिषु कोमलमाल्यमालिनीषु ।
पदमुपदधिरे कुलान्यलीनां
न परिचयो मलिनात्मनां प्रधानम् ॥

श्लथशिरसिजपाशपातभारा-
दिव नितरां नतिमद्भिरंसभागैः ।
मुकुलितनयनैर्मुखारविन्दै-
र्घनमहतामिव पक्ष्मणां भरेण ॥

अधिकमरुणिमानमुद्वहद्भि-
र्विलसदशीतमयूखरश्मिजालैः ।
परिचितपरिचुम्बनाभियोगा-
दपगतकुङ्कुमरेणुभिः कपोलैः ॥

अवसितललितक्रियेण बाह्वो-
र्ललिततरेण तनीयसा युगेन ।
सरसकिसलयानुरञ्जितैर्वा
करकमलैः पुनरुक्तरक्तभाभिः ॥

६५ स्मरसरसमुरःस्थलेन पत्यु-
र्विनिमयसंक्रमिताङ्गरागरागैः ।
भृशमतिशयखेदसंपदेव
स्तनयुगलैरितरेतरं निषण्णैः ॥

Swarms of bees had abandoned creepers stripped of their
    blossoms and settled on girls now garlanded with
    strings of delightful flowers. For those dark in color,
    as for those of an ungrateful disposition, an intimate
    connection counts for nothing.[11]

Their shoulders were drooping as if burdened by the loose
    falling braids of their hair, their eyes closed in their
    lotus-like faces as though burdened by their long,
    thick lashes,[12]

their cheeks, flushed from the fierce sunshine beating
    down upon them, had lost their coating of saffron
    powder through the passionate kisses of their lovers,

their slender elegant arms could no longer engage in any
    graceful activity, while the redness of their lotus-like
    hands increased twice over, as though colored by the
    sap-filled buds,

their breasts, pressing against each other tightly as if   65
    utterly exhausted, had given over their red unguent to
    their husbands' chests in the passionate exchange of
    love,

233

अनतकुचभरानतेन भूयः
क्रमजनितानतिना शरीरकेण ।
अनुचितगतिसादिनिःसहत्वं
कलभकरोरुभिरूरुभिर्दधानैः ॥

अपहृतनवयावकैश्चिराय
क्षितिगमनेन पुनर्वितीर्णरागैः ।
कथमपि चरणाम्बुजैश्चलद्भि-
र्भृशविनिवेशवशात्परस्परस्य ॥

मुहुरिति वनविभ्रमाभिषङ्गा-
दतमि तदा नितरां नितम्बिनीभिः ।
मृदुतरतनवो ऽलसाः प्रकृत्या
चिरमपि ताः किमुत प्रयासभाजः ॥

प्रथममलघुमौक्तिकाभमासी-
च्छ्रमजलमुज्ज्वलगण्डमण्डलेषु ।
कठिनकुचतटाग्रपाति पश्चा-
दथ शतशर्करतां जगाम तासाम् ॥

७० विपुलकमपि यौवनोद्धृतानां
घनपुलकोदयकोमलं चकाशे ।
परिमलितमपि प्रियैः प्रकामं
कुचयुगमुज्ज्वलमेव कामिनीनाम् ॥

234

their delicate bodies, already bending under the weight
of their full breasts, bent forward still farther with
fatigue; their thighs, tapering like elephants' trunks,
could not endure the weariness of unaccustomed
walking,

their lotus-like feet were regaining their natural redness
now that their fresh lac was fading after the long walk;
they could barely advance by deliberately planting
first one, then the next on the ground—

The lovely girls, naturally delicate and prone to fatigue
even when not greatly exerting themselves, were now
exhausted by their enthusiastic forest play.

At first the sweat on their round glowing cheeks had been
like perfect pearls; but as it dropped onto their firm
breasts, it broke into a hundred fragments.

The ample bosoms of these beauties glorying in their   70
youth were quite sumptuous. A thick down, soft and
smooth, arose on them when fondled by their lovers,
but despite this darkening their skin tone, they still
had a glow about them.[13]

अविरतकुसुमावचयखेदा-
न्निहितभुजलतयैकयोपकण्ठम् ।
विपुलतरनिरन्तरावलग्न-²
स्तनपिहितप्रियवक्षसा ललम्बे ॥

अभिमतमभितः कृताङ्गभङ्गा
कुचयुगमुन्नतिवित्तमुन्नमय्य ।
तनुरभिलषितं श्रमच्छलेन
व्यवृणुत वेल्लितबाहुवल्लरीका ॥

हिमलवसदृशः श्रमोदबिन्दू-
नपनयता किल नूतनोढवध्वाः ।
कुचकलशकिशोरकौ कथञ्चि-
त्तरलतया तरुणेन पस्पृशाते ॥

गत्वोद्रेकं जघनपुलिने रुद्धमध्यप्रदेशः
स्थित्वा नाभौ वलिषु वलयन्नाङ्गमम्भोविलासम् ।
प्राप्योरुत्वं स्तनतटभुवि³ प्लावयन्रोमकूपा-
न्स्वेदापूरो युवतिसरितां व्याप गण्डस्थलानि ॥

७५ प्रियकरपरिमार्गादङ्गनानां यदाभू-
त्पुनरधिकतरैव स्वेदतोयोदयश्रीः ।
अथ वपुरभिषेकुं तास्तदम्भोभिरीषु-
र्वनविहरणखेदम्लानमम्लानशोभाः ॥

Exhausted by plucking flowers all day long, a girl clung to
    her man; one slender arm was draped around his neck
    while her broad breasts, close set against each other,
    covered his chest.

She stretched her body, raising even higher her already
    prominent bosom, and twined her slender arms
    together; so she revealed her desire to him under the
    guise of weariness.

The young man's hands were trembling, but he still
    contrived to fondle the plump young breasts of
    his new bride while delicately removing drops of
    perspiration as if they were pieces of ice.

The girls were rivers in spate as sweat washed over them.
    It overflowed the sandbanks of their buttocks and
    washed over the middle regions of their waists; then
    after whirling in their navels it appeared like the
    Ganga's water streaming up over their stomach folds
    until, breaching the banks, their breasts, it flooded the
    wells, the pores of their skin, and reached the flatlands
    of their cheeks.[14]

When sweat sprang up again on the bodies of the young   75
    women, it was all the more delightful since it was the
    result of their lovers' caresses. Now, their attractions
    undiminished but worn out from the exertions of their
    forest amusements, they were eager to bathe.

CHAPTER 8

Water Games

आयासादलघुतरस्तनैः स्तनद्भि-
स्तान्तानामविशदलोचनारविन्दैः ।
अभ्यम्भः कथमपि योषितां समूहै-
स्तैरुर्वीनिमितचलत्पदं प्रचेले ॥

यान्तीनां सममसितभ्रुवां नतत्वा-
दंसानां महति नितान्तमन्तरे ऽपि ।
संसक्तैर्विपुलतया मिथो नितम्बैः
संबाधं बृहदपि तद्बभूव वर्त्म ॥

नीरन्ध्रद्रुमशिशिरां भुवं भजन्तीः
साशङ्कं मुहुरिव कौतुकात्करैस्ताः ।
पस्पर्श क्षणमनिलाकुलीकृतानां
शाखानामतुहिनरश्मिरन्तरालैः ॥

एकस्यास्तपनकरैः करालिताया
बिभ्राणः सपदि सितोष्णवारणत्वम् ।
सेवायै वदनसरोजनिर्जितश्री-
रागत्य प्रियमिव चन्द्रमाश्चकार ॥

५ स्वं रागादुपरि वितन्वतोत्तरीयं
कान्तेन प्रतिपथवारितातपायाः ।
सच्छत्रादपरविलासिनीसमूहा-
च्छायासीदधिकतरा तदापरस्याः ॥

All the girls were tired after their exertions; they were
    groaning from the weight of their breasts and their
    lotus-like eyes had lost their luster. Feet stumbling
    wherever they placed them, they only just managed to
    totter to the lake.

There was space enough between these dark-browed
    beauties as they moved along together, since they bent
    and contracted their shoulders in exhaustion, and the
    path itself was wide. But it soon became crowded as
    their broad hips pressed against one another.

Still, they continued on their way beneath the cool shade
    of the thick foliage. All the while the sun, reserved but
    filled with curiosity, went on stroking them with its
    rays through gaps in branches ruffled by the breeze.

One girl was distressed by the sun's burning rays, so the
    moon, its beauty surpassed by her lotus-like face,
    at once attended her, becoming a white sunshade, it
    seemed, to cool her.

The other young women may all have had their own   5
    fine parasols, but one of them appeared especially
    eye-catching in the shade, for her lover was keeping
    the heat at bay at every step by devotedly holding his
    jacket over her.[1]

संस्पर्शप्रभवसुखोपचीयमाने
सर्वाङ्गे करतललग्नवल्लभायाः ।
कौशेयं व्रजदपि गाढतामजस्रं
सस्रंसे विगलितनीवि नीराजाक्ष्याः ॥

आयान्तीरलसमवेक्ष्य विस्मयिन्य-
स्तास्तन्वीर्न विदधिरे गतानि हंस्यः ।
बुद्धा वा जितमपरेण काममावि-
ष्कुर्वीत स्वगुणमपत्रपः क एव ॥

श्रीमद्भिर्जितपुलिनानि माधवीना-
मारोहैर्निबिडबृहन्नितम्बबिम्बैः ।
पाषाणस्खलनविलोलमाशु नूनं
वैलक्ष्यादयुरवरोधनानि सिन्धोः ॥

मुक्ताभिः सलिलरयास्तशुक्तिपेशी-
मुक्ताभिः कृतरुचि सैकतं नदीनाम् ।
स्त्रीलोकः परिकलयांचकार तुल्यं
पल्यङ्कैर्विगलितहारचारुभिः स्वैः ॥

१० आघ्राय श्रमजमनिन्द्यगन्धबन्धुं
निःश्वासश्वसनमसङ्गमङ्गनानाम् ।
आरण्याः सुमनस ईषिरे न भृङ्गै-
रौचित्यं गणयति को विशेषकामः ॥

A lotus-eyed girl was clutching her lover's hand, and she
was shivering all over with the delight of touching
him; this loosened the tight knot on her skirt, and it
slowly slipped off.

Geese watched in awe and stopped moving as these
slender girls proceeded languidly on their way. No
wonder—who would shamelessly flaunt his qualities
knowing he has already been bested?[2]

Suddenly the rivers, the ocean's wives, felt embarrassed
as they splashed over their rocky beds. There could be
no doubt that their sandbanks had been surpassed in
shapeliness by the waists of Krishna's wives and their
beautiful round buttocks, so firm and broad.

These sandbanks stretching across the rivers glinted with
pearls loosened from broken oyster shells thrown up
by the watery spate. The women fancied them to be no
different from their own comfortable couches strewn
with discarded necklaces.

The forest flowers were spurned by bees that had caught   10
the scent of the womens' panting tinged with their
rich fragrance. Who concerns himself with the
ordinary when lured away by something special?

आयत्यां निजयुवतौ वनात्सशङ्कं
बर्हाणामितरशिखण्डिनीं भरेण ।
आलोक्य व्यवदधतं मयूरमारा-
द्धामिन्यः श्रदधुरनार्जवं नरेषु ॥

आलापैस्तुलितरवाणि वाणिनीनां
माधुर्यादमलपत्रिणां कुलानि ।
अन्तर्धामुपययुरुत्पलावलीषु
प्रादुःष्यात्क इव जितः पुरः परेण ॥

मुग्धायाः स्मरललितेषु चक्रवाक्या
निःशङ्कं दयिततमेन चुम्बितायाः१ ।
प्राणेशानभि विदधुर्विधूतहस्ताः
सीत्कारं समुचितमुत्तरं तरुण्यः ॥

उत्क्षिप्तस्फुरितसरोरुहार्धमुच्चैः
सस्नेहं विहगरवैरिवालपन्ती ।
नारीणामथ सरसी सफेनहासा
प्रीत्येव व्यतनुत पाद्यमूर्मिहस्तैः ॥

१५ नित्याया निजवसतेर्निरासिरे य-
द्रागेण श्रियमरविन्दतः कराग्रैः ।
व्यक्तं नियतमनेन निन्युरस्याः
सापत्न्यं क्षितिसुतविद्विषो महिष्यः ॥

The women saw an agitated peacock nearby concealing
a peahen with his thick plumage just as his mate was
emerging from the forest—confirmation that males
are always unfaithful!

The sweetness of excited female chatter matched the cries
of flocks of white-winged geese, who hid themselves
in the lotus clumps. Who would show off before a
successful rival?

A sheldrake hen,[3] inexperienced in love's intimacies,
called out when favored with a random peck from
her mate; the young women's hands trembled as
they uttered the same soft cry in response to their
husbands' kisses.

At last the lake welcomed the women. It produced as
guest-gift its opening lotuses, seemed to address them
affectionately with the cries of its birds, smiled with
its white foam in clear delight at seeing them, and with
its waves provided water for washing their feet.

The exquisite lotuses there were surpassed in redness   15
by the fingers of Krishna's consorts, who jealously
evicted the goddess Shri from her eternal home,[4]
demonstrating for all to see that they really were her
cowives.[5]

आस्कन्दन्कथमपि योषितो न याव-
द्ध्रीमत्यः प्रियकरधार्यमाणहस्ताः ।
औत्सुक्यात्त्वरितममूस्तदम्बु ताव-
त्संक्रान्तप्रतिमतया दधाविवान्तः ॥

ताः पूर्वं सचकितमागमय्य गाधं
कृत्वाथो मृदुपदमन्तराविशन्त्यः ।
कामिन्यो मन इव कामिनः सरागै-
रङ्गैस्तज्जलमनुरञ्जयांबभूवुः ॥

संक्षोभं पयसि मुहुर्महेभकुम्भ-
श्रीभाजा कुचयुगलेन नीयमाने ।
विश्लेषं युगमगमद्रथाङ्गनाम्नो-
रुद्वृत्तः क इव सुखावहः परेषाम् ॥

आसीना तटभुवि सस्मितेन भर्त्रा
रम्भोरूरवतरितुं सरस्यनिच्छुः ।
धुन्वाना करयुगमीक्षितुं विलासा-
न्शीतालुः सलिलगतेन सिच्यते स्म ॥

२० नेच्छन्ती समममुना सरो ऽवगाढुं
रोधस्तः प्रतिजलमीरिता सखीभिः ।
आश्लिक्षद्द्वयचकितेक्षणं नवोढा
वोढारं विपदि न दूषितातिभूमिः ॥

246

These women were now holding hands timidly with their
partners, but even before they had summoned the
courage to plunge into the lake, its water already
seemed to contain them as reflections on its surface.

At first they tested the water with trepidation, then they
stood in the shallows until eventually venturing in,
reddening the surface with their lac-colored limbs;
likewise they gradually roused their lovers' minds to
passion.[6]

As the lake's surface was repeatedly stirred up by breasts
round as the frontal lobes of mighty elephants, a
sheldrake couple separated in consternation. What
puffed-up person can truly make others happy?[7]

One slender-thighed girl sat on the bank wringing her
hands in dread of the chill and refused to venture
into the lake. Her smiling lover, already in the
water, splashed her just so he could watch her flinch
demurely.

A newly wed girl, unwilling to leap in after her husband,   20
was pushed off the bank into his embrace by her
friends, her eyes rolling in fear. There is nothing
wrong with breaching propriety if circumstances
demand.

तिष्ठन्तं पयसि पुमांसमंसमात्रे
तद्घ्नं तदवयती किलात्मनो ऽपि ।
अभ्येतुं सुतनुरभीरियेष मौग्ध्या-
दाश्लेषि द्रुतममुना निमज्जतीति ॥

आनाभेः सरसि नतभ्रुवावगाढे
चापल्यादथ सरसस्तरङ्गहस्तैः ।
उच्छ्रायिस्तनयुगमध्यरोहि लब्ध-
स्पर्शानां भवति कुतो ऽथ वा व्यवस्था ॥

कान्तानां कुवलयमप्यपास्तमक्ष्णोः
शोभाभिर्न मुखरुचाहमेकमेव ।
संहर्षादलिविरुतैरितीव गाय-
ह्लोलोर्मौ पयसि महोत्पलं ननर्त ॥

त्रस्यन्ती चलशफरीविघट्टितोरू-
र्वामोरूरतिशयमाप विभ्रमस्य ।
क्षुभ्यन्ति प्रततमहो विनापि हेतो-
र्लीलाभिः किमु सति कारणे रमन्यः ॥

२५ आकृष्टप्रतनुवपुर्लतैस्तरद्भि-
स्तस्याम्भस्तदथ सरोमहार्णवस्य ।
अक्षोभि प्रसृतविलोलबाहुपक्षै-
र्योषाणामुरुभिरुरोजगण्डशैलैः ॥

One young beauty saw her lover standing up to his
 shoulders in the water and naively thought, or so
 it seemed, that it would reach no higher on her.
 She moved boldly toward him, only to be quickly
 embraced before being completely submerged.

When another girl plunged grimacing into the lake
 up to her navel, hand-like waves rose from the
 splashing water to clutch her jutting breasts. Hardly
 surprising—how can people restrain themselves when
 they have already got hold of something?

A lotus danced on the lake's lapping waves, seeming to
 sing with delight as bees hummed around it: "I alone
 have not been surpassed by the lustrous faces of these
 beauties, unlike the blue water lily, outdone by their
 fair eyes."

As one lovely girl took fright when her thighs were
 nuzzled by darting carp, she became remarkably
 charming. Women get needlessly upset over trifles, let
 alone when there is good reason.

The lake's surface was no longer placid as the women   25
 jumped in, heavy breasts pulling their slender bodies
 after them, arms waving above their heads. So the
 mighty ocean had been stirred up when the towering
 mountains traversed them, wings flapping, trailing
 creepers in their wake.[8]

249

गाम्भीर्यं दधदपि रन्तुमङ्गनाभिः
प्रक्षोभं जघनविघट्टनेन नीतः ।
अम्भोधिर्विकसितवारिजाननो ऽसौ
मर्यादां सपदि विलङ्घ्यांबभूव ॥

आम्रष्टुं दयितमिवावगाढमारा-
दूर्मीणां ततिभिरभिप्रसार्यमाणः ।
कस्याश्चिद्द्रिततचलच्छिखाङ्गुलीको
लक्ष्मीवान्सरसि रराज केशहस्तः ॥

उन्निद्रप्रियकमनोरमं रमण्याः
संरेजे सरसि वपुः प्रकाशमेव ।
युक्तानां विमलतया तिरस्क्रियायै
नाक्रामन्नपि हि भवत्यलं जलौघः ॥

किं तावत्सरसि सरोजमेतदारा-
दाहोस्विन्मुखमवभासते तरुण्याः ।
संशय्य क्षणमिति निश्चिकाय कश्चि-
द्विव्वोकैर्बकसहवासिनां परोक्षैः ॥

३० शृङ्गाणि द्रुतकनकोज्ज्वलानि गन्धाः
कौसुम्भं पृथुकुचकुम्भसङ्गि वासः ।
मार्द्वीकं प्रियतमसंनिधानमास-
न्नारीणामिति जलकेलिसाधनानि ॥

That lake was already deep, but now that lotus-like faces
were bobbing everywhere upon its surface, it quickly
swelled further and inundated the shore. Caressing
these women's buttocks, it became amorous and,
despite its usual calm demeanor, soon abandoned
proper decorum.[9]

The luxuriously coiffured hair of one girl seemed like
hands, long finger-braids drifting on the water. The
waves pulled them farther out, as if to fondle her
lover, who had dived in nearby.

Another woman floated in the very center of the lake,
but she could still be easily seen, lovely as an opening
kadamba flower. While water may flow over bright
objects, it cannot conceal them, any more than
insolent fools can get the better of the intelligent.[10]

"Is that just a lotus in the distance glinting on the water's
surface or a girl's face?" A young man briefly voiced
his uncertainty but quickly arrived at the correct
conclusion—lotuses, those friends of the herons,[11] do
not arch their eyebrows suggestively!

Squirter toys bright as liquid gold, perfume, safflower-   30
dyed bodices clinging to full breasts, wine, their
lovers' proximity—all these were the women's aids to
love as they played in the water.

उत्तुङ्गादनिलचलांशुकास्तटान्ता-
च्चेतोभिः सह भयदर्शिनां प्रियाणाम् ।
श्रोणीभिर्गुरुभिरतूर्णमुत्पतन्त्य-
स्तोयेषु द्रुततरमङ्गना निपेतुः ॥

मुग्धत्वादविदितकैतवप्रयोगा
गच्छन्त्यः सपदि पराजयं तरुण्यः ।
ताः कान्तैः सह करपुष्करेरिताम्बु-
व्यात्युक्षीमभिसरणगलहामदीव्यन् ॥

योग्यस्य त्रिनयनलोचनानलार्चि-
र्निर्दग्धस्मरपृतनाधिराजलक्ष्म्याः ।
कान्तायाः करकलशोद्धृतैः पयोभि-
र्वक्रेन्दोरकृत महाभिषेकमेकः ॥

सिञ्चन्त्याः कथमपि बाहुमुन्नमय्य
प्रेयांसं मनसिजदुःखदुर्बलायाः ।
सौवर्णं वलयमवागलत्कराग्रा-
ल्लावण्यश्रिय इव शेषमङ्गनायाः ॥

३५ स्निह्यन्तीं दृशमपरा निधाय पूर्णं
मूर्तेन प्रणयरसेन वारिणेव ।
कन्दर्पप्रवणमनाः सखीसिसिक्षा-
लक्ष्येण प्रतियुवमञ्जलिं चकार ॥

Their hips were so heavy that they could not gain much
    height when they leapt from the lake's lofty bank,
    scarves fluttering in the breeze. But they fell quickly
    enough into the water—along with the hearts of those
    anxious spectators, their lovers.

These young women now held a gambling session with
    their partners, competing in splashing each other for
    the stake of an amorous encounter. But they were
    quite naive, knowing nothing of gamesmanship, and
    soon lost.[12]

A man filled his cupped hands with water and made a great
    lustration over his beloved's moon-like face; it was
    worthy of assuming command of the army of the god
    of love incinerated by the flame from Shiva's eye.[13]

One girl was so worn and wan from the exertions of
    lovemaking that when she finally managed to lift
    her arm to sprinkle water over her man, her golden
    bracelet slipped over her fingers, as if that was all that
    remained of her surpassing beauty.

With intense passion another woman fixed her loving gaze   35
    upon a young man. Then, on the pretext of sprinkling
    her girlfriend, she entreated him with cupped hands[14]
    filled with water, like love's essence in physical form.

आनन्दं दधति मुखे करोदकेन
श्यामाया दयिततमेन सिच्यमाने ।
ईर्ष्यन्त्या वदनमसिक्तमप्यनल्प-
स्वेदाम्भःस्नपितमजायतेतरस्याः ॥

उद्वीक्ष्य प्रियकरकुङ्कुलापविद्धै-
र्वक्षोजद्वयमभिषिक्तमन्यनार्याः ।
अम्भोभिर्मुहुरसिचद्बुधूरमर्षा-
दात्मीयं पृथुतरनेत्रयुग्ममुत्तैः ॥

कुर्वद्भिर्मुखरुचमुज्ज्वलामजस्रं
यैस्तोयैरसिचत वल्लभां विलासी ।
तैरेव प्रतियुवतेरकारि दूरा-
त्कालुष्यं शशधरदीधितिच्छटाच्छैः ॥

रागान्धीकृतनयनेन नामधेय-
व्यत्यासादभिमुखमीरितः प्रियेण ।
मानिन्या वपुषि पतन्निसर्गमन्दे
भिन्दानो हृदयमसाहि नोदवज्रः ॥

४० प्रेम्णोरः प्रणयिनि सिञ्चति प्रियाया-
स्तत्तापं नवजलविप्रुषो गृहीत्वा ।
उद्धूताः कठिनकुचस्थलाभिघाता-
दासन्नां भृशमपराङ्गनामधाक्षुः ॥

254

The face of one beautiful girl became suffused with joy
  when her lover sprinkled water upon her. Meanwhile,
  another's face was bathed with perspiration as her
  jealousy grew at being denied this favor.

Seeing her beloved pouring water from his cupped hands
  over a young woman's bosom, his wife proceeded to
  soak her own breasts with tears of anger pouring from
  her wide eyes.

An ardent lover continually sprinkled his favorite with
  water that shimmered like moonbeams; it made her
  fair face glow, but darkened her cowife's countenance.

Her lover, in the blindness of passion, addressed her by
  another's name as he threw water at her. The proud
  girl could not endure its crashing like a thunderbolt
  upon her body, never resilient at the best of times, and
  breaking her heart.

As a man was affectionately splashing his loved one, the 40
  drops of fresh water spattering up from her firm hard
  breasts absorbed their heat and scalded her cowife
  nearby.

संक्रान्तं प्रियतमवक्षसो ऽङ्गरागं
साध्वस्याः सरसि हरिष्यते ऽधुनाम्भः ।
तुष्टैवं सपदि हृते ऽपि तत्र तेपे
कस्याश्चित्स्फुटनखलक्षणः सपत्न्या ॥

हृतायाः प्रियसखि कामिनान्यनाम्ना
ह्रीमत्याः सरसि गलन्मुखेन्दुकान्तेः ।
अन्तर्धिं द्रुतमिव कर्तुमसुवर्षै-
र्भूमानं गमयितुमीषिरे पयांसि ॥

सिक्तायाः क्षणमभिषिच्य पूर्वमन्या-
मन्यस्याः प्रणयवता बताबलायाः ।
कालिम्ना समधित मन्युरेव वक्त्रं
प्रापाक्ष्णो गलदपशब्दमञ्जनाभः ॥

उद्ब्रोढुं कनकविभूषणान्यशक्तः
सध्रीचा वलयितपद्मनालसूत्रः ।
आरूढप्रतिवनिताकटाक्षभारः
साधीयो गुरुरभवद्भुजस्तरुण्याः ॥

४५ आबद्धप्रचुरपरार्ध्यकिङ्किणीको
रामाणामनवरतोद्गाहभाजाम् ।
आरावं व्यधित न मेखलाकलापः
कस्मिन्वा सजलगुणे गिरां पटुत्वम् ॥

One woman was overjoyed that the lake water would wash
 away the unguent smeared on her cowife's body by her
 husband's embrace. But when it disappeared, the nail
 marks she now saw there were a torment to her.

The beauty of another woman's moon-like face
 disappeared in her shame at her lover's mistaking her
 name in her girlfriend's hearing. As her tears flowed,
 the lake water seemed to yearn to swell up and hide
 her.

Anger had darkened a woman's face, for her husband who
 had just splashed her had a moment earlier done the
 same to her cowife—but the black kohl streaming
 from her eyes could perhaps take the blame for this.

The arm of one young woman was too weak to carry
 her golden ornaments and so her lover made her a
 bracelet from lotus-fiber threads; it became all the
 heavier since it was now weighed down by her jealous
 rival's bitter glances.

Though studded with many delightful little bells, the 45
 women's girdles did not jingle as, one after another,
 they jumped into the water. No surprise there! A belt
 cord sodden with water can no more make a sound
 than a fool can utter an articulate sentence.[15]

पर्यच्छे सरसि हृतें ऽशुके पयोभि-
र्लोलाक्षे सुरतगुरावपत्रपिष्णोः ।
सुश्रोण्या दलवसनेन वीचिहस्त-
न्यस्तेन द्रुतमकृताब्जिनी सखीत्वम् ॥

नारीभिर्गुरुजघनस्थलाहताना-
मास्यश्रीविजितविकासिवारिजानाम् ।
लोलत्वादपहरतां तदङ्गरागं
संजज्ञे स कलुष आशयो जलानाम् ॥

सागन्ध्यं दधदपि काममङ्गनानां
दूरत्वाद्द्रतमहमाननोपमानम् ।
नेदीयो जितमिति लज्जयेव तासां
लोलोर्मौ पयसि महोत्पलं ममज्ज ॥

प्रभ्रष्टैः सरभसमम्भसो ऽवगाह-
क्रिडाभिर्विदलितयूथिकापिशङ्गैः ।
आबन्ध्यैः सरसि हिरण्मयैर्वधूना-
मौर्वाग्निद्युतिशकलैरिव व्यराजि ॥

५० आस्माकी युवतिदृशामसौ तनोति
च्छायैव श्रियमनपायिनी किमेभिः ।
मत्वेव स्वगुणपिधानसाभ्यसूयैः
पानीयैरिति विदधाविरे ऽञ्जनानि ॥

To her embarrassment, one shapely girl's dress had
    been pulled off by the water, and her instructor in
    lovemaking was now staring into the pellucid lake.
    A lotus quickly became her close friend as hand-like
    ripples clothed her with its leaves.

Thanks to the women, the lake had become turbulent
    and dark; its water had been smitten by their heavy
    buttocks, its blossoming lotuses were surpassed in
    number and beauty by their faces, and its undulant
    waves were washing off their body cream. In the same
    way, fools are roused to excitement.[16]

A water lily sank in the rolling waves of the lake,
    apparently embarrassed: "When these women
    weren't around, I was reckoned their equal in
    fragrance and compared to their faces; but now that
    I'm actually near them, I clearly amount to nothing."

Gold ornaments, yellow as opening amaranth flowers,
    had fallen into the lake as the excited girls dived and
    played there; they blazed like flashes of submarine
    fire.

"It is my natural limpid purity that makes the young   50
    women's eyes so lustrous. So why do they need this
    makeup?" That's what the lake water seemed to think
    as it washed away their cream, annoyed that its own
    chief attribute had been discounted.

निर्धौते सति हरिचन्दने जलौचै-
रापाण्डोर्गतपरभागयाङ्गनायाः ।
अह्नाय स्तनकलशद्वयादुपेये
विच्छेदः सहृदययेव हारयष्ट्या ॥

अन्यूनं गुणममृतस्य धारयन्ती
संफुल्लस्फुरितसरोरुहावतंसा ।
प्रेयोभिः सह सरसी निषेव्यमाणा
रक्तत्वं व्यधित वधूदृशां सुरा च ॥

स्नान्तीनां बृहदमलोदबिन्दुचित्रौ
रेजाते रुचिरदृशामुरोजकुम्भौ ।
हाराणां मणिभिरिवाश्रितौ समन्ता-
दुत्सूत्रैर्गुणवदुपग्रहकाम्ययेव ॥

आरूढः पतित इति स्वसंभवो ऽपि
स्वच्छानां परिहरणीयतामुपैति ।
कर्णेभ्यश्श्रुतमसितोत्पलं वधूनां
वीचीभिस्तटमनु यन्निरासुरापः ॥

५५ दन्तानामधरमयावकं पदानि
प्रत्यग्रास्तनुमविलेपनां नखाङ्काः ।
आनिन्युः श्रियमधितोयमङ्गनायाः
शोभायै विपदि सदाश्रिता भवन्ति ॥

After the water had removed the red sandalwood from one
　　woman's pale round breasts, her pearl necklace lost
　　its superior hue and, as if it were aware, immediately
　　broke apart.

In the company of their lovers the women enjoyed both
　　the lake and wine with all their ambrosial delights.
　　One had full-blown lotuses floating on it, while the
　　other was garnished with them—both tinged eyes
　　with redness!

As these bright-eyed girls bathed in the lake, their bosoms,
　　sparkling with fat droplets of water, seemed spattered
　　with unstrung pearls. Perhaps their necklaces were
　　hoping that these sumptuous breasts could thread
　　them again!

The clearheaded shun even their own offspring when they
　　lose their position after rising high. In the same way,
　　billows washed to the shore the blue lilies fallen from
　　the women's ears.

Although one woman's lower lip may have had its balm　　55
　　washed away, its allure was still enhanced by traces of
　　love bites; her body was no longer coated with cream
　　but remained covered with fresh nail marks. Those
　　who stay loyal in the midst of difficulties are a source
　　of honor.

कस्याश्चिन्मुखमनु धौतपत्रलेखं
व्यतेने सलिलभरावलम्बिनीभिः ।
किञ्जल्कव्यतिकरपिञ्जरान्तराभि-
श्चित्रश्रीरलमलकाग्रवल्लरीभिः ॥

वक्षोभ्यो घनमनुलेपनं यदूना-
मुत्तंसानहरत वारि मूर्धजेभ्यः ।
नेत्राणां मदरुचिरक्षतैव तस्थौ
चक्षुष्यः खलु महतां परैरगम्यः ॥

यो बाह्यः स खलु जलैर्निरासि रागो
यश्चित्ते स तु तदवस्थ एव तेषाम् ।
धीराणां व्रजति हि सर्व एव नान्तः-
पातित्वादभिभवनीयतां परस्य ॥

फेनानामुरसिरुहेषु हारलीला
चेलश्रीर्जघनतटेषु शैवलानाम् ।
गण्डेषु स्फुटरचना च पत्रवल्ली
पर्याप्तं पयसि विभूषणं वधूनाम् ॥

६० भ्रश्यद्विर्जलमभि हेमभिर्वधूना-
मङ्गेभ्यो गुरुभिरमज्जि लज्जयेव ।
निर्माल्यैरथ ननृते ऽवधीरिताना-
मप्युच्चैर्भवति लघीयसां हि धाष्ट्र्यम् ॥

262

Another woman's face had lost its painted leaf
    decorations, but it was still as pretty as a picture,
    framed by her long curling hair drenched with water,
    half-smeared with yellow pollen.

While the water may have removed the thick cream from
    the Yadava women's breasts and the ornaments
    from their hair, the ardent light in their eyes was
    undimmed. Anyone viewed with favor[17] by the great is
    totally secure.

If the red lac on the women's bodies had been obliterated
    by the water, the passion they felt was undiminished.
    The innermost feelings of the single-minded are
    impervious to outside influence.[18]

Foam took shape as necklaces on their breasts, the
    pondweed was an elegant dress draped over their
    buttocks, while slender lotus leaves were prominently
    deployed on their cheeks as decorations—the lake was
    more than capable of adorning the women.

The heavy gold ornaments falling from the women's   60
    bodies sank as if from shame, while their discarded
    garlands bobbed confidently on the surface. The
    insignificant may be objects of contempt, but they can
    still prove most resilient.

आमृष्टस्तिलकरुचः स्रजो ऽद्रिरस्ता
नीरक्तं वसनमपाकृतो ऽङ्गरागः ।
कामः स्त्रीरनुशयवानिव स्वपक्ष-
व्याघातादिति सुतरां चकार चारूः ॥

शीतार्तिं बलवदुपेयुषेव नीरै-
रासेकाच्छिशिरसमीरकम्पितेन ।
रामाणामभिनवयौवनोष्मभाजो-
राश्लेषि स्तनतटयोर्नवांशुकेन ॥

श्रोतद्भिः समधिकमात्तमङ्गसङ्गा-
ल्लावण्यं तनुमदिवाम्बु वाससो ऽन्तैः ।
उत्तेरे तरलतरङ्गरङ्गलीला-
निष्णातैरथ सरसः प्रियासमूहैः ॥

दिव्यानामपि कृतविस्मयां पुरस्ता-
दम्भसः स्फुरदरविन्दचारुहस्ताम् ।
उद्वीक्ष्य श्रियमिव कांचिदुत्तरन्ती-
मस्मार्षीज्जलनिधिमन्थनस्य शौरिः ॥

६५ श्लक्ष्णं यत्परिहितमेतयोः किलान्त-
र्धानार्थं तदुदकसेकसक्तमूरू ।
नारीणां विमलतरौ समुल्लसन्त्या
भासान्तर्दधतुरुरू दुगूलमेव ॥

264

The water rubbed off bright forehead marks, tossed away
garlands, drained the color from clothes, and removed
body creams. The god of love seemed to resent this
rough treatment of his followers and made the women
appear still more seductive.

A freshly laundered bodice, fluttering in the cool breeze,
seemed to shiver with cold after receiving a soaking,
so it clung to gorgeous breasts, warm with fresh youth.

The women had all been skilled performers on the stage
provided by the tumbling waves. Finally, like beauty
incarnate extracted from the human body, they took
leave of the lake, water streaming from the hems of
their garments.

As one emerged from the water, she looked like the
goddess Shri; with fair lotus-like hands glinting, she
would have astonished even the gods. As Krishna
gazed at her, he recalled the churning of the ocean.[19]

Each of the women had pulled her dress around herself,   65
supposedly to hide her thighs. But every one of these
flimsy garments was now saturated and clung tightly
to them, and shapely contours stood out so clearly
their coverings went unnoticed.

265

वासांसि न्यवसत यानि योषितस्ताः
शुभ्राभ्रद्युतिभिरहासि तैर्मुदेव ।
अत्याक्षुः प्लवनगलज्जलानि यानि
स्थूलासुसुतिभिररोदि तैः शुचेव ॥

आर्द्रत्वादतिशयिनीमुपेयिवद्भिः
संसक्तिं भृशमपि भूरिशो ऽवधूतैः ।
अङ्गेभ्यः कथमपि वामलोचनानां
विश्लेषो बत नवरक्तकैः प्रपेदे ॥

प्रत्यंसं विलुलितमूर्धजा चिराय
स्नानार्द्रैं वपुरुदवापयत्किलैका ।
नाजानादभिमतमन्तिके ऽभिवीक्ष्य
स्वेदाम्बुद्रवमभवत्तरां पुनस्तत् ॥

सीमन्तं निजमवबध्नती कराभ्या-
मालक्ष्यस्तनतटबाहुमूलभागा ।
भर्त्रान्या मुहुरभिलष्यता निदध्ये
नैवाहो विरमति कौतुकं प्रियेभ्यः ॥

७० स्वच्छाम्भःस्नपनविधौतमङ्गमोष्ठ-
स्ताम्बूलद्युतिविशदो विलासिनीनाम् ।
वासश्च प्रतनु विविक्तमस्वितीया-
नाकल्पो यदि कुसुमेषुणा न शून्यः ॥

266

The clothes donned by the women were fresh as white
  clouds and seemed to be smiling with delight. Those
  they discarded, water dripping from them, appeared
  to weep copious tears of grief.

As for the other women emerging from the lake, their fine
  newly dyed dresses were of course soaked through and
  clung tightly to them. Although they repeatedly shook
  them, they could only disrobe with difficulty.[20]

Seemingly still wet after bathing, one woman went on
  drying herself, hair tumbling over her shoulders; she
  did not realize that she was dripping with sweat from
  seeing her lover beside her.

Another girl, arranging the part in her hair, gave a glimpse
  of her breasts and upper arms to her husband, who
  stared with mounting lust. How remarkable that
  fascination with objects of affection never ceases!

A body cleansed by bathing in pure water, lips bright red   70
  as betel nut, a fresh-laundered diaphanous dress—
  these will suffice to adorn lovely women, provided the
  god of love is present.

इति धौतपुरन्ध्रिमत्सरान्सरसि मज्जनेन
श्रियमात्तवतो ऽतिशायिनीमविरलाङ्गभासः ।
अवलोक्य तदेव यादवानपरवारिराशेः
शिशिरेतररोचिषाप्यपां ततिषु मङ्कुमीषे ॥

The hot-rayed sun observed how the Yadavas, by diving in the lake, had washed away their women's jealousy and gained vibrantly handsome physiques. So it conceived the desire to plunge into the waves of the western ocean.

CHAPTER 9

Romantic Encounters After Sunset

अतितापसंपदमथोष्णरुचि-
र्निजतेजसामसहमान इव ।
पयसि प्रपित्सुरपराम्बुनिधे-
रधिरोढुमस्तगिरिमभ्यपतत् ॥

गतया पुरः प्रतिगवाक्षमुखं
दधती रतेन भृशमुत्सुकताम् ।
मुहुरन्तरालभुवमस्तभुवः
सवितुश्च योषिदमिमीत दृशा ॥

विरलातपच्छविरनूष्मतनुः
परितो ऽतिपाण्डु दधदभ्रशिरः ।
अभवद्व्रतः परिणतिं शिथिलः
परिमन्दसूर्यनयनो दिवसः ॥

अपराह्णशीतलतरेण शनै-
रनिलेन लोलितलताङ्गुलये ।
निलयाय शाखिन इवाह्वयते
ददुराकुलाः खगकुलानि गिरः ॥

५ उपसंध्यमास्त तनु सानुमतः
शिखरेषु तत्क्षणमशीतरुचः ।
करजालमस्तसमये ऽपि सता-
मुचितं खलूच्चतरमेव पदम् ॥

The sun, apparently unable to endure the intense heat of
    its own rays, was eager to descend into the western
    ocean, and it hurried to climb the sunset mountain.[1]

Meanwhile, a woman repeatedly peered through a window
    and measured the distance between the sun and the
    mountain, hardly able to wait for lovemaking to start.

The day was winding down, a decrepit old man: its
    bright complexion was fading, it felt cold, a white
    halo of clouds on its head, and its eyes, the sun, were
    dimming.

Flocks of birds called excitedly to a tree seeming to invite
    them to nest, its finger-like vines waving gently in the
    cool breeze of late afternoon.

At twilight the sun's weakening rays rested for an instant   5
    on the mountain peaks. Even at the moment of
    decline, high rank remains the appropriate state for
    the virtuous.

प्रतिकूलतामुपगते हि विधौ
विफलत्वमेति बहुसाधनता ।
अवलम्बनाय दिनभर्तुरभू-
न्न पतिष्यतः करसहस्रमपि ॥

नवकुङ्कुमारुणपयोधरया
स्वकराग्रमुक्तरुचिराम्बरया ।
अतिसक्तिमेत्य वरुणस्य दिशा
भृशमन्वरज्यदतुषारकरः ॥

गतवत्यराजत जपाकुसुम-
स्तबकद्युतौ दिनकरे ऽवनतिम् ।
बहलानुरागकुरुविन्ददल-
प्रतिबद्धमध्यमिव दिग्वलयम् ॥

द्रुतशातकौम्भनिभमंशुमतो
वपुरर्धमग्रवपुषः पयसि ।
व्यरुचद्द्विरिञ्जिनखभिन्नबृह-
ज्जगदण्डकैकतरखण्डमिव ॥

१० अनुरागवन्तमपि लोचनयो-
र्दधतं वपुः सुखमतापकरम् ।
निरकासयद्द्विमपेतवसुं
वियदालयादपरदिग्गणिका ॥

274

But when fate has turned contrary, nothing can be gained
from abundant resources. Not even its infinite hand-
like rays could prop up the sun in the sky as it was
about to set.

So the reddening sun, infatuated, approached ever closer
to the western region, delicately removing the bright
bodice from its cloud-breasts orange as fresh saffron.[2]

While the sun was setting, pink as a clump of roses, the
entire horizon glowed, as if its waist were girdled with
a belt of crimson rubies.

The solar orb half-sunk in the ocean was ablaze like liquid
gold, seeming to be a fragment of the great egg of the
universe[3] pared off by Brahma the creator's fingernail.

The western region ejected the sun from the sky; even   10
though its redness was still pleasing to the eyes, its
rays had cooled and its luster had gone. So a prostitute
throws a customer out of her house when he lacks
staying power or money, even though he may be
handsome and besotted with her.[4]

275

अभितिग्मरश्मि चिरमा विषया-
दवधानखिन्नमनिमेषतया ।
विगलन्मधुव्रतकुलासुजलं
न्यमिमीलदब्जनयनं नलिनी ॥

अविभाव्यतारकमदृष्टहिम-
द्युतिबिम्बमास्तमितभानु नभः ।
विगतोरुतापमतमिस्रमभा-
दपदोषतैव विगुणस्य गुणः ॥

रुचिधाम्नि भर्तरि भृशं विमलाः
परलोकमभ्युपगते विविशुः ।
ज्वलनं त्विषः कथमिवेतरथा
सुलभो ऽन्यजन्मनि स एव पतिः ॥

विहिताञ्जलिर्जनतया दधती
विकसत्कुसुम्भकुसुमारुणताम् ।
चिरमुज्झितापि तनुरौज्झदसौ
न पितृप्रसूः प्रकृतिमात्मभुवः ॥

१५ अथ सान्द्रसांध्यकिरणारुणितं
हरिहेतिहूति मिथुनं पततोः ।
पृथगुत्पपात विरहार्तिदल-
द्धृदयसुतासृगनुलिप्तमिव ॥

276

Exhausted by long staring straight at the sun, the lotus
    clump closed its flowery eyes,[5] and the tears it shed
    were bees flying away.

As yet no stars could be seen in the sky. The moon's disc
    was not quite visible, while the sun had set; the intense
    heat had disappeared, yet it was not quite dark. For
    one who has no obvious talents, mere absence of faults
    represents his sole attribute.

When their lustrous lord had departed to the next world,
    its pure chaste rays immediately entered the fire. How
    else could they obtain the same husband in their next
    birth?[6]

Twilight was the embodiment of Brahma after he created
    the ancestors. It may have eventually been forsaken
    by him but has never renounced his main traits—to
    be red as the blossoming safflower and everywhere
    revered.[7]

A pair of sheldrakes, turned crimson by the deep rays   15
    of the twilight sun, flew up separately, as if smeared
    with blood flowing from hearts broken by the pain of
    separation.[8]

निलयः श्रियः सततमेतदिति
प्रथितं यदेव जलजन्म तया⁹ ।
दिवसात्ययात्तदपि मुक्तमसौ
चपलाजनं प्रति न चोद्यमदः ॥

दिवसो ऽनुमित्रमगमद्विलयं
किमिवास्यते बत मयाबलया ।
रुचिभर्तुरस्य विरहाधिगमा-
दिति संध्ययापि सपदि न्यशमि ॥

पतिते पतङ्गमृगराजि निज-
प्रतिबिम्बरोषित इवाम्बुनिधिम् ।
अथ नागयूथमलिनानि जग-
त्परितस्तमांसि परितस्तिरिरे ॥

व्यसरन्नु भूधरगुहान्तरतः
पटलं बहिर्बहलपङ्क्तरुचि ।
दिवसावसानपटुनस्तमसो
बहिरेत्य वाधिकमभक्त गुहाः ॥

२० किमलम्बताम्बरविलग्नमधः
किमवर्धतोर्ध्वमवनीतलतः ।
प्रससार तिर्यगथ दिग्भ्य इति
प्रचुरीभवन्न निरधारि तमः ॥

278

The lotus in Vishnu's navel is everywhere recognized as the eternal abode of the goddess Shri,[9] but she still abandons it when it closes at day's end—hardly a surprise in the case of the fickle.

The day followed after its friend, the sun, and at once the twilight also disappeared.[10] "I am a weak woman," she thought. "How can I remain in this world, now that I know that the lord of light has gone?"

After the sun had fallen lion-like upon the ocean as if raging at its reflection, darkness, black as an elephant herd, shrouded the whole world.

A cloud of gloom, the color of thick mud, manifested itself at day's ending. But did it emerge from mountain caves to spread everywhere, or did it arise in the outside world and then penetrate deep into the caverns?

Did it cling to the sky and hang downward? Did it emerge from the earth or stretch out sideways from the horizons? The gathering murk could not be truly assessed. 20

स्थगिताम्बरक्षितितले परित-
स्तिमिरे जनस्य दृशमन्धयति ।
दधिरे रसाञ्जनमपूर्वमतः
प्रियवेश्मवर्त्म सुदृशो दृदृशुः ॥

अवधार्य कार्यगुरुतामभव-
न्न भयाय सान्द्रतमसन्तमसम् ।
सुतनोः स्तनौ च दयितोपगमे
तनुरोमराजिपथवेपथवे ॥

दृदृशे ऽपि भास्कररुचाद्धि न यः
स तमीं तमोभिरधिगम्य तताम् ।
द्युतिमग्रहीद्द्रुहगणो लघवः
प्रकटीभवन्ति मलिनाश्रयतः ॥

अनुलेपनानि कुसुमान्यबलाः
कृतमन्यवः पतिषु दीपदशाः ।
समयेन तेन सुचिरं शयित-
द्रुतबोधितस्मरमबोधिषत ॥

२५ वसुधान्तनिःसृतमिवाहिपतेः
पटलं फणामणिसहस्ररुचाम् ।
स्फुरदंशुजालमथ शीतरुचः
ककुभं समस्कुरुत माघवनीम् ॥

While the gloom was everywhere concealing heaven and
earth and blinding the rest of the world, fair women
applied a miraculous collyrium to their eyes—with
its aid alone they could find their way to their lovers'
houses!

The pitch darkness certainly did not alarm one girl when
she considered the importance of her mission; nor, as
she was setting out to her lover, did her heavy breasts
make her slender waist shudder.

The planets, invisible during the bright glare of day, took
on a luminescence in night's deep blackness. The
insignificant become noticed only when they consort
with those of tarnished character.[11]

Now it was evening, women earlier annoyed with their
lovers turned their minds toward body creams,
flowers, and glowing lamps; these can quickly
reawaken strong affection, however long dormant.

Then the moon's glinting rays ornamented the eastern   25
horizon, as if they were the myriad coruscating jewels
in the hoods of Shesha, lord of snakes, risen from the
earth.

विशदप्रभापरिगतं विबभा-
वुदयाचलव्यवहितेन्दुवपुः ।
मुखमप्रकाशदशनं शनकैः
सविलासहासमिव शक्रदिशः ॥

कलया तुषारकिरणस्य पुरः
परिमन्दभिन्नतिमिरौघजटम् ।
क्षणमभ्यपद्यत जनैर्न मृषा
गगनं गणाधिपतिमूर्तिरिति ॥

नवचन्द्रिकाकुसुमकीर्णतमः-
कवरीभृतो मलयजाद्रिमिव ।
दद‍ृशे ललाटतटहारि हरे-
र्हरितो मुखस्य हिमरश्मिदलम् ॥

प्रथमं कलाभवदथार्धमथो
हिमदीधितिर्महदभूदुदितः ।
दधति ध्रुवं क्रमत एव न तु
द्युतिशालिनो ऽपि सहसाभ्युदयम् ॥

३० उदमज्जि कैटभजितः शयना-
दपनिद्रपाण्डुरसरोजरुचा ।
प्रथमप्रबुद्धनदराजसुता-
वदनेन्दुनेव तुहिनद्युतिना ॥

282

The face of the eastern horizon was glowing within a
corona of moonlight, like a seductive smile slowly
forming, with teeth just visible. Meanwhile, the
sunrise mountain concealed the moon's true shape.

The sky now swamped by thick darkness was a topknot of
matted hair pierced in the east by a digit of the moon;
for a moment all were certain it was one of Shiva's
bodies.[12]

Like a forehead damp with sandalwood paste, the crescent
moon could be seen on the eastern region's face;
darkness was its braided hair, early moonlight the
flowers scattered upon it.

The moon was at first no more than a single digit, then
it was half-full, until it rose completely. Even the
brilliant do not attain eminence immediately, only
gradually.

The moon, now bright as a white lotus, emerged from   30
the ocean couch of Vishnu, conqueror of the demon
Kaitabha, like the oval face of Shri, daughter of the
sea,[13] awaking before her husband.

अथ लक्ष्मणानुगतकान्तवपु-
र्जलधिं व्यतीत्य शशिदाशरथिः ।
परिवारितः परित ऋक्षबलै-
स्तिमिरौघराक्षसबलं बिभिदे ॥

उपजीवति स्म सततं दधतः
परिमुग्धतां वणिगिवोडुपतेः ।
घनवीथिवीथिमवतीर्णवतो
निधिरम्भसामुपचयाय कलाम् ॥

रजनीवशादुदयमाप शशी
सपदि व्यभूषयदसावपि ताम् ।
अविलम्बितक्रममहो महता-
मितरेतरोपकृतिमञ्चरितम् ॥

दिवसं भृशोष्णरुचिपादहतां
रुदतीमिवानवरतालिरुतैः ।
मुहुरामृशन्मृगधरो ऽग्रकरै-
रुदशिश्वसत्कुमुदिनीवनिताम् ॥

३५ प्रतिकामिनीति दृदृशुश्चकिताः
स्मरजन्मघर्मपयसेव चिताम् ।
सुदृशो ऽभिभर्तृ शशिरश्मिगल-
ज्जलबिन्दुमिन्दुमणिदारुवधूम् ॥

Then, truly lovely despite having one conspicuous flaw,[14]
    it crossed the ocean with all the other planets in its
    train and totally dispelled the deep darkness. So did
    handsome Rama, along with his brother Lakshmana
    and hordes of monkeys, bridge the sea and utterly
    destroy the demon army.[15]

In order that its waves could swell, the ocean took succor
    from the phases of the moon, the lord of the stars,
    in its eternal perfection now climbing into the sky,
    pathway of the clouds. It was like a merchant who
    battens on the resources of a gullible investor and
    enters the bazaar to enrich himself alone.[16]

The moon was able to rise thanks to the night, and in turn
    immediately made itself available as its ornament.
    How wonderful of the mighty to assist each other
    without hesitating over precedence!

The water lilies struck by the sun's fierce rays during the
    day seemed to sob with the continual buzzing of bees.
    As if caressing and comforting a spurned woman, the
    moon repeatedly stroked each one with its rays so that
    its flowers eventually opened.[17]

As their husband stood nearby, some women glared at a   35
    doll made out of moonstones, taking it for a rival wife;
    for moonbeams were making it ooze with water, as if
    coated with lovemaking's sweat.

अमृतद्रवैर्विदधदब्जहृशा-
मवमार्गमोषधिपतिः स्म करैः ।
परितो विसर्पि परितापि भृशं
वपुषो ऽवतारयति मानविषम् ॥

अमलात्मसु प्रतिफलन्नभित-
स्तरुणीकपोलफलकेषु मुहुः ।
विससार सान्द्रतरमिन्दुरुचा-
मधिकावभासितदिशां निकरः ॥

उपगूढवेलमलघूर्मिभुजैः
सरितामचुक्षुभदधीशमपि ।
रजनीकरः किमिव चित्रमदो
यदि रागिणां गणमनङ्गलघुम् ॥

भवनोदरेषु परिमन्दतया
शयितो लसत्स्फटिकयष्टिरुचः ।
अवलम्ब्य जालकमुखोपगता-
नुदतिष्ठदिन्दुकिरणान्मदनः ॥

४० अविभावितेषुविषयः प्रथमं
मदनो ऽपि नूनमभवत्तमसा ।
उदिते दिशः प्रकटयत्यमुना
यदघर्मधाम्नि धनुराचकृषे ॥

But the moon, master of healing herbs,[18] with its hand-
    like ambrosia-damp rays massaged these lotus-faced
    ladies and dispelled from their bodies the burning
    poison of the jealousy consuming them.[19]

The thick moonbeams illuminating the horizons became
    still more intense in their brilliance as they were
    reflected on each young woman's flawless cheeks.

The moon disturbed even the ocean, the lord of rivers,
    as it embraced the shore with its heavy arm-like
    breakers. What wonder, then, if it could also stir the
    world of amorous couples already made lightheaded
    by the god of love?

After sleeping off his languorous fatigue indoors, Love
    now roused himself, supporting his body on the
    moonbeams glinting like crystal sticks as they flooded
    through the window lattices.

No doubt because of the darkness he had not at first   40
    marked his arrow's target, since he drew back his bow
    only when moonrise revealed the horizon.

युगपद्विकासमुदयाद्द्विमिते
शशिनः शिलीमुखगणो ऽलभत ।
द्रुतमेत्य पुष्पधनुषो धनुषः
कुमुदे ऽङ्गनामनसि चावसरम् ॥

ककुभां मुखानि सहसोज्ज्वलय-
न्दधदाकुलत्वमधिकं रतये ।
अदिदीपदिन्दुरपरो दहनः
कुसुमेषुमत्रिनयनप्रभवः ॥

इति निश्चितप्रियतमागतयः
सितदीधितावुदयवत्यबलाः ।
प्रतिकर्म कर्तुमुपचक्रमिरे
समये हि सर्वमुपकारि कृतम् ॥

सममेकमेव दधतुः सुतनो-
र्गुरुहारभूषणमुरोजतटौ ।
घटते हि संहततया जनिता-
मिदमेव निर्विवरतां दधतोः ॥

४५   कदलीप्रकाण्डरुचिरोरुतरौ
जघनस्थलीपरिसरे महति ।
रशनाकलापकगुणेन वधू-
र्मकरध्वजद्विरदमाकलयत् ॥

As the moon ascended, swarms of bees and showers of
    arrows dispatched quickly from Love's flowery bow
    fell upon lotuses and women's hearts alike; together
    these blossomed and swelled with longing.[20]

The moon, sprung from Atri's* eye, immediately
    illuminated the horizons and stimulated the god of
    love, awaking eagerness for intercourse. But it was
    another form of fire, so it also agitated Rati† as it
    flooded her husband with refulgence—although on
    this occasion it did not flash from Shiva's forehead
    eye![21]

Now that the moon had risen in all its brilliance, ladies
    picked out the road to their lovers and proceeded to
    put on their finery. Everything done at the proper
    time brings a positive result.

One girl's breasts leagued together to support a heavy
    necklace—appropriate for two so close that there is no
    space between them.

Another woman tethered the elephant of love to the tree   45
    of her thighs, slender as a plantain stalk, with the
    girdle-string resting upon her broad round buttocks.[22]

---

* One of the seven sages and a son of the creator Brahma.
† Literally, "Sexual Pleasure."

अधरेष्वलक्तकरसः सुदृशां
विशदं कपोलभुवि रोध्ररजः ।
नवमञ्जनं नयनपङ्कजयो-
र्बिभिदे न शङ्खनिहितात्पयसः ॥

स्फुरदुज्ज्वलाधरदलैर्विलस-
दृशनांशुकेसरभरैः परितः ।
धृतमुग्धगण्डफलकैर्व्यरुच-
न्विकसद्द्विरास्यकुसुमैः प्रमदाः ॥

भजते विदेशमधिकेन जित-
स्तदनुप्रवेशमथ वा कुशलः ।
मुखमिन्दुरुज्ज्वलकपोलमतः
प्रतिमाच्छलेन सुदृशामविशत् ॥

ध्रुवमागताः प्रतिहतिं कठिने
मदनेषवः कुचतटे महति ।
इतराङ्गवन्न यदिदं गरिम-
ग्लपितावलग्रमगमत्तनुताम् ॥

५० न मनोरमास्वपि विशेषविदां
निरचेष्ट योग्यमिदमेतदिति ।
गृहमेष्यति प्रियतमे सुदृशां
वसनाङ्गरागसुमनःसु मनः ॥

The moist lac on the ladies' lips, the bright *lodhra* dust on
their cheeks, the fresh collyrium highlighting their
lotus-like eyes—suffused with moonlight, all were no
different from milk poured into a conch shell.

The women glowed as their flower-like faces blossomed:
their lower lips were leaves, trembling and gleaming,
the dancing rays from their teeth the filaments, their
fair cheeks the pericarps.

An intelligent man, if bested by a stronger, either goes
into exile or enters the other's service. Accordingly,
the moon merged into the women's gleaming cheeks
under the pretense of being reflected on them.

The women's broad firm breasts had obviously repulsed
Love's arrows, for they had not become slender and
weak like other parts of their bodies and never ceased
wearying their waists with their weight.

Their lovers[23] were already on their way to visit them,   50
so while normally discriminating about finery, the
women paid no attention to clothes, body creams,
and flowers—they merely tried to choose what was
glamorous and avoid what was not.

वपुरन्वलिम्प परिरम्भसुख-
व्यवधानभीरुकतया न वधूः ।
क्षममस्य बाढमिदमेव हि य-
त्रियसङ्गमेष्वनवलेपमदः ॥

निजपाणिपल्लवतटस्खलना-
दभिनासिकाविवरमुत्पतितैः ।
अपरा परीक्ष्य शनकैर्मुमुदे
मुखवासमास्यकमलश्वसनैः ॥

विधृते दिवा सवयसा च पुरः
परिपूर्णमण्डलविकासभृति ।
हिमधाम्नि दर्पणतले च मुहुः
स्वमुखश्रियं मृगदृशो ददृशुः ॥

अधिजानु बाहुमुपधाय नम-
त्करपल्लवार्पितकपोलतलम् ।
उदकण्ठि कण्ठपरिवर्तिकल-
स्वरशून्यगानपरया परया ॥

५५   प्रणयप्रकाशनविदो मधुराः
सुतरामभीष्टजनचित्तगृहः ।
प्रजिघाय कान्तमनु मुग्धतरा-
स्तरुणीजनो दृश इवाथ सखीः ॥

One girl avoided applying her body makeup, as she was
    afraid that it would spoil the pleasure of embracing.
    It is essential when making love not to wear too much
    cream—nor to display any self-regard.[24]

Another woman carefully tested her mouth-freshener[25]
    by blowing on it with little puffs of breath, already
    lotus-scented; to her delight they drifted back into her
    nostrils as she waved her delicate hand.

Each doe-eyed girl repeatedly inspected the perfect oval
    of her fair face in the full moon in the sky in front
    of her—and also as a reflection in the mirror in her
    friend's hand.

One woman, elbow on knee, cheeks cupped in slender
    hands, gave herself over to song, but her soft tones
    were stopped in her throat by her desire for her man.

The elegant young women then dispatched to their lovers   55
    their eloquent confidantes, like affectionate glances;
    both could reveal their strong attachment and enthrall
    the hearts of the objects of their desire.

न च मे ऽवगच्छति यथा लघुतां
करुणां यथा च कुरुते स मयि ।
निपुणं तथैनमभिगम्य वदे-
रभिदूति काचिदिति संदिदिशे ॥

दयिताय मानपरयापरया
त्वरितं ययावगदितापि सखी ।
किमु चोदिताः प्रियहितार्थकृतः
कृतिनो भवन्ति सुहृदः सुहृदाम्² ॥

प्रतिभिद्य कान्तमपराधकृतं
यदि तावदस्य पुनरेव मया ।
क्रियते ऽनुवृत्तिरुचितैष ततः
कलयेदमानमनसं सखि माम् ॥

अवधीर्य धैर्यकलिता दयितं
विदधे विरोधमथ तेन सह ।
तव गोप्यते किमिव कर्तुमिदं
न सहास्मि साहसमसाहसिकी ॥

६० तदवेत्य मास्म तमुपालभथा
न हि दोषमस्य किल विद्म वयम् ।
इति संप्रधार्य रमणाय वधू-
र्विहितागसे ऽपि विससर्ज सखीम् ॥

One instructed her go-between: "Go and speak subtly to
     him, so he won't think me flighty and will treat me
     with proper consideration."

Full of pride, she did not openly request her messenger to
     approach her lover; nonetheless, she set off post haste.
     Do the resourceful need to be asked to help allies?

"My dear! Though it may be right for me to run after
     my unfaithful lover once more after I have already
     rejected him, he would simply regard me as lacking
     self-respect.

I was headstrong right from the start; I spurned the one
     I love and then quarreled with him. But how could I
     hide it from you? I am not really so confident—
     I shouldn't behave in such an impulsive fashion!

Go to him, then, but don't scold him. We can pretend   60
     that his unfaithfulness has gone unnoticed." After
     assessing her situation thus, the girl dispatched her
     friend, even though her lover was manifestly at fault.

ननु संदिशेति सुदृशोदितया
त्रपया न किंचन किलाभिदधे ।
निजमैक्षि मन्दमनिशं निशितैः
क्रशितं शरीरमशरीरशरैः ॥

ब्रुवते स्म दूत्य उपसृत्य नरा-
न्नरवत्प्रगल्भमतिगर्भगिरः ।
सुहृदर्थमीहितमजिह्वधियां
प्रकृतेर्विराजति विरुद्धमपि ॥

मम रूपकीर्तिमहरद्भुवि य-
स्तमनुप्रसक्तहृदयेयमिति ।
त्वयि मत्सरादिव निरस्तदयः
सुतरां क्षिणोति खलु तां मदनः ॥

तव सा कथासु परिघट्ट्यते
श्रवणं यदङ्गुलिमुखेन मुहुः ।
घनतां ध्रुवं नयति तेन भव-
द्गुणपूगपूरितमतृप्ततया ॥

६५ उपताप्यमानमलघूष्णिमभिः
श्वसितैः सितेतरसरोजदृशः ।
द्रवतां न नेतुमधरं क्षमते
नवनागवल्लिदलराशिरसः ॥

296

Another fair-eyed woman appeared too embarrassed to
      reply when invited to provide a message for her lover.
      She simply looked at her feeble frame as it wilted from
      the pain of the bodiless love god's sharp arrows.[26]

One particular go-between knew how to speak like a man
      when she approached men, and her words were bold
      and confident. It is a fine thing when loyal friends do
      what is requested of them, even though it might not
      be in keeping with their true nature.

"Clearly Love is pitilessly causing that girl to waste away
      as if to vent his anger on you. Why? She is besotted
      with someone who has ended that god's universal
      reputation for good looks.

She inadvertently holds her fingertip to her ear whenever
      there is mention of you. Obviously it has already been
      filled by accounts of your virtues, so she is widening it
      in eagerness to hear more of them.[27]

The red sap oozing from fresh betel leaves cannot dampen   65
      that lovely girl's lower lip, for it has already been
      seared by her hot sighs.

दधति स्फुटं रतिपतेरिषवः
शिततां यदुत्पलपलाशदृशः ।
हृदयं निरन्तरबृहत्कठिन-
स्तनमण्डलावरणमप्यभिदन् ॥

कुसुमादपि स्मितदृशः सुतरां
सुकुमारमङ्गमिति नापरथा ।
अनिशं निजैरकरुणः करुणं
कुसुमेषुरुत्तपति यद्द्विशिखैः ॥

विषतां निषेवितमपक्रिययया
समुपैति सर्वमिति सत्यमदः ।
अमृतसुतो ऽपि विरहाद्द्रवतो
यदमूं दहन्ति हिमरश्मिरुचः ॥

उदितं प्रियां प्रति सहार्दमिति
श्रदधीयत प्रियतमेन वचः ।
विदितेङ्गिते पुरत एव जने
समुदीरिताः खलु लगन्ति गिरः ॥

७० दयिताहृतस्य युवभिर्मनसः
परिमूढतामिव गतैः प्रथमम् ।
उदिते ततः सपदि लब्धपदैः
क्षणदाकरे ऽनुपदिभिः प्रयये ॥

298

How sharp Love's arrows must be to pierce her heart, even
though it was shielded by firm, round breasts tight
pressed against each other.

That smiling girl's body is surely more delicate than a
blossom, if the cruel god of love uses flowery shafts to
torment and weaken it.

No doubt anything used inappropriately can turn to
poison. Moonbeams normally emit cool ambrosia, but
now that she is separated from you, they are burning
her instead."

The lover believed these heartfelt descriptions of his girl.
Assertions carry weight when made about one whose
true feelings are already known.

The young men initially appeared confused about what   70
path to take; then when the moon rose, they at once
perceived footprints and set off after their hearts,
already stolen by their girls.

निपपात संभ्रमभृतः श्रवणा-
दसितभ्रुवः प्रणदितालिकुलम् ।
दयितावलोकविकसन्नयन-
प्रसभप्रणुन्नमिव नीररुहम् ॥

उपनेतुमुन्नतिमतेव दिवं
कुचयोर्युगेन तरसा कलिताम् ।
रभसोत्थितामुपगतः सहसा
परिरभ्य कश्चन वधूमरुधत् ॥

अनुदेहमागतवतः प्रतिमां
परिणायकस्य गुरुमुद्वहता ।
मकुरेण वेपथुभृतो ऽतिभारा-
त्कथमप्यपाति न वधूकरतः ॥

अवनम्य वक्षसि निमग्रकुच-
द्वितयेन गाढमुपगूढवता ।
दयितेन तत्क्षणगलद्रशना-
कलकिङ्किणीरवमुदासि वधूः ॥

७५ कररुद्धनीवि दयितोपगतौ
हसितं त्वराविरहितासनया ।
क्षणवृष्टहाटकशिलासदृश-
स्फुरदूरुभित्ति वसनं ववसे ॥

300

One dark-eyed beauty became so excited that the lotus
ornament fell from her ear, accompanied by a swarm
of humming bees. It seemed to have been dislodged by
her eyes widening when she glimpsed her lover.

A man crept up on his girl; when she leapt to her feet, her
breasts heaved as if to lift her into the air. At this, he
embraced her tightly to hold her down.

A young wife almost dropped her mirror, apparently so
heavy it made her hand shake. In fact it was reflecting
the image of her husband—she was thinking of
nothing else—who had just stolen up behind her.

He bent amorously to embrace the girl, her breasts
pressing against his chest; then he lifted her up high,
and her belt immediately slipped down amid the
tinkling of tiny bells.

One young woman jumped from her seat when her lover   75
came near, tightly gripping the knot of her skirt as
she wrapped it round herself. It had been sliding
down and providing a quick flash of her firm thighs,
eye-catching as gold bars.

पिदधानमन्वगुपगम्य दृशौ
वदते जनाय वद को ऽयमिति ।
अभिधातुमध्यवससौ न गिरा
पुलकैः प्रियं नववधूर्न्यगदत् ॥

उदितोरुसादमतिवेपथुम-
त्सुदृशो ऽभिभर्तृ विधुरं त्रपया ।
वपुरादरातिशयशंसि पुरः
प्रतिपत्तिमूढमपि बाढमभूत् ॥

परिमन्थराभिरलघूरुभरा-
दधिवेश्म पत्युरुपचारविधौ ।
स्खलिताभिरप्यनुपदं प्रमदाः
प्रणयातिभूमिमगमन्नतिभिः ॥

मधुरोन्नतभ्रु ललितं च दृशोः
सकरप्रयोगचतुरं च वचः ।
प्रकृतिस्थमेव निपुणागमित-
स्फुटनाट्यलीलमभवत्सुतनोः ॥

८० तदयुक्तमङ्ग तव विश्वसृजा
न कृतं यदीक्षणसहस्रतयम् ।
प्रकटीकृता जगति येन खलु
स्फुटमिन्द्रताद्य मयि गोत्रभिदा ॥

Her husband had crept up and covered his new bride's
	eyes with his hands. Invited by her friend to identify
	who it was, she became lost for words and could only
	reply with the down rising on her body.

In her husband's presence, the fair-eyed girl's thighs
	weakened, she trembled and was helpless with
	embarrassment; although she had difficulty in
	welcoming him, her body betrayed her deep feelings.

While they were attentively welcoming their husbands to
	their apartments,[28] the women moved slowly because
	of their heavy thighs and stumbled at every step; as a
	result they excited passion still greater than before.

The graceful play of their eyes, their delicately raised
	eyebrows, and their conversation accompanied by
	eloquent gestures of the hands—all may have been
	quite natural to these lovely women, but they were
	also redolent of a striking dramatic performance
	prompted by a skillful director.

"Come on, don't you think that it was wrong of the creator 80
	not to give a thousand eyes to you as well? For today
	you have clearly shown yourself to be Indra, the
	mountain-destroyer, by getting my name wrong.[29]

न विभावयत्यनिशमक्षिगता-
मपि मां भवानतिसमीपतया ।
हृदयस्थितामपि पुरः परितः
कथमीक्षते बहिरभीष्टतमाम् ॥

इति गन्तुमिच्छुमभिधाय पुरः
क्षणदृष्टिपातविहसद्वदनाम् ।
सकरावलम्बनममुक्तगल-
त्कलकाञ्चि कांचिदरुणत्तरुणः ॥

अपयाति सरोषया निरस्ते
कृतकं कामिनि चुक्षुवे मृगाक्ष्या ।
कलयन्नपि सव्यथो ऽवतस्थे
ऽशकुनेन स्खलितः किलेतरो ऽपि ॥

आलोक्य प्रियतममंशुके विनीवौ
यत्तस्थे नमितमुखेन्दु मानवत्या ।
तन्नूनं पदमवलोकयांबभूवे
मानस्य द्रुतमपयानमास्थितस्य ॥

८५ सुदृशः सरसव्यलीकतप्त-
स्तरसा श्लिष्टवतः सयौवनोष्मा ।
कथमप्यभवत्स्मरानलोष्ण-
स्तनभारो न नखम्पचः प्रियस्य ॥

Here I am right beside you, but you never pay any
attention to me and take me for granted. Obviously I
am a pain to your eyes. How is that you can spot her
everywhere and anywhere, no matter how far off, even
though she is concealed within your heart?"[30]

With these words she was about to leave, but her
expression brightened when she glanced at her
young lover. He stopped her from going, holding her
with his hand and pulling on her flimsy belt, which
immediately began to unfasten.

A man had been angrily spurned by a doe-eyed girl and
was ready to leave; she pretended to sneeze in order
to make him stay. He understood what she meant
and, appearing to hesitate in irritation at the ill-omen,
ended up remaining with her.

The girl had indeed been annoyed, but when she glanced
at her lover, she stood with moon-like face bowed,
loosening the knot of her dress. What she had really
seen was her anger quickly slipping away.

Another lovely girl's heavy breasts were at one and the
same time burning with torment at her lover's recent
infidelity, hot with youth, and afire with love. For
some reason they did not scorch his fingernails as he
gave them a firm squeeze.

85

305

दधत्युरोजद्वयमुर्वशीतलं
भुवो गतेव स्वयमुर्वशी तलम् ।
बभौ मुखेनाप्रतिमेन काचन
श्रियाधिका तां प्रति मेनका च न ॥

इत्थं नारीर्घटयितुमलं कामिभिः काममास-
न्नालेयांशोः सपदि रुचयः शान्तमानान्तरायाः ।
आचार्यत्वं रतिषु विकसन्मन्मथश्रीविलासा
ह्रीप्रत्यूहप्रशमकुशलाः शीधवश्चक्रुरासाम् ॥

One girl endowed with warm round breasts was like the
heavenly nymph Urvashi come down to earth once
more. Her lovely face was so beyond compare, even
Menaka was not her superior in beauty.[31]

Moonlight quickly removed the obstacle of the women's
anger and brought about intimate union with
their lovers. Meanwhile, wine was equally adept
in removing the impediment of their modesty and
became their teacher in amorous activity, enabling
love's delights to manifest themselves to the full.

CHAPTER 10

Wine and Women

सज्जितानि सुरभीण्यथ यूना-
मुल्लसन्नयनवारिरुहाणि ।
आययुः सुघटितानि सुरायाः
पात्रतां प्रियतमावदनानि ॥

सोपचारमुपशान्तविचारं
सानुतर्षमनुतर्षपदेन ।
ते मुहूर्तमथ मूर्तमपीप्य-
न्प्रेम मानमवधूय वधूः स्वाः ॥

क्रान्तकान्तवदनप्रतिबिम्बे
भग्नबालसहकारसुगन्धौ ।
स्वादुनि प्रणदितालिनि शीते
निर्ववार मधुनीन्द्रियवर्गः ॥

कापिशायनसुगन्धि विघूर्ण-
न्नुन्मदो ऽधिशयितुं समशेत ।
फुल्लदृष्टि वदनं वनिताना-
मब्जचारु चषकं च षडङ्घ्रि ॥

५ बिम्बितं भृतपरिस्रुति जान-
न्भाजने जलजमित्यबलायाः ।
घ्रातुमक्षि मधुपः पतति स्म
भ्रान्तिभाजि भवति क्व विवेकः ॥

The women's perfectly symmetrical faces were tastefully
    made up, lotus-like eyes sparkling within them. Their
    fragrant mouths made suitably ornate goblets from
    which young men could sip sweet liquor[1] garnished
    with lotus fragments.[2]

So without hesitating they prevailed upon their partners
    to stop being annoyed with them for a while and
    instead eagerly consume love embodied as wine.

All the women's senses delighted in the wine: it reflected
    their lovers' faces, was fragrant with freshly crushed
    mango, sweet, surrounded by humming bees, and
    cool.

One bee, drunkenly meandering, was uncertain whether
    to alight upon the faces of the women, eyes wide open
    like flowers, or their drinking cup garnished with
    exquisite lotuses: both gave off the honeyed fragrance
    of sweet liquor.

Another bee hovered to smell a girl's eye, thinking it a   5
    lotus reflected in a wine-filled cup. Can the deluded
    ever distinguish correctly?

दत्तमिष्टतमया मधु पत्यु-
र्बाढमाप पिबतो रसवत्ताम् ।
यत्सुवर्णमुकुटांशुभिरासी-
च्चेतनाविरहितैरपि पीतम् ॥

स्वादनेन सुतनोरविचारा-
दोष्ठतः समचरिष्ट रसो ऽत्र ।
अन्यमन्यदिव यन्मधु यूनः
स्वादमिष्टमतनिष्ट तदेव ॥

बिभ्रतौ मधुरतामधिपात्रं
रागिभिर्युगपदेव पपाते ।
आननैर्मधुरसो विकसद्भि-
र्नासिकाभिरसितोत्पलगन्धः ॥

पीतवत्यभिमते मधु तुल्य-
स्वादमोष्ठरुचकं विदिदङ्क्षौ ।
लभ्यते स्म परिरक्ततयात्माः
यावकेन वियतापि युवत्याः ॥

१० कस्यचित्समदनं मदनीय-
प्रेयसीवदनपानपरस्य ।
स्वादितः सकृदिवासव एव
प्रत्युत क्षणविदंशपदे ऽभूत् ॥

312

The wine offered by one girl afforded an exquisite delight
　　to her lover as he sipped. The gold rays from her
　　bejeweled headdress did not merely turn the liquid
　　yellow—they were also drinking it in, despite their
　　insentience.[3]

Sweetness had undoubtedly transferred itself from
　　another girl's lips to the wine as she tasted it; for
　　her young man, its flavor became utterly fresh and
　　delicious, as if it were some quite unique substance.

The taste of the liquor and the fragrance of the blue water
　　lilies in the goblets were steeped in sweetness; lovers
　　imbibed both, their mouths and nostrils eagerly
　　opening wide.

A young woman's lover had taken wine with her and now
　　desired to nibble her glossy lip imbued with the same
　　sweet flavor; its lac coating was smudged, but the red
　　tinge soon came back.

Another man was intent on tasting his girl's intoxicating　　10
　　mouth, so he took no more than a preliminary sip
　　of the strong drink—it was just an aperitif on this
　　occasion.

पीतशीधुमधुरैर्मिथुनाना-२
माननैः परिहृतं चषकान्तः ।
व्रीडया रुदिदवालिविरावै-
र्नीलिनीरजमगच्छदधस्तात् ॥

प्रातिभं त्रिसरकेण गतानां
वक्रवाक्यरचनारमणीयः ।
गूढसूचितरहस्यसहास्यः
सुभ्रुवां प्रववृते परिहासः ॥

हावहारि हसितं वचनानां
कौशलं दृशि विकारविशेषाः ।
चक्रिरे भृशमृजोरपि वध्वाः
कामिनेव तरुणेन मदेन ॥

अप्रसन्नमपराद्धुरि पत्यौ
कोपदीप्तमुररीकृतधैर्यम् ।
क्षालितं नु शमितं नु वधूनां
द्राविनं नु हृदयं मधुवारैः ॥

१५ सन्तमेव चिरमप्रकृतत्वा-
दप्रकाशितमदिद्युतदङ्के ।
विभ्रमं मधुमदः प्रमदानां
धातुलीनमुपसर्ग इवार्थम् ॥

314

Loving couples had drunk deeply of the sweet liquor,
    ignoring the blue water lily in the middle of their
    goblet; it sank toward the bottom, the humming of
    bees masquerading as its embarrassed lament.

Lovely women became emboldened from imbibing
    the powerful drink and started laughing; they told
    amusing anecdotes full of double entendres, while
    their smiles slyly hinted at secret delights.

As tipsiness took hold, even an unsophisticated girl could
    not stop smiling suggestively, as though prompted by
    a lover; she became brilliant in conversation and had a
    distinct twinkle in her eye.

Women whose hearts had formerly darkened, filled with
    rage, and hardened against their erring husbands now
    renounced such thoughts; drinking wine had made
    them relaxed and tolerant.

The intoxicating effects of the liquor brought to the fore   15
    the women's flirtatiousness, dormant for a while,
    since immediate opportunities to exercise it had been
    rare. It was like a prefix clarifying the meaning of a
    verbal root.[4]

सावशेषपदमुक्तमुपेक्षा
स्रस्तमाल्यवसनाभरणेषु ।
गन्तुमुत्थितमकारणतः स्म
द्योतयन्ति मदविभ्रममासाम् ॥

मद्यमन्दविगलत्तपमीष-
च्चक्षुरुच्छ्वसितपक्ष्म दधत्या ।
वीक्ष्यते स्म शनकैर्नववध्वा
कामिनो मुखमधोमुखयैव ॥

या कथञ्चन सखीवचनेन
प्रागभिप्रियतमं प्रजगल्भे ।
व्रीडजाड्यमभजन्मधुपा सा
स्वां मदात्मकृतिमेति हि सर्वः ॥

छादितः कथमपि त्रपयान्त-
र्यः प्रियं प्रति चिराय तरुण्याः ।
वारुणीमदविशङ्कमथावि-
श्चक्षुषो ऽभवदसाविव रागः ॥

२० आगतानगणितप्रतियाता-
न्वल्लभानभिसिसारयिषूणाम् ।
प्रापि चेतसि सविप्रतिसारे
सुभ्रुवामवसरः सरकेण ॥

Words half uttered, indifference toward garlands, clothes,
    and jewelry carelessly arranged, getting up to leave
    for no reason—all revealed the women's delightful
    drunkenness.

A young wife's modesty was slowly disappearing under
    the wine's influence; even as her eyelashes fluttered
    slightly and her head began to droop, she still gazed
    steadily at her man.

Earlier, at her friends' urging, one woman had been severe
    toward her lover, but now when drinking she was
    overcome by bashfulness. All betray their true nature
    when drunk.

One girl had modestly managed to conceal her passion for
    her man within herself; but as the wine took hold, it
    seemed to be manifesting itself clearly as a red tinge in
    her eye.[5]

The drink penetrated these women's hearts; now full of   20
    regret, they yearned to meet lovers who had earlier
    come and gone without being acknowledged.

मा पुनस्तमभिसीसरमाग-
स्कारिणं मदविमोहितचेताः ।
योषिदित्यभिललाष न हालां
दुस्त्यजः खलु सुखादपि मानः ॥

ह्रीविमोहमहरद्द्वियताना-
मन्तिकं रतिसुखाय निनाय ।
सप्रसादमिति सेवितमासी-
त्सद्य एव फलदं मधु तासाम् ॥

दत्तमात्तमदनं दयितेन
व्याप्तमातिशयिकेन रसेन ।
सस्वदे मुखसुरं प्रमदानां
नाम रूढमपि च व्युदपादि ॥

लब्धसौरभगुणो मदिराया
अङ्गनास्यकमलस्य च गन्धः ।
मोदितालिरितरेतरयोगा-
दन्यतामभजतातिशयं नु ॥

२५ मानभङ्गपटुना सुरतेच्छां
तन्वता प्रथयता हृदि रागम् ।
लेभिरे सपदि भावयतान्त-
र्योषितः प्रणयिनेव मदेन ॥

318

Another woman rejected the strong liquor, claiming she
could not visit her unfaithful lover again if befuddled
by its influence. It is clearly more difficult to abandon
self-esteem than pleasure.

Other women drank the wine and it took effect
immediately; it dispelled their embarrassed confusion
and led them straight to their partners to enjoy
lovemaking.

A mouthful of liquor, saturated with rich flavor, was
offered by a lover along with his eager desire; after
tasting it, these young madams became completely
maddened. Thereby the accuracy of a popular
etymology was confirmed![6]

The scent of wine and the women's lotus-like mouths were
each steeped in fragrance, intoxicating to the bees, but
they attained a unique intensity when they mingled.

These women were immediately gripped by drunkenness,   25
as if by a lover skilled in dispelling sulking; it made
them eager for intercourse, revealed the red tinge of
passion in their eyes, and awoke intense emotions in
their hearts.[7]

पानधौतनवयावकपङ्कुं
सुभ्रुवो निभृतचुम्बनदक्षाः ।
प्रेयसामधररागरसेन
स्वं किलाधरमुपालि ररञ्जुः ॥

अर्पितं रसितवत्यपि नाम-
ग्राहमन्ययुवतेर्दयितेन ।
उज्झति स्म मदमप्यपिबन्ती
वीक्ष्य मद्यमपराथ ममाद ॥

अन्ययान्यवनितागतचित्तं
चित्तनाथमभिशङ्कितवत्या ।
पीतभूरिसुरयापि न मेदे
निर्वृतिर्हि मनसो मदहेतुः ॥

कोपवत्यनुनयानगृहीत्वा
प्रागथो मधुमदाहितमोहा ।
कोपिनं विरहखेदितचेताः
कान्तमेव कलयन्त्यनुनिन्ये ॥

३० कुर्वता मुकुलिताक्षियुगाना-
मङ्गसादमवसादितवाचा ।
ईर्ष्यतेव हरता ह्रियमासां
तद्रुणः स्वयमकारि मदेन ॥

The wine washed away the rouge of fresh lac from the
      women's mouths, expert at stealing kisses. When
      their friends were present, they pretended to redden
      them again with betel juice from their partners' lips.

One woman tasted the wine offered by her husband but
      remained sober, for he had addressed her by the
      wrong name. Her cowife, without drinking at all,
      became drunk with delight on realizing what had
      happened.

Another woman feared that her beloved's heart belonged
      elsewhere, and so even after taking much wine, she
      did not become drunk. Mere happiness can truly
      intoxicate.

A girl, infuriated with her lover, had earlier rejected his
      apologies, and then, upset by his departure, became
      bewildered by drink; thinking him the aggrieved
      party, she begged his forgiveness!

Drunkenness compelled these women to lower their eyes,   30
      adopt a restrained pose, and keep quiet; in removing
      their modesty, it made itself an attribute of that very
      same quality, as if in jealousy.

गण्डभित्तिषु पुरा सदृशीषु
व्याञ्जि नाञ्जितदृशां प्रतिमेन्दुः ।
पानपाटलितकान्तिषु पश्चा-
द्रोध्रचूर्णतिलकाकृतिरासीत् ॥

उद्धतैरिव परस्परसङ्घ-
दीरितान्युभयतः कुचकुम्भैः ।
योषितामतिमदेन जुघूर्णु-
र्विभ्रमाभिभवपूषि वपूंषि ॥

चारुता वपुरभूषयदासां
तामनूननवयौवनयोगः ।
तं पुनर्मकरकेतनलक्ष्मी-
स्तां मदो दयितसङ्गमभूषः ॥

क्षीबतामुपगतास्वनुवेलं
तासु रोषपरितोषवतीषु ।
अग्रहीन्नु सशरं धनुरुज्झा-
मास नूज्झितनिषङ्गमनङ्गः ॥

३५ शङ्कयान्ययुवतौ वनिताभिः
प्रत्यभेदि दयितः स्फुटमेव ।
न क्षमं भवति तत्त्वविचारे
मत्सरेण हतसंवृति चेतः ॥

At first the moon was not reflected clearly on the long-
eyed women's high cheeks since it was equally pale;
with their complexions flushed from drinking,
however, it stood out as a decoration of white *lodhra*
powder.

Their breasts, heaving as they pressed tightly together,
appeared to be pulling their bodies from side to side.
This seemed a novel form of flirtatiousness, but the
women were simply swaying from the effects of drink.

Beauty embellished their appearance and full fresh youth
in turn complemented their good looks; their youth
was enhanced by strong feelings of emotion. All were
heightened by intoxication made still more delightful
by the company of their lovers.

In their drunkenness these women were continually
alternating between feelings of anger and delight. So
did Love take his bow and aim an arrow at them, or
did he simply throw down his quiver and abandon it?

Suspicious of a cowife, some women openly rebuked their   35
husband. When jealousy undermines confidence, it is
impossible to appreciate what is true.

आननैर्विचकसे हृषिताभि-
र्वल्लभानभि तनूभिरभावि ।
आर्द्रता हृदयमाप च रोषो
लोलति स्म वचनेषु वधूनाम् ॥

रूपमप्रतिविधानमनोज्ञं
प्रेम कार्यमनपेक्ष्य विकासि ।
चाटु चाकृतकसंभ्रममासां
कार्मणत्वमगमद्रमनेषु ॥

हेलयैव सुतनोस्तुलयित्वा
गौरवाढ्यमपि लावणिकेन ।
मानवज्ञनविदा वचनेन
क्रीतमेव हृदयं दयितस्य ॥

स्पर्शभाजि विषदच्छविचारौ
कल्पिते मृगदृशां सुरताय ।
संनतिं दधति पेतुरजस्रं
दृष्टयः प्रियतमे शयने च ॥

४० यूनि रागतरलैरपि तिर्य-
क्पातिभिः श्रुतिगुणेन युतस्य ।
दीर्घदर्शिभिरकारि वधूनां
लङ्घना न नयनैः श्रवणस्य ॥

In the presence of their lovers,[8] their expressions
blossomed into smiles, their bodies thrilled with goose
bumps, and affection entered their hearts. It was only
when they spoke that the young women showed any
irritation with their men.

Their appearance was effortlessly delightful, their
burgeoning emotion totally genuine, and their speech
charming and free of pretense—all this enchanted
their lovers.

One lovely girl knew well how to dispel the pride of the
man she fancied. After quickly sizing him up, she
won his heart with her delightful conversation, even
though he was full of self-importance.[9]

Doe-eyed women gazed at their partners and then at
the couch; both were soft to the touch, well-built
and tempting, made for love, continually pliant and
yielding.

Passionate, knowing sidelong glances were darted at the   40
young men, although the girls' eyes did not extend
quite as far as their ears![10]

संकथेच्छुरभिधातुमनीशा
संमुखी च न बभूव दिदृक्षुः ।
स्पर्शनेन दयितस्य नतभ्रू-
रङ्गसङ्गचपलापि चकम्पे ॥

उत्तरीयविनयात्तपमाणा
रुन्धती किल तदीक्षणमार्गम् ।
आवरिष्ट विकटेन विवोढु-
र्वक्षसैव कुचमण्डलमन्या ॥

अंशुकं हृतवता तनुबाहु-
स्वस्तिकापिहितमुग्धकुचाग्रा ।
भिन्नशङ्खवलयं परिणेत्रा
पर्यरम्भि रभसादचिरोढा ॥

संजहार सहसा परिरब्ध-
प्रेयसीषु विरहय्य विरोधम् ।
संहितं रतिपतिः स्मितभिन्न-
क्रोधमाशु तरुणीषु महेषुम् ॥

४५ स्रंसमानमुपयन्तरि वध्वाः
श्लिष्टवत्युपसपत्नि रसेन ।
आत्मनैव रुरुधे कृतिनेव
स्वेदसज्जि वसनं जघनेन ॥

326

A young woman[11] with arching eyebrows yearned to speak
    to her beloved but could not address him; she wanted
    to see him, yet would not look him in the face, and
    despite eagerness for contact she trembled when he
    touched her.

Another woman became embarrassed when her husband
    removed her bodice, so she pulled his broad chest to
    her round breasts—as if to prevent him seeing any
    more.

A newly wed girl received a passionate embrace from her
    husband, but when he started to undress her, she
    folded her slender arms over her lovely breasts—and
    broke her conch-shell armlets.

The young women stopped quarreling with their lovers
    and fell into their arms; so Rati's husband, the god of
    love, immediately withdrew the mighty arrow he had
    aimed at them, his anger dispelled by a satisfied smile.

When her husband embraced her ardently as her rival   45
    watched, his wife's clinging sweat-soaked dress
    began to slip down, held back only by her hips like a
    resourceful friend.

पीडिते पुर उरःप्रतिपेषं
भर्तरि स्तनयुगेन युवत्या ।
स्पष्टमेव दलतः प्रतिनार्या-
स्तन्मयत्वमभवद्धृदयस्य ॥

दीपितस्मरमुरस्युपपीडं
वल्लभे घनमपि स्वजमाने ।
चक्रतां न ययतुः कुचकुम्भौ
सुभ्रुवः कठिनतातिशयेन ॥

संप्रवेष्टुमिव योषित ईषुः
श्लिष्यतां हृदयमिष्टतमानाम् ।
आत्मनः सततमेव तदन्त-
र्वर्तिनो न खलु नूनमजानन् ॥

स्नेहनिर्भरमधत्त वधूना-
मार्द्रतां वपुरसंशयमन्तः ।
यूनि गाढपरिरम्भिणि वस्त्र-
क्षोपमम्बु ववृषे यदनेन ॥

५० न स्म माति वपुषः प्रमदाना-
मन्तरिष्टतमसङ्गमजन्मा ।
यद्बहुर्बहिरवाप्य विकासं
व्यानशे तनुरुहाण्यपि हर्षः ॥

As the young woman squeezed and rubbed her breasts
    against her husband's chest for all to see, it was
    obvious that her cowife had already taken him into her
    heart—because it burst apart.

The girl's lover was on fire with lust when he folded her to
    his chest in a tight embrace, but her breasts were so
    hard that he could not squeeze them flat.

As they hugged their lovers, the women appeared eager
    to penetrate the very core of their hearts; clearly they
    were unaware that they had always occupied a place
    there.

There can be no arguing that the young women's bodies
    were moist with desire; when the young men squeezed
    them tightly, a flood of sweat drenched their clothes.

The rush of joy felt by the women as their lovers fondled   50
    them was not confined within; it surged outward and
    made their body hair thrill all over.[12]

यत्प्रियव्यतिकराद्व्रनिताना-
मञ्जनेन पुलकेन बभूवे ।
प्रापि तेन भृशमुच्छ्वसिताभि-
र्नीविभिः सपदि बन्धनमोक्षः ॥

ह्रीभरादवनतं परिरम्भे
रागवानवटुजेष्ववकृष्य ।
अर्पितोष्ठदलमाननपद्मं
योषितो मुकुलिताक्षमधासीत् ॥

पल्लवोपमितिसाम्यसपक्षं
दष्टवत्यधरबिम्बमभीष्टे ।
पर्यकूजि सरुजेव तरुण्या-
स्तारलोलवलयेन करेण ॥

केनचिन्मधुरमुल्वणरागं
बाष्पतप्तमधिकं विरहेषु ।
ओष्ठपल्लवमपास्य मुहूर्तं
सुभ्रुवः सरसमक्षि चुचुम्बे ॥

५५ रेचितं परिजनेन महीयः
केवलाभिरतदम्पति धाम ।
साम्यमाप कमलासखविश्व-
क्सेनसेवितयुगान्तपयोधेः ॥

So thick was the thrilling hair on the women's bodies when
they were with their lovers that their skirts billowed
out and their belts became loosened.[13]

The woman's head dropped in modesty during an
embrace; her lover tugged her hair from behind so
that she was compelled to offer her petal-like lips. As
he drank from her lotus-mouth, her eyelids folded
shut in ecstasy.

When her lover nibbled her round lower lip (to be
compared to a crimson bud, if one were constructing a
formal analogy!),[14] the young woman's bangles jingled
noisily on her wrists so that her lac-covered palms
seemed to cry out in sympathy.

Another man momentarily left his girl's shoot-like lip,
sweet and deep red but now scorched by sighs when
the two of them were apart, and eagerly kissed her
eye.

The pavilion[15] was empty of servants; just a husband and   55
wife were there, making love. It was like the cosmic
ocean at the end of a world age where only Vishnu and
Shri are present.

आवृतान्यपि निरन्तरमुच्चै-
र्योषितामुरसिजद्वितयेन ।
रागिणामित इतो विमृशद्भिः
पाणिभिर्जगृहिरे हृदयानि ॥

कामिनामसकलानि विभुग्रैः
स्वेदवारिमृदुभिः करजाग्रैः ।
अक्रियन्त कठिनेषु कथञ्चि-
त्कामिनीकुचतटेषु पदानि ॥

सोष्मणः स्तनशिखाशिखराग्रा-
दात्तधर्मसलिलैस्तरुणानाम् ।
उच्छ्वसत्कमलचारुषु हस्तै-
र्निम्ननाभिसरसीषु निपेते ॥

आमृशद्भिरभितो वलिवीची-
र्लोलमानवितताङ्गुलिहस्तैः ।
सुभ्रुवामनुभवात्प्रतिपेदे
मुष्टिमेयमिति मध्यमभीष्टैः ॥

६० प्राप्तनाभिनदमज्जनमाशु
प्रस्थितं निवसनग्रहणाय ।
औपनीविकमरुन्ध किल स्त्री
वल्लभस्य करमात्मकराभ्याम् ॥

Although the women's hearts were completely concealed
    by their close-set jutting breasts, their lovers still
    contrived to get hold of them, touching them now
    here, now there.

Their breasts were hard and firm; their men could barely
    leave a few faint scratches on them with their curving
    nails, softened by love's sweat.

The young men's perspiring hands moved from the girls'
    warm nipples down to their navels, alluring as opening
    lotuses.[16]

Their lovers stroked the women's rippling stomach
    folds with their long fingers roaming and probing
    everywhere; they established that their waists were so
    slender they could be gripped by one clenched hand.

One woman had to be nimbly dexterous while pretending   60
    to restrain her lover's hand; it had been fumbling
    around her navel and was now heading swiftly toward
    her belt in order to pull off her dress.

कामिनः कृतरतोत्सवकाल-
क्षेपमाकुलवधूकरसङ्गि ।
मेखलागुणविलग्रमसूयां
दीर्घसूत्रमकरोत्परिधानम् ॥

अम्बरं विनयतः प्रियपाणे-
र्योषितश्च करयोः कलहस्य ।
वारणामिव विधातुमभीक्ष्णं
कक्ष्यया च वलयैश्च शिशिञ्जे ॥

ग्रन्थिमुद्ग्रथयितुं हृदयेशो
वाससः स्पृशति मानधनायाः ।
भ्रूयुगेन सपदि प्रतिपेदे
रोमभिश्च सममेव विभेदः ॥

आशु लङ्घितवतीष्टकराग्रे
नीविमर्धमुकुलीकृतदृष्ट्या ।
रक्तवैणिकहताधरतन्त्री-
मण्डलक्वणितचारु चुकूजे ॥

६५ आयताङ्गुलिरभूदतिरिक्तः
सुभ्रुवां क्रशिमशालिनि मध्ये ।
श्रोणिषु प्रियकरः पृथुलासु
स्पर्शमाप सकलेन तालेन ॥

334

As the flustered girl held on to her skirt, it slowly became
    entangled with her belt and infuriated her lover, for it
    was delaying lovemaking's delights.

While he was finally removing her dress and she was still
    trying to prevent him, belt and armlets jingled as if to
    put an end to the hands' squabbling.

As an angry woman's lover was tugging on the knot of
    her dress to loosen it, simultaneously her eyebrows
    contracted in a frown and the down on her body
    thrilled with desire.

Now, as her lover was running his fingers over the knot of
    her dress, the girl half closed her eyes and moaned as
    sweetly as the thrumming of lute strings when their
    lower notes are sounded by an inspired virtuoso.

Their lovers' fingers were longer than these ladies' slender   65
    waists, while the entire palm of their hands could
    cover their broad buttocks.

चक्रुरेव ललनोरुषु राजीः
स्पर्शलोभवशलोलकराणाम् ।
कामिनामनिहितान्यपि रम्भा-
स्तम्भकोमलतरेषु नखानि ॥

ऊरुमूलचपलेक्षणमग्न-
न्यैर्वतंसकुसुमैः प्रियमेताः ।
चक्रिरे सपदि तानि यथार्थं
मन्मथस्य कुसुमायुधनाम ॥

धैर्यमुल्वणमनोभवभावा
वामतां च वपुरर्पितवत्यः ।
व्रीडितं ललितसौरतधाच्छर्या-
स्तेनिरे ऽभिरुचितेषु रमण्यः ॥

पाणिरोधमनिरोधितवाञ्छं
भर्त्सनाश्च मधुरस्मितगर्भाः ।
कामिनः स्म कुरुते करभोरू-
र्हरि शुष्करुदितं च सुखे ऽपि ॥

७० वारणार्थपदगद्गदवाचा-
मीर्ष्यया मुहुरपत्रपया च ।
कुर्वते स्म सुदृशामनुकूलं
प्रातिकूलिकतयैव युवानः ॥

The lovers' wandering hands were eager to caress;
    although their fingernails barely brushed the girls'
    thighs, they still left marks on skin quite as soft as
    banana stalks.

When the lovers stared eagerly at the women's intimate
    places, they were smacked with blossom garlands. At
    once, "flower-armed" became an appropriate epithet
    for the god of love.

The young women were experiencing the pangs of
    love, but they still showed obstinacy toward their
    lovers; although they surrendered their bodies, they
    remained contrary, and despite being committed to
    the delights of intercourse, their demeanor stayed
    bashful.

A slender-thighed woman restrained her lover's hand
    without holding back his lust, reproached him but
    with a sweet smile, and in the joy of lovemaking
    sobbed delightfully without shedding tears.

These lovelies behaved perversely, repeatedly stammering   70
    words of rejection with a mixture of anger and
    embarrassment. For their part, the young men simply
    humored them.

अन्यकालपरिहार्यमजस्रं
तद्द्वयेन विदधे द्वयमेव ।
धृष्टता रहसि भर्तृषु ताभि-
र्निर्दयत्वमितरैरबलासु ॥

बाहुपीडनकचग्रहणाभ्या-
माहतेन नखदन्तनिपातैः ।
बोधितस्तनुशयस्तरुणीना-
मुन्मिमील विशदं विषमेषुः ॥

कान्तया सपदि को ऽप्युपगूढः
प्रौढपाणिरपनेतुमियेष ।
संहतस्तनतिरस्कृतदृष्टि-
र्भ्रष्टमेव न दुगूलमपश्यत् ॥

आहतं कुचतटेन तरुण्याः
साधु सोढममुनेति पपात ।
त्रुट्यतः प्रियतमोरसि हारा-
त्पुष्पवृष्टिरिव मौक्तिकवर्षः ॥

७५ सीत्कृतानि मणितं करुणोक्तिः
स्निग्धमुक्तमलमर्थवचांसि ।
हासभूषणरवाश्च रमण्या
कामसूत्रपदतामुपजग्मुः ॥

Boldness toward husbands and lack of concern for wives'
frailty are two things generally to be avoided. But
when they made love, the couples paid no heed to
such advice.

The five-arrowed god of love had been dozing within the
young women's bodies; his eyes opened wide as he
was rudely awoken by fierce embraces, pulling of hair,
passionate slaps, scratchings, and bitings.

A man was suddenly embraced by his beloved and
stretched out his arms to remove her dress; blinded by
her taut breasts full in his face, he could not see it had
already slipped off.

A girl's necklace came unstrung during lovemaking and a
stream of pearls fell onto her lover's chest, like flowers
raining from heaven to celebrate his heroic endurance
of buffetings from her breasts.[17]

A young woman's sharp cries, moaning, and helpless   75
gasps, her passionate words and remonstrations—all
these sounds represented the textbook topics of the
Kama Sutra.

उद्धतैर्निभृतमेकमनेकै-
श्छेदवन्मृगदृशामविरामैः ।
श्रूयते स्म मणितं कलकाञ्ची-
नूपुरध्वनिभिरक्षतमेव ॥

ईदृशस्य भवतः कथमेत-
ल्लाघवं मुहुरितीव रतेषु ।
क्षिप्तमायतमदर्शयदुर्व्या
काञ्चिदाम जघनस्य महत्त्वम् ॥

प्राप्यते स्म गतचित्रकचित्रै-
श्चित्रमार्द्रनखलक्ष्म कपोलैः ।
दधिरे च रभसच्युतपुष्पाः
स्वेदबिन्दुकुसुमान्यलकान्ताः ॥

यद्यदेव रुरुचे रुचितेभ्यः
सुभ्रुवो रहसि तत्तदकुर्वन् ।
आनुकूलिकतया हि नराणा-
माक्षिपन्ति हृदयानि रमण्यः ॥

८० प्राप्य मन्मथमदादतिभूमिं
दुर्वहस्तनभराः सुरतस्य ।
शश्रमुः श्रमजलार्द्रललाट-
श्लिष्टकेशमसितायतकेश्यः ॥

The soft, unaccompanied, sporadic moaning of the
doe-eyed women as they made love could be heard
over the loud, interweaving, relentless jingling of belts
and anklets.

The long belt string discarded on the ground made clear
the broadness of the girl's backside; it seemed to pose
the question: "How is it that someone as heavy as you
is always so agile in lovemaking?"

Cheeks with makeup rubbed away were now decorated by
fresh nail scratches; hair that had lost its decorative
flowers in love's excitement was blossoming with
drops of sweat.

In the course of lovemaking those lovely girls did whatever
pleased their partners. Women can capture men's
hearts through indulging their desires.

What beauties these women were, with their long dark   80
tresses and breasts they could barely support! They
reached the heights of erotic ecstasy as they made
passionate love and then rested in exhaustion, hair
sticking to foreheads damp with perspiration.

सङ्गताभिरुचितैश्चलितापि
प्रागमुच्यत चिरेण सखीव ।
भूय एव समगंस्त रतान्ते
ह्रीर्वधूभिरसहा विरहस्य ॥

प्रेक्षणीयकमिव क्षणमास-
न्ह्रीतभङ्गुरविलोचनपाताः ।
संभ्रमद्रुतगृहीतदुगूल-
च्छाद्यमानवपुषः सुरतान्ताः ॥

अप्रभूतमतनीयसि तन्वी
काञ्चिधाम्नि पिहितैकतमोरूः ३ ।
क्षौममाकुलकरा विचकर्ष
क्रान्तपल्लवमभीष्टतमेन ॥

मृष्टचन्दनविशेषकभक्ति-
र्भ्रष्टभूषणकदर्थितमाल्यः ।
सापराध इव मण्डनमासी-
दात्मनैव सुदृशामुपभोगः ॥

८५ योषितः पतितकाञ्चनकाञ्चौ
मोहनातिरभसेन नितम्बे ।
मेखलेव परितः स्म विचित्रा
राजते नवनखक्षतलक्ष्मीः ॥

Their modesty was like one of their girlfriends—at first
    continually in their company, then keeping a distance
    when the lover was about, and finally dismissed for
    good; it was only reunited with them at the end of
    intercourse, as if it could not bear separation.

The conclusion of lovemaking was for an instant like a
    dramatic performance, with the women assuming
    expressions of exaggerated modesty and in
    consternation screening their bodies with costumes
    quickly pulled on.

One slender girl pulled up her skirt with fumbling hands,
    as her lover tugged on its hem; it would not fit over her
    broad hips and covered only one thigh.

Carefully applied sandalwood cream had been rubbed
    away, jewelry discarded, and garlands crushed—
    seemingly responsible for rough behavior, lovemaking
    actually enhanced these women's beauty.

One woman's golden girdle had fallen off in the   85
    excitement of intercourse, and her buttocks were
    decorated all over with fresh scratches from the recent
    love bout—she now seemed to be wearing a delectable
    belt.

भातु नाम सुदृशां दशनाङ्कः
पाटलो धवलगण्डतलेषु ।
दन्तवाससि समानगुणश्रीः
संमुखो ऽपि परभागमवाप ॥

सुभ्रुवामधिपयोधरपीठं
पीडनैस्त्रुटितवत्यपि पत्युः ।
मुक्तमौक्तिकतनुर्गुणशेषा
हारयष्टिरभवद्भुरुरेव ॥

विश्रमार्थमुपगूढमजस्रं
यत्प्रियैः प्रथमरत्यवसाने ।
योषितामुदितमन्मथमादौ
तद्द्वितीयसुरतस्य बभूव ॥

आस्तृते ऽभिनवपल्लववपुष्पै-
रप्यनारतरताभिरताभ्यः ।
दीयते स्म शयितुं शयनीये
न क्षणः क्षणदयापि वधूभ्यः ॥

९० योषितामतितरां नखलूनं
गात्रमुज्ज्वलतया न खलूनम् ।
क्षोभमाशु हृदयं नयदूनां
रागवृद्धिमकरोन्न यदूनाम् ॥

Granted the red bite-marks already stood out clearly on
the women's pale cheeks because makeup had been
kissed away, but their true glory came from occupying
a place of prominence on faces and sharing the deep
hue of lower lips.

When her husband squeezed his wife's[18] breasts, her
slender necklace broke and its pearls fell off. Although
now worthless since it had been reduced to just a
thread, the necklace still possessed one significant
virtue—it had, after all, been unstrung by a lover![19]

At the end of the first bout of love, men invariably
embrace their partners so they can both relax, but that
only rouses the god of love and signals the start of the
next session.

For women absorbed in unceasing intercourse there was
no chance even at night to fall asleep on the bed,
despite its being strewn with fresh leaves and flowers.

The womens' bodies may have been covered all over with   90
love scratches, but that certainly did not diminish
their beauty. Although they could infatuate the minds
of the Yadava men in an instant, their own surging
passion was not weakened in any degree.

इति मदमदनाभ्यां रागिणः स्पष्टरागा-
ननवरतरतश्रीसङ्गिनस्तानवेक्ष्य ।
अभजत परिवृत्तिं साथ पर्यस्तहस्ता
रजनिरवनतेन्दुलर्ज्जयाधोमुखीव ॥

As the constellation Hasta* disappeared from the sky and
the moon set, night came to an end, like a woman
casting down her gaze in embarrassment, hands
thrown over her face.[20] It had witnessed the couples
giving themselves over to the delights of unceasing
lovemaking, with their emotions clearly enflamed by
drunkenness and lust.

---

* The eleventh or thirteenth lunar asterism.

CHAPTER 11

The Court Bards Welcome the Dawn

श्रुतिसमधिकमुच्चैः पञ्चमं पीडयन्तः
सततमृषभहीनं भिन्नकीकृत्य षड्जम् ।
अभिजगदुरकाकिश्रावकस्निग्धकण्ठाः१
परिणतिमिति रात्रेर्मागधा माधवाय ॥

रतिरभसविलासाभ्यासतान्तं न याव-
न्नयनयुगममीलीत्तावदेवाहतो ऽसौ ।
रजनिविरतिशंसी कमिनीनां भविष्य-
द्विरहविहितनिद्राभङ्गमुच्चैर्मृदङ्गः ॥

स्फुटतरमुपरिष्टादल्पमूर्तेर्ध्रुवस्य
स्फुरति सुरमुनीनां मण्डलं व्यस्तमेतत् ।
शकटमिव महीयः शैशवे शार्ङ्गपाणे-
श्चपलचरणकाब्जप्रेरणोत्तुङ्गिताग्रम् ॥

प्रहरकमपनीय स्वं निदिद्रासतोच्चैः
प्रतिपदमुपहूतः केनचिज्जागृहीति ।
मुहुरविशदवर्णां निद्रया शून्यशून्यां
दददपि खलु वाचं बुध्यते नो मनुष्यः ॥

५ विपुलतरनितम्बाभोगरुद्धे रमण्याः
शयितुमनधिगच्छञ्जीवितेशो ऽवकाशम् ।
रतिपरिचयनश्यैत्रैद्रतन्द्रः कथञ्चि-
द्रमयति शयनीये शर्वरीं किं करोतु ॥

Smooth-voiced bards sang to Krishna of the night's
ending. Their melody was steady and sonorous; within
it they separated out the tonic into its many intervals,
carefully suppressing the "fifth" note and avoiding the
"bull" note, unsuitable in a morning song.[1]

"Exhausted eyes have barely closed after repeated bouts
of ardent lovemaking when the drum proclaiming
night's end is sounded. It disturbs beautiful women's
slumber with thoughts of coming separation.

Here spread out in the sky is the constellation of the Seven
Seers,* glowing brightly above the waning pole star.
It looks like the mighty Wagon[2] flying through the air
after being playfully kicked in the chest by the child
Krishna's lotus-like feet.

At the end of his shift the watchman wants to go to bed;
he shouts in his colleague's ear to rouse him, but that
fellow just mutters sleepily and will not wake.

The girl's hips are so broad she takes up all the space on   5
the bed and her partner can find no room. He had
been drowsily relaxed after many love bouts, but that
is wearing off and he must pass the remaining night
uncomfortably. What else can he do?

---

* Ursa Major, or the Great Bear.

351

क्षणशयितविबुद्धाः कल्पयन्तः प्रयोगा-
नुदधिमहति राज्ये काव्यवद्दुर्विगाहे ।
गहनमपररात्रप्राप्तबुद्धिप्रसादाः
कवय इव महीपाश्चिन्तयन्त्यर्थजातम् ॥

क्षितितटशयनान्तादुत्थितं दानपङ्क-
प्लुतबहलशरीरं शाययत्येष भूयः ।
मृदुचलदपरान्तोदीरितान्दूनिनादं
गजपतिमधिरोहः पक्षकव्यत्ययेन ॥

द्रुततरकरदक्षाक्षिप्तवैशाखशैले
दधति दधनि धीरानारवान्वारिणीव ।
शशिनमिव सुरौघाः सारमुद्धर्तुमेते
कलशिमुदधिगुर्वीं वल्ववा लोडयन्ति ॥

अनुनयमगृहीत्वा व्याजसुप्ता पराची
स्वरमथ कृकवाकोस्तारमाकर्ण्य काले ।
कथमपि परिवृत्ता निद्रयान्धा किल स्त्री
मुकुलितनयनैव श्लिष्यति प्राणनाथम् ॥

Kings are wakeful after sleeping for a while, their minds
    clear in the night's last watch; they mull over
    stratagems to be used against some impregnable
    kingdom vast as the sea and brood on the principal
    aims of men. They are like poets reflecting upon the
    complex meaning of their poems as they consider the
    literary devices to be employed.[3]

Over here a mighty elephant stirs from its bed on the
    ground, its body smeared with ichor; chains jangle as
    it gently shakes its rear foot, while its driver coaxes the
    beast back to sleep by making it turn over.

And over here cowherds run their nimble hands up and
    down a long pole; they are churning milk noisily
    sloshing in a tub almost as wide as the sea, so they can
    extract its essence. Thus the gods once used Mount
    Mandara to churn the vast deep-roaring ocean and
    draw out the moon, its treasure within.[4]

A woman averts her face from her lover when he fails
    to respond and feigns sleep. But on hearing the
    cockerel's sharp morning cry, she laboriously turns
    over again, pretending to be groggily drowsy, and
    embraces him, eyes squeezed shut.

१० गतमनुगतवीणैरेकतां वेणुनादैः
कलमविकलतालं गाथकैर्बोधहेतोः ।
असकृदनवगीतं गीतमाकर्णयन्तः
सुखमुकुलितनेत्रा यान्ति निद्रां नरेन्द्राः ॥

परिशिथिलितकर्णग्रीवमामीलिताक्षः
क्षणमयमनुभूय स्वप्रमूर्ध्वञ्जुरेव ।
रिरसयिषति भूयः शष्पमग्रे विकीर्णं
पटुतरचपलौष्ठप्रस्फुरत्प्रोथमश्वः ॥

उदयमुदितदीप्रियाति यः सङ्गतौ मे
पतति नवरमिन्दुः सो ऽपरामेष गत्वा ।
स्मितरुचिरिव सद्यः साभ्यसूयं प्रभेति
स्फुरति विशदमेषा पूर्वकाष्ठाङ्गनायाः ॥

चिररतिपरिखेदप्राप्तनिद्रासुखानां
चरममपि शयित्वा पूर्वमेव प्रबुद्धाः ।
अपरिचलितगात्राः कुर्वते न प्रियाणा-
मशिथिलभुजचक्राश्लेषभेदं तरुण्यः ॥

कृतधवलिमभेदैः कुङ्कुमेनेव किंचि-
न्मलयरुहरजोभिर्भूषयन्पश्चिमाशाम् ।
हिमरुचिररुणिम्ना राजते रज्यमानै-
र्जरढकमलकन्दच्छेदगौरैर्मयूखैः ॥

Kings close their eyes in restful ease and drift back into   10
    slumber. All the while they hear the regular rhythm
    of a sweet melody of awakening repeatedly intoned
    by singers against a background of flutes and lutes
    blending harmoniously.

Over here a horse, ears and neck relaxed, eyes closed,
    has momentarily fallen asleep on its feet; but its lips
    continue champing busily and its nostrils twitch, for it
    is still hungry for the hay spread before it.

The glow of the heavenly lady of the eastern quarter
    appears like a quick smile of jealous satisfaction: 'The
    moon was bright and waxed full when united with me,
    but now that it has gone to that other lady in the west,
    it can only fall from the sky.'

Young women may have fallen asleep last and woken
    first, but they do not budge an inch lest they disturb
    the tight embrace of their partners dozing off in
    exhaustion after long lovemaking.

The moon still shines, adorning the western quarter with
    rays white as slivers of mature lotus bulbs, yet now as
    it sets, tinged with red. It is like a man decorating his
    beloved with pale sandalwood powder blended with a
    pinch of saffron.

१५ दधदसकलमेकं खण्डितामानमद्रिः
श्रियमपरमपूर्णामुच्छ्वसद्भिः पलाशैः ।
कलरवमुपगीते षद्पदौघेन धत्तः
कुमुदकमलषण्डे तुल्यरूपामवस्थाम् ॥

मदरुचिमरुणेनोद्वच्छता लम्भितस्य
त्यजत इव चिरावस्थायिनीमाशु लज्जाम् ।
वसनमिव मुखस्य स्रंसते संप्रतीदं
सितकरकरजालं वासवाशायुवत्याः ॥

अविरतरतलीलायासजातश्रमाणा-
मुपशममुपयान्तं निःसहे ऽङ्गे ऽङ्गनानाम् ।
पुनरुषसि विविक्तैर्मातरिश्वावचूर्ण्य
ज्वलयति मदनाग्निं मालतीनां रजोभिः ॥

अनिमिषमविरामा रागिणां सर्वरात्रं
नवनिधुवनलीलाः कौतुकेनाभिवीक्ष्य ।
इदमुदवसितानामस्फुटालोकसंप-
न्नयनमिव सनिद्रं घूर्णते दैपमर्चिः ॥

विकचकमलगन्धैरन्धयन्भृङ्गमालाः
सुरभितमकरन्दं मन्दमावाति वायुः ।
समदमदनमाद्यद्यौवनोद्दामरामा-
रमणरभसखेदस्वेदविच्छेददक्षः ॥

A clump of white water lilies and a cluster of lotuses are   15
     alike in enjoying the same soft serenade of humming
     bees. But the charm of one has faded with the dawn
     closing of its petals, while for the other it is yet to
     emerge, as its blossoms have not fully opened.

Now the thick moonbeams are disappearing, like a veil
     falling from the face of the damsel of the eastern
     quarter; suffused with a pink glow she appears
     intoxicated, hurrying to abandon her normal modesty.

The fire of lust is subsiding within the weak bodies of
     women tired from love-play's unceasing toil; at dawn
     the breeze stirs up its flame again with a fine dusting
     of jasmine pollen.

Over here a lamp, now burning with dim flame, flickers
     like the sleepy eye of the pavilions; without respite
     it has watched with unblinking curiosity as lovers
     renewed their exchanges through the night.

A breeze blows softly, blinding the swarms of bees with
     the perfume of opening lotuses, rousing the jasmine
     to blossom. It deftly removes the sweat from lovely
     women weak from lovemaking, intoxicated with
     wanton desire in the joy of youth.

२० लुलितनयनताराः क्षामवक्त्रेन्दुबिम्बा
रजनय इव निद्राक्रान्तनीलोत्पलाक्ष्यः ।
तिमिरमिव दधानाः स्रंसिनः केशपाशा-
नवनिपतिगृहेभ्यो यान्त्यमूर्वारवध्वः ॥

शिशिरकिरणकान्तं वासरान्ते ऽभिसार्य
श्वसनसुरभिगन्धिः सांप्रतं सत्वरेव ।
व्रजति रजनिरेषा तन्मयूखाङ्गरागैः
परिमलितमनिन्द्यैरम्बरान्तं वहन्ती ॥

नवकुमुदवनश्रीहासकेलिप्रसङ्ग-
दधिकरुचिरशेषामप्युषां जागरित्वा ।
अयमपरदिशो ऽङ्के मुञ्चति स्रस्तहस्तः
शिशयिषुरिव पाण्डुम्लानमात्मानमिन्दुः ॥

सरभसपरिरम्भारम्भसंरम्भभाजो
यदधिनिशमपास्तं वल्लभेनाङ्गनायाः ।
वसनमपि निशान्ते नेष्यते तत्प्रदातुं
रथचरणविशालश्रोणिलोलेक्षणेन ॥

सपदि कुमुदिनीभिर्मीलितं हा क्षपापि
क्षयमगमदपेतास्तारकास्ताः समस्ताः ।
इति दयितकलत्रश्चिन्तयन्नङ्गमिन्दु-
र्वहति कृशमशेषं भ्रष्टशोभं शुचेव ॥

Over here, beauties are creeping from the royal pavilions　　20
　　like night approaching its end. The star-like pupils
　　of their eyes flicker weakly, their moon-like faces are
　　pallid, while their eyes, like dark lilies, are drowsily
　　closing, and their braided hair falls over their bodies
　　like pitch darkness.

Night, exhaling a perfumed breeze, disappears quickly at
　　dawn after its union with the moon, while still trailing
　　a portion of the sky illuminated by its bright rays. It
　　is like a woman panting with sweet-scented breath as
　　she picks up the hem of her dress, richly fragrant with
　　cosmetic creams, to hurry back at daybreak from her
　　nocturnal assignation.[5]

The moon shone brightly as it stayed awake all night from
　　fondness for the sweet smile of the blossoming water
　　lilies. Now with rays disappearing, as if with hands
　　drooping in desire for sleep,[6] it falls, pale and wan,
　　onto the lap of the western quarter of the sky.

During the night a girl's lover had pulled off her dress as
　　the excitement of passionate embraces overcame her;
　　in the morning he will not return it, for he is eager to
　　see her hips, broad as a chariot wheel.

The moon adores its wives, but now seems worn out, its
　　beauty gone. It is grieving piteously for the water lilies
　　suddenly closing, the night reaching its end, and all
　　the stars disappearing.

२५ व्रजति विषयमक्ष्णामंशुमाली न याव-
त्तिमिरमखिलमस्तं तावदेवारुणेन ।
परपरिभवि तेजस्तन्वतामाशु कर्तुं
विभवति हि विपक्षोच्छेदमग्रेसरो ऽपि ॥

विगततिमिरपङ्कं पश्यति व्योम याव-
द्द्रुवति विरहखिन्नः पक्षती यावदेव ।
रथचरणसमाह्वस्तावदौत्सुक्यनुन्ना
सरिदपरतटान्तादागता चक्रवाकी ॥

मुदितयुवमनस्कास्तुल्यमेव प्रदोषे
रुचिमदधुरुभय्यः कल्पिता भूषिताश्च ।
परिमलरुचिराभिर्न्यक्कृतास्तु प्रभाते
युवतिभिरुपभोगान्नीरुचः पुष्पमालाः ॥

विलुलितकमलौघः कीर्णवल्लीवितानः
प्रतिदिशमवधूताशेषशाखिप्रसूनः ।
क्वचिदयमनवस्थः स्थासुतामेति वायु-
र्मधुकुसुमविमर्दोद्गन्धिवेश्मान्तरेषु ॥

नखपदवलिनाभीसंधिभागेषु लक्ष्यः
क्षतिषु च दशनानामञ्जनायाः सशेषः ।
अपि रहसि कृतानां वाग्विहीनो ऽपि जातः
सुरतविलसितानां वर्णको वर्णको ऽसौ ॥

360

Before the sun comes into full view, its charioteer Aruna   25
    has already dispelled the darkness with the pink glow
    of dawn.[7] A mere servant of the illustrious can quickly
    dispose of enemies.

The sheldrake, distressed by separation, looks at the sky,
    free from the mud of darkness; as he shakes his wings,
    his mate, driven by longing, has flown to him from the
    far riverbank.[8]

Elaborate flowery garlands and women in their finery—
    they once possessed beauty in equal measure,
    enchanting young men during the night. By
    morning the garlands, faded from rough handling,
    are worthless compared with girls suffused with
    lovemaking's afterglow.

The breeze does not linger anywhere, disturbing the lotus
    clumps, scattering the long creepers, and shaking all
    the blossoms from the trees; but now it is settling in
    the pavilions amid the mingling scent of wine and
    flowers.

Sandalwood makeup can be seen clearly overlaid on the
    scratches on the body of the woman over there, in
    her stomach folds and navel, and around her intimate
    parts, while it is just discernible on the bites on her
    lips—it may lack the power of speech but can still
    describe lovemaking's pleasures, however discreetly
    enjoyed.[9]

३० प्रकटमलिनलक्ष्मा मृष्टपत्राङ्गुलीकै-
रधिगतरतिशोभैः प्रत्युषः प्रोषितश्रीः ।
उपहसित इवासौ चन्द्रमाः कामिनीनां
परिणतशरकाण्डापाण्डुभिर्गण्डभागैः ॥

सकलमपि निकामं कामलोलान्यनारी-
रतरभसविमर्दे भिन्नवत्यङ्गरागम् ।
इदमतिमहदेवाश्चर्यमाश्चर्यधाम्न-
स्तव खलु मुखरागो यन्न भेदं प्रयातः ॥

प्रकटतरमिमं मा द्राक्षुरन्या रमण्यः
स्फुटमिति सविशङ्कं कान्तया तुल्यवर्णः ।
चरणतलसरोजाक्रान्तसंक्रान्तयासौ
वपुषि नखविलेखो लाक्षया रञ्जितस्ते ॥

तदवितथमवादीर्यन्मम त्वं प्रियेति
प्रियजनपरिभुक्तं यद्दुगूलं दधानः ।
मदधिवसतिमागाः कामिनां मण्डनश्री-
र्व्रजति हि सफलत्वं वल्लभालोकनेन ॥

नवनखपदमङ्कं गोपयस्यंशुकेन
स्थगयसि मुहुरोष्ठं पाणिना दन्तदष्टम् ।
प्रतिदिशमपरस्त्रीसङ्गशंसी विसर्प-
न्वद परिमलगन्धः केन शक्यो वरीतुम् ॥

The dark mark stands out on the moon, its beauty   30
    disappearing with the morning. It seems to be mocked
    by the fair women's cheeks, where signs of lovemaking
    are clear—now that their makeup has been rubbed off,
    they are pale as stalks of straw.[10]

'A miracle! Your passionate lovemaking with some lusty
    lady has completely removed the cream coloring your
    body. But it's you who are the real wonder—your face
    hasn't changed color with shame![11]

Your sweetheart is worried that other women might have a
    clear view of an obvious love mark, so she has covered
    your scratch with lac by pressing her delicate foot
    upon you.[12] Now it's the same shade of red!

You swore to that me that I was the only one you cared for.
    That must be true, since you have come to my place
    draped in your beloved's dress. Finery only achieves
    its purpose when seen by one's real sweetheart.[13]

Your body is covered with fresh scratches, so you hide it
    with your upper garment. Your lip has been bitten,
    so you keep on masking it with your hand. Tell me,
    though—how can you conceal that wafting fragrance
    proclaiming your infidelity?'

३५ इति कृतवचनायाः कश्चिदभ्येति बिभ्य-
द्दलितनयनवारेर्याति पादावनामम् ।
करुणमपि समर्थं मानिनां मानभेदे
रुदितमुदितमस्तं योषितां विग्रहेषु ॥

मदमदनविकासस्पष्टधाष्र्योदयानां
रतिकलहविकीर्णैर्भूषणैरञ्चितेषु ।
विदधति न गृहेषूत्फुल्लपुष्पोपकारं
विफलविनययत्नाः कामिनीनां वयस्याः ॥

करजदशनचिह्नं नैशमङ्के ऽन्यनारी-
जनितमिति सरोषामीर्ष्यया शङ्कमानाम् ।
स्मरसि न खलु दत्तं मत्तयैतत्त्वयैव
स्त्रियमनुनयतीत्थं क्रीडमानां विलासी ॥

कृतगुरुतरहारच्छेदमालिङ्ग्य पत्यौ
परिशिथिलितगात्रे गन्तुमापृच्छमाने ।
विगलितनवमुक्तास्थूलबाष्पाम्बुबिन्दु
स्तनयुगमबलायास्तत्क्षणं रोदतीव ॥

बहु जगद परस्तात्तस्य मत्ता किलाहं
चकर च किल चाटु प्रौढयोषिद्वदस्य ।
विदितमिति सखीभ्यो रात्रिवृत्तं विचिन्त्य
व्यपगतमदयाद्धि व्रीडितं मुग्धवध्वा ॥

She stopped, giving way to tears, and her man ran up in 35
   distress to fall at her feet. In quarrels a woman's pitiful
   weeping is a weapon, they say, to destroy the esteem
   of the proud.

Visibly emboldened as their drunkenness and passion
   increased, the women had carpeted the pavilions
   with ornaments thrown off in their love bouts. With
   morning now come, there is no point in their friends
   attempting to pick them up[14] and they need not
   scatter decorative blossoms.

In a jealous rage she accused her lover of flaunting bites
   and scratches made by another woman during the
   night. That ladies' man soothes her: 'Don't you
   remember it was you who did this to me when you
   were drunk?' Now it is she who is embarrassed!

When her lord asked leave to depart, his embrace broke
   her heavy necklace; and as he pulled away, her breasts
   seemed at that moment to weep fat tear drops as the
   bright pearls dropped off.

'Apparently when I was drunk I flattered him a great
   deal, as if I were a woman of the world.' A demure
   girl, sobering up in the morning, has heard from her
   friends about the night's events and cringes with
   embarrassment to think of them.[15]

४० अरुणजलजराजीमुग्धहस्ताग्रपादा
बहलमधुपमालाकज्जलेन्दीवराक्षी ।
अनुपतति विरावैः पत्रिणां व्याहरन्ती
रजनिमचिरजाता पूर्वसन्ध्या सुतेव ॥

प्रतिशरणमशीर्णज्योतिरध्याहितानां
विधिविहितविरिब्धैः सामिधेनीरधीत्य ।
कृतगुरुदुरितौघध्वंसमध्वर्युवर्यै-
र्हुतमयमुपलीढे साधु सान्नाय्यमग्निः ॥

प्रकृतजपविधीनामास्यमुद्रश्छिदन्तं
मुहुरपिहितमोष्ठैरक्षरैरलक्ष्यमन्यैः ।
अनुकृतिमनुवेलं घट्टितोद्धट्टितस्य
व्रजति नियमभाजां मुग्धमुक्तापुटस्य ॥

नवकनकपिशङ्गं वासराणां विधातुः
ककुभि कुलिशपाणेर्भाति भासां वितानम् ।
जनितभुवनदाहारम्भमम्भांसि दग्ध्वा
चलितमिव महाब्धेरूर्ध्वमौर्वानलार्चिः ॥

विततपृथुवरत्रातुल्यरूपैर्मयूखैः
कलश इव गरीयान्दिग्भिराकृष्यमाणः ।
कृतकलकलविङ्क्षालापकोलाहलाभि-
र्जलनिधिजलमध्यादेष उत्तार्यते ऽर्कः ॥

The morning twilight, teeming with gloriously red lotuses   40
    and water lilies dark with swarms of bees,[16] follows
    the night, calling to it with birdsong. It is like a little
    child running in tears after her mother, hands and feet
    covered with lac, eyes blackened with kohl.[17]

A fire burns brightly in every householder's sacrificial
    enclosure. Offerings are made in the prescribed
    manner by priests, masters of the verses appropriate
    to the ritual kindling;[18] while they intone the liturgy
    in conformity to its melody, the morning oblation[19] is
    consumed, and with it heavy burdens of sin.

As Brahmans[20] begin the regular dawn chanting of the
    Veda, their mouths repeatedly close when they
    encounter labial sounds and gape wide with a display
    of flashing teeth to enunciate dentals—they look like
    an oyster opening and shutting to reveal its fine pearls!

In the east, Indra's region, the ray-canopy of the
    day-bringing sun is yellow as new-beaten gold. It looks
    like blazing fire bursting upward from the mighty
    ocean to burn the universe after the water has been
    consumed.

Amid the uproar of excited birds the horizon hauls the sun
    into the sky from the ocean with rays like thick taut
    ropes, in the same way that chattering women heave a
    heavy bucket from a well.

४५ पयसि सलिलराशेर्नक्तमन्तर्निमग्नः
स्फुटमनिशमतापि ज्वालया वाडवाग्रे: ।
यदयमिदमिदानीमङ्गमुद्यन्दधाति
ज्वलितखदिरकाष्ठाङ्गारगौरं विवस्वान् ॥

अतुहिनरुचिनासौ केवलं नोदयाद्रि:
क्षणमुपरिगतेन क्ष्माभृत: सर्व एव ।
नवकरनिकरेण स्पृष्टबन्धूकसून-
स्तबकरचितमेते शेखरं बिभ्रतीव ॥

उदयशिखरिशृङ्गप्राङ्गणेष्वेष रिङ्ग-
न्नसकमलमुखहासं वीक्षित: पद्मिनीभि: ।
विततमृदुकराग्र: शब्दयन्त्या वयोभि:
परिपतति दिवो ऽङ्कं लीलया बालसूर्य: ॥

क्षणमयमुपविष्ट: क्ष्मातलन्यस्तपाद:
प्रणतिपरमवेक्ष्य प्रीतमह्याय लोकम् ।
भुवनतलमशेषं प्रत्यवेक्षिष्यमाण:
क्षितिधरतटपीठादुत्थित: सप्तसप्ति: ॥

परिणतमदिराभं भास्करेणांशुबाणै-
स्तिमिरकरिघटाया: सर्वदिक्षु क्षताया: ।
रुधिरमिव वहन्त्यो भान्ति बालातपेन
च्छुरितमुभयरोधोवारितं वारि नद्य: ॥

368

The sun, sunk by night within the ocean's depths, had   45
    clearly been roasted by the flame of the underwater
    fire; as it now rises, its orb is yellow as sparks from
    blazing *khadira* wood.

The sun did not scale the eastern mountain alone, but with
    dense morning rays it struck all these towering peaks,
    seeming to crown them with blossoming *bandhujīvaka*
    flowers.[21]

The opening lotuses gaze at the morning sun wandering
    among the heights of the eastern mountain; it extends
    its soft finger-like rays and expands over the sky, as
    birds shriek aloud.[22]

The sun had rested for an instant and settled upon its rays.
    Then after quickly surveying its faithful devotee, the
    earth, bowing in worship, it has risen from the eastern
    mountain slopes to oversee the universe.[23]

Now rivers are glowing, the water between their banks
    reddened by the light of the newly risen sun; it looks
    like the blood, flowing like mature wine, of the
    elephant herd of darkness wounded all over by the sun
    with its arrow-rays.

५० दधति परिपतन्त्यो जालवातायनेभ्य-
स्तरुणतपनभासो मन्दिराभ्यन्तरेषु ।
प्रणयिषु वनितानां प्रातरिच्छत्सु गन्तुं
कुपितमदनमुक्तोत्तप्रनाराचलीलाम् ॥

अधिरजनि वधूभिः पीतमैरेयरिक्तं
कनकचषकमेतत्प्रातरालोहितेन ।
उदयदहिमरोचिज्ज्योतिषाक्रान्तमन्त-
र्मधुन इव तथैवापूर्णमद्यापि भाति ॥

सितरुचि शयनीये नक्तमेकान्तमुक्तं
दिनकरकरसङ्गाव्यङ्गकौसुम्भकान्ति ।
निजमिति रतबन्धोर्जानतीमुत्तरीयं
परिहसति सखी स्त्रीमाददानां दिनादौ ॥

प्लुतमिव शिशिरांशोरंशुभिर्यत्रिशासु
स्फटिकमयमराजद्राजताद्रिस्थलाभम् ।
अरुणितमकठोरैर्वेश्म कश्मीरजाम्भः-
स्नपितमिव तदेतद्भानुभिर्भाति भानोः ॥

सरसनखपदान्तर्दष्टकेशप्रमोकं
प्रणयिनि विदधाने योषितामुल्लसन्त्यः ।
विदधति दशनानां सीत्कृताविष्कृताना-
मभिनवरविभासः पद्मरागानुकारम् ॥

The morning sunbeams falling through latticed windows   50
    into the pavilions are like blazing arrows shot by the
    god of love in anger at lovers about to abandon their
    women at dawn.

This golden goblet, emptied of wine drunk by women
    through the night, overflows in the morning with
    the pinkish light of the rising sun, apparently still
    brimming with liquid.

A woman's partner in lovemaking threw off his white
    jacket beside their bed during the night. Now it has
    become yellow as a safflower in the morning sunshine;
    her girlfriend laughs at her when she picks it up,
    thinking it is her own.

The crystalline pavilion over here is like the slopes of
    Kailasa, the silver mountain; washed by moonbeams
    at night and now reddened by the sun's soft rays, it
    seems to have been drenched by saffron water.

As her lover pulls away the girl's hair stuck to fresh nail
    wounds, she shows her teeth in squeals of pain; the
    flashing rays of the newly risen sun make them gleam
    like rubies.

५५ अविरतदयिताङ्गासङ्गसंचारितेन
च्छुरितमभिनवासृक्कान्तिना कुङ्कुमेन ।
कनकनिकषलेखाकोमलं कामिनीनां
भवति वपुरवाप्तच्छायमेवातपे ऽपि ॥

सरसिजवनकान्तं बिभ्रदभ्रान्तवृत्तिः
करनयनसहस्रं हेतुमालोकशक्तेः ।
अखिलमतिमहिम्ना लोकमाक्रान्तवन्तं
हरिरिव हरिदश्वः साधु वृत्रं हिनस्ति ॥

अवतमसभिदायै भास्वताभ्युद्गतेन
प्रसभमुडुगणो ऽयं दर्शनीयो ऽप्यपास्तः ।
निरसितुमरिमिच्छोर्ये तदीयाश्रयेण
श्रियमधिगतवन्तस्ते ऽपि हन्तव्यपक्षे ॥

प्रतिफलति करौघे संमुखावस्थितायां
रजतकटकभित्तौ सान्द्रचन्द्रांशुगौर्याम् ।
बहिरभिहतमद्रेः संहतं कन्दरान्त-
र्गतमपि तिमिरौघं घर्मभानुर्भिनत्ति ॥

बहिरपि विलसन्त्यः काममानिन्यिरे य-
द्दिवसकररुचो ऽन्तं ध्वान्तमन्तर्गृहेभ्यः ।
नियतविषयवृत्तेरप्यनल्पप्रताप-
क्षतसकलविपक्षस्तेजसः स स्वभावः ॥

Fair women's bodies are smeared with saffron bright as   55
    fresh blood, transferred by constant rubbing against
    their lovers; soft as a golden streak on a touchstone,
    they possess a cool beauty even in the heat.

The sun, beloved of lotuses, moves across the sky with
    countless eye-like rays, enabling sight, dispelling the
    darkness overpowering the world.[24]

Once-lovely stars have been driven away by the sun, risen
    to conquer the gloom. When an enemy must be put to
    flight, those who have prospered in his service become
    included among the doomed.

The fierce sunrays are reflected on the silvery slopes of
    the valleys opposite, white as luminous moonbeams.
    Their brightness still destroys the profound darkness,
    even when it has squeezed into mountain caves after
    being vanquished in the wide world.[25]

Despite shining outside the pavilions, the sunlight has
    easily dispelled the dimness within. Even when its
    sphere of action is restricted, brilliance musters its
    resources to overcome any opposition.

६० चिरमतिरसलौल्याद्वन्धनं लम्बितानां
पुनरयमुदयाय प्राप्य धाम स्वमेव ।
दलितदलकवाटः षद्रुदानां सरोजे
सरभस इव गुप्तिस्फोटमर्कः करोति ॥

युगपदयुगसप्तिस्तुल्यसंख्यैर्मयूखै-
र्दशदलशतभेदं कौतुकेनाशु कृत्वा ।
श्रियमलिकुलगीतैर्ललितां पङ्कजान्त-
र्भवनमधिशयानामादरात्पश्यतीव ॥

अदयमिव कराग्रैरेष निष्पीड्य सद्यः
शशधरमहरादौ रागवानुष्णरश्मिः ।
अवकिरति नितान्तं कान्तिनिर्यासमब्द-
सुतनवजलपाण्डुं पुण्डरीकोदरेषु ॥

प्रविकसति चिराय द्योतिताशेषलोके
दशकरशतमूर्तावक्षिणीव द्वितीये ।
सितरुचिवपुषासौ लक्ष्यते संप्रति द्यौ-
र्विगलितकिरणेन न्यञ्जितैकेक्षणेव² ॥

कुमुदवनमपश्रि श्रीमदम्बोजषण्डं
त्यजति मुदमुलूकः प्रीतिमांश्चक्रवाकः ।
उदयति दिननाथो याति शीतांशुरस्तं
बत विधिललितानां ही विचित्रो विपाकः ॥

Now rising high again, the sun has regained its proper   60
    rank. As if in celebration, it opens the closed lotuses
    and releases from prison the bees long held captive
    through their lust for honey.[26]

At once the sun eagerly pries open the petals of the
    thousand-leafed lotuses with rays of equal number.
    It seems to be inspiring the divine beauty reclining in
    their inner chambers,[27] serenaded by bees' humming.

As soon as dawn breaks, the sun, red with rage,[28] appears
    to squeeze the moon remorselessly with its finger-like
    rays and lavishly sprinkles the decoction of its beauty,
    pale as rain new-fallen from clouds, on the calyxes of
    white lotuses.

When the myriad-rayed sun, illuminator of the universe,
    finally appears like a second eye, the sky looks as if it
    has lost its other orb, for the moon no longer possesses
    any light.

The clump of water lilies is bereft of its beauty, while the
    lotus cluster has increased in loveliness. The owl is
    no longer happy and the sheldrake rejoices,[29] the sun
    rises and the moon sets. How different are the results
    of destiny's workings!

६५ क्षणमतुहिनधाम्नि प्रोष्य भूयः पुरस्ता-
दुपगतवति पाणिग्राहवद्दिग्वधूनाम् ।
द्रुततरमुपयातः स्रंसमानांशुको ऽसा-
वुपपतिरिव नीचैः पश्चिमान्तेन चन्द्रः ॥

प्रलयमखिलतारालोकमह्लाय नीत्वा
श्रियमनतिशयश्रीः सानुरागां दधानः ।
गगनसलिलराशिं रात्रिकल्पावसाने
मधुरिपुरिव भास्वानेष एको ऽधिशेते ॥

कृतसकलजगद्विबोधो ऽविधूतान्धकारोदयः
क्षपितकुमुदतारकश्रीर्वियोगं नयन्कामिनः ।
गुरुतरगुणदर्शनादभ्युपेताल्पदोषः कृती
तव वरद करोतु सुप्रातमह्वामयं नायकः ॥

The sun ascends in the east, as if it were the husband of 65
    the directions, approaching the entrance to his house
    after a brief absence. The moon now puts away its
    rays and swiftly sinks in the west, like a lover fleeing
    through the back door, half-dressed and head down.[30]

The sun, unrivaled in glory, has quickly destroyed all the
    stars and at dawn lies in rosy splendor alone in the sky.
    So Vishnu in his supreme majesty sleeps in solitude
    on the ocean with his beloved Shri at the world age's
    end.[31]

Krishna, granter of boons! With consummate ease the
    sun has wakened all the world and overthrown the
    power of darkness. It may have ended the beauty of
    water lilies and stars and separated the lover from his
    darling, but trifling faults can be tolerated in the face
    of manifestly greater virtues. May it bring you a good
    morning!"

CHAPTER 12

The Yadava Army on the March Again

इत्थं रथाश्वेभनिषादिनां प्रगे
गणो नृपाणामथ तोरणाद्बहिः ।
प्रस्थानकालक्षमवेषकल्पना-
कृतक्षणक्षेपमुदैक्षताच्युतम् ॥

स्वक्षं सुपत्रं कनकोज्ज्वलद्युतिं
जवेन नागाञ्जितवन्तमुच्चकैः ।
आरुह्य तार्क्ष्यं नभसीव भूतले
ययावनुद्घातसुखेन सो ऽध्वना ॥

हस्तस्थिताखण्डितचक्रशालिनं
द्विजेन्द्रकान्ताः श्रितवक्षसं श्रिया ।
सत्यानुरक्तं नरकस्य जिष्णवो
गुणैर्नृपाः शार्ङ्गिणमन्वयासिषुः ॥

शुक्लैः सतारैर्मुकुलीकृतैस्थुलैः
कुमुद्वतीनां कुमुदाकरैरिव ।
व्युष्टं प्रयाणं च वियोगवेदना-
विदूननारीकमभूत्समं तदा ॥

Now that morning had come, the assembled kings
    mounted their chariots, horses, and elephants outside
    the ceremonial gateway, waiting for Krishna, who
    had delayed a while to put on clothes suitable for a
    journey.

At last he mounted his lofty chariot, secure on the ground,
    firm of axle, bright as shining gold, swifter than
    elephants. So Vishnu rides on the divine bird Garuda
    in the heavens, sharp-eyed and gleaming with fine
    yellow plumage, dealing instant death to serpents.[1]
    Then he moved off by a smooth and comfortable
    route.

The kings, Krishna's vassals, were favored by eminent
    Brahmans and overcame hell through their virtuous
    behavior.[2] But they followed their lord because of
    his particular attributes—he was resplendent with
    the invincible discus Sudarshana in his hand, his
    handsome chest bore the mark of majesty, and he was
    devoted to truth.[3]

The morning and the army's preparations for departure
    were for that moment no different: white tents were
    folded away along with guy ropes, like water lilies
    closing in ponds after the stars had fled,[4] while women
    lamented as lovers departed.

५ उत्क्षिप्तगात्रः स्म विडम्बयन्नभः
समुत्पतिष्यन्तमगेन्द्रमुच्चकैः ।
आकुञ्चितप्रौढनिरूपितक्रमं
करेणुरारोहयते निषादिनम् ॥

स्वैरं कृतास्फालनलालनान्पुरः
स्फुरत्तनून्दर्शितलाघवक्रियाः ।
वङ्काबलग्रैकसवल्गपाणय-
स्तुरङ्गमानारुरुहुस्तुरङ्गिणः ॥

अह्नाय यावन्न चकार भूयसे
निषेदिवानासनबन्धमध्वने ।
तीक्ष्णोत्थितास्तावदसह्यरंहसो
विश‍ृङ्खलं श‍ृङ्खलकाः प्रतस्थिरे ॥

गण्डोज्ज्वलामुज्ज्वलनाभिचक्रया
विराजमानां नवयोदरश्रिया ।
कश्चित्सुखं प्राप्तुमनाः सुसारथी
रथीं युयोजाविधुरां वधूमिव ॥

उत्थातुमिच्छुर्विधृतः पुरो बला-
न्निधीयमाने भरभाजि यन्त्रके ।
अर्धोद्धृतोद्दारविजर्जरस्वरः
स्वनाम निन्ये रवणः स्फुटार्थताम् ॥

382

An elephant raised its forequarters, like a towering 5
  mountain about to fly into the sky; then it bent its leg
  to indicate to the mahout where he should mount and
  lifted him onto its back.

As the horses trembled with anticipation, their riders took
  hold of the reins, gripping the saddle pommel with
  their other hand; then in a display of easy skill they
  vaulted onto their mounts, coaxing them forward with
  gentle slaps.

Before their drivers could leap into their seats to
  commence the long journey, the camels, released from
  their chains, rose abruptly and set off at a resolute
  pace.

One warrior intent on traveling comfortably was assisted
  by his expert driver in yoking his chariot which was
  like a wife to him; it was fitted with a strong axle and
  powerful shaft, its wheels furnished with an excellent
  central hub and fine new spokes.[5]

As a camel was fitted with its heavy bit, it tried to rise to
  its feet but was held back by the muzzle and made
  terrible noises, spitting out half-chewed cud—its
  nickname "Groaner" was quite appropriate!

१० नस्यागृहीतो ऽपि धुवन्विषाणयो-
युगं सशूत्कारविवर्तितत्रिकः ।
गोणीं जवेन स्म निधातुमुद्धता-
मनुक्षणं नोक्षतरः प्रतीच्छति ॥

नानाविधाविष्कृतसामजस्वरः
सहस्रवर्त्मा चपलैर्दुरध्ययः ।
गान्धर्वभूयिष्ठतया समानतां
स सामवेदस्य दधौ बलोदधिः ॥

प्रत्यन्यनागं चलितस्वरावता
निरस्य कुण्ठं दधतान्यमङ्कुशम् ।
मूर्धानमूर्ध्वायतदन्तमण्डलं
धुवन्नरोधि द्विरदो निषादिना ॥

संमूर्छदुच्छृङ्खलशङ्खनिःस्वनः
स्वनः प्रयाते पटहस्य शार्ङ्गिणि ।
सत्त्वानि निन्ये नितरां महान्त्यपि
व्यथां द्वयेषामपि मेदिनीभृताम् ॥

कालीयकक्षोदविलेपनश्रियं
दिशद्दिशामुल्लसदंशुमच्छुति ।
खातं खुरैर्मुद्भुजां विपप्रथे
गिरेरधः काञ्चनभूमिजं रजः ॥

384

Although pulled by the nose, a huge bull, turning its back   10
    with a bellow and a shake of its horns, repeatedly
    rejected the sack being hoisted onto it.

The ocean-like army was like the hymns of the Sama
    Veda*; resounding to the repeated trumpetings of
    its elephants, it surged down a thousand roads, but
    thanks to its superiority in cavalry was immune to any
    sudden assault.[6]

An elephant had charged toward a rival, tossing its head
    and lifting its long sharp tusks to strike; it was only
    restrained by its mahout after he threw away the goad
    he had broken on its head and hastily applied another.

As Krishna set out, the sound of the drum mingling with
    the all-pervading blare of the conch-shell trumpets
    rose in a crescendo; it greatly disturbed two mighty
    entities—the valor of rival rulers and the wild beasts
    of the mountains.[7]

Dust, kicked up by the hooves of bean-fed horses, seemed
    to smear the air with turmeric powder; yellow as the
    blazing sun, it rose from the golden earth and spread
    below the mountain.

---

* The third of the four Veda collections.

१५ मन्द्रैर्गजानां रथमण्डलस्वनै-
र्निजुह्वे तादृशमेव बृंहितम् ।
तारैर्बभूवे परभागलाभतः
परिस्फुटैस्तेषु तुरङ्गहेषितैः ॥

अन्वेतुकामो ऽगणिताङ्कुशग्रह-
स्तिरोगतं साङ्कुशमुद्वहञ्छिरः ।
स्थूलोच्चयेनागमदन्तिकाद्द्रुतां
गजो ऽग्रयाताग्रकरः करेणुकाम् ॥

यान्तो ऽस्पृशन्तश्चरणैरिवावनिं
जवात्प्रकीर्णैरभितः प्रकीर्णकैः ।
अद्यापि सेनातुरगाः सविस्मयै-
रलूनपक्षा इव मेनिरे जनैः ॥

ऋज्वीर्दधानैरवतत्य कन्धरा-
श्चलावचूलाकुलघर्घरारवैः ।
भूमिर्महत्यप्यविलम्बितक्रमं
क्रमेलकैस्तत्क्षणमेव विच्छिदे ॥

तूर्णं प्रवेत्रा कृतनादमुच्चकैः
प्रचोदितं वेसरयुक्तमध्वनि ।
आत्मीयनेमिक्षतसान्द्रमेदिनी-
रजश्चयाक्रान्तिभयादिवाद्रवत् ॥

The elephants' bellowing was drowned by the rumbling   15
    chariots emitting the same deep thunder, but the
    shrill neighing of the horses could be heard distinctly
    above the tumult.

One elephant was eager to pursue a female marching
    nearby; ignoring the commands of its mahout, it
    stretched out its trunk and set off at a stolid pace,
    averting its head when beaten by the goad.

The cavalry chargers galloped forth, barely touching the
    ground with their hooves. As yak tail pennants flew
    around them, captivated onlookers fancied they still
    possessed wings.[8]

Camels extended their long necks, then in an instant,
    surrounded by flowing streamers, bells lightly
    jingling, they set off, covering a great distance at an
    unrelenting trot.

Urged on by their driver, the mules pulling a wagon brayed
    noisily and galloped so fast they seemed terrified of
    being overtaken by the billowing dust thrown up by
    the wheels.

२० व्यावृत्तवक्त्रैरखिलैश्वमूचरै-
र्व्रजद्भिरेव क्षणमीक्षिताननाः ।
वल्गद्वरीयःकुचकम्प्रकञ्चुकं
ययुस्तुरङ्गाधिरुहो ऽवरोधिकाः ॥

पादैः पुरः कूवरिणां विदारिताः
प्रकाममाक्रान्ततलास्ततो गजैः ।
भग्नोन्नतानन्तरपूरितानता
बभुर्भुवः कृष्टमतीकृता इव ॥

दुर्दान्तमुत्प्लुत्य निरस्तसादिनं
सहासहाकारमलोकयज्जनः ।
पर्याणतस्त्रस्तमुरोविलम्बिन-
स्तुरङ्गमं प्रद्रुतमेकया दिशा ॥

भूभृद्भिरप्यस्खलिता९ खलून्नतै-
रपह्नुवाना सरितः पृथूरपि ।
अन्वर्थसंज्ञैव परं त्रिमार्गगा
ययावसंख्यैः पथिभिश्रमूरसौ ॥

त्रस्तौ समासन्नकरेणुशूत्कृता-
न्नियन्तरि व्याकुलमुक्तरज्जुके
क्षिप्तावरोधाङ्गनमुत्पथेन गां
विलङ्घ्य लङ्घीं करभौ बभञ्जतुः ॥

388

The harem women rode by on their palfreys, bodices   20
   rippling on their heavy bouncing breasts; their faces
   were momentarily glimpsed by all the soldiers, heads
   turning as they marched.

The ground was torn up by chariot wheels, then firmly
   trampled down by the elephants; with ridges broken
   and hollows immediately filled in, its surface seemed
   to have been plowed and leveled.

Everyone laughed delightedly as they watched a skittish
   horse; it reared up after unseating its rider, and then
   took fright at the empty saddle hanging on its chest
   and galloped off into the distance.

That army was unhindered by mountains and kings,[9] no
   matter how high and mighty; it could render rivers
   insignificant, whatever their width. It was like the
   Ganga, the "Triple Stream"—but whereas the river
   flows in only three regions of the universe, as its name
   makes clear,[10] Krishna's mighty host advanced along
   countless routes.

Two mules[11] were startled by the bellowing of a nearby
   elephant. When their driver dropped the reins in
   fright, they rushed straight off the road and wrecked
   their carriage, throwing out its passenger, a harem
   woman.

२५ स्रस्ताङ्गसंधौ विगताक्षपाटवे
रुजा निकामं विकलीकृते रथे ।
आप्तेन तक्ष्णा भिषजेव तत्क्षणं
प्रचक्रमे लङ्घनपूर्वकः क्रमः ॥

धूर्भङ्गसंक्षोभविदारितोष्ट्रिका-
गलन्मधुप्लावितदूरवर्त्मनि ।
स्थाणौ निषङ्गिण्यनसि क्षणं पुरः
शुशोच लाभाय कृतक्रयो वणिक् ॥

भेरीभिराकृष्टगुहामुखो मुहु-
र्ध्वजांशुकैस्तर्जितकन्दलीवनः ।
उत्तुङ्गमातङ्गजितालघूपलो
बलैः स पश्चात्क्रियते स्म भूधरः ॥

वन्येभदानानिलगन्धदुर्धराः
क्षणं तरूच्छेदविनोदितक्रुधः ।
व्यालद्विपा यन्तृभिरुन्मदिष्णवः
कथञ्चिदारादपथेन निन्यिरे ॥

निम्नानि दुःखादवतीर्य सादिभिः
सयत्नमाकृष्टकशाः शनैः शनैः ।
उत्तेरुरुत्तालखुरारवं द्रुताः
श्लथीकृतप्रग्रहमर्वतां व्रजाः² ॥

A chariot had broken down and come to a halt, its   25
    bodywork collapsed, its axles useless. Instantly a
    skilled carpenter leapt onto it and tried to effect
    repairs, as if he were an experienced doctor.[12]

A wagon struck a tree trunk, breaking its yoke pole; its
    load of casks burst from the impact and wine poured
    out, flooding the road as far as the eye could see. The
    merchant who had just purchased it in hope of a fine
    profit gave a sharp cry of lamentation.

Mount Raivataka was altogether outclassed by the army.
    Its cavernous hollows resounded to the thunder
    of kettledrums, its groves of banana trees were
    repeatedly mocked by banners, and its mighty rocks
    were outmeasured by lofty elephants.

The fearsome elephants were unruly, for the ichor
    scent borne on the wind from wild tuskers had
    made them difficult to control. They diverted their
    anger for a while by tearing up trees, and then their
    mahouts managed to lead them a good way off by an
    unfrequented detour.

Troops of horses laboriously edged down the slopes of
    gorges, their riders carefully withdrawing the whip;
    then with reins loosened, they galloped quickly up the
    other side, hooves drumming.

३० अध्यध्वमारूढवतैव केनचि-
त्प्रतीक्षमाणेन जनं मुहुर्धृतः ।
दाक्ष्यं हि सद्यःफलदं यदग्रत-
श्वरखाद शाखादयुवा वनावलीः ॥

तैर्वैजयन्तीवनराजिराजिभि-
र्गिरिप्रतिच्छन्दमहामतङ्गजैः ।
बह्व्यः प्रसर्पज्जनतानदीशतै-
र्भुवो बलैरन्तरयांबभूविरे ॥

तस्थे मुहूर्तं हरिणीविलोचनैः
सटंशि दृष्ट्वा नयनानि योषिताम् ।
मत्वाथ सत्रासमनेकविभ्रम-
क्रियाविकाराणि मृगैः पलाय्यत ॥

शौरेः प्रतापोपनतैरितस्ततः
समागतैः प्रश्रयनम्रमूर्तिभिः ।
एकातपत्रा पृथिवीभृतां गणै-
रभूद्बुहुच्छत्रतया पताकिनी ॥

आगच्छतोऽनूचि गजस्य घण्टयोः ३
स्वनं समाकर्ण्य समाकुलाङ्गनाः ।
दूरादपावर्तितभारवाहणाः
पथो ऽपसस्रुश्चपलं चमूचराः ॥

A young camel was repeatedly pulled back by its driver as   30
    he waited for his companions to catch up, so it ate the
    forest creepers before it. Opportunism is immediately
    rewarded.

Its banners like rows of forest trees, its mighty elephants
    like mountains, its troops spread in all directions
    like hundreds of rivers, the army far surpassed the
    wilderness.

On seeing the women's doe-like eyes, the deer stood
    motionless a moment; then realizing their frequent
    darting looks were flirtatious, they fled in fright.

Krishna's army was transformed into one huge sunshade
    by the many parasols of the hosts of kings who, cowed
    by his energy, came from every direction to bow in
    homage.

Some camp followers heard the jangling bells of an
    elephant approaching behind them and, to the noise
    of women's screaming, fled headlong from the road,
    abandoning the pack animals.

३५ ओजस्विवर्णोज्ज्वलवृत्तशालिनः
प्रसादिनो ऽनुज्झितगोत्रसंविदः ।
श्लोकानुपेन्द्रस्य पुरः स्म भूयसो
गुणान्समुद्दिश्य पठन्ति वन्दिनः ॥

निःशेषमाक्रान्तमहीतलो जलै-
श्चलन्समुद्रो ऽपि समुज्झति स्थितिम् ।
ग्रामेषु सैन्यैरकरोद्वारितैः
किमव्यवस्थां चलितो ऽपि केशवः ॥

कौशातकीपुष्पगुलुच्छकान्तिभि-
र्मुखैर्विनिद्रोल्वणबाणचक्षुषः ।
ग्रामीणवध्वस्तमलक्षिता जनै-
श्चिरं वृतीनामुपरि व्यलोकयन् ॥

गोष्ठेषु गोष्ठीकृतमण्डलासना-
न्सनादमुत्थाय मुहुः स वल्गतः ।
ग्राम्यानपश्यत्कपिशं पिपासतः
स्वगोत्रसंकीर्तनभावितात्मनः ॥

पश्यन्कृतार्थैरपि वल्लवीजनो
जनाधिनाथं न ययौ वितृष्णताम् ।
एकान्तमौग्ध्यादविबुद्धविभ्रम-
प्रसिद्धविस्तारगुणैर्विलोचनैः ॥

394

Bards preceded Krishna, reciting verses lauding his   35
    many qualities as a true member of the warrior class,
    gracious and mindful of the duties of his lineage. In
    heaping praise on his name and family, they employed
    sonorous syllables and virtuoso meters to achieve a
    lucid poetic effect.[13]

Even the ocean abandons its limits when it surges up at the
    end of a world age and floods the world. But although
    Krishna was setting out on an expedition with his
    invincible armies, he never transgressed the bounds of
    proper behavior toward the hamlets through which he
    passed.

Above boundary hedges, village women, unnoticed by
    Krishna's people, stared at him for a long time, their
    faces fair as clusters of white *kauśātikī* flowers,[14] eyes
    like huge *bāṇa* blossoms.

Krishna watched villagers convivially seated in groups in
    their cow pens drinking liquor; they repeatedly leapt
    up with a shout to dance, filled with emotion as they
    praised his name.[15]

The cowherd girls could not get enough of gazing at
    Krishna, the lord of the world; they fixed their wide-
    open eyes upon him, but, totally artless, showed no
    trace of flirtatiousness.

४० प्रीत्या नियुक्तॉल्लिहतीः स्तनन्धया-
स्त्रिगृह्य पारीमुभयेन जानुनोः ।
वर्धिष्णुधाराध्वनि रोहिणीः पय-
श्चिरं निदध्यौ दुहतः स गोदुहः ॥

अभ्याजतो ऽभ्यागततूर्णतर्णकां
नियानहस्तस्य पुरो दुधुक्षतः ।
वर्गाद्द्वां हुङ्कृतिचारु निर्यती-
मरिर्मधौरैक्षत गोमतल्लिकान् ॥

स व्रीहिणां यावदपासितुं द्रुताः
शुकान्मृगैस्तावदुपद्रुतश्रियाम् ।
कैदारकाणामभितः समाकुलाः
सहासमालोकयति स्म गोपिकाः ॥

व्यासेङ्मस्मानवधानतः पुरा
चलत्यसावित्युपकर्णयन्नसौ ।
गीतानि गोप्याः कलमं मृगव्रजो
न नूनमत्तीति हरिर्व्यकल्पयत् ॥

लीलाचलस्त्रीचरणारुणोत्पल-
स्खलत्तुलाकोटिनिनादकोमलः ।
शौरेरुपानूपमवाच्छिनन्मनः
स्वनान्तरादुन्मदसारसारवः ॥

Krishna, once upon a time himself a cowherd,[16] passed   40
   some moments inspecting these girls; they were
   gripping pails between their knees amid the din of
   flowing liquid as they milked cows affectionately
   licking their calves tied alongside.

Krishna, Madhu's foe, then watched a fine cow, its calf
   frisking alongside, gently lowing as it left the herd at
   the coaxing of a milker holding a rope.[17]

Krishna looked with a smile at the girls guarding the paddy
   fields; they had just run up to shoo away the parrots
   from the rice, but were now caught in two minds, since
   deer had started despoiling their crop.

He fancied the deer were so fascinated on hearing one
   cowherd girl's singing that they did not eat the rice,
   lest she stop and hurry to drive them away.

When he came upon marshy ground, the crying of excited
   geese, soft as the noise of anklets shaking on the
   reddened feet of women gracefully walking, diverted
   his mind from any other sounds.

४५ उच्चैर्गतामस्खलितां गरीयसीं
तदातिदूरादपि तस्य गच्छतः ।
एके ऽग्रहीषुर्बलरेणुसंहतिं
शिरोभिराज्ञामपरे महीभृतः ॥

प्रायेण नीचानपि मेदिणीभृतो
जनः समेनैव पथाधिरोहति ।
सेना मुरारेः पथ एव सा पुन-
र्महामहीध्रान्परितो ऽध्यरोपयत् ॥

दन्ताग्रनिर्भिन्नपयोदमुन्मुखाः
शिलोच्चयानारुरुहुर्महीयसः ।
तिर्यक्कटप्लाविमदाम्बुनिम्नगा-
विपूर्यमाणश्रवणोदरं द्विपाः ॥

श्योतन्मदाम्भःकटकेन केनचि-
ज्जनस्य जीमूतकदम्बकद्युता ।
नागेन नागेन गरीयसोच्चकै-
ररोधि पन्थाः पृथुदन्तशालिना ॥

भग्नद्रुमाश्चक्रुरितस्ततो दिशः
समुल्लसत्केतनकाननाकुलाः ।
पिष्टाद्रिपृष्ठास्तरसा च दन्तिन-
श्चलन्निजाङ्घ्राचलदुर्गमा भुवः ॥

As Krishna proceeded on the march, some—they were 45
  mountains—even though very far off, carried on
  their peaks the thick dust thrown up in the air by
  his army, pervasive and quite stifling; others—they
  were kings—bore on their heads his command, lofty,
  unimpeded, and authoritative.[18]

Mountains, if not too high, can usually be climbed by a
  well-trodden route, but Krishna's army was blazing
  paths all over towering peaks as it ascended.

Elephants conquered the colossal rock massifs, carrying
  their heads high; they ripped open the clouds with the
  tips of their tusks, while their ears filled with streams
  of ichor flowing across their temples.

It was only an elephant—gray as a cloud bank and temples
  dripping ichor, powerful, tall, with broad tusks—that
  could block the path of the army, rather than any
  mountain—cliffs flooding with rainwater, clouds
  lowering over it, mighty and lofty, with formidable
  peaks.[19]

The elephants, destroying trees around them, tossed up
  forests and covered the sky with waving banners;
  in pulverizing the mountain slopes they made the
  ground impassable for those moving massifs, their
  own bodies.

५० आलोकयामास हरिर्महीधरा-
नधिश्रयन्तीर्गजताः परःशताः ।
उत्पातवातप्रतिकूलपातिनी-
रुपत्यकाभ्यो बृहतीः शिला इव ॥

शैलाध्यरोहाभ्यसनाधिकोद्धुरैः
पयोधरैरामलकीवनाश्रिताः ।
तं पर्वतीयप्रमदाश्चायिरे
विकासविस्मारितविभ्रमेक्षणाः ॥

सावज्ञमुन्मील्य विलोचने सकृ-
त्क्षणं मृगेन्द्रेण सुषुप्सुना पुनः ।
सैन्यात्र यातः समयापि विव्यथे
कथं सुराजंभवमन्यथाथ वा ॥

उत्सेधनिर्धूतमहीरुहं ध्वजै-
र्हयौघरुद्धोद्धतसिन्धुरंहसाम् ।
नागैरधिक्षिप्तमहाशिलं मुहु-
र्बलं बभूवोपरि तन्महीभृताम् ॥

रमश्रूयमाणे मधुजालके तरो-
र्गजेन गण्डं कषतावधूनिते ।
क्षुद्राभिरक्षुद्रतराभिराकुलं
विदश्यमानेन जनेन दुद्रुवे ॥

400

That is what Krishna saw as the troops of elephants scaled   50
the mountains in vast numbers, like colossal boulders
flying up from the foothills, driven by a prodigious
gale.

Meanwhile, hill women watched Krishna from myrobalan
groves; their breasts heaved from the exertion of
climbing the mountain, and their eyes forgot to dart
flirtatious glances since they were already wide open
in admiration.

In disdain a lion momentarily opened its eyes just once,
then turned back to sleep unperturbed, even though
the army was marching nearby. If it did not behave
like that, how could it possibly be king of the beasts?

The army repeatedly found itself above the mountain
range; its banners overtopped lofty trees, turbulent
rivers flowing in spate were dammed by the crossing
cavalry squadrons, while the elephants tossed great
rocks up in the air.

A honeycomb, looking like the beard of a tree, was
dislodged by an elephant rubbing his temples against
it; those nearby were set upon by huge bees and fled in
terror.

५५ नीते पलाशिन्युचिते शरीरव-
द्व्रजान्तकेनान्तमदान्तकर्मणा ।
संचेरुरात्मान इवापरं क्षणा-
त्क्ष्मारुहं देहमिव प्लवङ्गमाः ॥

प्रह्वानतीव क्वचिदुद्धतिश्रितः
क्वचित्प्रकाशानथ गह्वरानपि ।
साम्यादपेतानिति वाहिनी हरे-
स्तदातिचक्राम गिरीनगुरूनपि ॥

स व्याप्तवत्या परितो ऽपथान्यपि
स्वसेनया सर्वपथीनया तया ।
अम्भोभिरुल्लङ्घिततुङ्गरोधसः
प्रतीपनाम्रीः कुरुते स्म निम्नगाः ॥

यावद्व्यगाहन्त न दन्तिनां घटा-
स्तुरङ्गमैस्तावदुदीरितं खुरैः ।
क्षिप्तं समीरैः सरितां पुरः पत-
ज्जलान्यनैषीद्व्रज एव पङ्क्तताम् ॥

रन्तुं क्षतोत्तुङ्गनितम्बभूमयो
मुहुर्व्रजन्तः प्रमदं मदोद्धताः ।
पङ्कं करापाकृतशेवलांशुकाः
समुद्रगानामुदपादयन्निभाः ॥

A monkey tribe's ancestral tree home had been destroyed   55
    by a rampaging elephant, as death ends a mortal body.
    So they moved to another dwelling in an instant, like
    souls migrating to their next host.

In this way Krishna's army crossed the mountains, all
    massive, but otherwise very different—here quite low
    with humped ridges, there towering high: here with
    no hidden dangers, there dark and impassable.[20]

The high river banks were flooded with water by the army
    advancing on all fronts, surging over even inaccessible
    places. Rivers are normally styled "deep flowing,"
    but Krishna now changed their designation to "high
    rising."

Before the elephants could plunge into the rivers, the
    water had already turned into mud the dust kicked up
    by the horses' hooves and scattered before them by
    the wind.

In a frenzy of delight the rutting elephants muddied
    the rivers, the ocean's wives. They playfully tore at
    their high banks like excited lovers scratching their
    partners' ample buttocks in intercourse, and threw up
    the waterweed with their trunks as if pulling off their
    clothes.[21]

६० रुग्नोरुरोधःपरिपूरिताम्भसः
समस्थलीकृत्य पुरातनीर्नदीः ।
कूलङ्कषौघाः सरितस्तथापराः
प्रवर्तयामासुरिभा मदाम्बुभिः ॥

पद्यैरनन्वीतवधूमुखद्युतो
गता न हंसैः श्रियमातपत्रजाम् ।
दूरे ऽभवन्भोजबलस्य गच्छतः
शिलोपमातीतगजस्य निम्नगाः ॥

स्निग्धाञ्जनश्यामतनूभिरुन्नतै-
र्निरन्तराला करिणां कदम्बकैः ।
सेना सुधाक्षालितसौधसंपदां
पुरां बहूनां परभागमाप सा ॥

प्रासादशोभातिशयालुभिः पथि
प्रभोर्निवासाः पटवेश्मभिर्बभुः ।
नूनं सहानेन वियोगविक्लवा
पुरः पुरश्रीरपि निर्ययौ तदा ॥

वर्ष्म द्विपानां विरुवन्त उच्चकै-
र्वनेचरेभ्यश्चिरमाचचक्षिरे ।
गण्डस्थलाघर्षगलन्मदोदक-
द्रवद्रुमस्कन्धनिलायिनो ऽलिनः ॥

The elephants had filled the water with the earth from the 60
high banks that they had broken down, transforming
what had once been rivers into a solid level mass; then
with their ichor they set fresh streams flowing, quite
undermining the banks.

The rivers were far inferior to the Yadava host as it
marched onward. Their lotuses lacked the beauty
of the women's faces, their geese could not rival
the charm of its parasols, and their rocks were far
surpassed in bulk by the army elephants.

Thronging with troops of elephants, their towering bodies
dark as damp unguent, the army was more imposing
than many cities with whitewashed mansions.

Krishna's marching-camp was packed with tents more
splendid than palaces. When he left Dvaraka, the
magnificence of his capital was so distressed by
separation it had obviously set forth with him.

Bees, humming busily, settled on tree trunks dripping
with ichor as the elephants rubbed their temples
against them; their passage was long after discernible
to forest people.[22]

६५ आयामवद्भिः करिणां घटाशतै-
रधःकृताट्टालकपङ्क्तिरुच्चकैः ।
दूष्यैर्जितोदग्रगृहाणि सा चमू-
रतीत्य भूयांसि पुराण्यवर्तत ॥

उद्भूतमुच्चैर्ध्वजिनीभिरंशुभिः
प्रतप्तमभ्यर्णतया विवस्वतः ।
आह्लादिकह्लारसमीरणाहते
पुरः पपाताम्भसि यामुने रजः ॥

या घर्मभासस्तनयापि शीतलैः
स्वसा यमस्यापि जनस्य जीवनैः ।
कृष्णापि शुद्धेरधिकं विधातृभि-
र्विहन्तुमंहांसि जलैः पटीयसी ॥

यस्या महानीलतटीरिव द्रुताः
प्रयान्ति पीत्वा हिमपिण्डपाण्डवः ।
कालीरपस्ताभिरिवानुरञ्जिताः
क्षणेन भिन्नाञ्जनवर्णतां घनाः ॥

व्यक्तं बलीयान्यदि हेतुरागमा-
दपूरयत्सा जलधिं न जाह्नवी ।
गङ्गौघनिर्भस्मितशंभुकन्धरा-
सवर्णमर्णः कथमन्यथास्य तत् ॥

With hundreds of lengthy elephant columns, the army   65
    surpassed a chain of watchtowers; it was superior to
    many cities, its tents grander than great palaces.

The dust thrown high into the air by the soldiers reached
    close to the sun to be burned by its rays. Then in the
    east it plummeted upon the water of the Yamuna
    rippled by the fragrant breeze blowing through the
    white water lilies.

Although the daughter of the sun, the Yamuna can readily
    destroy sins with its cooling streams; although the
    sister of Yama, ruler of the underworld, it enlivens
    mortals, and although dark in hue, it brings great
    purity.

After drinking its black waters, clouds took on the
    Yamuna's kohl-powder hue; once white as heaps of
    snow, they were now like scudding sapphire crags.

If inference is truly more authoritative than scriptural
    testimony, it must be concluded that the Yamuna and
    not the Ganga fills the ocean.[23] Otherwise why is it the
    same dark color as Shiva's throat after the white flood
    of the Ganga had washed away its coating of ashes?[24]

७० अभ्युद्यतस्य क्रमितुं जवेन गां
तमालनीला नितरां धृतायतिः ।
सीमेव सा तस्य पुरः क्षणं बभौ
बलाम्बुराशेर्महतो महापगा ॥

लोलैररित्रैश्चरणैरिवाभितो
जवाद्रजन्तीभिरसौ सरिज्जनैः ।
नौभिः प्रतेरे ऽनुचितप्लवोदित-
भ्रमीनिमीलल्ललनावलम्बितैः ॥

तत्पूर्वमंसद्वयसं द्विपाधिपाः
क्षणं सहेलाः परितो जगाहिरे ।
सद्यस्ततस्तेरुरनारतसुत-
स्वदानवारिप्रचुरीकृतं पयः ॥

प्रोथैः स्फुरद्भिः स्फुटशब्दमुन्मुखै-
स्तुरङ्गमैरायतकीर्णवालधि ।
उत्कर्णमुद्ग्राहितधीरकन्धरै-
रतीर्यतागे तटदत्तदृष्टिभिः ॥

तीर्त्वा जवेनैव नितान्तदुस्तरां
नदीं प्रतिज्ञामिव तां गरीयसीम् ।
शृङ्गैरपस्कीर्णबृहत्तटीभुवा-
मशोभतोच्चैर्ननदितं ककुद्मताम् ॥

408

That vast stream, stretching far into the distance, dark as   70
a *tamāla* flower, seemed like a boundary ahead of the
mighty ocean-like army as it aspired for that moment
to flood the earth.

But using speedy boats propelled by dipping oars, as if by
feet scurrying on each side, the soldiers forded that
river. Their women clung to them with eyes tight shut
in alarm at the unaccustomed sensation of floating on
water.

At first the mighty elephants plunged playfully in the
water that reached to their shoulders, but when the
river surged up as the ichor poured from them, they
forded it in due haste.

The horses crossed in the vanguard, muzzles glistening,
heads lifted high as they neighed loudly, long tails
spread out, ears pricked up, their steady necks
stretched forward, eyes fixed on the opposite bank.

That mighty river was most treacherous to ford, but the
oxen crossed over quickly. As they ripped up the
high embankments with their horns, their bellowing
pleased the ear, as if they had honored a solemn
promise difficult to fulfill.[25]

७५ सीमन्त्यमाना यदुभूभृतां बलै-
बंभौ तरद्भिर्गवलावलिद्युतिः⁴ ।
सिन्दूरितानेकपकङ्कणाङ्कित
तरङ्गिणी वेणिरिवायता भुवः ॥

अव्याहतक्षिप्रगतैः समुच्छ्रिता-
ननुज्झितद्राघिमभिर्वरीयसः ।
नाव्यं पयः केचिदतारिषुर्भुजैः
क्षिपद्भिरूर्मीनपरैरिवोर्मिभिः ॥

विदलितमहाकूलमुक्षणां विषाणविघट्टनै-
रलघुचरणाकृष्टग्राहां विषाणिभिरुन्मदैः ।
सपदि सरितं सा श्रीभर्तुर्बृहद्रथमण्डल-
स्खलितसलिलामुल्लङ्घ्यैनां जगाम वरूथिनी ॥

410

The Yamuna looked like a long braid of hair on the earth;   75
    parted in the middle by the troops of the Yadava kings
    fording it, dark as a buffalo's horn, it was decorated all
    over with vermilion-smeared elephants.

The river was best forded by boat, but some soldiers
    swam over, throwing up high, heavy waves, their
    outstretched arms moving so relentlessly they looked
    like another shoal of billows.

Although lofty and broad, the river banks were destroyed
    by the scraping of the oxen's horns, its crocodiles
    beached by the heavy tread of excited elephants,
    and its waters convulsed by the great squadrons of
    chariots. Thus the army of Krishna, the husband of
    Shri, quickly mastered the flood and proceeded on the
    march.

CHAPTER 13

Arrival at Indraprastha

यमुनामतीतमथ शुश्रुवानमुं
तपसस्तनूज इति नाधुनोच्यते ।
स यदाचलन्निजपुरादहर्निशं
नृपतेस्तदादि समचारि वार्तया ॥

यदुभर्तुरागमनलब्धजन्मनः
प्रमदादमानिव पुरे महियसि ।
सहसाधनः सह ततो ऽनुजन्मभि-
र्वसुधाधिपो ऽभिमुखमस्य निर्ययौ ॥

रभसप्रचक्रकुरुचक्रदुन्दुभि-१
ध्वनिभिर्जनस्य बधिरीकृतश्रुतेः ।
समवादि वक्तृभिरभीष्टसंकथा-
प्रकृतार्थशेषमथ हस्तसंज्ञया ॥

अपदान्तरं च परितः क्षितिक्षिता-
मपतन्द्रुतभ्रमितहेमनेमयः ।
जवमारुताञ्छितपरस्परोपम-
क्षितिरेणुकेतुवसनाः पताकिनः ॥

५ द्रुतमध्वनन्नुपरिपाणिवृत्तयः
पणवा इवाश्वचरणाहता भुवः ।
ननृतुश्च वारिधरधीरधोरण-
ध्वनिधृष्टकूजितकलाः कलापिनः ॥

It could not be said that Yudhishthira, son of austerity,[1]
　　had recently heard that Krishna had forded the
　　Yamuna; rather, from the very moment Krishna
　　marched out of his capital, tidings of him had been
　　reaching that king day and night.

So Yudhishthira, accompanied by his younger brothers,[*]
　　went with their army to meet him. It was if he could
　　not be physically contained inside his huge city from
　　the joy swelling within him at the Yadava leader's
　　arrival.

People engrossed in conversation had to convey with
　　gestures the rest of what they wanted to discuss, for
　　they were deafened by the thundering of the drums of
　　the Kuru[2] army marching out on the double.

Packed tightly together, the regal chariots sped all around;
　　their golden wheels whirled, while their flapping
　　banners and the dust blowing in the gale were
　　indistinguishable.

The ground resounded to the thunder of the horses'　　　5
　　hooves, like drums slapped rhythmically. Peacocks
　　danced in delight, their cries loud and sweet amid the
　　tumult of galloping deep as storm clouds' rumbling.[3]

---

* Bhima, Arjuna, Nakula, and Sahadeva.

व्रजतोरपि प्रणयपूर्वमेकतां
कुकुराधिनाथकुरुराजसैन्ययोः ।
ररुषे विषाणिभिरनुक्षणं मिथो
मदमूढबुद्धिषु विवेकिता कुतः ॥

अवलोक एव नृपतेः² स्म दूरतो
रभसाद्रथादवतरीतुमिच्छतः ।
अवतीर्णवान्प्रथममात्मना हरि-
र्विनयं³ विशेषयति संभ्रमेण सः ॥

वपुषा पुराणपुरुषः पुरः क्षितौ
परिपुञ्ज्यमानपृथुहारयष्टिना ।
भुवनैर्नतो ऽप्यरहिताप्यगौरवः
प्रणनाम नाम तनयं पितृष्वसुः ॥

मुकुटांशुरञ्जितपरागमग्रतः
स न यावदाप शिरसा महीतलम् ।
क्षितिपेन तावदविलम्बितक्रमं
भुजपञ्जरेण रभसादगृह्यत ॥

१० न ममौ कवाटतटविस्तृतं तनो-
र्मुरवैरिवक्ष उरसि क्षमाभुजः ।
भुजयोस्तथापि युगलेन दीर्घयो-
र्विकटीकृतेन परितो ऽभिषस्वजे ॥

As the armies of Krishna and Yudhishthira met in
    comradeship, their elephants continued to rage at
    each other. How can those in the grip of passion—
    or maddened by the scent of ichor[4]—exercise any
    judgment?

When he saw Yudhishthira in the distance about to leap
    from his chariot, Krishna got down first, outdoing the
    king's courtesy with his own eagerness.

Krishna, the primal being,[5] may have been an object of
    homage to the whole universe, but he did not neglect
    to show respect to his relatives. He gave a conspicuous
    bow to his father's sister's son, so low that the long
    pearl string on his chest piled up on the ground before
    him.

As he bowed, his head reddened the dust with the rays
    from his crown; before it could touch the ground,
    Yudhishthira had swiftly grasped Krishna in a close
    embrace.

Krishna's chest was broad as a door panel and far exceeded   10
    in size the breast of the king, emaciated from fasting
    prior to his sacrifice. But Yudhishthira still clasped
    him tightly, his long arms thrown wide.

गतया निरन्तरनिवासमध्युरः
परिनाभि नूनमवमुच्य वारिजम् ।
कुरुराजनिर्दयनिपीडनाभया-
न्मुखमध्यरोहि मुरविद्विषः श्रिया ॥

शिरसि स्म जिघ्रति सुरारिबन्धन-
च्छलवामनं[४] विनयवामनं तदा ।
यशसेव वीर्यविजितामरद्रुम-
प्रसवेन वासितशिरोरुहे नृपः ॥

सुखवेदनाह्रषितरोमकूपया
शिथिलीकृते ऽपि वसुदेवजन्मनि ।
कुरभर्तुरङ्गलतया न तत्यजे
विदलत्कदम्बनिकुरुम्बचारुता ॥

इतरानपि क्षितिभुजो ऽनुजन्मनः
प्रमनाः प्रमोदपरिफुल्लचक्षुषः ।
स यथोचितं जनसभाजनोचितः[५]
प्रसभोद्धृतासुरसभो ऽसभाजयन् ॥

१५ समुपेत्य तुल्यमहतः शिलाघना-
न्घनपक्षदीर्घतरबाहुशालिनः ।
परिशिशिलिषुः क्षितिपतीन्क्षितीश्वराः
कुलिशात्परेण गिरयो गिरीनिव ॥

The goddess Shri, beauty's embodiment,[6] who had
    previously left the lotus in Krishna's navel and
    stationed herself on his breast, now ascended to his
    handsome face in fear of the intense embrace of the
    Kuru monarch.

Krishna had once become a dwarf as a ruse to defeat the
    demon Bali,[7] but his frame was now bent low only
    in politeness. Then Yudhishthira kissed him on his
    head, perfumed as if by fame with a blossom from the
    heavenly tree won by his boldness.[8]

Although he had released the son of Vasudeva from his
    embrace, the Kuru king's slender body, fair as a cluster
    of opening *kadamba* flowers, still thrilled from the
    pleasurable feeling.

Krishna had destroyed the demons and was accustomed to
    being honored by all, but he willingly paid his respects
    in the appropriate manner to the other kings, the
    younger brothers of Yudhishthira; at this their eyes
    opened wide in delight.

Princes from one army mingled on equal terms with those   15
    from the other, men hard as rocks. As they embraced
    with their long arms, their alliance secure, they were
    like mountains clasping each other when they still
    possessed wings, before Indra's mace struck them.[9]

इभकुम्भतुङ्गघटितेतरेतर-
स्तनभारदूरविनिवारितोदराः ।
प्रतिफुल्लगण्डफलकाः परस्परं
परिरेभिरे कुकुरकौरवस्त्रियः ॥

रथवाजिपत्तिकरिणीसमाकुलं
तदनीकयोः समगतं द्वयं मिथः ।
दधिरे पृथक्करिण एव दूरतो
महतां हि सर्वमथ वा जनातिगम् ॥

अधिरुह्य तामिति महीभृतोदितः
कपिकेतनार्पितकरो रथं हरिः ।
अवलम्बितैडबिडपाणिपल्लवः
श्रयति स्म मेघमिव मेघवाहनः ॥

रथमास्थितस्य च पुराभिवर्तिन-
स्तिसृणां पुरामिव रिपोर्मधुद्विषः ।
अथ धर्ममूर्तिरनुरागभावितः
स्वयमादित प्रवयणं प्रजापतिः ॥

२० शनकैश्च तस्य तनुजालकान्तर-
क्षरितक्षपाकरकरोत्कराकृतिः ।
पृथु फेनकूटमिव निम्नगापते-
र्मरुदस्य सूनुरधुवत्प्रकीर्णकम् ॥

The Vrishni and Kuru women also embraced, the down on
their cheeks thrilling in delight. Their stomachs could
not touch, however, since their heavy breasts jutted
forward like elephants' forehead lobes.

Thronging with chariots, horses, infantry, and cow
elephants, those two hosts came together. But the
bull elephants kept their distance—no wonder,
for everything about the mighty transcends the
conventional.

Invited by King Yudhishthira to mount, Krishna took
Arjuna's hand and got into his chariot, as Indra
ascends a cloud leaning on the delicate arm of Kubera,
god of wealth.

When Krishna, Madhu's foe, had mounted his chariot
to set off for Indraprastha, King Yudhishthira, the
embodiment of duty, filled with affection for him,
took up his whip unprompted, as did red-skinned
Brahma when driving the chariot of Shiva, enemy of
the three cities.[10]

And Bhima, son of the wind, looking like a flood of   20
moonlight pouring through a window's lattice holes,
slowly waved over him a yak-tail pennant like a broad
plume of foam drifting on the ocean.

विकसत्कलायकुसुमासितद्युते-
रलघूडुपाण्डु जगतामधीशितुः ।
यमुनाह्रदोपरिगहंसमण्डल-
द्युतिजिष्णु जिष्णुरभृतोष्णवारणम् ॥

पवनात्मजेन्द्रसुतमध्यवर्तिना
नितरामरोचि रुचिरेण चक्रिणा ।
दधतेव योगमुभयग्रहान्तर-
स्थितकारितं दुरुधुरार्ख्यमिन्दुना ॥

वशिनं क्षितेरयनयाविवेश्वरं
नियमो यमश्च नियतं यतिं यथा ।
विजयश्रिया वृतिमिवार्कमारुता-
वनुससस्तुस्तमथ दस्रयोः सुतौ ॥

मुदितैस्तदेति दितिजन्मनां रिपा-
वविनेयसंभ्रमविकासिभक्तिभिः ।
उपसेदिवद्भिरुपदेष्टरीव तै-
र्ववृते विनीतमविनीतशासिभिः ॥

२५ गतयोरभेदमिति सैन्योस्तयो-
रथ भानुजह्नुतनयाम्भसोरिव ।
प्रतिनादितामरविमानमानकै-
र्नितरां मुदा परमयेव दध्वने ॥

Arjuna carried a parasol, white as a great star, brighter
   than a flock of geese gliding on the Yamuna, which he
   held over Krishna, the lord of the universe, dark as a
   blossoming *kalāya* flower.

Handsome Krishna was now standing between Bhima
   and Arjuna, bright as the moon entering its station
   between the sun and the earth.

Nakula and Sahadeva came behind him, as luck and skill
   in policy result for a king exercising self-control, as
   discipline and restraint ensue for a dedicated ascetic,
   as the sun and wind follow one who has gained
   victory's glory.

So at that moment the Pandava brothers, those chastisers
   of the wicked, politely surrounded Krishna, the
   demons' foe. Their devotion to him appeared as
   sincere enthusiasm, and in their delight they looked
   like eager pupils thronging round their teacher.

While both armies mingled like the waters of the Yamuna,   25
   daughter of the sun, and the Ganga, daughter of the
   sage Jahnu, their drums boomed forth as if rejoicing
   so that the heavenly realms resounded.

मखमीक्षितुं क्षितिपतेरुपेयुषां
परितः प्रकल्पितनिकेतनं बहिः ।
उपरुध्यमानमिव भूभृतां बलैः
पुटभेदनं दनुसुतारिरैक्षत ॥

प्रतिशब्दपूरितदिगन्तरः पत-
न्पुरगोपुरं प्रति स सैन्यसागरः ।
रुरुचे हिमाचलगुहामुखोन्मुखः
पयसां प्रवाह इव सौरसैन्धवः ॥

असकृद्गृहीतबहुदेहसंभव-
स्तदसौ विभक्तनवगोपुरान्तरम् ।
पुरुषः पुरं प्रविशति स्म पञ्चभिः
सममिन्द्रियैरिव नरेन्द्रसूनुभिः ॥

तनुभिस्त्रिनेत्रनयनानवेक्षित-
स्मरविग्रहद्युतिभिरद्युतन्नराः ।
प्रमदाश्च यत्र खलु राजयक्ष्मणः
परतो निशाकरमनोहरैर्मुखैः ॥

३० अवलोकनाय सुरविद्विषां द्विषः
पटहप्रणादविहितोपहूतयः ।
अवधीरितान्यकरणीयसत्वराः
प्रतिरथ्यमाजिहत पौरयोषितः ॥

Krishna, enemy of the sons of Danu,* fancied that
    Yudhishthira's capital, Indraprastha, was besieged on
    all sides, for encampments had been erected outside
    its walls by the forces of princes come to witness the
    king's ceremony.

The commotion of the ocean-like armies echoed
    throughout the heavens. Surging in the direction
    of the main city gate, they glittered like the flood of
    divine Ganga water tumbling toward a cavernous
    channel in Mount Himalaya.

That city had been provided with several new gates and so
    Krishna, the primal being, repeatedly reborn in many
    forms, entered along with the Pandava princes, as the
    soul takes up residence in a body with its five senses
    and nine orifices.[11]

There the men were as lustrously handsome as the god of
    love until Shiva had cast his third eye upon his body;
    the women's faces were fair as the moon before it
    wastes away.

The city women, summoned by the noisy drumming,   30
    hurried along the highway to see the foe of the gods'
    foes, spurning other tasks in their haste.

———

* The mother of the demons.

अभिवीक्ष्य सामिकृतमण्डनं यतीः
कररुद्धनिर्लसदुरोंशुकाः स्त्रियः ।
दधिरे ऽधिभित्ति पटहप्रतिस्वनैः
स्फुटमट्टहासमिव सौधपङ्क्तयः ॥

रभसेन हारपददत्तकाञ्चयः
प्रतिमूर्धजं निहितकर्णपूरकाः ।
परिवर्तिताम्बरयुगाः समापत-
न्वलयीकृतश्रवणकुण्डलाः स्त्रियः ॥

व्यतनोदपास्य चरणं प्रसाधिका-
करवल्लवाद्रसवशेन काचन ।
द्रुतयावकैकपदचित्रितावनिं
पदवीं गतेव गिरिजा हरार्धताम् ॥

व्यलगन्निशङ्कुटकटीरकस्थली-
शिखरस्खलन्मुखरमेखलाकुलाः ।
भवनानि तुङ्गतपनीयसंक्रम-
क्रमणक्रणत्कनकनूपुराः स्त्रियः ॥

३५ अधिरुक्ममन्दिरगवाक्षमुल्लस-
त्सुदृशो रराज मुरजिद्दिदृक्षया ।
वदनारविन्दमुदयाद्रिकन्दरा-
विवरोदरस्थितमिवेन्दुमण्डलम् ॥

As the drumbeats echoed from their walls, the avenues of
     whitewashed mansions seemed to laugh aloud at the
     sight of the women rushing on their way, half made
     up, clutching their bodices to stop them slipping off.

The women ran on. In excitement they had put their belts
     round their necks instead of necklaces and tied floral
     ear ornaments on their hair; they wore their clothes
     inside out and the wrong way round, while their
     earrings had been turned into armlets.

In her eagerness to see Krishna, one woman had pulled
     away her foot from the slender hand of the servant
     decorating it; the other, already covered with wet lac,
     marked out her path as she went, as if she were Parvati
     after becoming half of Shiva's body.*

Women thronged the mansions, impeded by jingling belts
     bouncing above their full hips, gold anklets ringing as
     they climbed long gilded ladders.

The lotus-like face of one beautiful woman, bobbing in a   35
     window of a golden palace as she tried to get a glimpse
     of Krishna, glowed like the moon's disc framed in a
     cavern entrance on the eastern mountain.

---

* The androgynous deity Ardhanarishvari.

अधिरूढया निजनिकेतमुच्चकैः
पवनावधूतवसनान्तयैकया ।
विहितोपशोभमभियाति यादवे
नगरं व्यरोचत पताकयेव तत् ॥

करयुग्मपद्ममुकुलापवर्जितैः
प्रतिवेश्म लाजकुसुमैरवाकिरन् ।
अवदीर्णशुक्तिपुटमुक्तमौक्तिक-
प्रकरैरिव प्रियरथाङ्गमङ्गनाः ॥

हिममुक्तचन्द्ररुचिरः सपद्मको
मदयन्द्विजाञ्जनितमीनकेतनः ।
अभवत्प्रसादितसुरो महोत्सवः
प्रमदाजनस्य स चिराय माधवः ॥

धरणिधरेन्द्रदुहितुर्भयादसौ
विषमेक्षणः स्फुटममूर्न पश्यति ।
मदनेन वीतभयमित्यधिष्ठिताः
क्षणमीक्षते स्म स पुरो विलासिनीः ॥

४० विपुलेन सागरशयस्य कुक्षिणा
भुवनानि यस्य पपिरे युगक्षये ।
मदविभ्रमासकलया पपे पुरः
स पुरस्त्रियैकतमयैकया दृशा ॥

428

Another woman had ascended to the top story of her
house with her dress fluttering in the breeze; the city
seemed to be flying a resplendent banner as Krishna
went by.

Women on every roof pelted their adored Krishna with
parched rice grain and flowers from hands like lotus
buds, as if with powdered pearls released from oyster
shells pried open.

Krishna was a constant source of delight to the women,
like the spring season,[12] beautified by the moon freed
from winter, with lotuses blossoming everywhere,
charming the birds and stimulating love, the time
when wine is at its best.[13]

For an instant he glanced at the city beauties possessed
by the god of love, who was confident that Shiva,
fearful of Parvati's jealousy, would not look in their
direction.[14]

Krishna had absorbed the universe into his capacious   40
stomach at the end of the world age as he slept on the
ocean,[15] but a single woman by the road was able to
drink him in with one quick glance flirtatiously cut
short.

अधिकोन्नमद्धनपयोधरं मुहुः
प्रचलत्कलाचिकलशङ्खकस्वना ।
अभिकृष्णमङ्गुलिमुखेन काचन
द्रुतमेककर्णविवरं व्यघट्टयत् ॥

परिपाटलोर्ध्वतलचारुणासकृ-
च्चलिताङ्गुलीकिसलयेन पाणिना ।
सशिरःप्रकम्पमपरा रिपुं मधो-
रनुदीर्णवर्णनिभृतार्थमाह्वयत ॥

नलिनान्तिकोपहितपल्लवश्रिया
व्यवधाय चारु मुखमेकपाणिना ।
स्फुरदङ्गुलीविवरनिःसृतोल्लस-
द्दशनप्रभाङ्कुरमजृम्भतापरा ॥

वलयार्पितासितमहोपलप्रभा-
बहलीकृतप्रतनुरोमराजिना ।
हरिवीक्षणाक्षणिकचक्षुषान्यया
करपल्लवेन गलदम्बरं दधे ॥

४५ निजसौरभभ्रमितभृङ्गपक्षति-
व्यजनानिलोल्ललितघर्मवारिणा ।
अभिशौरि काचिदनिमेषदृष्टिना
पुरदेवतेव वपुषा व्यभाव्यत ॥

Another woman, plump breasts jutting, conch-shell
    ornaments jingling on her forearms as they moved up
    and down, assiduously scratched one of her ears with
    her fingertip[16] while looking straight at him.

Yet another woman nodded her head and beckoned
    Krishna with her hand, alluring lac-red palm held
    upward, slender fingers moving suggestively—she did
    not need to express in words what she meant.

One beauty was yawning,[17] covering her lovely mouth
    with a hand fair as a leaf placed near a lotus; light from
    her sparkling teeth poured through the gaps between
    her trembling fingers.

A girl fixed her gaze on Krishna while clutching her skirt
    with her slender hand as it slipped down; the dark
    glow of sapphires set in her armlet lengthened the
    thin line of her navel hair.

Another woman could have been taken for the city's   45
    divine protector. As she stared unblinkingly at
    Krishna, the perspiration was removed from her
    body[18] by the breeze from the beating wings of bees
    confused by her fragrance.

अभियाति नः सतृष एव चक्षुषो
हरिरित्यखिद्यत नितम्बिनीजनः ।
न विवेद यः सततमेनमीक्षते
न वितृष्णतां व्रजति खल्वसावपि ॥

अकृतस्वसद्मगमनादरः क्षणं
लिपिकर्मनिर्मित इव व्यतिष्ठत ।
गतमच्युतेन सह शून्यतां गतः
प्रतिपालयन्मन इवाङ्गनागणः ॥

अलसैर्मदेन सुदृशः शरीरकैः
स्वगृहान्प्रति प्रतिययुः शनैः शनैः ।
अलघुप्रसारितविलोचनाञ्जलि-
द्रुतपीतमाधवरसौघनिर्भरैः ॥

नवगन्धवारिविरजीकृताः पुरो
घनधूपधूमकृतरेणुविभ्रमाः ।
प्रचुरोद्धतध्वजविलम्बिवाससः
पुरवीथयो ऽथ हरिणातिपेतिरे ॥

५० उपनीय बिन्दुसरसान्मयेन या
मणिदारु चारु किल वार्षपर्वणम् ।
विदधे ऽवधूतसुरसद्मसंपदं
समुपासदत्सपदि संसदं स ताम् ॥

"Here is Krishna actually walking toward us, and yet we
   still cannot get enough of looking at him." Though
   saddened by the thought, these beauties did not
   realize that even one meditating upon him continually
   never becomes satiated.

The women lost interest in going home and stood for an
   instant as if painted in a picture, totally preoccupied;
   they appeared to be waiting for their imaginations to
   return after eloping with Krishna.

But they gradually went back to their own homes, their
   weak bodies intoxicated with the sweet liquor of
   Krishna[19] gulped down from the cupped hands of
   their wide-open eyes.

Krishna continued on his way through the city streets.
   Earlier they had been cleansed with fresh perfumed
   water, but now the thick smoke of incense whirled
   around like dust; banners hung down upon them from
   many a lofty flagpole.

Krishna proceeded briskly to the Pandava assembly hall,   50
   built, so it was said, by Maya after bringing from the
   Bindusaras lake fine bejeweled wood, the property
   of the demon king Vrishaparvan; in its splendor it
   surpassed Indra's palace.[20]

अधिरात्रि यत्र निपतन्नभोलिहः
कलधौतधौतमणिवेशमनां रुचः ।
पुनरप्यवापदिव दुग्धवारिधि-
क्षणगर्भवासमनिदाघदीधितिः ॥

लयनेषु लोहितकनिर्मिता भुवः
शितिरत्नरश्मिहरितीकृतान्तराः ।
जमदग्निसूनुपितृतर्पणीरप-
स्तनुते स्म या विरलशेवला इव ॥

विषदाश्मकूटघटिताः क्षपाकृतः
क्षणदासु यत्र च रुचैकतां गताः ।
गृहपङ्क्त्यश्चिरमतीयिरे जनै-
स्तमसीव हस्तपरिमर्शसूचिताः ॥

निलयेषु नक्तमसिताश्मनां चयै-
र्बिसिनीवधूपरिभवस्फुटागसः ।
मुहुरत्नसद्भिरपि यत्र गौरवा-
च्छशलाञ्छनांशव उपांशु जघ्निरे ॥

५५ सुखिनः पुरो ऽभिमुखतामुपागतैः
प्रतिमासु यत्र गृहरत्नभित्तिषु ।
नवसङ्गमैरबिभरुः प्रियाजनैः
प्रमदं त्रपाभरपराङ्मुखैरपि६ ॥

There at night the moon encountered the luster of its
    jeweled chambers, white as silver, reaching into the
    sky, and seemed for a instant to dwell once again
    within the ocean of milk whence it had emerged long
    ago.

In its apartments there were ruby floors, joists turned
    green by emerald rays, looking like Parashurama's[21]
    bloody lakes of oblation to his ancestors, flecked with
    aquatic weed.

The hall's terraces of residences built of crystal bricks
    were as brilliant as the moon. Wayfarers inevitably
    passed them by, identifying their presence solely by
    touch as if they were groping in the dark.

In those buildings at night the guilt of the moon's rays
    was obvious, for they had despised those women,
    the lotuses. So time and again they were secretly
    overpowered by blazing sapphires, emboldened since
    female honor was to be preserved.[22]

There, contented lovers experienced bliss with their new   55
    brides. Overcome by coyness, the girls averted their
    faces from their husbands, but they were reflected
    on the jeweled walls of the apartments, still staring
    straight at them.

तृणवाञ्छया मुहुरवाञ्छितानना-
त्रिचयेषु यत्र हरिताश्मवेश्मनाम् ।
रसनाग्रलग्नकिराणाङ्कुराञ्ज्ञनो
हरिणाग्नृहीतकवलानिवैक्षत ॥

विपुलालवालभृतवारिदर्पण-
प्रतिमागतैरभिविरेजुरात्मभिः ।
यदुपान्तिकेषु दधतो महीरुहः
सपलाशराशिमिव मूलसन्ततिम् ॥

उरगेन्द्रमूर्धरुहरत्नसंनिधे-
र्मुहुरुन्नतस्य रसितैः पयोमुचः ।
अभवन्यदङ्गनभुवः समुच्छ्वस-
न्नववालवायजमणिस्थलाङ्कुराः ॥

नलिनी निगूढसलिला च यत्र सा
स्थलमित्यदः पतति या सुयोधने ।
अनिलात्मजप्रहसनाकुले ऽखिल-
क्षितिपक्षयागमनिमित्ततां ययौ ॥

६० हसितुं परेण परितः परिस्फुर-
त्करवालकोमलरुचावुपेक्षितैः ।
उदकर्षि यत्र जलशङ्क्या जनै-
र्मुहुरिन्द्रनीलभुवि दूरमम्बरम् ॥

There could be seen deer repeatedly dropping their
    muzzles upon the mansions' emerald bricks in
    expectation of grass; as shoot-like rays settled on the
    end of their tongues, they appeared to be chewing
    mouthfuls of greenery.

Nearby trees were mirrored on the surface of the broad
    encircling water channels, seemingly crowned with a
    thick-leafed mass of roots.

As a mighty raincloud thundered upon nearing the
    gem-studded heads of serpent princes, the hall's
    courtyards became spangled with fresh beryl slivers
    sprouting on its jeweled pavements.[23]

There a lotus pond concealed by leaves was to cause the
    death of every king, when Duryodhana, thinking
    it solid ground, tumbled in and was humiliated by
    Bhima's mockery.[24]

There strangers, kept in the dark for a joke, repeatedly   60
    hitched up their robes when crossing its sapphire
    walkway glinting like a sword blade, taking it to be
    water.

अभितः सदो ऽथ हरिपाण्डवौ रथा-
दमलांशुमण्डलसमुल्लसत्तनू ।
अवतेरतुर्नयननन्दनौ दिवं
शशिभार्गवावुदयपर्वतादिव ॥

तदलक्ष्यरत्नमयकुड्यमादरा-
दभिधातरीत इत इत्थो नृपे ।
धवलाश्मरश्मिपटलाविभावित-
प्रतिहारमाविशदसौ सदः शनैः ॥

नवहाटकेष्टकचितं ददर्श सः
क्षितिपस्य पस्त्यमथ तत्र संसदि ।
गगनस्पृशां मणिरुचां चयेन य-
त्सदनान्युदस्मयत नाकिनामिव ॥

उदयाद्रिमूर्ध्नि युगपच्चकासतो-
रहिमांशुपूर्णशशिनोरसंभवाम् ।
रुचिमासने रुचिरधाम्नि बिभ्रता-
वलघुन्यथ न्यषदतां नृपाच्युतौ ॥

६५ सुतरां सुखेन सकलक्कुमच्छिदा
सनिदाघमङ्गमिव मातरिश्वना ।
यदुनन्दनेन तदुदन्वतः पयः
शशिनेव राजकुलमाप नन्दथुम् ॥

Finally Krishna and Yudhishthira, glowing within a bright
    penumbra, a delight to the eye, got down from their
    chariot in front of the hall, like the moon and Venus in
    the sky descending from the eastern mountain.

As the king courteously ushered him in, Krishna
    slowly entered the assembly hall, its bejeweled
    walls invisible, its portal vanishing within the light
    streaming from crystals.

Then he saw within that hall Yudhishthira's chambers
    built of bright gold bricks; the dense light emanating
    from its gems reached the heavens, seeming to taunt
    the palaces of the gods.

Yudhishthira and Krishna sat down on a great shining
    throne. They were as brilliant as the sun and full moon
    blazing simultaneously on the peak of the eastern
    mountain—an unlikely event!

The royal court was filled with delight at the arrival of   65
    Krishna, the scion of Yadu,* for he brought happiness
    and removed all suffering, as a body tormented by
    heat is refreshed by a breeze and the ocean swells
    under the moon.

---

* The progenitor of the Yadava clan.

अनवद्यवाद्यलयगामि कोमलं
नवगीतमप्यनवगीततां दधत् ।
स्फुटसात्त्विकाङ्गिकमनृत्यदुज्ज्वलं
सविलासलासकविलासिनीजनः ॥

सकले च तत्र नगरे हरौ गृहा-
नततवत्यकालमहमादिदेश सः ।
सततोत्सवं तदिति नूनमुन्मदो
रभसेन विस्मृतमभून्महीभृतः ॥

हरिराकुमारमखिलाभिधानवि-
त्स्वजनस्य वार्तमयमन्वयुङ्क सः ।
महतीमपि श्रियमवाप्य विस्मयः
सुजनो न विस्मरति जातु किञ्चन ॥

मर्त्यलोकदुरवापमवाप्तरसोदयं
नूतनत्वमतिरिक्ततयानुपदं[9] दधत् ।
श्रीपतिः पतिरसाववनेश्व परस्परं
सङ्कथामृतमनेकमसिष्वदतामुभौ ॥

Then beautiful dancers performed with grace and
    brilliance, artfully projecting inner feelings and bodily
    responses for all to see. The accompanying music
    was original yet traditional in style, with instruments
    immaculately laying down a steady beat.

Now that Krishna had finally arrived at his palace,
    Yudhishthira proclaimed a special festival throughout
    the city; no doubt in his enthusiasm he had suddenly
    forgotten that celebration there was unending.

Krishna, familiar with all the names of his relatives to the
    very youngest, enquired about their well-being. A
    virtuous man lacking pride never forgets anything,
    even when he has attained great prosperity—or
    married the goddess of good fortune herself.[25]

Then the husband of Shri and that ruler of the earth
    enjoyed the ambrosia of long conversation; it was of a
    mode unique among mortals, tasteful in every respect,
    continually fresh because so out of the ordinary.

CHAPTER 14

Yudhishthira's Sacrifice

तं जगाद गिरमुद्धिरन्निव
स्नेहमाहितविकासया दृशा ।
यज्ञकर्मणि मनः समादध-
द्वाग्विदां वरमकद्धदो नृपः ॥

लज्जते न गदितः प्रियं परो
वक्तुरेव भवति त्रपाधिका ।
व्रीडमेति न तव प्रियंवदो
ह्रीमता तु भवतैव भूयते ॥

तेषामेति वितथस्तवैः पर-
स्ते च तस्य सुकराः शरीरिभिः ।
अस्ति न स्तुतिवचो ऽनृतं तव
स्तोत्रयोग्य न च तेन तुष्यसि ॥

बह्वपि प्रियमयं तव ब्रुव-
न्न व्रजत्यनृतवादितां जनः ।
संभवन्ति यददोषदूषिताः
सार्व सर्वगुणसंपदस्त्वयि ॥

५ सा विभूतिरनुभावसंपदां
भूयसी तव यदायतायति ।
एतदूढगुरुभार भारतं
वर्षमद्य मम वर्तते वशे ॥

Yudhishthira now turned his mind to performing the
    sacrifice.[1] Seeming to exude affection from his very
    eyes, he spoke sincerely to Krishna, himself the best of
    orators.

"As a rule a person unlike you is unabashed when flattered,
    while the one offering the compliment is embarrassed.
    But whoever speaks well of you never feels awkward,
    while you, sir, always remain modest.

Someone different from you is gratified by the false praise
    readily proffered by the world at large. You, however,
    truly deserve to be lauded, and no encomium of you
    can be insincere, even though you yourself take no
    pleasure in it.

That I extol you greatly does not make me a liar. All virtues
    in their most pristine form manifest themselves in
    you, Krishna.

You have borne the universe's great weight. This supreme   5
    power of yours now makes itself felt so completely
    that the continent of Bharata* will be under my sway
    for a long time to come.

---

* South Asia.

समतन्तुमधिगन्तुमिच्छतः
कुर्वनुग्रहमनुज्ञया मम ।
मूलतामुपगते खलु त्वयि
प्रापि धर्ममयवृक्षता मया ॥

संभृतोपकरणेन निर्मलां
कर्तुमिष्टिमभिवाञ्छता मया ।
त्वं समीरण इव प्रतीक्षितः
कार्षकेण वलजं पुपोषता ॥

वीतविघ्नमनघेन भाविता
सन्निधेस्तव मखेन मे ऽधुना ।
को विहन्तुमलमास्थितोदये
वासरश्रियमशीतदीधितौ ॥

स्वापतेयमधिगम्य धर्मतः
पर्यपालयमवीवृधं च यत् ।
तीर्थगामि करवै विधानत-
स्तज्जुषस्व जुहवानि चानले ॥

१० पूर्वमङ्ग जुहुधि त्वमेव वा
स्नातवत्यवभृथे ततस्त्वयि ।
सोमपायिनि भविष्यते मया
वाञ्छितोत्तमवितानयाजिना ॥

I wish now to perform a sacrifice and so beg you to grant
me permission. For you, my lord, are the root of every
religious action, while I am just the tree.

Having gathered together the necessary materials for the
ritual, I desire to carry it out to perfection. To that
end I have awaited you, as the farmer anticipates the
wind when he has assembled his tools[2] and prepares to
winnow his grain.

Through your presence today my sacrifice will be
complete and unimpeded. When the sun has risen,
who can remove daytime's beauty?

As a ruler I have gained wealth, I have guarded and
increased it; now in accordance with precept I will
make it accessible to worthy recipients. Do I have your
leave to offer it up in sacrifice?

Wait, though! It is you who should be the first to perform   10
the ritual. When you have drunk *soma*[3] and taken the
concluding purificatory bath, only then will I perform
the royal consecration ceremony in conformity with
my intention.

किं विधेयमनया विधीयतां
त्वत्प्रतापजितयार्थसंपदा ।
शाधि शासक जगत्त्रयस्य मा-
माश्रवो ऽस्मि भवतः सहानुजः ॥

तं वदन्तममिति विष्टरश्रवाः
श्रावयन्नथ समस्तभूभृतः ।
व्याजहार दशनांशुमण्डल-
व्याजहारशवलं दधद्वपुः ॥

साधिताखिलनृपं महन्मह-
त्संप्रति स्वनयसंपदैव ते ।
किं परस्य स गुणः समश्रुते
पथ्यवृत्तिरिह यद्घरोगिताम् ॥

तत्सुराज्ञि भवति स्थिते परः
कः क्रतुं यजतु राजलक्षणम् ।
उद्धृतौ भवतु कस्य वा भुवः
श्रीवराहमपहाय योग्यता ॥

१५ शासने ऽपि गुरुणि व्यवस्थितं
कृत्यवस्तुषु नियुङ्क्ष्व कामतः ।
त्वत्प्रयोजनधनं धनञ्जया-
दन्य एव इति मां च मावगाः ॥

448

It is yours to command what should be done with my
wealth, for it has been gained through your goodwill.
Instruct me, ruler of the universe. I and my brothers
are at your service."

The celebrated Krishna smiled, and his dark body was
dappled with what appeared to be a necklace, the rays
of light from his teeth. He replied to Yudhishthira so
that every prince could hear him.

"You have mastered all other rulers and gained today a
far-flung kingdom through the excellence of your
strategy. Is it to another's credit if a man following a
proper diet enjoys lifelong health?

So when you, a worthy ruler, are present, who else could
perform that sacrifice that defines a king? Who was
suitable to lift the earth other than Vishnu in his Boar
incarnation?[4]

Nonetheless, although I too am involved in the onerous 15
duties of government,[5] employ me at your pleasure in
any immediate tasks. My riches are at your disposal;
do not think of me as any different in this respect from
your brother Arjuna, the wealth-winner.

यस्तवेह सवने न भूपतिः
कर्म कर्मकरवत्करिष्यति ।
तस्य नेष्यति वपुः कबन्धतां
बन्धुरेष जगतां सुदर्शनः ॥

इत्युदीरितगिरं नृपस्त्वयि
श्रेयसि स्थितवति स्थिराꣳ मम ।
सर्वसंपदिति शौरिमुक्त्वा-
नुद्वहन्मुदमुदस्थित क्रतौ ॥

आननेन शशिनः कलां दध-
द्दर्शनक्षपितकामविभ्रमः ।
आप्लुतः स विमलैर्जलैरभू-
दष्टमूर्तिधरमूर्तिरष्टमी ॥

तस्य सांख्यपुरुषेण तुल्यतां
बिभ्रतः स्वयमकुर्वतः क्रियाः ।
कर्तृता तदुपलम्भतो ऽभव-
द्वृत्तिभाजि करणे यथर्त्विजि ॥

This discus of mine, Sudarshana, is a friend to the
universe, but it will behead any king who does
not participate in this sacrifice of yours as a vassal
should."[6]

When Krishna had finished, Yudhishthira replied,
"Since you are concerned with my welfare, my good
fortune is totally secure." He then applied himself
enthusiastically to performing the sacrifice.

Yudhishthira's face was by now as pale as a sliver of the
moon,[7] and strong emotion had disappeared from
his gaze. After taking a purifying bath, he became the
eighth form of the god of eight forms[8]—Shiva, bearer
of the crescent moon on his head, destroyer of Love
with a glance, he who is washed by the pure water of
the Ganga.[9]

In his role as sacrificial sponsor, the king was akin to the
self in Samkhya philosophy:[10] inactive in respect to
actual ritual performance, he exercised controlling
agency through witnessing the actions of the principal
priest who, like active consciousness undergoing
transformations, supervised the necessary
procedures.[11]

२० शब्दितामनपशब्दमुच्चकै-
र्वाक्यलक्षणविदो ऽनुवाक्यया ।
याज्यया यजनधर्मिणो ऽत्यज-
न्द्रव्यजातमपदिश्य देवताम् ॥

सप्तभेदकरकल्पितस्वरं
साम सामविदसङ्घमुज्जगौ ।
तत्र सूनृतगिरश्च सूरयः
पुण्यमृग्यजुषमध्यगीषत ॥

बद्धदर्भमयकाञ्चिदामया
वीक्षितानि यजमानजायया ।
शुष्मणि प्रणयनाभिसंस्कृते
तैर्हवींषि जुहुवांबभूविरे ॥

नाञ्जसा निगदितं विभक्तिभि-
र्व्यक्तिभिश्च निखिलाभिरागमे ।
तत्र कर्मसु विपर्ययिणीनम-
न्मन्त्रमूहकुशलाः प्रयोगिनः ॥

संशयाय दधतोः सरूपतां
दूरभिन्नफलयोः क्रियां प्रति ।
शब्दशासनविदः समासयो-
र्विग्रहं व्यवससुः स्वरेण ते ॥

452

To the accompaniment of the ritual formulas, the other   20
    priests, fully proficient in the significance of the
    liturgy, offered up the material substances to the deity
    summoned by invocatory verses enunciated clearly
    and precisely.

The priest responsible for the appropriate chants sang
    the sacred melodies without interruption, indicating
    their seven different notes with motions of his hand.
    The other officiants, their voices true, recited the
    auspicious hymns and liturgical sentences.

The sacrificer's wife, Draupadi,* girdled with a string of
    sacred *darbha* grass, witnessed the oblations offered
    up in the fire after it had been formally consecrated.[12]

When the sacrifice was under way, priests expert in the
    rules for formalizing meaning[13] made the wording
    of the hymns suitable for ritual use by adding all the
    necessary verbal components not already transmitted.

Experts in grammar, they could determine on the basis
    of accent[14] how to interpret compounds of differing
    meaning whose identical structure might have
    rendered them ambiguous.

---

* Married to all five Pandava brothers.

२५ लोलहेतिरसनाशतप्रभा-
मण्डलेन लसता हसन्निव ।
प्राज्यमाज्यमसकृद्दृषट्कृतं
निर्मलीमसमलीढ पावकः ॥

तत्र मन्त्रपवितं हविः क्रता-
वश्रतो न वपुरेव केवलम् ।
वर्णसंपदमतिस्फुटां दध-
न्नाम चोज्ज्वलमभूद्द्विभुजः ॥

स्पर्शमुष्णमुचितं दधच्छिखी
यद्दाह हविरद्भुतं न तत् ।
गन्धतो ऽपि हुतहव्यसंभवा-
देहिनामदहदोघमंहसाम् ॥

उन्नमन्सपदि धूम्रयन्दिशः
सान्द्रतां दधदधःकृताम्बुदः ।
व्यामियाय दहनस्य केतनः
केतयन्निव दिवौकसां प्रियम् ॥

निर्जिताखिलमहार्णवौषधि-
स्यन्दसारममृतं ववल्भिरे२ ।
नाकिनः कथमपि प्रतीक्षितुं
हूयमानमनले विषेहिरे ॥

The sacrificial fire seemed to smile with a blaze of light   25
    from its hundreds of flickering tongue-like flames. It
    continually licked the rich pure ghee offered up to the
    sound of the invocation "*vaṣaṭ*."[15]

As it consumed the oblation ritually purified by mantras,
    the fire did not merely blaze brightly; its very name—
    "offering-eater"[16]—was formed of luminously clear
    syllables.

Fire is always scorching, so no wonder that it easily
    incinerated the oblation; the mere odor of the offering
    consumed the accumulation of mortals' sins.

The ascending smoke, fire's banner, was denser than rain
    clouds and quickly turned the sky gray; it then rose to
    heaven as if to proffer the gods a friendly invitation.

They had already partaken of the ambrosia churned from
    the ocean; but although that surpassed the essence of
    the juices of every healing herb, they could scarcely
    wait for what had been offered up in the fire.

३० तत्र नित्यविहितोपहूतिषु
प्रोषितेषु पतिषु द्युयोषिताम् ।
गुम्फिताः शिरसि वेणयो ऽभव-
न्न प्रफुल्लसुरपादपस्रजः ॥

प्राशुराशु हवनीयमत्र य-
त्तेन दीर्घममरत्वमध्यगुः ।
उद्धृतानधिकमेधितौजसो
दानवांश्च विबुधा विजिग्यिरे ॥

नापचारमगमन्क्कचित्क्रियाः
सर्वमत्र समपादि साधनम् ।
अत्यशेरत परस्परं धियः
सत्रिणां नरपतेश्च संपदः ॥

दक्षिणीयमधिगम्य पङ्क्तिशः
पङ्क्तीपावनमथ द्विजव्रजम् ।
दक्षिणः क्षितिपतिर्व्यशिश्रण-
द्दक्षिणाः सदसि राजसूयिकीः ॥

वारिपूर्वमखिलासु संस्क्रिया-
लब्धशुद्धिषु धनानि बीजवत् ।
भावि बिभ्रति फलं महद्द्विज-
क्षेत्रभूमिषु नराधिपो ऽवपत् ॥

Their divine husbands were continually away in response   30
to regular invitations to sacrifices, so the goddesses
arranged only braids on their heads, not flowery
wreaths from heaven's trees.[17]

The gods quickly consumed the oblation at the sacrifice
and thereby gained full immortality.[18] Thus, with
strength enhanced, they could overcome the arrogant
demons.

In the course of the sacrifice no ritual failed in any way;
rather, each procedure brought about a positive
outcome. The skill of the priests and the resulting
prosperity of the king surpassed each other.

At the conclusion, the openhanded[19] Yudhishthira
disbursed the sacrificial fees to the priests one after
another in the ritual enclosure.[20] He knew that
Brahmans purified all the social classes by their
activities and so were worthy of recompense.

That king sowed money like seeds yielding plentiful crops
in the future; his fields were the Brahmans, thriving
through proper cultivation and the application of pure
water.

३५ किं नु चित्रमधिवेदि भूपति-
दर्क्षयन्द्विजगणानपूयत ।
राजतः पुपुविरे विरेपसः
प्राप्य ते ऽपि विमलं प्रतिग्रहम् ॥

स स्वहस्तकृतचिह्वशासनाः
पाकशासनसमानशासनः ।
आ शशाङ्कतपनार्णवस्थिते-
र्विप्रसादकृत भूयसीर्भुवः ॥

शुद्धमश्रुतिविरोधि बिभ्रतं
शास्त्रमुज्ज्वलमवर्णसंकरैः ।
पुस्तकैः सममसौ गणं मुहु-
र्वाच्यमानमशृणोद्विजन्मनाम् ॥

तत्प्रतीतमनसामुपेयुषां
द्रष्टुमाहवनमग्रजन्मनाम् ।
आतिथेयमनिवारितातिथिः
कर्तुमाश्रमगुरुः स नाश्रमत् ॥

मृग्यमाणमपि यद्दुरासदं
भूरिसारमुपनीय तत्स्वयम् ।
आसतावसरकाङ्क्षिणो बहि-
स्तस्य रत्नमुपदीकृतं नृपाः ॥

It is no surprise that Yudhishthira himself attained purity   35
    by rewarding the Brahmans beside the altar. They too
    were purified through receiving a flawless gift from
    such a blameless monarch.

Ruling like the king of the gods, he bestowed numerous
    landholdings on Brahmans, confirming with his
    personal signature their ownership for as long as the
    moon, sun, and ocean endure.[21]

Yudhishthira then listened while at his urging the
    Brahmans in the fullness of their purity engaged in
    scholarly debate. It was a pleasure to hear; on the basis
    of clearly formulated and orthodox textbooks [22] they
    adumbrated at length their brilliant philosophical
    system, logically correct, but fully in accord with the
    Veda.[23]

That king who presided over the four orders of life [24] had
    never turned away a guest, so when other Brahmans
    came in delight to witness his sacrifice, he was not
    slow to perform the guest-offering.

Meanwhile, princes awaiting an audience with
    Yudhishthira remained outside the sacrificial
    enclosure. They had each brought him the gift of a
    valuable jewel whose equal would be difficult to find
    even after long searching.

४० एक एव वसु यद्ददौ नृप-
स्तत्समापकमलक्ष्यत क्रतोः ।
त्यागशालिनि तपःसुते ययुः
सर्वपार्थिवधनान्यपि क्षयम् ॥

प्रीतिरस्य ददतो ऽभवत्तथा
येन तत्प्रियचिकीर्षवो नृपाः ।
स्पर्शितैरधिकमागमन्मुदं
नाधिवेश्म निहितैरुपायनैः ॥

यं लघुन्यपि लघूकृताहितः
शिष्यभूतमशिषत्स कर्मणि ।
सस्पृहं नृपतिभिर्नृपो ऽपरै-
र्गौरवेण दद‍ृशेतरामसौ ॥

आदिकोलतुलितां प्रकम्पनैः
कम्पितां मुहुरनीदृगात्मनि ।
वाचि रोपितवतामुना महीं
राजकाय विषया विलेभिरे ॥

आगताद्व्यवसितेन चेतसा
सत्त्वसंपद्विकारिमानसः ।
तत्र नाभवदसौ महाहवे
शात्रवादिव पराङ्मुखो ऽर्थिनः ॥

460

The wealth bestowed by just one of the princes was 40
    reckoned equivalent to the sacrifice's entire cost, but
    when Yudhishthira, the son of austerity, engaged in
    liberality, the riches of all of them became as nothing.

Yudhishthira took such delight in giving that the princes,
    in their desire to please him, were more gratified by
    the gifts they bestowed on him than by what they had
    stored up in their own treasuries.

Any prince to whom Yudhishthira, diminisher of his
    enemies, had given advice as to a pupil about even a
    minor matter was gazed at with envy and respect by
    the others.[25]

He had already stabilized the earth, once lifted by the
    primal Boar[26] after being repeatedly wracked by
    disasters, and grounded it on his word, unique in its
    reliability. Now he granted lands to kings.

In that great sacrifice Yudhishthira through his noble
    character remained uninfluenced by desire; nor did he
    turn away from a petitioner approaching in confident
    anticipation of assistance, any more than he did from a
    foe in battle.[27]

४५ नैक्षितार्थिनमवज्ञया मुहु-
र्याच्यते स्म स न कालमक्षिपत् ।
नादिताल्पमथ न व्यकत्थत
प्रत्तमिष्टमपि नान्वशोत सः ॥

निर्गुणो ऽपि विमुखो न भूपते-
र्दानशौण्डमनसः परो ऽभवत् ।
वार्षुकस्य किमपः कृतोन्नते-
रम्बुदस्य परिहार्यमूषरम् ॥

प्रेम तस्य न गुणेषु नाधिकं
न स्म वेद न गुणान्तरं च सः ।
दित्सया तदपि पार्थिवो ऽर्थिनं
गुण्यगुण्य इति न व्यचारयत् ॥

दर्शनानुपदमेव कामतः
स्वं वनीपकजने ऽधिगच्छति ।
प्रार्थनार्थरहितं तदाभव-
द्दीयतामिति वचो ऽतिसर्जने ॥

नानवाप्तवसुनार्थकाम्यता
नाचिकित्सितगदेन रोगिणा ।
इच्छताशितुमनाशुषा च न
प्रत्यगामि तदुपेयुषा सदः ॥

He never viewed a suppliant with disdain; if repeatedly   45
    solicited, he was not hesitant. He did not give an
    insignificant amount, nor did he boast about it;
    he would not express regret about what had been
    bestowed, although it might be precious to him.

Even a worthless enemy was not rejected by Yudhishthira,
    for he was intoxicated with generosity. Must barren
    ground be avoided by a lofty cloud as it rains down
    water?

It was not that his devotion to virtues was insignificant,
    nor that he failed to differentiate between them.
    Rather, in his eagerness to give, the king simply did
    not consider whether a suppliant was meritorious or
    not.

Since the needy gained the wealth they desired immedi-
    ately on seeing Yudhishthira, the expression "Give
    to me!" lost its sense of supplication in the face of his
    extraordinary liberality.

No one approaching that sacrificial enclosure in hope of
    money departed without obtaining wealth, no invalid
    went away with his ailment uncured, and no hungry
    person left unsated.

५० स्वादयत्रसमनेकसंस्कृत-
प्राकृतैरकृतपात्रसंकरैः ।
भावशुद्धिविहितैर्मुदं जनो
नाटकैरिव बभार भोजनैः ॥

रक्षितारमिति तत्र कर्मणां
न्यस्य दुष्टदमनक्षमं हरिम् ।
अक्षतानि निरवर्तयत्तदा
दानहोमयजनानि पार्थिवः ॥

एक एव सुसखैष सुन्वतां
शौरिरित्यभिनयं वितन्वती ।
यूपमङ्गुलिमिवोदनीनम-
द्धूश्वशालतुलिताङ्गुलीयकम् ॥

इत्थमत्र विततक्रमे क्रतौ
वीक्ष्य धर्ममथ धर्मजन्मना ।
अर्घदानमनु चोदितो वचः
सभ्यमभ्यधित शन्तनोः सुतः ॥

आत्मनैव गुणदोषकोविदः
किं नु वेत्थ करणीयवस्तुषु ।
यत्तथापि न गुरून्न पृच्छसि
त्वं क्रमो ऽयमिति तत्र कारणम् ॥

464

Then, as if appreciating the aesthetic flavor of a drama,   50
    all partook with relish of tasty food, provided with
    requisite impartiality,[28] consisting of many types of
    dressed meat and fruit served on individual dishes.[29]

Yudhishthira had appointed Krishna, well capable of
    punishing the evil, to prevent any impediment to
    the performance of the sacrifice. So he could carry
    out unhindered the rituals of giving, oblation, and
    offering.

The earth raised up the sacrificial post crowned with its
    wooden pommel[30] like a finger adorned with a ring to
    indicate that Krishna alone was the staunch friend of
    sacrificers[31] who press the *soma* plant.

In this way the various stages of the ritual were completed.
    Then Bhishma,* the son of Shamtanu, replied to
    Yudhishthira who, aware of traditional custom, had
    asked him about the honor offering to be performed at
    the end of the ceremony.[32]

"You are knowledgeable about virtues and vices, so
    what issues of obligation can you not comprehend?
    Nonetheless, the reason you consult your teacher is
    because that is the proper procedure in this matter.

---

* Yudhishthira's great-uncle.

५५ स्नातकं गुरुमभीष्टमृत्विजं
संयुजा च सह मेदिनीपतिम् ।
अर्घभाज इति कीर्तयन्ति षट्
ते च ते युगपदागताः सदः ॥

शोभयन्ति परितः प्रभाविणो
मन्त्रशक्तिविनिवारितापदः ।
त्वन्मखं मुखभुवः स्वयंभुवो
भूभुजश्च परलोकजिष्णवः ॥

आभजन्ति गुणिनः पृथक्पृथ-
क्पार्थ सत्कृतिमकृत्रिमाममी ।
एक एव गुणवत्तमो ऽथ वा
पूज्य इत्ययमपीष्यते विधिः ॥

अत्र चैष सकले ऽपि भाति मां
प्रत्यशेषगुणबन्धुरर्हिति ।
भूमिदेवनरदेवसङ्गमे
पूर्वदेवरिपुरर्हणां हरिः ॥

मर्त्यमात्रमवदीधरद्भवा-
न्नैनमानमितदैत्यदानवम् ।
अंश एष जनतातिवर्तिनो
वेधसः प्रतिजनं कृतस्थितेः ॥

466

Tradition has it that six people—a Brahman householder,   55
    a teacher, an intimate of the sacrificer, a sacrificial
    priest, a king, and a son-in-law—are appropriate
    recipients of the gift of honor. All have come to this
    ritual enclosure at the same time.

There are present here illustrious Brahmans, emerged
    from the mouth of Brahma;[33] they have warded off
    evil by the power of their sacred formulas and gained
    heavenly realms. Along with them are mighty rulers
    who have kept misfortune at bay by their sagacity and
    conquered their enemies' realms; they add luster to
    your sacrifice in every respect.[34]

These men of quality individually deserve sincere respect,
    son of Pritha. But it has been laid down as a principle
    that only the most meritorious individual should be
    honored.

And among this entire assembly of Brahmans and kings
    it is Krishna, friend of every virtue and enemy of
    demons, who seems to me to merit the honor.

However, do not think that he who has brought low every
    demon is a mere mortal. In reality he is a portion of
    the creator, transcending mortality while also existent
    in every human being.

६० ध्येयमेकमपथि स्थितं धियः
स्तुत्यमुत्तममतीतवाक्पथम् ।
आमनन्ति यमुपास्यमादरा-
दूरवर्तिनमतीव योगिनः ॥

पद्मभूरिति सृजञ्जगद्रजः
सत्त्वमच्युत इति स्थितिं नयन् ।
संहरन्हर इति श्रितस्तम-
स्त्रैधमेष भजति त्रिभिर्गुणैः ॥

सर्ववेदिनमनादिमास्थितं
देहिनामनुजिघृक्षया वपुः ।
क्लेशकर्मफलभोगवर्जितं
पुंविशेषममुमीश्वरं विदुः ॥

भक्तिमन्त इह भक्तवत्सले
सन्ततस्मरणरीणकल्मषाः ।
यान्ति निर्वहणमस्य संसृति-
क्लेशनाटकविडम्बनाविधेः ॥

ग्राम्यभावमपहातुमिच्छवो
योगमार्गपतितेन चेतसा ।
दुर्गमेकमपुनर्निवृत्तये
यं विशन्ति वशिनं विमोक्षवः ॥

468

Yogis declare him the sole focus of contemplation even   60
    though he is beyond conception, the supreme object
    of praise despite being outside the realm of speech, to
    be worshiped devoutly although totally transcendent.

He is tripartite through comprising the three natural
    powers: as the lotus-born Brahma who creates the
    world, he is passion; as Vishnu who maintains it, he is
    clarity; and as Shiva who ends it, he is darkness.[35]

Yogis recognize him as all-knowing, beginningless,
    embodied in order to aid mortals, free from afflictions
    and the consequences of action, the supreme self, the
    lord.

He loves his devotees, so those devoted to him lose their
    sin by continually calling him to mind. They can then
    proceed to the denouement of the drama named 'The
    Anguish of Wandering through Existence.'[36]

Aspirants to deliverance striving to abandon the sensory
    world should apply their minds to the path of yoga.
    They can then merge with him, remote,[37] unique, and
    autonomous though he may be, to end rebirth.

६५ आदितामजननाय देहिना-
मन्ततां च दधते ऽनपायिने ।
बिभ्रते भुवमधः सदाथ च
ब्रह्मणो ऽप्युपरि तिष्ठते नमः ॥

केवलं दधति कर्तृवाचिनः
प्रत्ययानिह न जातु कर्मणि ।
धातवः सृजतिसंहृशास्तयः
स्तौतिरत्र विपरीतकारकः ॥

पूर्वमेष किल सृष्ट्वानप-
स्तासु वीर्यमनिवार्यमादधौ ।
तत्र कारणमभूद्धिरण्मयं
ब्रह्मणो ऽसृजदसाविदं जगत् ॥

मत्कुणाविव पुरा परिप्लवौ
सिन्धुनाथशयने निषेदुषः ।
गच्छतः स्म मधुकैटभौ विभो-
र्यस्य नैद्रसुखविघ्नतां क्षणम् ॥

श्रौतमार्गसुखगानकोविद-
ब्रह्मषड्चरणगर्भमुज्ज्वलम् ।
श्रीमुखेन्दुसविधे ऽपि शोभते
यस्य नाभसरसीसरोरुहम् ॥

Pay homage to the one who, birthless and eternal himself,   65
    embodies the beginning of mortal creatures and their
    end, everlastingly supporting the earth below while
    still dwelling beyond even Brahma's heaven.[38]

When used in relation to him, the verbs 'create,' 'destroy,'
    and 'rule,' employ only the active voice, never the
    passive, whereas the verb 'praise' is employed only in
    the passive sense. So he should be regarded as solely
    the object, never the agent in any act of praising.

Tradition has it that the Lord first created the waters;
    within that he placed irresistible male energy as
    semen. That generated a golden egg from which
    Brahma emerged; it is he who brought this universe
    into being.[39]

When at the time of creation the lord was lying on his
    ocean-couch, the demons Madhu and Kaitabha could
    hinder his easeful repose only for an instant, no more
    than buzzing mosquitoes.

The lotus in Vishnu's deep navel held a sweetly humming
    bee, Brahma, expert in mellifluous chanting of the
    Veda;[40] it opened to display its beauty despite Shri's
    moon-like face being near.[41]

७० सत्यवृत्तिमपि मायिनं जग-
द्ब्रूह्मप्युचितनिद्रमर्भकम् ।
जन्म बिभ्रतमजं नवं नवं
यं पुराणपुरुषं प्रचक्षते ॥

स्कन्धधूननविसारिकेसर-
क्षिप्तसागरमहाप्लवामयम् ।
उद्धृतामिव मुहूर्तमैक्षत
स्थूलनासिकवपुर्वसुन्धराम् ॥

दिव्यकेसरिरिपुः सुरद्विषो
नैव लब्धशममायुधैरपि ।
दुर्निवाररणकण्डु कोमलै-
र्वक्ष एष निरवापयन्नखैः³ ॥

वारिधेरिव कराग्रवीचिभि-
र्दिह्नतङ्गजमुखान्यभिघ्नतः ।
यस्य चारुनखशुक्तयः स्फुर-
न्मौक्तिकप्रकरगर्भतां दधुः ॥

दीप्तिनिर्जितविरोचनादयं
द्यां विरोचनसुतादभीच्छतः ।
आत्मभूरवरजाखिलप्रजः
स्वर्पतेरवरजत्वमाययौ ॥

He is described as a wonder-worker although he conforms   70
    to what is truly real, an infant fast asleep[42] although
    the ancient of the universe, unborn although taking
    birth, the primal being although continually renewing
    himself.

Assuming the form of a thick-snouted boar, he seemed for
    a moment to find the earth already raised to safety,
    for as he shook his shoulders, his bristles stiffened and
    drove back the ocean surging over it.[43]

He was next embodied as a divine lion and with his
    smooth claws soothed the breast of the demon
    Hiranyakashipu, who suffered an itch for battle too
    insatiable even for weapons to relieve.[44]

When, like the ocean striking the sky with talon-like
    waves, he slashed open the heads of the elephants
    of the directions, his elegantly curved claws were
    filled with gleaming clusters of pearls as if they were
    shells.[45]

He is self-born, all other creatures come into being in his
    wake. Still, he took birth as the younger brother of
    Indra, for that god desired to regain heaven from Bali,
    the son of Virocana, by then grown more brilliant than
    the sun.

७५ किं क्रमिष्यति किलैष वामनो
यावदित्थमहसन्न दानवः ।
तावदस्य न ममौ नभस्तले
लङ्घितार्कशशिमण्डलः क्रमः ॥

गच्छतापि गगनाग्रमुच्चकै-
र्यस्य भूधरगरीयसाङ्घ्रिणा ।
क्रान्तकन्धर इवाबलो बलिः
स्वर्गभर्तुरगमत्सुबन्धताम् ॥

क्रामतो ऽस्य दद‍ृशुर्दिवौकसो
दूरमूरुमलिनीलमायतम् ।
व्योम्नि दिव्यसरिदम्बुपद्धति-
स्पर्धयेव यमुनौघमुत्थितम् ॥

यस्य किंचिदपकर्तुमक्षमः
कायनिग्रहगृहीतविग्रहः ।
कान्तवक्रसद‍ृशाकृतिं कृती
राहुरिन्दुमधुनापि बाधते ॥

संप्रदायविगमादुपेयुषी-
रेष नाशमविनाशिविग्रहः ।
स्मर्तुमप्रतिहतस्मृतिः श्रुती-
र्दत्त इत्यभवदत्रिगोत्रजः ॥

'Let us see what sort of distance this dwarf can pace out!'[46]   75
    The demon had hardly finished mocking him when
    Vishnu had already marched over the sun and moon
    and disappeared beyond the sky.

Bali became as helpless as if Vishnu, in the act of
    ascending to heaven's heights, had actually trod on
    his neck with his foot heavy as a mountain. So he was
    easily captured by Indra.

As Vishnu strode far into the distance, the gods could
    see his long legs, dark as a swarm of bees, like the
    Yamuna's flood risen up into the sky to rival the
    celestial Ganga's stream.[47]

Clever Rahu!* He cannot injure Vishnu in any way but
    harbors a grudge against him for doing away with his
    body. Even now he menaces the moon just because its
    orb is as beautiful as his enemy's face.

Vishnu's own body is eternal and his memory flawless,
    so he took birth in the clan of Atri as Datta to rescue
    the Vedic scriptures disappearing from lack of
    transmission.[48]

———

* The bodiless eclipse demon.

८० रेणुकातनयतामुपगतः
शातितप्रचुरपत्रसंहतिः ।
लूनभूरिभुजशाखमुज्झित-
च्छायमर्जुनवनं व्यधादयम् ॥

एष दाशरथिभूयमेत्य च
ध्वंसितोद्धतदशाननामपि ।
राक्षसीमकृत रक्षितप्रज-
स्तेजसाधिकविभीषणां पुरीम् ॥

निग्रहर्तुममरेशविद्विषा-
मर्थितः स्वयमथ स्वयंभुवा ।
संप्रति श्रयति सूनुतामयं
कश्यपस्य वसुदेवरूपिणः ॥

तात नोदधिविलोडनं प्रति
त्वद्विनाद्य वयमुत्सहामहे ।
यः सुरैरिति सुरौघवल्लभो
वल्लवैश्च जगदे जगत्पतिः ॥

नात्तगन्धमवधूय शत्रुभि-
श्छायया च शमितामरश्रमम् ।
यो ऽभिमानमिव वृत्रविद्विषः
पारिजातमुदमूलयद्दिवः ॥

476

Reborn next as Parashurama, son of Renuka, he dealt   80
    with Arjuna Kartavirya[49] as if felling *arjuna* trees.
He destroyed his horses, elephants, and chariots,
countless as leaves, lopped off his many arms as if they
were branches, and robbed him of his good looks like a
forest stripped of its shade.[50]

He had always protected mortals, so he was reborn as
    Rama, son of Dasharatha. Through his heroic energy
he made Lanka still more terrible to the demons after
the haughty ten-faced Ravana had been destroyed,
for he consecrated his upright younger brother
Vibhishana as ruler.[51]

Requested by Brahma himself to destroy the gods'
    enemies, he has now become the son of Kashyapa
who had assumed the form of Vasudeva.

He is lord of the universe and beloved of the gods, who
    told him, 'Father, we certainly cannot churn the ocean
in your absence.' In just the same way the cowherds
once said, 'We can't churn the curd if you're off
somewhere, lad.'[52]

He violently shook the divine coral tree and uprooted it
    from heaven;[53] until then its shade had eased the gods'
weariness, and its fragrance had never been smelled
by enemies. It was as if he had removed Indra's self-
esteem, not hitherto undermined by any foe, shielding
the gods from danger.[54]

477

८५ यं समेत्य च ललाटलेखया
मुञ्चतः सपदि शाम्भुविभ्रमम् ।
चण्डमारुतमिव प्रदीपव-
च्छेदिपस्य निरवादि्दलोचनम् ॥

यः कोलतां वल्लवतां च बिभ्र-
द्दंष्ट्रामुदस्याशु भुजां च गुर्वीम् ।
मग्नस्य तोयापदि दुस्तरायां
गोमण्डलस्योद्धरणं चकार ॥

धन्यो ऽसि यस्य हरिरेष समक्ष एव
दूरादपि क्रतुषु यज्वभिरिज्यते यः ।
दत्तार्घमत्रभवते भुवनेषु याव-
त्संसारमण्डलमवाप्नुहि साधुवादम् ॥

भीष्मोक्तं तदिति वचो निशम्य सम्य-
क्साम्राज्यश्रियमथ बिभ्रता नृपेण ।
दत्ते ऽर्घे महति महीभृतां पुरो ऽपि
त्रौलोक्ये मधुभिदभूदनर्घ एव ॥

When Shishupala first encountered him, he was like a   85
     hurricane. The Chedi king's third eye was blown out
     like a lamp, and at that very moment his forehead
     abandoned any similarity to Shiva's.[55]

He has assumed the form of both a boar and a cowherd;
     with his mighty tusks he lifted up the orb of the earth
     sunk in the calamitous flood at doomsday, while with
     his strong arms he rescued a herd of cows trapped in a
     deep, dangerous swamp.[56]

You are fortunate to behold Krishna right before your
     very eyes, for even priests can only make oblations to
     him from afar.[57] In giving the honor offering to this
     eminent person, you will be applauded throughout
     the universe as long as the wheel of time turns."

Yudhishthira, now ritually imbued with the majesty
     of kingship, listened respectfully to Bhishma's
     advice, and then made the great honor offering in
     the presence of all the kings. So Krishna, the enemy
     of Madhu, never required such an offering again
     anywhere in the universe.

CHAPTER 15

Shishupala's Anger

अथ तत्र पाण्डुतनयेन
सदसि विहितं मधुद्विषो ।
मानमसहत न चेदिपतिः
परवृद्धिमत्सरि मनो हि मानिनाम् ॥

पुर एव शार्ङ्गिणि सवैर-
मथ पुनरमुं तदर्चया ।
मन्युरभजदवगाढतरः
समदोषकाल इव देहिनं ज्वरः ॥

अभितर्जयन्निव॰ समस्त-
नृपगणमसावकम्पयत् ।
लोलमुकुटमणिरश्मि शनै-
रशनैः प्रकम्पितजगत्त्रयं शिरः ॥

स वमन्नुषासु घनघर्म-
विगलदुरुगण्डमण्डलः ।
स्वेदजलकणकरालकरो
निरभात्प्रभिन्न इव कुञ्जरस्त्रिधा ॥

५ सनिकामघर्मितमभीक्ष्ण-
मधुवदवधूतराजकः ।
क्षिप्तबहलजलबिन्दु वपुः
प्रलयार्णवोत्थित इवादिसूकरः ॥

482

But Shishupala, lord of the Chedis, could not endure the
respect shown in that gathering to Krishna, the enemy
of Madhu, by Yudhishthira, son of Pandu. When
others prosper, the self-absorbed harbor envious
thoughts.

A deep rage possessed him because of the honor proffered
to Krishna, in previous births his foe. So fever grips
a man when the state of his bodily humors and a due
period of incubation coincide.

He slowly tossed his head, as if threatening all the kings.
The jewels flashed in his crown, and the whole
universe immediately trembled.

As he wept tears of rage, thick drops of perspiration
poured down his high cheeks, and beads of sweat
stood out on his hands—he looked like an elephant
with ichor streaming from three different parts of its
body.[1]

Ignoring the assembled kings, he went on shaking his   5
burning body, throwing off a thick spray of sweat, like
the primal Boar risen from the ocean when the world
ends.

क्षणमाश्लिषद्घटितशैल-
शिखरकठिनांसमण्डलः ।
स्तम्भमुपहितविधूनिमसा-
वधिकावधूनितसमस्तसंसदम् ॥

कनकाङ्गदद्युतिभिरस्य
गमितमरुचत्पिशङ्गताम् ।
क्रोधमयशिखिशिखापटलैः
परितः परीतमिव बाहुमण्डलम् ॥

कृतसन्निधानमिव तस्य
पुनरपि तृतीयचक्षुषा ।
क्रूरमजनि कुटिलभ्रु गुरु-
भ्रुकुटीकठोरितललाटमाननम् ॥

अतिरक्तभावमुपगम्य
कृतमतिरमुष्य साहसे ।
दृष्टिरगणितभयासिलता-
मवलम्बते स्म समया सखीमिव ॥

१०   करकुड्मलेन निजमूरु-
मुरुतरनगाश्मकर्कशम् ।
त्रस्तचपलवलमानजन-
श्रुतभीमनादमयमाहतोच्चकैः ॥

Flexing shoulders hard as lofty mountain, Shishupala
    seized the hall's central pillar and shook it, making the
    entire building shudder.

His muscular biceps glowed yellow from the rays from his
    golden armlets, as if enveloped by the flames of his
    fiery anger.

He took on a cruel look, his brows arching, his forehead
    furrowed as though a third eye had been placed there
    again.[2]

His face became flushed, for he was turning his thoughts
    to a desperate enterprise without reckoning the
    danger involved. He stared intently at the sword at
    his side, as a woman bent on amorous adventure puts
    away all apprehension and glances meaningfully at her
    confidante.[3]

With his fist he noisily struck his thigh, hard as a great slab   10
    of mountain rock; on hearing the terrible sound, all
    scattered in fear and consternation.

इति चुक्रुधे भृशमनेन
ननु महदवाप्य विप्रियम् ।
याति विकृतिमपि संवृतिम्-
त्किमु यन्निसर्गनिरवग्रहं मनः ॥

प्रथमं शरीरजविकार-
कृतमुकुलबन्धनमव्यथी ।
भाविकलहफलयोगमसौ
वचनेन कोपकुसुमं व्यचीकसत् ॥

ध्वनयन्सभामथ सनीर-
घनरवगभीरवागभीः ।
वाचमवददिति रोषवशा-
मतिनिष्ठुरस्फुटतराक्षरामसौ ॥

यदपूपुजस्त्वमिह पार्थ
मुरजितमपूजितं सताम् ।
प्रेम विलसति महत्तदहो
दयितं जनः खलु गुणीति मन्यते ॥२

१५ यदराज्ञि राजवदिहार्घ्य-
मुपहितमिदं मुरद्विषि ।
ग्राम्यमृग इव हविस्तदयं
भजते ज्वलत्सु न महीशवह्निषु ॥

In short, he was quite beside himself with fury. Apprehen-
ding an unpleasant fact disturbs even a mind under
control, let alone when it is naturally undisciplined.

Without wavering, Shishupala now began to speak,
opening wide the flower of his anger; its buds had
already appeared as physical reactions to his inner
feelings, and it was soon to blossom in the form of
conflict.

This is what he said to Yudhishthira in his rage, fearlessly,
rousing echoes throughout the assembly hall, his tone
deep as a storm cloud's thundering, enunciating every
syllable sharply and clearly.

"Son of Pritha, the honor you have shown here to Krishna,
the conqueror of Mura, someone whom decent people
do not respect, simply demonstrates your excessive
partiality for him. Everyone thinks the one he loves is
the most attractive.

Krishna is not a true ruler, but you have given him the   15
honor offering as if he were.[4] When real kings,
lustrous as sacrificial fires, are actually present, he no
more merits the distinction than a cur deserves the
oblation.

अनृतां गिरं न गदसीति
जगति पटहैर्विघुष्यसे ।
निन्द्यमथ च हरिमर्चयत-
स्तव कर्मणैव विकसत्यसत्यता ॥

तव धर्मराज इति नाम
कथमिदमपष्टु पठ्यते ।
भौमदिनमभिदधत्यथ वा
भृशमप्रशस्तमपि मङ्गलं जनाः ॥

यदि वार्चनीयतम एष
किमपि भवतां पृथासुताः ।
शौरिरवनिपतिभिर्निखिलै-
रवमाननार्थमिह किं निमन्त्रितैः ॥

अथ वा धर्ममसुबोध-
समयमवयात बालिशाः ।
काममयमिह वृथापलितो
हतबुद्धिरप्रणिहितः सरित्सुतः ॥

२० स्वयमेव शन्तनुतनूज
यमपि गणमर्घ्यैभ्यधाः ।
तत्र मुररिपुरयं कतमो
यमनिन्द्यबन्दिवदभिष्टुषे वृथा ॥

You proclaim with great fanfare throughout the world that
you never utter an untrue word. However, in paying
homage to the odious Krishna your actions reveal your
insincerity.

How can the patent falsehood that you are a righteous
king be so widely believed? Still, I suppose that the
world at large persists in calling unlucky Tuesday
auspicious.[5]

Listen, you other sons of Pritha! If Krishna was going to
be honored from the start, why did you invite all these
kings here and then treat them with contempt?

But should I be surprised? The precepts defining proper
behavior are complicated at the best of times, and you
idiots have certainly not grasped them. Bhishma, son
of Ganga, has not derived any benefit from his gray
hair; he has lost his wits and cannot think straight
about this matter.

You yourself specified the types of individual deserving   20
of the honor, Bhishma.[6] So which one of them is
represented by the enemy of Mura on whom you
lavish such misplaced praise, like a hired bard in full
cry?

अवनीभृतां त्वमपहाय
गणमतिजडः समुन्नतम् ।
नीचि नियतमिह यच्चपलो
निरतः स्फुटं भवसि निम्नगासुतः ॥

प्रतिपत्तुमङ्ग घटते च
न तव नृपयोग्यमर्हणम् ।
कृष्ण कलय ननु को ऽहमिति
स्फुटमापदां पदमनात्मवेदिता ॥

असुरस्त्वया न्यवधि को ऽपि
मधुरिति कथं प्रतीयते ।
दण्डदलितसरघः प्रथसे
मधुसूदनस्त्वमिति सूदयन्मधु ॥

मुचकुन्दतल्पशरणस्य
मगधपतिशातितौजसः ।
सिद्धमबल सबलत्वमहो
तव रोहिणीतनयसाहचर्यतः ॥

२५ छलयन्प्रजास्त्वमनृतेन
कपटपटुरैन्द्रजालिकः ।
प्रीतिमनुभवसि नग्नजितः
सुतयेष्टसत्य इति संप्रतीयसे ॥

You are a rash fool to spurn these distinguished rulers and
    take the part of somebody of no rank. It's obvious
    you are the offspring of a river—chilly and incapable
    of reaching lofty heights, while continually veering
    toward anything low and base.[7]

Come on now, Krishna! It is simply wrong of you to receive
    an honor appropriate for a king. Just think about who
    you actually are. Lack of self-knowledge invariably
    ends in ruin.

And does anyone really believe that you killed some sort
    of honey monster called Madhu? You got the moniker
    'Honey Squeezer' because you shooed away bees
    with a stick and put the squeeze on—the contents of a
    honeycomb![8]

You fled for refuge beneath Muchukunda's couch,[9] while
    Jarasandha, king of Magadha, got the better of you.[10]
    Any power you might possess depends on your
    connection with Balarama, son of Rohini.[11]

You lie and deceive; you are a con man, a trickster, a cheap   25
    showman! You are perceived as sincere simply because
    Satya, daughter of Nagnajit, became your true love.[12]

धृतवान्न चक्रमरिचक्र-
भयचकितमाहवे निजम् ।
चक्रधर इति रथाङ्गमदः
सततं बिभर्षि भुवेनषु रूढये ॥

जगति श्रिया विरहितो ऽपि
यदुदधिसुतामुपायथाः ।
ज्ञातिजनजनितनामपदां
त्वमतः श्रियः पतिरिति प्रथामगाः ॥

अभिशत्रु संयति कदाचि-
द्विहितपराक्रमो ऽपि यत् ।
व्योम्नि कथमपि चकर्थ पदं
व्यपदिश्यते जगति विक्रमीत्यतः ॥

पृथिवीं बिभर्थ यदि पूर्व-
मिदमपि गुणाय वर्तते ।
भूमिभृदिति परहारितभू-
स्त्वमुदाहियस्व कथमन्यथा जनैः ॥

३० तव धन्यतेयमपि सर्व-
नृपतितुलितो ऽपि यत्क्षणम् ।
क्रान्तकरतलधृताचलकः
पृथिवीतले तुलितभूभृदुच्यसे ॥

When you are on the battlefield, you are not shielded
by a circle of allies—they are too terrified of being
surrounded by enemy hosts! It is only because you
always carry that round discus that you are popularly
known as one who turns the wheels of power.[13]

Although lacking any regal dignity,[14] you somehow
contrived to marry the daughter of the ocean.[15] It was
her relatives who gave her the glorious name of 'Shri';
it was this marital connection alone that made you
known as majesty's lord.[16]

You have never displayed any conspicuous gallantry in
combat with your enemies, but after managing to take
just a single step in the sky you became known as the
'brave strider.'[17]

Supposing you did once lift up the earth, then all to the
good! How else could you be called a ruler who bears
the world[18] when you have been stripped of your
realm by your foes?[19]

And since every king has vanquished you, it must have   30
been through some past merit that you could hold a
tiny hillock for a second in your trembling hand. This
is what led to you being widely called 'the mountain
lifter!'[20]

त्वमशक्नुवन्नशुभकर्म-
निरत परिपाकदारुणम् ।
जेतुमकुशलमतिर्नरकं
यशसे ऽधिलोकमजयः सुतं भुवः ॥

सकलैर्वपुः सकलदोष-
समुदितमिदं गुणैस्तव ।
व्यक्तमपगुण गुणत्रितय-
त्यजनप्रयासमुपयासि किं मुधा ॥

त्वयि पूजनं जगति जाल्म
कृतमिदमपाकृते गुणैः ।
हासकरमघटते नितरां
शिरसीव कङ्कतमपेतमूर्धजे ॥

मृगविद्विषामिव यदित्थ-
मजनि मिषतां पृथासुतैः ।
अस्य वनशुन इवापचितिः
परिभाव एव भवतां भुवो ऽधिपाः ॥

३५ अवधीज्जनङ्गम इवैष
यदि हतवृषो वृषं ननु ।
स्पर्शमशुचिवपुरर्हति न
प्रतिमाननां तु नितरां नृपोचिताम् ॥

You are devoted to dark deeds but lack the wit to escape
   hell, the terrible outcome of every evil action. So
   instead, to gain notoriety, you got the better of the
   demon Naraka.[21]

Good-for-nothing! You exemplify every possible fault
   and lack any worthwhile qualities. Why make futile
   efforts to cast off the three natural forces in hope of
   liberation?[22]

Buffoon! The reverence offered by the world to your
   mediocrity is as big a joke as combing a bald head.

You kings! While you look on impassively like lions, the
   sons of Kunti* have honored one who is no better than
   a jackal. This is an insult to you.

If Krishna really did abandon any sense of morality and,   35
   like a casteless butcher, slaughter a bull,[23] then he is
   an untouchable and all should avoid him. He certainly
   does not merit the respect befitting rulers.

---

* The Pandava brothers.

यदि नाङ्गनेति मतिरस्य
मृदुरजनि पूतनां प्रति ।
स्तन्यमघृणमनसः पिबतः
किल धर्मतो भवति सा जनन्यपि ॥

शकटव्युदासतरुभङ्ग-
धरणिधरधारणादिकम् ।
कर्म यदयमकरोत्तरलः
स्थिरचेतसां क इव तेन विस्मयः ॥

अयमुग्रसेनतनयस्य
नृपशुरपरः पशूनवन् ।
स्वामिवधमसुकरं पुरुषैः
कुरुते स्म यत्परममेतदद्भुतम् ॥

इति वाचमुद्धतमुदीर्य
सपदि सह वेणुदारिणा ।
सोढरिपुभरबलोऽसहनः
स जहास दत्तकरतालमुच्चकैः ॥

४० कटुनापि चैद्यवचनेन
विकृतिमगमन्न माधवः ।
सत्यनियतवचसं वचसः
सुजनं जनाश्चलयितुं क ईशते³ ॥

He never showed any fine feeling toward Putana, despite
    the fact she was female. And just consider this—as
    he pitilessly sucked her life from her breast, she had
    thereby legally become his mother![24]

Overturning a wagon, knocking down trees, and lifting up
    a mountain—what levelheaded person is impressed by
    these childish actions?[25]

It is his beastliness that makes him unique. While
    guarding Kamsa's cattle, he killed his employer,[26]
    something that no normal person would do. That is
    the real miracle he performed!"

Grim and relentless, Shishupala finished his arrogant
    tirade and gave a great laugh, slapping Venudarin's*
    palms in glee.

But Krishna was undisturbed by Shishupala's speech,   40
    bitter though it had been. Who can say anything
    to disconcert a virtuous man whose words embody
    truth?

---

* A follower of Shishupala's.

न च तं तदेति शपमान-
मपि यदुनृपाः प्रचुक्रुधुः ।
शौरिसमयनिगृहीतधियः
प्रभुचित्तमेव हि जनो ऽनुवर्तते ॥

विहितागसो मुहुरलङ्घ्य-
निजवचनदामसंयतः ।
तस्य कतिथ इति तत्प्रथमं
मनसा समाख्यदपराधमच्युतः ॥

स्मृतिवर्त्म तस्य न सम-
स्तमपकृतमियाय विद्विषः ।
स्मर्तुमधिगतगुणस्मरणाः
पटवो न दोषमखिलं खलूत्तमाः ॥

नृपतावधिक्षिपति शौरि-
मथ सुरसरित्सुतो वचः ।
स्माह चलयति भुवं मरुति
क्षुभितस्य नादमनुकुर्वदम्बुधेः ॥

४५ अथ गौरवेण परिवाद-
मपरिगणयंस्तमात्मनः ।
प्राह मुररिपुतिरस्करण-
क्षुभितः स्म वाचमिति जाह्नवीसुतः४ ॥

And the Yadava princes too were not angry with Shishu-
pala. Although he had just uttered such execrations,
their reaction was governed by Krishna's pledge to
be tolerant of him.[27] Servants follow the will of their
lord.

Krishna was certainly restrained by the bond of his
unbreakable promise, but he still turned the
insult over in his mind to see where it stood in the
enumeration of the many offenses already committed
against him.

However, he could not call to mind his enemy's
misdemeanors. The excellent readily remember
virtues but do not recollect every fault.

When Shishupala was finished with abusing Krishna,
Bhishma, son of Ganga, replied to him in tones like
the ocean's booming when tempest batters the earth
on doomsday.

Natural dignity led him to ignore the personal insult   45
directed at him, but he was infuriated by Shishupala's
contempt for Krishna and so could not remain silent.

विहितं मयाद्य सदसीद-
मपमृषितमच्युतार्चनं ।
यस्य नमयतु स चापमयं
चरणः कृतः शरसि सर्वभूभृताम् ॥

इति भीष्मभाषितवचो ऽर्थ-
मधिगतवतामिव क्षणात् ।
क्षोभमगमदतिमात्रमथो
शिशुपालपक्ष्यपृथिवीभृतां गणः ॥

शितितारकानुमितताम्र-
नयनमरुणीकृतं क्रुधा ।
बाणवदनमुददीपि भिये
जगतः सकीलमिव सूर्यमण्डलम् ॥

अनिशान्तवैरदहनेन
विरहितवतान्तरार्द्रताम् ।
कोपमरुदभिहतेन भृशं
नरकात्मजेन तरुणेन जज्वले ॥

५० अभिधित्सतः किमपि राहु-
वदनविकृतं व्यभाव्यत ।
ग्रस्तशशधरमिवोपलस-
त्सितदन्तपङ्क्ति मुखमुत्तमौजसः ॥

"I have offered honor to Krishna today in this assembly
   hall. Let anyone who rejects what I have done bend his
   bow in battle. I will be ready to crush any such king!"

The kings loyal to Shishupala all seemed to grasp in an
   instant that Bhishma's remark referred to them, and
   they immediately became outraged.

Bana's face flushed with anger, and the presence of eyes
   there could only be inferred from their dark pupils;
   its glow was enough to cause universal consternation,
   like the sun's disc when marked with dark spots.

As the son of Naraka, Hayagriva had long ago lost any
   personal warmth toward Krishna, the killer of his
   father,[28] and now his undimmed enmity stoked by
   anger caught fire like a blazing tree fanned by the
   wind.

Uttamaujas's teeth flashed white in his mouth as he   50
   opened it to retort; it looked as terrifying as Rahu's
   gaping maw after he has devoured the moon.

प्रविदारितारुणतरोग्र-
नयनकुसुमोज्ज्वलः स्फुरन् ।
प्रातरहिमकरताम्ररुचि-
विषविद्रुमो ऽपर इवाभवद्द्रुमः ॥

कुपिताकृतिं प्रथममेव
हसितमशनैरसूचयत् ।
क्रुद्धमशनिदलिताद्रितट-
ध्वनि दन्तवक्रमरिचक्रभीषणम् ॥

प्रतिघः कुतो ऽपि समुपेत्य
नरपतिगणं समाश्रयत् ।
जामिहरणजनितो ऽनुशयः
समुदाचचार निज एव रुक्मिणः ॥

चरणेन हन्ति सुबलः स्म
शिथिलितमहीध्रबन्धनाम् ।
तीरतरलजलराशिजला-
मवभुग्रभोगिफणमण्डलां भुवम् ॥

५५ रुषितेषु राजसु तथापि
रथचरणपाणिपूजया ।
चित्तकलितकलहागमनो
मुदमाह्वृतिः५ सुहृदिवाधिकां दधौ ॥

Druma's eyes were bulging in a bloodshot glare like
     crimson blossoms. He blazed with indignation, red as
     morning sunrays, like a new type of poison tree.[29]

A laugh could be heard, grating like a mountain
     escarpment split open by a thunderbolt—Dantavakra,
     the terror of his enemies, had at first only appeared
     angry but was now truly enraged.

Wrath arose from nowhere and overwhelmed these kings.
     But hatred of a different order consumed Rukmin,
     for it had been caused by Krishna making off with his
     sister.[30]

Subala stamped his foot on the ground and destabilized
     the mountains binding the earth together like thongs.
     He made the ocean's waters overflow its shores and
     crash over the hoods of the serpent Shesha, already
     bending under the strain of supporting the earth.

Although these kings were so outraged by the honor   55
     shown to Krishna, Bhishmaka was actually overjoyed,
     for he recognized imminent conflict as if he were its
     friend.

गुरुकोपरुद्धपदमाप-
दसितयवनस्य रौद्रताम् ।
व्यात्तमशितुमिव सर्वजग-
द्विकरालमास्यकुहरं विवक्षतः ॥

विवृढोरुबाहुपरिघेन
सरभसपदं निपित्सता ।
हन्तुमखिलनृपतीन्वसुना
वसने ऽवलम्बिनि निजे विचस्खले ॥

इति तत्तदा विकृतरूप-
मभजदविभिन्नचेतसम् ।
मारबलमिव भयङ्करतां
हरिबोधिसत्त्वमभि राजमण्डलम् ॥

रभसादुदस्थुरथ युद्ध-
मनुचितभियो ऽभिलाषुकाः ।
सान्द्रमुकुटकिरणोच्छलित-
स्फटिकांशवः सपदि मेदिनीभृतः ॥

६० स्फुरमाणनेत्रकुसुमोष्ठ-
दलमभृत भूभृदङ्घ्रिपैः ।
धूतपृथुभुजलतं चलितै-
र्द्रुतवातवानवनविभ्रमं सदः ॥

504

Kalayavana bared his teeth in his cavernous mouth, as
   though about to devour the world. His deep anger
   stopped his words in his throat when he tried to speak,
   and he became a terrifying sight.

Vasu threw up his huge club-like arms, intending to fall
   upon all Krishna's royal followers immediately and
   kill them—but it was his robe that fell down, and he
   tripped over it.[31]

In all such ways the host of kings gave vent to their
   emotions and menaced the impassive Krishna. They
   were like the demonic army of Mara,[32] magically
   changing shape to threaten the Buddha-to-be as he
   meditated serenely.[33]

Immediately they sprang up, strangers to fear, eager for
   battle, as shafts of light flashing from the crystal walls
   of the hall shot upward to merge with the dense rays
   from their crowns.

These excited princes transformed the assembly hall into   60
   a forest with a storm raging through it. They could be
   taken for waving trees, their twitching eyes and lips
   the shaking flowers and leaves, their long trembling
   arms the vine tendrils blown by the wind.

505

हरिमप्यमंसत तृणाय
कुरुपतिमजीगणन्न वा ।
मानतुलितभुवनत्रितयाः
सरितः सुतादबिभयुर्न भूभुजः ॥

गुरु निःश्वसन्नथ विलोल-
सदवथुवपुर्वचोविषम् ।
कीर्णदशनकिरणाग्निकणः
फणवानिवेति विससर्ज चेदिपः ॥

किमहो नृपाः समममीभि-
रुपपतिसुतैर्न पञ्चभिः ।
वध्यमभिहथ भुजिष्यममुं
सह चानया स्थविरराजकन्यया ॥

विदतुर्यमुत्तममशेष-
परिषदि नदीजधर्मजौ ।
यातु निकषमधियुद्ध्मसौ
वचनेन किं भवति साध्वसाधु वा ॥

६५ अचिरान्मया सह गतस्य
समरमुरगारिलक्ष्मणः ।
तीक्ष्णविशिखमुखपीतमसृ-
क्पततां गणैः पिबतु साकमुर्वरा ॥

506

Their arrogance was as vast as the universe; they did not
    reckon Krishna worth a straw, while they despised
    Yudhishthira, king of the Kurus, and had no fear at all
    of Bhishma, Ganga's son.

Then Shishupala, hissing loudly, spat out these venomous
    words like a snake. His body swayed and glowed,
    scattering the rays from his teeth like sparks.

"Royal comrades, this slave deserves to die, and you
    should kill him along with these five Pandava bastards
    and this old maid of a warrior, Bhishma.[34]

The sons of Ganga and Dharma* reckon Krishna to be
    supreme among this entire assembly, so let him put it
    to the test in battle. Nothing, good or bad, comes from
    words alone.

When Krishna of the Garuda ensign faces me in combat,   65
    may the earth and carrion birds drink his blood
    already sipped by the points of my sharp arrows!"

---

* Bhishma and Yudhishthira.

अभिधाय रूक्षमिति मा स्म
गम इति पृथासुतेरिताम् ।
वाचमनुनयपरां स ततः
सहसावगण्य निरियाय संसदः ॥

गृहमागताय कृपया च
कथमपि निसर्गदक्षिणाः ।
क्षान्तिमहितमनसो जननी-
स्वसुरात्मजाय चुकुपुर्न पाण्डवाः ॥

चलितं ततो ऽनभिहतेच्छ-
मवनिपतियज्ञभूमितः ।
तूर्णमथ ययुमिवानुययु-
र्दमघोषसूनुमवनीशसूनवः ॥

विशिखान्तराण्यतिपपात
सपदि जवनैः स वाजिभिः ।
द्रष्टुमलघुरभसापतिता
वनिताश्वकार न सकामचेतसः ॥

७० क्षणमीक्षितः पथि जनेन
किमिदमिति जल्पता मिथः ।
प्राप्य शिविरमविशङ्किमनाः
समनीनहद्द्रुतमनीकिनीमसौ ॥

So Shishupala ferociously spoke and immediately left
    the assembly, ignoring Yudhishthira's conciliatory
    invitation to remain.

The Pandavas for their part were naturally gracious and
    of a generous disposition, but only pity made them
    restrain their anger toward the son of their mother's
    sister as he returned home.

His royal followers had to rush after Shishupala, son
    of Damaghosha, for he had left impetuously, like
    a sacrificial horse galloping from a king's ritual
    enclosure.[35]

At once he flew over the intervening roads with his swift
    stallions, frustrating women hurrying in excitement to
    see him.

Bystanders could only catch a brief glimpse and asked   70
    each other what the commotion was. Finally he
    reached his camp and straightaway issued a curt
    command to his forces to take up arms.

त्वरमाणशाङ्किकसवेग-
वदनपवनाभिपूरितः ।
शैलकटकतटभिन्नरवः
प्रणनाद सांनहनिको ऽस्य वारिजः ॥

जगदन्तकालसमवेत-
विषदविषमेरितारवम् ।
धीरनिजरवविलीनगुरु-
प्रतिशब्दमस्य रणतूर्यमावधि ॥

सहसा च संभ्रमविलोल-
सकलजनतासमाकुलम् ।
स्थानमगमदथ तत्परित-
श्चलितोडुमण्डलनभस्तलोपमाम् ॥

दधतो भयानकतरत्व-
मुपगतवतः समानताम् ।
धूमपटलपिहितस्य गिरेः
समवर्मयन्सपदि मेदिनीभृतः ॥

७५ परिमोहिणा परिजनेन
कथमपि चिरादुपाहृतम् ।
वर्म करतलयुगेन बृह-
त्तनुचूर्णपेषमपिषद्रुषा परः ॥

The trumpeter, now on the alert, filled his conch shell
with a forceful breath, and the call to muster blared
out, echoing through the uplands and valleys of the
mountains.

Shishupala's battle drums were struck up, thundering as
terribly as the lowering storm clouds at doomsday,
their deep echo muffled by their own rumbling.

Immediately the encampment was crowded with people
bustling around in excitement; it looked like the
heavens thronged with constellations of whirling
stars.

The princes at once donned their armor, like mountains
swathed in clouds of black smoke, terrible to behold.

When after some delay one warrior was presented with his   75
heavy armor by a flustered attendant, he pulverized it
with his bare hands in impatient fury.

रणसंमदोदयविकासि-
बलकलकलाकुलीकृते ।
शारिमतरदधिरोपयितुं
द्विरदे मदश्च्युति जनः कथञ्चन ॥

परितश्च धौतमुखरुक्म-
विलसदहिमांशुमण्डलाः ।
तेनुरतनुवपुषः पृथिवीं
स्फुटमलक्ष्यतेजस इवात्मजाः श्रियः ॥

प्रधिमण्डलोद्धतपराग-
घनवलयमध्यवर्तिनः ।
पेतुरशनय इवाशनकै-
र्गुरुनिस्वनव्यथितजन्तवो रथाः ॥

दधतः शशाङ्कितशशाङ्क-
रुचि लसदुरश्छदं वपुः ।
चक्रुरथ सह पुरन्ध्रिजनै-
रयथार्थसिद्धिसरकं महीभृतः ॥

८० दयिताय सासवमुदस्त-
मपतदवसादिनः करात् ।
कांस्यमुपहितसरोजपत-
द्ध्रमरौघभारगुरु राजयोषितः ॥

512

Only with a struggle could protective armor be attached to
    an elephant pouring forth ichor; it had been disturbed
    by the army's uproar, rising in a crescendo as battle
    approached.

Mighty chargers, the goddess Lakshmi's offspring,[36]
    raced all round the encampment; the sun's energy
    was almost palpable within them as it flashed on their
    bright golden muzzle guards.

Chariots, engulfed by thick clouds of dust thrown up
    by their wheels, terrified everyone with their deep
    rumble as they flew along, swift as thunderbolts.

The princes, now wearing gleaming breastplates so that
    each looked like the moon overlaid by its hare mark,[37]
    took a good luck drink with their consorts, though it
    was to have no effect.

The wife of one warrior proffered a cup of wine to her   80
    beloved, but it was weighed down by bees flying into
    the lotus floating within and fell from her enfeebled
    hand.[38]

भृशमङ्गसादमरुणत्व-
मविशादृशः कपोलयोः ।
वाक्यमसकलमपास्य मदं
विदधुस्तदीयगुणमात्मना शुचः ॥

सुदृशः समीकगमनाय
युवभिरथ संबभाषिरे ।
शोकपिहितगलरुद्धगिर-
स्तरसागतासुजलकेवलोत्तराः ॥

विपुलाचलस्थलघनेन
जिगमिषुभिरङ्गनाः प्रियैः ।
पीनकुचतटनिपीडदल-
द्द्रवारबाणमुरसालिलिङ्गिरे ॥

न मुमोच लोचनजलानि
दयितजयमङ्गलैषिणी ।
यातमवनिमवसन्नभुजा-
न्न गलद्विवेद वलयं विलासिनी ॥

८५ प्रविवित्सतः प्रियतमस्य
निगडमिव चक्षुरक्षिपत् ।
नीलनलिनदलदामरुचि
प्रतिपादयुग्ममचिरोढसुन्दरी ॥

514

Another woman had given way to tears, so her pangs of
grief kept wine's influence at bay; yet her weeping had
the same effect—total listlessness, flushed cheeks, and
incoherent speech.[39]

When the young warriors took their leave to go off to
battle, their wives' words were stopped in their grief-
choked throats, and they replied simply with floods of
tears.

The women were embraced by their husbands on the point
of departing, but when those warriors pressed them to
their chests broad and hard as mountain slopes, their
splendid armor split open from the pressure of their
firm breasts.

One beautiful woman held back her tears, since she
desired the good luck that would bring victory for her
beloved. She did not notice that her bangles had fallen
off as her arms hung down in grief.[40]

A newly married beauty cast a glance, dark as a chain of   85
lotus petals, toward the feet of her husband, as if to
fetter him while he prepared to leave.

व्रजतः क्व तात वजसीति
परिचयगतार्थमस्फुटम् ।
धैर्यमभिनदुदितं शिशुना
जननीनिभर्त्सनविवृद्धमन्युना ॥

शठ नाकलोकललनाभि-
रविरतरसं रिरंससे ।
तेन वहसि मुदमित्यवद-
द्रणरागिणं रमणमीर्ष्ययापरा ॥

ध्रियमाणमप्यगलदसु
चलति दयिते नतभ्रुवः ।
स्नेहमकृतकरसं दधता-
मिदमेव युक्तमतिमुग्धचेतसाम् ॥

सह कज्जलेन विरराज
नयनकमलाम्बुसंततिः ।
गण्डफलकमभितः सुतनोः
पदवीव शोकमयकृष्णवर्त्मनः ॥

९० क्षणमात्ररोधि गलितेन
कतिपयपदं नतभ्रुवः ।
स्रस्तभुजयुगगलद्वलय-
स्वनितं प्रतिक्षिपदिवोपशुश्रुवे ॥

A wailing child had been scolded by his mother and was
    turning still more petulant. When he wept, "Daddy,
    where you koing?" his father, long familiar with his
    son's way of talking, lost his resolve to depart.

Another woman jealously addressed her husband, who
    was eager for battle: "You cheat! You just want to
    spend an eternity making love with apsarases in
    heaven. That's why you are so pleased to be off!"[41]

Although she was restraining her tears, a beautiful girl still
    sobbed as her beloved departed. This reaction comes
    naturally to the artless, since their love is totally
    sincere.

Another woman's cheeks were marked with traces of tears
    and kohl, like a dark path blazed by grief's flame.

A warrior had only taken a few paces as he left, but when   90
    he heard the jingle of the ornaments falling from
    his wife's powerless arms,[42] he was held back for an
    instant as if by a reproach.

अनुवर्त्म वल्लभतमस्य
विगलदमलायतांशुकम् ।
भूमिनभसि रभसेन यती
विरराज काचन समं महोल्कया ॥

समरोन्मुखे नृपगणे ऽपि
तदनुसरणोद्यतैकधीः ।
दीनपरिजनकृतासुजलो
न भटीजनः स्थिरमना विचक्लवे ॥

विदुषीव दर्शनममुष्य
युवतिरतिदुर्लभं पुनः ।
यान्तमनिमिषमतृप्तमनाः
पतिमीक्षते स्म भृशमा दृशः पथः ॥

संप्रत्युपेयाः कुशली पुनर्युधः
सस्नेहमाशीरिति भर्तुरीरिता ।
सद्यः प्रसह्य द्वितयेन नेत्रयोः
प्रत्याचचक्षे गलता भटस्त्रिया ॥

One woman rushing after her beloved with the bright train
of her skirt trailing in her wake looked like a comet
flying across the sky.[43]

Although the kings were bent on battle, their warrior
wives did not lose heart, for they had loyally resolved
to die after them on the funeral pyre, despite the
lamentation of their unhappy servants.

As her beloved went off to war, a young woman's
unblinking gaze followed him as far as her eye could
reach. But she was in no way gratified, apparently
aware that it would be difficult ever to catch sight of
him again.

Another warrior's wife gave her husband a loving farewell
blessing, bidding him return immediately, unscathed
from the battle. This was set at naught by her eyes
breaking into a flood of tears.

९५ कांचित्कीर्णा रजोभिर्दिवमनुविदधौ मन्दवक्रेन्दुलक्ष्मी-
रश्रीकाः कश्चिदन्तर्दिश इव दधिरे दाहमुद्भ्रान्तसत्त्वाः ।
भ्रेमुर्वर्त्या इवान्याः प्रतिपदमपरा भूमिवत्कम्पमाप
प्रस्थाने पार्थिवानामशुभमिति पुरोभावि नार्यः शशंसुः ॥

One woman poured earth over herself;[44] her face no longer   95
possessed any allure, appearing like a wan moon in
a dust-clogged sky. Other women, now lacking any
gracefulness, were consumed by grief and lost their
will, as when a raging fire strips an entire forest of its
luxuriant foliage and animals flee in terror.[45] Some
roamed aimlessly as the wind blows, while others
trembled with every step they took as if the earth were
quaking. So their wives signaled the ill fortune in store
when Shishupala's followers went forth to war.

CHAPTER 16

The Emissary from Shishupala

दमघोषसुतेन कश्चन
प्रतिशिष्टः प्रतिभानवानथ ।
उपगम्य हरिं सदस्यदः
स्फुटभिन्नार्थमुदाहरद्वचः ॥

अभिधाय तदा तदप्रियं
शिशुपालो ऽनुशयं परं गतः ।
भवतो ऽभिमनाः समीहते
सरुषः कर्तुमुपेत्य माननाम् ॥

विपुलेन निपीड्य निर्दयं
मुदमायातु नितान्तमुन्मनाः ।
प्रचुराधिगताङ्गनिर्वृतिं
परितस्त्वां खलु विग्रहेण सः ॥

प्रणतः शिरसा करिष्यते
सकलैरेत्य समं नराधिपैः ।
तव शासनमाशु भूपतिः
परवानद्य यतस्त्वयैव सः ॥

५   अधिवह्निपतङ्गतेजसो
नियतस्वान्तसमर्थकर्मणः ।
तव सर्वविधेयवर्तिनः
प्रणतिं बिभ्रति के न भूभृतः ॥

524

Then an emissary, instructed by Shishupala,
    Damaghosha's son, came to Krishna in the assembly
    hall. He was a man crafty with words and his message
    was ambiguous, as everybody realized.[1]

His message to Krishna appeared to be this:
    "Earlier Shishupala spoke aggressively, but he has
        now become full of regret. He sincerely wishes to
        come and pay his respects to you, for you must be
        angry with him.

He is impatient to experience the genuine delight of
    clasping you tightly in his strong embrace. May you
    feel equal enthusiasm.

King Shishupala has received homage from all rulers
    united together. But he will immediately carry out
    your command, for it is you who are now his overlord.

Are there any kings owing you fealty who refuse to pay   5
    obeisance? Your luster is greater than fire or the sun,
    while your deeds fully match your ambitions.

जनतां भयशून्यधीः परै-
रभिभूतामवलम्बसे यतः ।
तव कृष्ण गुणास्ततो नरै-
रसमानस्य दधत्यगण्यताम् ॥

अहितादनपत्रपस्त्रस-
न्नतिमात्रोज्झितभीरनास्तिकः ।
विनयोपहितः कुतस्त्वया
सदृशो ऽन्यो गुणवानविस्मयः ॥

कृतगोपवधूरतेर्व्रतो
वृषमुग्रे नरके ऽपि संप्रति ।
प्रतिपत्तिरधःकृतैनसो
जनताभिस्तव साधु वर्ण्यते ॥

विहितापचितिर्महीभुजा
द्विषतामाहितसाध्वसो बलैः ।
भव सानुचरस्त्वमुच्चकै-
र्महतामप्युपरि क्षमाभृताम् ॥

१० घनजालनिभैर्दुरासदाः
परितो नागकदम्बकैस्तव ।
नगरेषु भवन्तु वीथयः
परिकीर्णा वनजैर्मृगादिभिः ॥

Fearlessly you support the world when oppressed by
enemies, Krishna. For that reason your merits are
unrivaled among men and beyond reckoning.

Another might be virtuous, unashamed of dreading evil,
supremely valiant, affirming the traditional order
of things, disciplined in behavior, and with no sense
of pride. Nonetheless, despite these attributes, how
could he truly be your equal?

You may have made love to cowherd girls and killed
the buffalo demon,[2] but no sin accrued to you from
these deeds. Your bravery in the face of yet another
ferocious demon, Naraka, is now everywhere
acclaimed.[3]

As one honored by King Shishupala, you can instill fear
in your enemies with your strength in arms. May you
and your followers be exalted above other rulers,
however great.

May the avenues of your capital be a haven of security,   10
thronged with troops of elephants like banks of rain
clouds, teeming with tame forest animals of every
kind.

सकलापिहितस्वपौरुषो
नियतव्यापदवर्धितोदयः ।
रिपुरुन्नतधीरचेतसः
सततव्याधिरनीतिरस्तु ते ॥

विकचोत्पलचारुलोचन-
स्तव चैद्येन घटामुपेयुषा ।
यदुपुङ्गव बन्धुगौरवा-
दपि पाता ससुरो नवासवः ॥

चलितानकदुन्दुभिः पुरः
सबलस्त्वं सह सारणेन तम् ।
समितौ रभसादुपागतं
सगदः संप्रतिपत्तुमर्हसि ॥

समरेषु रिपून्विनिघ्नता
शिशुपालेन समेत्य संप्रति ।
सुचिरं सह सर्वसात्त्वतै-
र्भव विश्वस्तविलासिनीजनः ॥

१५ विजितक्रुधमीक्षितामसौ
महतां त्वा महितं महीभृताम् ।
असकृज्जितसंयतं पुरो
मुदितः सप्रमदं महीपतिः ॥

Your motives are noble and profound. So may each of
    your enemies lose all resolve and weaken in the face of
    continual disaster. May he be ravaged by disease and
    incapable of exercising any political judgment.

Mighty Yadava, the king of the Chedis respects you as his
    maternal uncle and feels appropriate affection. You
    will soon toast him with fresh double-strength liquor
    garnished with an exquisite lotus blossom winking in
    the goblet.

So far as honoring Shishupala is concerned, your father
    Vasudeva ought to proceed first in this respect, and
    then you and your brothers, Balarama, Gada, and
    Sarana, should follow. For, after all, my master did
    come to the assembly with positive intent.

Then having made peace with Shishupala, always
    victorious over his enemies, you and the entire Yadava
    clan will emphatically confirm your fair women's
    security.

May Shishupala delight in viewing you as one has   15
    overcome anger, an individual honored by mighty
    kings who has continually experienced the joy of
    victory in battle."

अभिधाय तदा तदप्रियं
शिशुपालो ऽनुशयं परं गतः ।
भवतो ऽभिमनाः समीहते
सरुषः कर्तुमुपेत्य माननाम् ॥१

विपुलेन निपीड्य निर्दयं
मुदमायातु नितान्तमुन्मनाः ।
प्रचुराधिगताङ्गनिर्वृतिं
परितस्त्वां खलु विग्रहेण सः ॥

प्रणतः शिरसा करिष्यते
सकलैरेत्य समं नराधिपैः ।
तव शासनमाशु भूपतिः
परवानद्य यतस्त्वयैव सः ॥

५ अधिवह्निपतङ्गतेजसो
नियतस्वान्तसमर्थकर्मणः ।
तव सर्वविधेयवर्तिनः
प्रणतिं बिभ्रति के न भूभृतः ॥

जनतां भयशून्यधीः परै-
रभिभूतामवलम्बसे यतः ।
तव कृष्ण गुणास्ततो नरै-
रसमानस्य दधत्यगण्यताम् ॥

But his message to Krishna was also this:
  "Earlier Shishupala may have spoken harshly enough,
      but he has become still more aggrieved. Now he is
      eager to go on the offensive and pay due honor to
      the rage he feels against you.

May that proud king derive deep pleasure from
      relentlessly destroying you with his mighty army.
      May your deep anguish rob you of your health.

King Shishupala has received homage from all rulers
      united together and now he will punish you, for today
      he has become your implacable foe.

Why should any king offer you fealty? Your power fades   5
      like a moth flying into a flame, while your actions will
      bring your certain demise. In short, you should really
      be everybody's servant.

Wretch! You've lost your wits through fear. Through
      associating with people everywhere despised,[4] you
      yourself have become an object of contempt and none
      will acknowledge you possess any virtues.

अहितादनपत्रपस्त्रस-
न्नतिमात्रोज्झितभीरनास्तिकः ।
विनयोपहितः कुतस्त्वया
सदृशो ऽन्यो गुणवानविस्मयः ॥

कृतगोपवधूरतेर्व्रतो
वृषमुग्रे नरके ऽपि संप्रति ।
प्रतिपत्तिरधःकृतैनसो
जनताभिस्तव साधु वर्ण्यते ॥

विहितापचितिर्महीभुजा
द्विषतामाहितसाध्वसो बलैः ।
भव सानुचरस्त्वमुच्चकै-
र्महतामप्युपरि क्षमाभृताम् ॥

१०   घनजालनिभैर्दुरासदाः
परितो नागकदम्बकैस्तव ।
नगरेषु भवन्तु वीथयः
परिकीर्णा वनजैर्मृगादिभिः ॥

सकलापिहितस्वपौरुषो
नियतव्यापदवर्धितोदयः ।
रिपुरुन्नतधीरचेतसः
सततव्याधिरनीतिरस्तु ते ॥

532

Where can be found another like you—totally lacking
    in qualities, unashamedly terrified of his enemies,[5]
    feeling secure only through abasement, rejecting
    proper social and religious custom, pursuing unsound
    policy, puffed up with arrogance?

You have sinned greatly through having illicit sex with
    cowherd girls and killing a bull. As a result, your
    descent into hell's terrible suffering is confidently
    predicted by all.[6]

You have been bested by Shishupala and are now terrified
    of your enemies' forces. So flee with your followers
    over the mountains, however lofty they may be.

After your defeat, may the deserted thoroughfares of   10
    your cities be infested with hordes of snakes thick as
    strands of netting, and haunted by all sorts of wild
    beasts.

You are a fool! May your enemy Shishupala, secure in his
    vigor and invincible, be unimpeded on his march to
    success. May he experience no dangers and avoid
    calamity.

विकचोत्पलचारुलोचन-
स्तव चैद्येन घटामुपेयुषा ।
यदुपुङ्गव बन्धुगौरवा-
दपि पाता ससुरो नवासवः ॥

चलितानकदुन्दुभिः पुरः
सबलस्त्वं सह सारणेन तम् ।
समितौ रभसादुपागतं
सगदः संप्रतिपत्तुमर्हसि ॥

समरेषु रिपून्विनिघ्नता
शिशुपालेन समेत्य संप्रति ।
सुचिरं सह सर्वसात्त्वतै-
र्भव विश्वस्तविलासिनीजनः ॥

१५ विजितक्रुधमीक्षितामसौ
महतां त्वा महितं महीभृताम् ।
असकृज्जितसंयतं पुरो
मुदितः सप्रमदं महीपतिः ॥

इति जोषमवस्थितं द्विषः
प्रणिधिं गामभिधाय सात्यकिः ।
वदति स्म वचो ऽथ चोदित-
श्चलितैकभ्रु रथाङ्गपाणिना ॥

Yadava donkey! If Shishupala goes to war with you, not
    even Indra, eyes glinting like lotus blossoms, will
    afford you protection, irrespective of any concern he
    might have for a relative[7]—nor will any other god.

So strike up the drums of war; muster your army and,
    mace in hand, march forward at once to engage with
    Shishupala in battle. He for his part is committed to
    conflict.

Fight now with the invincible Shishupala, and you and the
    entire Yadava clan can make all your women widows
    for the rest of their lives.

May Shishupala once again rejoice in seeing you and   15
    your wives humiliated by mighty kings, for when
    giving way to wrath in the past you have always been
    overpowered and made captive."[8]

The enemy's envoy delivered his message and fell silent.
    Then Krishna raised an eyebrow and indicated to
    Satyaki that he should reply.

मधुरं बहिरन्तरप्रियं
कृतिनावाचि वचस्तथा त्वया ।
सकलार्थतया विभाव्यते
प्रियमन्तरबहिरप्रियं यता ॥

अतिकोमलमेकतो ऽन्यतः
सरसाम्भोरुहवृन्तकर्कशम् ।
वहति स्फुटमेकमेव ते
वचनं शाकपलाशदेश्यताम् ॥

प्रकटं मृदु नाम जल्पतः
परुषं सूचयतो ऽर्थमन्तरा ।
शकुनादिव मार्गवर्तिभिः
पुरुषादुद्द्विजितव्यमीदृशात् ॥

२० हरिमर्चितवान्महीपति-
र्यदि राजंस्तव को ऽत्र मत्सरः ।
न्यसनाय ससौरभस्य क-
स्तरुसूनस्य शिरस्यसूयति ॥

सुकुमारमहो लघीयसां
हृदयं तद्द्रुतमप्रियं यतः ।
सहसैव समुद्धिरन्त्यमी
जरयन्त्येव हि तन्मनीषिणः ॥

"You have delivered a cunning speech embodying a double meaning. Its message is amenable on the surface but disagreeable within, and can just as well be interpreted the other way round.

On the one hand, what you have said is cordial, on the other, unpalatable and tough as wet lotus fibers. It is akin to the leaf of a teak tree, simultaneously soft and hard.

Beware of the man who can articulate an ostensibly pleasing message while signaling another harsher meaning hidden within. Travelers fear a bird that sings sweetly but portends ill.

If Yudhishthira has shown honor to Krishna, why should your master resent it? Who is jealous of a fragrant blossom when it is plucked from a tree and fixed in someone's hair?   20

The hearts of insignificant people are certainly not large. If any unfriendly disposition arises in them, they immediately give voice and expel it, whereas the intelligent let it fade away within. In the same way, those of feeble constitution and delicate stomachs vomit out anything unpalatable, while the robust simply digest it.[9]

उपकारपरः स्वभावतः
सततं सर्वजनस्य सज्जनः ।
असतामनिशं तथाप्यहो
गुरुह्द्रोगकरी तदुन्नतिः ॥

परितप्यत एव नोत्तमः
परितप्तो ऽप्यपरः सुसंवृतः ।
परवृद्धिभिराहितव्यथः
स्फुटनिर्भिन्नदुराशयो ऽधमः ॥

अनिराकृततापसंपदं
फलहीनां सुमनोभिरुज्झिताम् ।
खलतां खलतामिवासतीं
प्रतिपद्येत कथं बुधो जनः ॥

२५ प्रतिवाचमदत्त केशवः
शपमानाय न चेदिभूभृते ।
अनुहुंकुरुते घनध्वनिं
न हि गोमायुरुतानि केसरी ॥

जितरोषरया महाधियः
सपदि क्रोधजितो लघुर्जनः ।
विजितेन जितस्य दुर्मते-
र्मतिमद्भिः सह का विरोधिता ॥

A virtuous man is by nature always intent on aiding others.
But how deeply and incessantly it gnaws at the hearts
of the wicked when such an individual prospers.

The best type of person is untroubled when others
flourish. While an average man might become
agitated, he can conceal his feelings well enough.
However, a worthless individual is deeply pained by
another's good fortune, and his mean-spiritedness
stands out clearly.

How could any intelligent man adopt wicked ways, for
such behavior involves relentless troubling of others,
has no good result, and is shunned by the wise as
altogether evil. It is like cultivating barren ground,
exposed to the heat of the sun, unproductive of fruit
or flowers, everywhere infertile.[10]

Krishna certainly did not acknowledge the lord of the   25
Chedis as he cursed him. The lion roars in response to
monsoon thunder, not the jackal's shrieks.

Intelligent men control the course of their wrath, but the
low are swiftly consumed by rage. When the fool is
overcome by anger while the wise can master it, how
can there be a quarrel between them?

वचनैरसतां महीयसो
न खलु व्येति महत्त्वमुद्धतैः ।
किमपैति रजोभिरौवैरै-
रवकीर्णस्य मणेर्महार्घता ॥

परितोषयिता च कश्चन
स्वगतो यस्य गुणो ऽस्ति देहिनः ।
परदोषकथाभिरल्पकः
स जनं तोषयितुं किलेच्छति ॥

सहजान्धदृशः स्वदुर्नये
परदोषेक्षणदिव्यचक्षुषः ।
स्वगुणोच्चगिरो मुनिव्रताः
परवर्णग्रहणेष्वसाधवः ॥

३० प्रकटान्यपि नैपुणं मह-
त्परवाच्यानि चिराय गोपितुम् ।
विवरीतुमथात्मनो गुणा-
न्भृशमाकौशलमार्यचेतसाम् ॥

किमिवाखिललोककीर्तितं
कथयत्यात्मगुणं महामनाः ।
वदिता न लघीयसो ऽपरः
स्वगुणं तेन वदत्यसौ स्वयम् ॥

The dignity of the mighty does not desert them through
  the haughty words of the wicked. Does a gem's high
  value vanish when it is sullied with dust?

However, the man lacking any specific talent worthy
  of applause is truly insignificant; he aspires only to
  charm the world by telling tales of others' weaknesses.

The wicked are by nature blind to their own bad behavior
  but have supernatural vision when it comes to seeing
  others' faults. They loudly proclaim their own virtues,
  while taking a vow of silence when it comes to praising
  anyone else.

The high-minded, on the other hand, will persistently   30
  exercise great skill to avoid drawing attention to
  others' weaknesses, however obvious, but they are
  completely artless about revealing their own virtues.

Why should a truly great man point to his own gifts
  when they are praised by the entire world? Nobody
  discusses the virtues of an insignificant person, so he
  has to talk about them himself.

विसृजन्त्यविकत्थिनः परे
विषमाशिर्विषवन्नराः क्रुधम् ।
दधतो ऽन्तरसाररूपतां
ध्वनिसाराः पटहा इवेतरे ॥

नरकच्छिदमिच्छतीक्षितुं
विधिना येन स चेदिभूपतिः ।
दूतमेतु न हापयिष्यते
सदृशं तस्य विधातुमुत्तरम् ॥

समनद्ध किमङ्ग भूपति-
र्यदि संधित्सुरसौ किलामुना ।
हरिराक्रमणेन सन्नतिं
किल बिभ्रीत भियेत्यसंभवः ॥

३५ महतस्तरसा विलङ्घय-
न्निजदोषेण विधीर्विनश्यति ।
कुरुते न खलु स्वयेच्छया
शलभानिन्धनमिद्धदीधितिः ॥

यदपूरि पुरा मधुद्विषो[2]
न मुखेन स्वयमागसां शतम् ।
अथ संप्रति पर्यपूपुर-
त्तदसौ दूतमुखेन चेदिपः[3] ॥

Men who do not boast instead direct their anger toward
their enemy, like a mute snake releasing its venom.
Those with nothing substantial within themselves
make an empty noise like drums.

Let Shishupala come! It is no matter how he wishes to
encounter Krishna, destroyer of Naraka, whether
aggressively or peacefully. An appropriate answer will
not be slow in coming.

But please tell me—if Shishupala does really intend to
make peace with Krishna, why has he put on his
armor? Don't you know it is impossible for a lion to
cower in fear of attack?[11]

The fool who assaults the powerful brings about his own   35
destruction by his error. It is hardly of fire's own
volition that it consumes moths in its flames.

The Chedi king could not complete his hundred sins[12]
against Krishna by his own speech, so he has got his
emissary to round them off now.

यदनर्गलगोपुरानन-
स्त्वमतो वक्ष्यसि किंचिदप्रियम् ।
विवरिष्यति तच्चिरस्य नः
समयोदीक्षणरक्षिताः क्रुधः ॥

निशमय्य तदूर्जितं शिने-
र्वचनं नमुरनामुरेनसाम् ।
पुनरुज्झितसाध्वसं द्विषा-
मभिधत्ते स्म वचो वचोहरः ॥

विविनक्ति न बुद्धिदुर्विधः
स्वयमेव स्वहितं पृथग्जनः ।
यदुदीरितमप्यदः परै-
र्न विजानाति तद्द्भुतं महत् ॥

४० विदुरेष्यदपायमात्मना
परतः श्रद्दधते ऽथ वा बुधाः ।
न परोपहितं न च स्वतः
प्रमिमीते ऽनुभवाट्टते ऽल्पधीः ॥

कुशलं खलु तुभ्यमेव त-
द्वचनं कृष्ण यदभ्यधामहम् ।
उपदेशपराः परेष्वपि
स्वविनाशाभिमुखेषु साधवः ॥

Your mouth gapes as wide as the city gate. If you open
     it to utter another hostile remark, it will reveal our
     anger held in reserve till now in anticipation of an
     appropriate moment to attack."

The enemy's emissary listened to the forceful speech of
     Satyaki, upright grandson of Shini, and then gave a
     brazen response.

"An ordinary person cannot consider what is to his
     immediate advantage if he lacks acumen, but it is truly
     remarkable when he is incapable of grasping what
     others have told him.

The intelligent know of their own accord when a disaster   40
     is about to befall them; alternatively, they pay heed
     when warned by another. But a fool will not accept as
     direct evidence someone else's assertion or what he
     himself realizes as self-evident,[13] unless he personally
     experiences it.

What I declared in my message, Krishna, will undoubtedly
     be to your advantage. The virtuous take pains to
     counsel even their enemies when bent on their own
     destruction.

उभयं युगपन्मयोदितं
त्वरया सान्त्वमथेतरच्च ते ।
प्रविभज्य पृथङ्ङनीषया
सगुणं यत्किल तत्करिष्यसि ॥

अथ वाभिनिविष्टबुद्धिषु
व्रजति व्यर्थकतां सुभाषितम् ।
रविरागिषु शीतरोचिषः
करजालं कमलाकरेष्विव ॥

अनपेक्ष्य गुणागुणं जनः
स्वरुचिं निश्चयतो ऽनुधावति ।
अपहाय महीपमार्चिच-
त्सदसि त्वां ननु भीमपूर्वजः ॥

४५ त्वयि भक्तिमता न सत्कृतः
कुरुराजा गुरुरेव चेदिपः ।
प्रियमांसमृगाधिपोज्झितः
किमवद्यः करिकुम्भजो मणिः ॥

क्रियते धवलः खलूच्चकै-
र्धवलैरेव सितेतरैरधः ।
शिरसौघमदत्त शङ्करः
सुरसिन्धोर्मधुशत्रुरङ्घ्रिणा ॥

546

I simultaneously conveyed two messages, mild and severe,
   because there was little time available. You must
   employ your intelligence to distinguish between them,
   and then do what appears appropriate.

However, good advice proffered to the obsessed is
   pointless, like moonbeams fondling lotuses that still
   adore the sun.

People undoubtedly follow their own whims without
   reference to what is good or bad. After all, didn't
   Bhima's elder brother Yudhishthira ignore my master
   in the assembly and do honor to you instead?

Despite his loyalty, the king of the Chedis was not honored   45
   by the king of the Kurus. Nonetheless, my master
   is still a most eminent person. Is the pearl in the
   elephant's temple lobe worthless because the lion
   pushes it aside in his craving for flesh?[14]

The good exalt the good, while the evil diminish them.
   Shiva, white with ashes, bore the pure flood of the
   Ganga on his head, but it only splashed over the foot
   of the dark enemy of Madhu.[15]

अबुधैः कृतमानसंविद-
स्तव पार्थैः कथमेव योग्यता ।
सहसि प्लवगैरुपासितं
न हि गुञ्जाफलमेति सोष्मताम् ॥

अपराधशतक्षमं नृपः
क्षमयात्येति भवन्तमेकया ।
हतवत्यपि भीष्मकात्मजां
त्वयि चक्षाम समर्थ एव यत् ॥

गुरुभिः प्रतिपादितां वधू-
मपहृत्य स्वजनस्य भूपतेः ।
जनको ऽसि जनार्दन स्फुटं
हतधर्मार्थतया मनोभुवः ॥

५० अनिरूपितरूपसंपद-
स्तमसो वान्यभृतच्छदच्छवेः ।
तव सर्वगतस्य संप्रति
क्षितिपः क्षिप्रभीशुमानिव ॥

क्षुभितस्य महीभृतस्त्वयि
प्रशमोपन्यसनं वृथा मम ।
प्रलयोल्ललितस्य वारिधेः
परिवाहो जगतः करोति किम् ॥

Why should you be regarded as worthy simply because
    your behavior is applauded by Kunti's foolish sons?
    The red *guñjā* berry does not emit heat just because
    monkeys grab it in the winter cold.

You may have had to put up with a hundred insults, but my
    lord has outdone this by a solitary act of forbearance.
    Powerful as he is, he had to endure your abducting
    Rukmini, daughter of Bhishmaka.[16]

Krishna, you are a tyrant! In making off with the wife of
    a king and relative, a woman formally bestowed in
    marriage by her elders, you clearly gave yourself over
    to sexual pleasure at the expense of your obligations
    to personal duty and general polity.[17]

Your true nature is inscrutable and your appearance is   50
    appropriately black as a cuckoo's feather.[18] You may
    be all powerful, but my lord will soon destroy you, as
    the sun destroys the pitch darkness concealing the
    world.[19]

Shishupala is justifiably aggrieved at you and my attempts
    to placate him have failed. When the ocean swells at
    doomsday, what benefit to the world is an overflow
    pipe?

प्रहितः प्रधनाय माधवा-
नहमाकारयितुं महीभृता ।
न परेषु महौजसश्छला-
दपकुर्वन्ति मलिम्लुचा इव ॥

तदयं समुपैति भूपतिः
पयसां पूर इवानिवारितः ।
अविलम्बितमेधि वेतस-
स्तलवन्माधव मा स्म भज्यथाः ॥

परिपाति स केवलं शिशू-
निति तन्नामनि मा च विश्वसीः ।
तरुणानपि रक्षति क्षमी
स शरण्यः शरणागतान्द्विषः ॥

५५ न विदध्युरशङ्कमप्रियं
महतः स्वार्थपराः परे कथम् ।
भजते कुपितो ऽप्युदात्तधी-
रनुनीतिं नतिमात्रकेण यः ॥

हितमप्रियमिच्छसि श्रुतं
यदि संधत्स्व पुरा विनश्यसि ।
अनृतैरथ तुष्यसि प्रियै-
र्जयताज्जीव भवावनीश्वरः ॥

I have been dispatched by my lord to summon the Yadavas
openly to battle. The strong do not injure their
enemies by treachery, as do thieves.

Shishupala is advancing against you like a river in spate
bursting through a dam. Krishna, you should behave
like a reed and bend, lest you be swept away like a
palm tree.

Do not trust in the literal meaning of Shishupala's name
and assume he protects only children.[20] Merciful and
sheltering, he can also succor enemies in the vigor of
youth who have come to him for help.

A powerful monarch may adopt a high-minded position   55
even when enraged and conciliate an opponent who
abases himself. But how can foes with only their
own interests at heart refrain from attacking such an
individual?

If you want to hear something to your advantage, however
distasteful, then I say, make peace before you are
destroyed. But if you are satisfied with plausible
falsehoods, then victory to you, live forever, and rule
the universe!

प्रतिपक्षजिदप्यसंशयं
युधि चैद्येन भवान्विजेष्यते ।
ग्रसते हि तमोपहं मुहु-
र्ननु राह्वाह्ममहर्पतिं तमः ॥

अचिराज्जितमीनकेतनो
विलसन्वृष्णिगणैर्नमस्कृतः ।
क्षितिपः क्षपितोद्धतान्धको
हरलीलां स विडम्बयिष्यति ॥

निहतोन्मददुष्टकुञ्जरा-
द्दधतो भूरि यशः क्रमार्जितम् ।
न बिभेति रणे हरेरपि
क्षितपः का गणनास्य वृष्णिषु ॥

६० न तद्द्रुतमस्य यन्मुखं
युधि पश्यन्ति भिया न शत्रवः ।
द्रवतां ननु पृष्ठमीक्षते
वदनं सो ऽपि न जातु विद्विषाम् ॥

Even though you may regularly get the better of your
enemies,[21] you will undoubtedly be overthrown in
battle by the Chedi king. The sun may dispel darkness,
but does not Rahu, the eclipse, repeatedly devour it?

The glorious Shishupala will quickly overcome your son
Pradyumna and receive the obeisance of the Yadava
armies, while obliterating the haughty Andhaka
clan.* So he will replicate the deeds of Shiva—he
who conquered the god of love and rides on the bull
Nandin, an object of worship to his loyal devotees and
destroyer of the arrogant demon Andhaka.[22]

Shishupala is not afraid to meet you in combat, Krishna,
any more than he fears a tawny cat.[23] Your great
fame has been gained very slowly; it derives from
nothing more than taking a few strides and killing a
bad-tempered elephant in rut. And what respect could
my master have for the Vrishnis, who are no better
than cattle?[24]

It is hardly surprising that Shishupala's terrified enemies   60
never confront him in battle; bear in mind that he only
ever sees their backs, not their faces, as they flee.

---

* A lineage within the Yadava clan.

प्रतनूल्लसिताचिरद्युतः
शरदं प्राप्य विखण्डितायुधाः ।
दधते ऽरिभिरस्य तुल्यतां
यदि नासारभृतः पयोभृतः ॥

मलिनं रणरेणुभिर्मुहु-
र्द्विषतां क्षालितमङ्गनासुभिः ।
नृपमौलिमरीचिवर्णकै-
रथ यस्याङ्घ्रियुगं विलिप्यते ॥

समराय निकामकर्कशं
क्षणमाकृष्टमुपैति यस्य च ।
धनुषा सममाशु विद्विषां
कुलमाशङ्कितभङ्गमानतिम् ॥

तुहिनांशुममुं सुहृज्जनाः
कलयन्त्युष्णरुचिं विरोधिनः ।
कृतिभिः कृतदृष्टिविभ्रमाः
स्रजमेके भुजगं यथापरे ॥

६५ दधतो ऽसुलभक्ष्यागमा-
स्तनुमेकान्तरताममानुषाः ।
भुवि सांप्रतमप्रतिष्ठिताः
सदृशा यस्य सुरैररातयः ॥

554

Were the autumnal clouds not to pour down rain, shafts
of lightning to flash from them only intermittently,
rainbows no longer to arch above, a comparison could
be made to Shishupala's enemies, neutralized and
lethargic, their weapons destroyed by his arrows when
they attack him.[25]

Shishupala's feet, when grimy with dust from battle, are
washed clean by the tears of his enemies' wives and
then anointed with sandalwood paste, the rays of
light streaming from the diadems of kings bowing in
homage before him.

His enemies, summarily invited to battle, fear destruction
and make obeisance to him forthwith, strong and
hard though they may be. They are like his bow—
drawn back in an instant as battle begins, it bends so
quickly that it nears breaking, despite its wood's great
toughness.[26]

Shishupala's allies see him as the cooling moon, but his
foes view him as the burning sun. Some people, their
eyes deceived by skillful conjurors, mistake a rope for
a garland, while others take it for a snake.

Shishupala's foes can never return to their palaces and   65
now live in remote regions, wifeless and insecure. In
their remoteness they might be compared to gods—
but the immortals will never know ruin, and they
spend all their time in heaven making love.[27]

अतिविस्मयनीयकर्मणो
नृपतेः पश्य विरोधि चेष्टितम् ।
यदमुक्तनयो नयत्यसा-
वहितानां कुलमक्षयं क्षयम् ॥

चलितोर्ध्वकबन्धसंपदो
मकरव्यूहनिरुद्धवर्त्मनः ।
अतरत्स्वभुजौजसा मुहु-
र्महतः सङ्करसागरानसौ ॥

न चिकीर्षति यः समयोद्धतं
नृपतिस्तच्चरणोपगं शिरः ।
चरणं कुरुते गतस्मयः
स्वमसावेव तदीयमूर्धनि ॥

स भुजद्वयकेवलायुध-
श्चतुरङ्गामपहाय वाहिनीम् ।
बहुशः सह शक्रदन्तिना
सचतुर्दन्तमगच्छदाहवम् ॥

७० अविचालितचारुचक्रयो-
रनुरागादुपगूढयोः श्रिया ।
युवयोरियदेव भिद्यते
यदुपेन्द्रस्त्वमतीन्द्र एव सः ॥

His actions are quite astonishing. Just consider his
    contradictory behavior[28]—exercising wily strategy to
    overwhelm hitherto indestructible enemies and then
    restoring them from exile to their domains.[29]

With his mighty arms he has traversed great oceans
    of battle, where ranks of headless corpses bob like
    waves on the watery surface and avenues of attack
    are blocked by enemy formations like shoals of sea
    monsters.[30]

A king, swollen with pride, might refuse to touch his head
    to Shishupala's foot in homage. But quite without any
    arrogance my master will himself place his foot upon
    it in token of subjugation.

With his only weapons his two arms and without the help
    of a 'four-limbed' army, he has frequently engaged in
    'four-tusked' battle with Indra's elephant.[31]

Both you and Shishupala possess invincible discuses   70
    and fine kingdoms,[32] and both of you are lovingly
    embraced by good fortune. But this much separates
    you, Krishna: you are merely Indra's younger
    brother,[33] while Shishupala actually excels that god in
    strength.

भृतभूतिरहीनभोगभा-
ग्विजितानेकपुरो ऽपि विद्विषाम् ।
रुचिमिन्दुदले करोत्यजः
परिपूर्णेन्दुरुचिर्महीपतिः ॥

नयति द्रुतमुद्धतिश्रितः
प्रसभाद्भङ्गमभङ्गुरोदयः ।
गमयत्यवनीतलस्फुर-
द्द्रुजशाखाभृतमन्यमानतिम् ॥

अधिगम्य च रन्ध्रमन्तरा
जनयन्मण्डलभेदमन्ततः ।
खनति क्षतसंहतिः क्षणा-
दपि मूलानि महान्ति कस्यचित् ॥

घनपत्रभृतो ऽनुगामिन-
स्तरसाकृष्य करोति कांश्चन ।
दृढमप्यपरं प्रतिष्ठितं
प्रतिकूलं नितरां निरस्यति ॥

Shiva, smeared with ashes, with a snake coiling round
   him, conquered the three cities of the demons;[34] yet
   he takes pleasure in a mere sliver of the moon, his
   ornament. Shishupala is similar yet superior to him—
   wielding vast power and a great voluptuary, he has
   captured many enemy fortresses while still remaining
   fair as the full lunar orb.[35]

Shishupala's rise has been inexorable; he will speedily
   bring down the haughty, like lofty trees, and make
   any other ruler bow down so that his arms brush the
   ground like branches.[36]

He can identify internal weakness and from the outside
   foment division within a kingdom; he is able to
   destroy confederacies and quickly undermine the
   strong foundations of any state. So a river can pour
   through a breach in a dam, washing away the ground
   at the foot of a tree; such a flood can pull apart and
   tear up strong roots.

He can also quickly win over kings, irrespective of the
   number of chariots in their armies, and compel them
   to be his followers; he can equally overthrow a hostile
   monarch even if he is well established. Likewise a river
   in spate can drag down thickly leaved trees, sweeping
   them away in its swift current. In short, it can cast
   upon its banks any tree, however firmly rooted, if it
   stands in the way.[37]

७५ इति पूर इवोदकस्य यः
सरितां प्रावृषिजस्तटद्रुमैः ।
क्वचनापि महानखण्डित-
प्रसरः क्रीडति भूभृतां गणैः ॥

अलघूपलपङ्क्तीशालिनीः
परितो रुद्धनिरन्तराम्बराः ।
अधिरूढनितम्बभूमयो
न विमुञ्चन्ति चिराय मेखलाः ॥

कटकानि भजन्ति चारुभि-
र्नवमुक्ताफलभूषणैर्भुजैः ।
नियतं दधते च चित्रकै-
रवियोगं पृथुगण्डशैलतः ॥

इति यस्य ससंपदः पुरा
यदवापुः सदनेश्वरिस्त्रियः ।
स्फुटमेव समस्तमापदा
तदिदानीमवनीध्रमूर्धसु ॥

महतः कुकुरान्धकद्रुमा-
नतिमात्रं दववद्दहन्नपि ।
अतिचित्रमिदं महीपति-
र्यदकृष्णामवनिं करिष्यति ॥

560

Thus, like a mighty flood swelling in the monsoon and   75
   surging unabated, Shishupala has his own way with
   other rulers, wherever they may be.

In the past his enemies' firm-buttocked wives were
   accustomed to wearing heavy jewel-studded belts
   to hold their dresses tight around them. Now they
   scramble up escarpments and haunt mountain
   uplands covered with huge rocks everywhere blocking
   out the sky.

Once they wore on their shapely arms bangles dripping
   with fresh pearls, and their high cheeks were
   decorated with makeup. Now using these same arms
   they clamber over crags, quickly abandoning their
   ornaments, useless for widows, as they pass their days
   on stony moors, wandering with the dappled deer.

You could say that the luxury these women enjoyed
   during their palace lives is still manifestly theirs—of
   course, after their lord's demise, to be enjoyed only on
   mountain heights![38]

Shishupala will completely immolate the mighty Yadava
   clans, as fire consumes a forest's trees. But quite
   remarkably, in ridding the world of Krishna he will not
   leave the slightest trace of ashes.[39]

८० परितः प्रमिताक्षरापि सर्वं
विषयं प्राप्नुवती गता प्रतिष्ठाम् ।
न खलु प्रतिहन्यते कुतश्चि-
त्परिभाषेव गरीयसी यदाज्ञा ॥

यामूढवानूढवराहमूर्ति-
र्मुहूर्तमादौ पुरुषः पुराणः ।
तेनोह्यते सांप्रतमक्षतैव
क्षतारिणा सम्यगसौ पुनर्भूः ॥

भूयांसः क्वचिदपि काममस्खलन्त-
स्तुङ्गत्वं दधति च यद्यपि द्वये ऽपि ।
कल्लोलाः सलिलनिधेरवाप्य पारं
क्षीयन्ते न गुणमहोर्मयस्तदीयाः४ ॥

लोकालोकव्याहतं घर्मरश्मेः
शालीनं वा धाम नालं प्रसर्तुम् ।
लोकस्याग्रे पश्यतो धृष्टमाशु
क्रामत्युच्चैर्भूभृतो यस्य तेजः ॥

562

While his royal decree may be succinct, it is weighty in
    implication, encompassing all regions and enacted
    everywhere, meeting no opposition. It is like a
    governing rule in grammar—highly condensed while
    covering every possibility, sound and authoritative,
    uncontradicted by another rule.[40]

80

The earth may have been borne for a moment at the
    beginning of the world age by the primal being in the
    form of a boar, but now after Shishupala has destroyed
    his enemies it will be properly ruled in full security
    once again.[41]

There are two kinds of ocean wave, both huge, relentless,
    and surging to great heights; but the sea's billows
    recede when they reach the shore, while the rolling
    breakers of my master's merits never reach their
    limit.[42]

The course of the sun's light is blocked by the Bright-
    Dark mountain range at the edge of the world[43] and,
    apparently embarrassed by the gaze of men, cannot
    proceed beyond its peaks. However, Shishupala's
    brilliance quickly overtops every mountain—and
    every king, as all can see.

विच्छित्तिर्नवचन्दनेन वपुषां भिन्नो ऽधरो ऽलक्तकै-
रच्छाच्छे पतिताञ्जने च नयने श्रोण्यो लसन्मेखलाः ।
प्राप्तो मौक्तिकहारमुन्नतकुचाभोगस्तदीयद्विषा-
मित्थं नित्यविभूषणा युवतयः संपद्रुदापद्यपि ॥

८५   विनिहत्य भवन्तमूर्जितश्री-
      र्युधि सद्यः शिशुपालतां यथार्थाम् ।
      रुदतां भवदङ्गनागणानां
      करुणान्तःकरणः करिष्यते ऽसौ ॥

Once the womenfolk of Shishupala's enemies were
    habitually decked out in finery—they were anointed
    with fresh sandalwood cream, their lower lips rouged
    with lac, and their flashing eyes rimmed with kohl;
    jeweled belts bounced on their hips, while pearl
    necklaces ornamented their jutting breasts. It is the
    same for them after the defeat of their lord as it was
    when he prospered—apart from the fact that they
    no longer have sandalwood cream on their bodies or
    lac on their lips, there is no kohl on their bright eyes,
    they have ceased to wear belts, and no pearl necklaces
    adorn their breasts![44]

So my lord will increase in majesty by killing you in battle.   85
    Then he will justify his name Shishupala, "Child
    Protector," through taking pity on your weeping
    women."[45]

CHAPTER 17

The Yadavas Prepare for War

इतीरिते वचसि वचस्विनामुना
युगक्षयक्षुभितमरुद्ररीयसि ।
प्रचुक्षुभे सपदि तदम्बुराशिना
समं महाप्रलयसमुद्धतं सदः ॥

सरागया स्तुतघनघर्मतोयया
कराहितिध्वनितपृथूरुपृष्ठया ।
मुहुर्मुहुर्दशनविलङ्घितौष्ठया
रुषा नृपाः प्रियतमेव भेजिरे ॥

अलक्ष्यत क्षणदलिताङ्घ्रदे गदे
करोदरप्रहतनिजांसधामनि ।
समुच्छलच्छकलितपाटलोपल-
स्फुलिङ्गवान्स्फुटमिव कोपपावकः ॥

अवज्ञया यदहसदुच्चकैर्बलः
समुल्लसद्दशनमयूखमण्डलः ।
रुषारुणीकृतमपि तेन तत्क्षणा-
न्निजं वपुः पुनरनयन्निजां रुचम् ॥

५ यदुत्पतत्पृथुतरहारमण्डलं
व्यवर्तत द्रुतमभिदूतमुल्मुकः ।
बृहच्छिलातटकठिनांसघट्टितं
ततो ऽभवद्भ्रमितमिवाखिलं जगत् ॥

568

That smooth-tongued man finished his speech, pitched
    as violently as the hurricane that roars at the end of a
    world age. At once his audience in the assembly hall
    was roused to uproar, like the ocean readying for the
    final cataclysm.

The kings flushed with rage, as if they had been embraced
    tightly by a passionate lover;[1] sweat coursed freely,
    thighs resounded to the slap of hands, and lips were
    gnawed.

Gada* smote his own shoulders so hard his armlets
    immediately burst; the fire of his anger was almost
    palpable, with shards of rubies spurting from him like
    sparks.

As Balarama laughed aloud in derision, his teeth flashed,
    and at that very instant his whole body, glowing with
    rage, regained its normal pale hue.

Ulmuka† spun in a flash toward the envoy, his long pearl   5
    necklace swinging; the whole world seemed to reel
    from the blow of his shoulder, hard as a slab of rock.

---

* Krishna's younger brother.
† According to V, a son of Krishna.

प्रकुप्यतः श्वसनसमीरणाहति-
स्फुटोष्मभिस्तनुवसनान्तमारुतैः ।
युधाजितः कृतपरितूर्णवीजनं
पुनस्तरां वदनसरोजमस्विदत् ॥

प्रजापतिक्रतुनिधनार्थमुत्थितं
व्यतर्कयञ्ज्वरमिव रौद्रमुद्धृतः ।
समुद्धतं सपदि वधाय विद्विषा-
मधिक्रुधं निषधमनौषधं जनः ॥

परस्परं परिकुपितस्य पिंषतः
क्षतोर्मिकाकनकपरागपङ्कितम् ।
करद्वयं सपदि सुधन्वनः स्वजै-
रनारतस्नुतिभिरधाव्यताम्बुभिः ॥

निरायतामनलशिखोज्ज्वलज्वल-
न्नखप्रभाकृतपरिवेशसंपदम् ।
अबिभ्रमद्भ्रमदमलोल्मुकाकृतिं
प्रदेशिनीं जगदिव दग्धुमाहुकः ॥

१० दुरीक्षतामभजत मन्मथस्तथा
यथा पुरा परिचितदाहधाष्ट्र्यया ।
ध्रुवं पुनः सशरममुं तृतीयया
हरो ऽपि न व्यषहत वीक्षितुं दृशा ॥

To cool his anger Yudhajit fanned himself fiercely with the
   hem of his fine robe, but the breeze became heated up
   as it merged with his panting, and his lotus-like face
   sweated all the more.

To general consternation the implacable Nishadha was
   straining in fury to kill his enemies on the spot; he had
   been mistaken for Shiva's deadly fever, taking shape to
   destroy the king's sacrifice.[2]

Sudhanvan's hands, smeared with golden dust from his
   broken rings as he furiously ground them together,
   were straightaway washed clean by streams of sweat.

Ahuka stretched out a finger, wagging it in admonition;
   surrounded by the shimmer of his bright nails
   gleaming like flames, it appeared to be a blazing torch
   whirled around to consume the world.

As he stroked his arrows, Pradyumna became so terrible   10
   to behold that not even Shiva, who had nonchalantly
   immolated him in a previous existence, would have
   had the audacity to cast his third eye upon him again.[3]

विचिन्तयन्नुपनतमाहवं रसा-
दुरः स्फुरत्तनुरुहमग्रपाणिना ।
परामृशत्कठिनकठोरकामिनी-
कुचस्थलप्रमुषितचन्दनं पृथुः ॥

विलङ्घितस्थितिमभिवीक्ष्य रूक्षया
रिपोर्गिरा गुरुमपि गान्दिनीसुतम् ।
जनैस्तदा युगपरिवर्तवायुभि-
र्विवर्तिता गिरिपतयः प्रतीयिरे ॥

विवर्तयन्मदकलुषीकृते दृशौ
कराहतक्षिति कृतभैरवारवः ।
क्रुधा दधत्तनुमतिलोहिनीमभू-
त्प्रसेनजिद्द्रज इव गैरिकारुणः ॥

सकुङ्कुमैरविरलमम्बुबिन्दुभि-
र्गवेषणः परिणतदाडिमारुणैः ।
समत्सरस्फुटितवपुर्विनिःसृतै-
र्बभौ चिरं निचित इवासृजां लवैः ॥

१५ ससंभ्रमश्चरणतलाभिताडन-
स्फुटन्महीविवरवितीर्णवर्त्मभिः ।
रवेः करैरनुचिततापितोरुगं
प्रकाशतां शिनिरनयद्रसातलम् ॥

572

Sensing that battle was imminent, Prithu rubbed his
hand over his chest; its hair had already wiped the
sandalwood cream from the full taut breasts of his
lovers and was now standing on end again in his
excitement.

On seeing that even Akrura, the grave son of Gandini, had
lost his composure through the enemy's harsh words,
all became convinced that towering mountains would
really be overthrown by the hurricanes as the next
world age comes round.

Prasenajit became flushed all over in his anger; he rolled
his eyes bloodshot with drunkenness and pounded
the ground with his hands, roaring constantly. He was
like a rutting elephant smeared red with vermilion,
trumpeting as it lashes its trunk.[4]

Drops of sweat mixed with saffron cream, russet as
pomegranate, appeared on Gaveshana so that he
throbbed and glowed; it was as if he was spattered
with gobbets of blood spurting from his body as it
burst apart in anger.

Shini* split open the ground with his excited stamping; the 15
sun's rays penetrated the clefts he had made to reveal
the underworld, subjecting the serpents below to
unaccustomed heat.

---

* Grandfather of Satyaki.

प्रतिक्षणं विधुवति सारणे शिरः
शिखिद्युतः कनककिरीटरश्मयः ।
अशङ्कितं युधमधुना विशन्त्वमी
क्षमापतीनिति निरराजयन्निव ॥

दधौ चलत्पृथुरसनं विवक्षया
विदारितं विततबृहद्भुजालतः ।
विडूरथः² प्रतिभयमास्यकन्दरं
ललत्फणाधरमिव कोटरं तरुः ॥

समाकुले सदसि तथापि विक्रियां
मनो ऽगमन्न मुरभिदः परोदितैः ।
घनाम्बुभिर्बहलितनिम्नगाजलै-
र्जलं न हि व्रजति विकारमम्बुधेः ॥

परानमी यदपवदन्त आत्मनः
स्तुवन्ति च स्थितिरसतामसाविति ।
मुमोच न प्रकृतिमविस्मितः स्मितं
मुखं दधच्छशधरमुग्धमुद्भवः ॥

२० निराकृते यदुभिरिति प्रकोपिभिः
स्पशे शनैर्गतवति तत्र विद्विषाम् ।
मुरद्विषः स्वनितभयानकानकं
बलं क्षणादथ समनह्यदाजये ॥

As Sarana shook his head up and down, the fire-like rays
of light shooting from his golden crown seemed to be
consecrating[5] the weapons of the other kings so that
they could go at once into battle with full confidence.

In his eagerness to reply, Viduratha stretched out wide his
vine-like arms and opened his terrifying mouth where
his long tongue was darting; he looked like a tree cleft
with a hole where a slithering snake was lurking.

The assembly was in uproar, but Krishna's thoughts were
unperturbed by the enemy's words. The ocean's
depths remain unchanged by the rain swelling the
rivers' flood.

Since he knew that reviling others and extolling
themselves was the habit of the evil, Uddhava also
felt no surprise and did not lose his equanimity; his
smiling face remained as fair as the autumn moon.

So the enemy's agent was spurned by the angry Yadavas   20
and slunk away. Then, to the terrifying thunder of
drums, Krishna's army immediately prepared for war.

मुहुः प्रतिस्खलितपरायुधा युधि
स्थवीयसीरचलनितम्बनिर्वराः ।
अदंसयन्नरहितशौर्यदंसना-
स्तनूरयं नय इति वृष्णिभूभृतः ॥

दुरुद्वहाः क्षणमपरैस्तदन्तरे
रणश्रवादुपचयमाशु बिभ्रति ।
महीभृतां महिमभृतां न संममु-
र्मुदो ऽन्तरा वपुषि बहिश्च कञ्चुकाः ॥

सकल्पनं द्विरदगणं वरूथिन-
स्तुरङ्गिनो जयनयुजश्च वाजिनः ।
त्वरावतः स्वयमपि कुर्वतो नृपाः
पुनः पुनस्तदधिकृतानतत्वरन् ॥

युधे परैः सह दृढबद्धकक्ष्यया
कलक्कणन्मधुपगणोपगीतया ।
अदीयत द्विपघटया सवारिभिः
करोदरैः स्वयमथ दानमक्षयम् ॥

२५ सुमेखलाः सिततरदन्तचारवः
समुल्लसत्तनुपरिधानसंपदः ।
रणैषिणां पुलकभृतो ऽधिकन्धरं
ललम्बिरे सदसिलताः प्रिया इव ॥

The Vrishni princes had always repelled their opponents'
weapons in combat. Now they encased their huge
bodies, solid as mountain crags, in armor simply
because it was military procedure; otherwise they
always wore their real armor—heroism.

When they realized the battle was imminent, the mighty
kings immediately puffed out their chests; neither
their excitement nor their armor, so difficult for their
foes to cope with at any time, could find a place within
or outside their bodies.

They repeatedly exhorted their officers who in turn urged
on the battle-ready elephants, the chariots now yoked
to their horses, and the stallions decked out with full
military accoutrements.

As the troops of elephants, tightly armored for battle
with the foe, released a steady stream of ichor down
their damp trunks, they were serenaded by a gently
humming swarm of bees.[6]

Fine slender swords attached to ornate baldrics hung   25
like lovers from the necks of the eager soldiers; their
pommels were inlaid with ivory and their magnificent
scabbards gleamed.[7]

मनोरमैः प्रकृतिमनोरमाकृति-
र्भयप्रदैः समितिषु भीमदर्शनः ।
सदैवतैः सततमथानपायिभि-
र्निजाङ्गवन्मुरजिदसेव्यतायुधैः ॥

अवारितं गतमुभयेषु भूरिशः
क्षमाभृतामथ कटकान्तरेष्वपि ।
मुहुर्युधि क्षतसुरशत्रुशोणित-
प्लुतप्रधिं रथमधिरोहति स्म सः ॥

उपेत्य च स्वनगुरुपक्षमारुतं
दिवस्त्विषा कपिशितदूरदिङ्मुखः ।
अकम्पितस्थिरतरयष्टि तत्क्षणं
पतत्पतिः पदमधिकेतनं दधौ ॥

गभीरताविजितमृदङ्गनादया
स्वनश्रिया हतरिपुहंसहर्षया ।
प्रमोदयन्नथ मुखरान्कलापिनः
प्रतिष्ठते नवघनवद्रथः स्म सः ॥

३० निरन्तरस्थगितदिगन्तरं तत-
स्तदुच्चलद्धूलमवलोकयञ्जनः ।
विकौतुकः प्रकृतमहाप्लवे ऽभव-
द्विश्रृङ्खलप्रचलितसिन्धुवारिणि ॥

Then Krishna, the enemy of Mura, most times gentle to
the eye but in battle terrible to behold, took up his
splendid, fearsome weapons endowed with divine
power, always unfailing, just like his own person.

He mounted his chariot, moving freely and unimpeded
along mountain defiles and the avenues of royal
encampments alike, for its wheels had been repeatedly
washed by demons' blood.

At that moment Garuda, lord of birds, descended from
heaven, beating wings booming. He perched on
Krishna's banner without shaking its firm pole, and
turned the entire sky golden with his luster.

The chariot rolled forth like a fresh storm cloud; its
rumbling resonance, surpassing the deep thunder
of drums, delighted the screeching peacocks, but
destroyed the ease of enemies and geese.[8]

When onlookers saw the army blocking out the horizon as   30
it set out on the march, they lost all curiosity about the
ocean's unrelenting surge when the huge tidal wave
rises at doomsday.

579

बबृंहिरे गजपतयो महानकाः
प्रदध्वनुर्जयतुरगा जिहेषिरे ।
असंभवद्धूतगिरिगह्वरैरभू-
त्तदारवैर्दलित इव स्व आश्रयः ॥

अनारतं रसति जयाय दुन्दुभौ
मधुद्विषः फलदलघुप्रतिस्वनैः ।
विनिष्पतन्मृगपतिभिर्गुहामुखै-
र्गताः परां मुदमहसन्निवाद्रयः ॥

जडीकृतश्रवणपथे दिवौकसां
चमूरवे विशति सुराद्रिकन्धराः ।
अनर्थकैरजनि विदग्धकामिनी-
रतान्तरक्वणितविलासकौशलैः ॥

अरातिभिर्युधि सहयुध्वनो हता-
न्निजघृक्षवः श्रुतरणतूर्यनिःस्वनाः ।
अकुर्वत प्रथमसमागमोचितं
चिरोज्झितं सुरगणिकाः प्रसाधनम् ॥

३५ प्रचोदिताः परिगतयन्तृकर्मभि-
र्निषादिभिर्विदितयताङ्कुशक्रियैः ³ ।
गजाः सकृत्करतललोललालिका-
हता मुहुःप्रणदितघण्टमाययुः ⁴ ॥

The mighty elephants trumpeted, the great drums
      boomed, and the warhorses whinnied. The
      cacophony impalpably filled the mountain caverns
      to overflowing, and then seemed to rupture the very
      ether, its natural location.

Krishna's kettledrum beat out incessantly for victory,
      and the mountains resounded to its loud echoes;
      they appeared to be laughing in delight when lions
      leapt out in alarm from their cavernous lairs.

As the tumult of the army penetrated Mount Meru's
      ravines and deafened even the gods, the artfully
      amorous sighs and moans of their partners, versed in
      love's wiles, became pointless.

When heaven's courtesans heard the thunder of the battle
      drums, they yearned to possess the warriors slain in
      combat, putting on long-unused finery suitable for a
      first passionate encounter.[9]

The elephants were readied by their drivers, men expert   35
      in the mahout's duties who understood how to control
      their beasts with foot and goad. Coaxed forward
      with a single brisk slap of the hand, they moved into
      position amid the incessant jangling of bells.

सविक्रमक्रमणचलैरितस्ततः
प्रकीर्णकैः क्षिपत इव क्षिते रजः ।
व्यरंसिषुर्न खलु जनस्य दृष्टय-
स्तुरङ्गमादभिनवभाण्डभारिणः ॥

चलाङ्गुलीकिसलयमुच्छ्रितैः करै-
रनृत्यत स्फुटकृतकर्णतालया ।
मदोदकद्रवकटभित्तिसङ्गिभिः
कलस्वनं भ्रमरगणैरगीयत ॥

असिच्यत प्रशमितपांसुभिर्मही
मदाम्बुभिर्धृतनवपूर्णकुम्भया ।
अवाद्यत श्रवणसुखं समुन्नम-
त्पयोधरध्वनिगुरु तूर्यमाननैः५ ॥

उदासिरे पवनविधूतवासस-
स्ततस्ततो गगननलिहश्च केतवः ।
यतः पुरः प्रतिरिपु शार्ङ्गिणः स्वयं
व्यधीयत द्विपघटयेति मङ्गलम् ॥

४० न शून्यतामगमदसौ निवेशभूः
प्रभूततां दधति बले चलत्यपि ।
पयस्यभिद्रवति भुवं युगावधौ
सरित्पतिर्न हि समुपैति रिक्तताम् ॥

582

A squadron of freshly caparisoned horses galloping past
    seemed to throw up a cloud of dust as their yak-tail
    pennants fluttered around them—it was impossible to
    stop staring at them.[10]

Trunks held high, shoot-like tips waving from side to side,
    and ears flapping rhythmically, the elephants danced,
    while bees clinging to their ichor-streaming temples
    gently serenaded them.[11]

They sprinkled the earth and damped down the dust with
    ichor pouring from lobes like freshly filled pots;[12]
    they made a music most pleasing to the ear as they
    bellowed sonorously, like the rumbling of gathering
    storm clouds.

Standards flew above them; banners fluttered in the wind,
    everywhere reaching high into the sky. So, as Krishna
    went forth against the enemy, the elephant brigade,
    rather than the city women, spontaneously performed
    the auspicious rituals for him.

The mustering ground did not empty in the slightest,   40
    even as that vast army was marching out. When its
    tide floods the earth at doomsday, the ocean does not
    diminish in size.

यियासितामथ मधुभिद्दिवस्वता
जनो जरन्महिषविषाणधूसराम् ।
पुरः पतत्परबलरेणुमालिनी-
मलक्षयद्दिशमभिधूमितामिव ॥

मनस्विनामुदितगुरुप्रतिश्रुतः
श्रुतास्तथा न निजमृदङ्गनिःस्वनाः ।
यथा पुरः समरमुखोद्धतद्दिष-
द्बलानकध्वनिरुदकर्षयन्मनः ॥

यथा यथा पटहरवः समीपता-
मुपाययौ स हरिवराग्रतःसरः ।
तथा तथा हृषितवपुर्मुदाकुला
द्विषां चमूरजनि जनीव चेतसा ॥

प्रसारिणी सपदि नभस्तले ततः
समीरणभ्रमितपरागरूषिता ।
व्यभाव्यत प्रलयजकालिकाकृति-
र्विदूरतः प्रतिबलकेतनावली ॥

४५ क्षणेन च प्रतिमुखतिग्मदीधिति-
प्रतिप्रभास्फुरदसिदुःखदर्शना ।
भयंकरा भृशमपि दर्शनीयतां
ययावसावसुरचमूश्रमूभृताम् ॥

Then all looked toward the distant horizon, the goal of
    sun-like Krishna; gray as the tusks of an aged bull,
    shrouded with dust from the advancing enemy army,
    it seemed to be filled with smoke.

The sound of their own drums' booming echo did not stir
    the valiant warriors as much as the thunder of the foe
    advancing to battle against them.

The nearer drew the beating of the drums preceding
    Krishna, the more the enemy host grew excited
    and dizzy with delight—it was like a bridegroom
    approaching a young wife.

At last the column of banners of the opposing army could
    be glimpsed in the distance, suddenly reaching up
    into a sky enveloped with dust whirling in the wind; it
    seemed to be a bank of storm clouds gathering at the
    world's destruction.

The demonic Shishupala's army was difficult to catch   45
    sight of, as its swords reflected the fierce sunlight,
    but painful to the eyes though it was, it immediately
    became a cynosure for Krishna's generals.

पयोमुचामभिपततां दिवि द्रुतं
विपर्ययः परित इवातपस्य सः ।
समक्रियः समविषमेष्वथ क्षणा-
त्क्षमातलं बलजलराशिरानशे ॥

ममौ पुरः क्षणमिव पश्यतो मह-
त्तनूदरश्रितभुवनस्य तस्य तत् ।
विशालतां दधति नितान्तमायते
बलं द्विषां मधुमथनस्य चक्षुषि ॥

भृशस्विदः पुलकविकासिमूर्तयो
रसाधिके मनसि निविष्टसाहसाः ।
मुखे युधः सपदि रतेरिवाभव-
न्ससंभ्रमाः क्षितिपचमूवधूगणाः ॥

ध्वजांशुकैर्ध्रुवमनुकूलमारुत-
प्रसारितैः प्रसभकृतोपहूतयः ।
यदूनभि द्रुततरमुद्यतायुधाः
क्रुधारयः परमरयं प्रपेदिरे ॥

५० हरेरपि प्रति परकीयवाहिनी-
रधिस्यदं प्रववृतिरे चमूचराः ।
विलम्बितुं न खलु सहाः सहस्विनो
विधित्सतः कलहमवेक्ष्य विद्विषः ॥

Then in an instant the ocean-like forces of Krishna flowed
over high and low terrain alike, covering the earth
everywhere, like the shadow of rain clouds racing
across the sky.

As Krishna looked out for no more than a second, the vast
host of the enemy was encompassed within his wide-
open eyes—he does, after all, contain the universe in
his slender belly.[13]

Now that battle was imminent, Krishna's troops broke
out in a profuse sweat and hair bristled all over their
bodies. They had bold deeds on their minds and
their hearts were swelling with emotion—in their
excitement they had become like women about to
make love.

Their foes did not doubt they had been aggressively
challenged to fight by the banners blowing fiercely in
the following wind. They charged angrily toward the
Yadavas, brandishing their weapons as they ran.

Krishna's soldiers advanced on the double toward the   50
enemy army. When the mighty see their rivals bent on
conflict, they will not brook any delay.

587

निवाततां दधदपि वर्म बिभ्रतः
स्फुरन्मणिप्रसृतमरीचिसूचिभिः ।
निरन्तरं नरपतयो रणाजिरे
रराजिरे शरनिकराचिता इव ॥

अथोच्चकैर्जरढकपोतकन्धरा-
तनूरुहप्रकरविपाण्डुरद्युति ।
बलैश्चलच्चरणविधूतमुच्चर-
द्ध्वनावलीरुदचरत क्षमारजः ॥

विषञ्जिभिर्भृशमितरेतरं क्वचि-
त्तुरङ्गमैरुपरि निरुद्धनिर्गमाः ।
चलाचलैरनुपदमाहताः खुरै-
र्विबभ्रमुश्चिरमध एव धूलयः ॥

गरीयसः प्रचुरमुखस्य रागिणो
रजो ऽभवद्व्यवहितसत्त्वमुत्कटम् ।
सिसृक्षतः सरसिजजन्मनो जनं
बलस्य तु क्षयमुपनेतुमिच्छतः ॥

५५ पुरा शरक्षतिगलितानि संयुगे
नयन्ति नः प्रसभमसृञ्जि पङ्क्तताम् ।
इति ध्रुवं व्यलगिषुरात्तभीतयः
खमुच्चकैरनलसखस्य केतवः ॥

The kings wore armor without a chink, set with flashing
jewels emitting shafts of light; standing on the edge of
the battlefield they looked as if they had already been
stuck full with showers of arrows.

Now dust, deep-white as the neck feathers of a full-grown
pigeon, was kicked up by the advancing armies' feet
and rose to touch the clouds massed in the sky.

Elsewhere it had been stirred up by the constant passage
of hooves; the horsemen were so tightly packed
together that it could rise no further and kept floating
back down to the ground.

The army was an elite band with many divisions, and in its
lust for battle it yearned to destroy all its opponents,
but now a great cloud of dust had risen up and hidden
everybody.[14]

The dust, in mortal fear that the blood flowing from arrow   55
wounds during battle would immediately transform it
into mud, sprang into the air and clung fast there.

समुन्नमद्धूननिकुरुम्बकर्बुरः
क्वचिद्धिरण्मयकणपुञ्जपिञ्जरः ।
क्वचिच्छरच्छशधरखण्डपाण्डुरः⁶
खुरक्षतः क्षितितलरेणुरुद्ययौ ॥

महीयसां महति दिगन्तदन्तिना-
मनीकजे रजसि मुखानुषञ्जिणि ।
विसारितामजिहत कोकिलावली-
मलीमसा जलदमदाम्बुराजयः ॥

शिरोरुहैरलिकुलकोमलैरमी
मुधा मृधे मृषत युवान एव मा ।
बलोद्धतं धवलितमूर्धजानिति
ध्रुवं जनाञ्जरत इवाकरोद्रजः ॥

सुसंहतैर्दधदपि धाम नीयते
तिरस्कृतिं बहुभिरसंशयं परः ।
यतः क्षितेरवयवसंपदो ऽणव-
स्त्विषां निधेरपि वपुरावरीषत ॥

६० द्रुतद्रवद्रथचरणक्षतक्षमा-
तलोल्ललद्बहलरजोऽवगुण्ठितम् ।
युगक्षयक्षणनिरवग्रहे जग-
न्महोदधेर्जल इव मग्नमाबभौ ॥

Kicked up by hooves, it floated around, here gray as
    lowering monsoon clouds, there yellow as heaped
    golden grain, elsewhere white as the autumn moon's
    crescent.

As the thick dust rising from both armies settled on
    the heads of the mighty elephants of the heavenly
    quarters,[15] cloudy streaks of ichor,[16] dark as a flock of
    cuckoos,[17] spread all over them.

The dust flying up from the armies did not want the young
    warriors, their glossy locks dark as bee swarms, to
    die pointlessly in battle, so it turned them into white-
    haired dotards.

A single foe, no matter how brilliant, can undoubtedly be
    reduced to obscurity by many united together. A mass
    of minute fragments of the earth could conceal the
    shape of even the sun.

The world was veiled by the thick dust drifting up from   60
    the ground as it was disturbed by speeding chariot
    wheels; it appeared to have sunk in the water of the
    mighty ocean unleashed when it is time for a world
    age to end.

591

अनुलसद्दिनकरवक्रकान्तयो
रजस्वलाः परिमलिनाम्बरश्रियः ।
दिगङ्गनाः क्षणमविलोकनक्षमाः
शरीरिणामविहरणीयतां ययुः ॥

निरीक्षितुं वियति समेत्य कौतुका-
त्पराक्रमं समरमुखे महीभृताम् ।
रजस्तताविनिमिषलोचनोत्पल-
व्यथाकृति त्रिदशगणः पलायत ॥

विषङ्क्षिणि प्रतिपदमापिबत्यपो
हताचिरद्युतिनि समीरलक्ष्मणि ।
शनैः शनैरुपचितपङ्कभारिकाः
पयोधराः प्रययुरपेतवृष्टयः ॥

नभोनदीव्यतिकरधौतमूर्तिभि-
र्वियद्द्वतैरनधिगतानि लेभिरे ।
चलच्चमूतुरगखुराहतोत्पत-
न्महीरजःस्नपनसुखानि दिग्गजैः ॥

६५ गजव्रजक्रमणभरावनम्रया
रसातलं यदखिलमानशे भुवा ।
नभस्तलं बहलतरेण रेणुना
ततो ऽगमत्त्रिभुवनमेकतामिव ॥

Shrouded in dust, the horizon for a moment became
   invisible, the sun no longer shone clearly, the blue sky
   darkened, and nobody could move freely.[18]

The gods were curious to see the valor of the kings as
   battle approached; but when they assembled in
   the sky, it was smothered in dust, tormenting their
   unblinking lotus-like eyes,[19] and so they fled.

The clinging dust swiftly destroyed the clouds' whiteness
   and began to absorb their water; lacking rain and
   laden with masses of mud, they floated ponderously in
   the sky.

The elephants of the directions, high in the heavens, were
   always washed by the flood of the celestial Ganga, but
   now they experienced the novel pleasure of bathing in
   the floating dust of the earth, kicked up by the hooves
   of the galloping cavalry.[20]

The earth buckled so much from the weight of the   65
   elephants' tread that it merged with the underworld
   below, while the sky was clogged everywhere with a
   thick layer of dust—the three worlds seemed to have
   become one.

समस्थलीकृतविवरेण पूरिताः
क्षमाभृतां बलरजसा महागुहाः ।
रहस्तपाविधुरवधूरतार्थिनां
नभःसदामुपकरणीयतां ययुः ॥

गते मुखच्छदपटसाट्टशीं दृशः
पथस्तिरोदधति घने रजस्यपि ।
मदानिलैरधिमधुचूतगन्धिभि-
र्द्विपा द्विपानभिययुरेव रंहसा ॥

मदाम्भसा परिगलितेन सम्मदा
गजाञ्जनः शमितमरुद्धुजानधः ।
उपर्यवस्थितघनपांसुमण्डला-
नलोकयत्ततपटमण्डपानिव ॥

अन्यूनोन्नतयो ऽतिमात्रपृथवः पृथ्वीधरश्रीभृत-
स्तन्वन्तः कनकावलीभिरुपमां सौदामिनीदामनि ।
वर्षन्तः शाममानयन्नुपलसच्छृङ्गारलेखायुधाः
काले कालियकायकालवपुषः पांसुं गजाम्भोमुचः ॥

The dust from the army filled the deep mountain caverns,
    blocking and concealing their entrances; it aided
    wizards[21] seeking to make love in seclusion, for their
    wives were cringing with embarrassment at being
    spied.

Although the thick dust covered their eyes like a cloth
    mask, the elephants still charged toward each other;
    they could smell, borne on the wind, the scent of ichor
    fragrant as pollen-rich mango blossom.

The elephants had damped down the ground with ichor
    flowing from their seven orifices,[22] but they remained
    wreathed in the thick floating dust—they could be
    taken for long avenues of tents.

These cloud-like elephants were of exceptional height
    and breadth, as imposingly majestic as mountains;
    their golden chains looked like lightning flashes,
    and their decorations of red orpiment glinted like
    rainbows. Dark as the serpent Kaliya,* they poured
    down torrents of ichor as the moment required and
    eventually dampened the flurrying dust.

---

* Defeated by the young Krishna.

CHAPTER 18

The Battle Begins

संजग्माते तावपायानपेक्षौ
सेनाम्भोधी धीरनादौ रयेण ।
पक्षच्छेदात्पूर्वमेकत्र देशे
वान्छन्तौ वा सह्यविन्ध्यौ निलेतुम् ॥

पत्तिः पत्तिं वाहमेयाय वाजी
नागं नागः स्यन्दनी स्यन्दनस्थम् ।
इत्थं सेना वल्लभस्येव रागा-
दङ्गेनाङ्गं प्रत्यनीकस्य भेजे ॥

रथ्याघोषैर्बृंहया वारणाना-
मैक्यं गच्छन्वाजिनां हेषया च ।
व्योमव्यापी संततं दुन्दुभीना-
मव्यक्तो ऽभूदीशितेव प्रणादः ॥

रोषावेशाद्द्रावतः प्रत्यमित्रं
दूरोत्क्षिप्तस्थूलबाहुध्वजस्य ।
दीर्घास्तिर्यग्वैजयन्तीसदृश्यः
पादातस्य भ्रेजिरे खड्गलेखाः ॥

५ वध्राबद्धा धोरितेन प्रयाता-
मश्वीयानामुच्चकैरुच्छलन्तः ।
रौक्मा रेजुः स्थासका मूर्तिभाजो
दर्पस्येव व्याप्तदेहस्य शेषाः ॥

Then the two ocean-like armies charged each other with
    a mighty roar, heedless of danger; they were like the
    Sahya and Vindhya mountains* vying to settle in the
    same place before Indra cut off their wings.[1]

Foot soldier clashed with foot soldier, stallion with
    stallion, elephant with elephant, and charioteer with
    charioteer; each army embraced its foe as passionately
    as if making love.

Beating of drums mingled with thundering of chariots,
    trumpeting of elephants, and neighing of horses;
    the din pervaded the heavens and became
    undifferentiated, like Brahma the all-encompassing.[2]

As the infantry rushed toward the enemy, they lifted
    their arms like muscular flagpoles; the sword blades
    slanting beside them seemed like ensigns celebrating
    victory.

The cavalry advanced at a canter, golden ornaments on   5
    their girth straps bouncing high; they glowed like
    visible fragments of the spirit suffusing the horses'
    bodies.

---

* Both these mountain ranges are located in the Deccan.

सान्द्रत्वक्कास्तल्पलाश्लिष्टकक्ष्या-१
माझीं शोभामाप्नुवन्तश्चतुर्थीम् ।
कल्पस्यान्ते मारुतेनापनुन्ना-
श्चेलुश्चण्डा गण्डशैला इवेभाः ॥

संक्रीडन्ती तेजिताश्वस्य रागा-
दुद्दम्याराद्ग्रकायोत्थितस्य२ ।
रंहोभाजामक्षधूः स्यन्दनानां
हाकारं नु प्राजितुः प्रत्यनन्दत् ॥

कुर्वाणानां संपरायान्तरायं
भूरेणूनां मृत्युना मार्जनाय ।
संमार्जन्यो नूनमुद्धूयमाना
भान्ति स्मोच्चैः केतनानां पताकाः ॥

उद्यन्नादं धन्विभिर्निष्ठुराणि
स्थूलान्युच्चैर्मण्डलत्वं दधन्ति ।
आस्फाल्यन्ते कार्मुकाणि स्म कामं
हस्त्यारोहैः कुञ्जराणां शिरांसि ॥

१० घण्टानादा निःस्वना दिण्डिमानां
ग्रैवेयाणामारवा बृंहितानि ।
आमित्येव प्रत्यवोचनगजाना-
मुत्साहार्थं वाचमाधोरणस्य ॥

Thick-hided elephants, turrets strapped on their backs,
    charged with the majesty of full maturity, like
    terrifying blocks of rock driven by the doomsday
    hurricane.

As the chariots raced forward, each rattling axle
    echoed with enthusiastic applause the shouted
    encouragement of the charioteer leaning far out to
    wield the whip.

The banners atop their flagstaffs looked just like cloths
    shaken by death to wipe away the dust obscuring the
    battle.

With a shout the archers lustily slapped their bows, made
    of hard wood, strong, with a long, natural curve;
    they looked like mahouts striking the heads of their
    elephants.

There arose a jangling of bells, thundering of drums,   10
    rattling of chains, and trumpeting—the elephants
    were responding with a will to the cries of drivers
    urging them on.

यातैश्चतुर्विध्यमस्त्रादिभेदा-
दव्यासङ्गैः सौष्ठवाल्लाघवाच्च ।
शिक्षाशक्तीः प्राहरन्दर्शयन्तो
मुक्तामुक्तैरायुधैरायुधीयाः ॥

रोषावेशादाभिमुख्येन कौचि-
त्पाणिग्राहं रंहसैवोपयातौ ।
हित्वा हेती मल्लवन्मुष्टिघातं
घ्नन्तौ बाहूबाहवि व्यासजेताम् ॥

शुद्धाः सङ्गं न क्वचित्प्राप्नुवन्तो
दूरान्मुक्ताः शीघ्रतां दर्शयन्तः ।
अन्तःसेनं विद्विषामाविशन्तो
युक्तं चक्रुः सायका वाजितायाः ॥

आक्रम्याजेरग्रिमस्कन्धमुच्चै-
रास्थायाथो वीतशङ्कं शिरश्च ।
हेलालोला वर्त्म गत्वातिमर्त्यं
घ्रामारोहन्मानभाजः सुखेन ॥

१५ रोदोरन्ध्रं व्यश्नुवानानि लोलै-
रङ्गस्यान्तर्मापितैः स्थावराणि ।
केचिद्द्वीरित्य संयन्निषद्याः
क्रीणन्ति स्म प्राणमूल्यैर्यशांसि ॥

602

The warriors displayed their professional skill as they
    fought; their weapons may have been diverse—
    thrown or held, and of four main types, such as the
    bow[3]—but deployed with dexterity and speed, they all
    proved irresistible.

However, one pair of warriors simply threw away their
    weapons and angrily rushed together; pummeling
    each other, they fell to grappling hand to hand like
    wrestlers.

Well-honed, totally overwhelming, released from afar, and
    picking up speed before descending upon the enemy
    army—the feathered arrows seemed just like the
    cavalry.[4]

Intrepid warriors successfully negotiated the preliminary
    stages of battle; then, after fearlessly reaching
    combat's climax, they nonchalantly entered on the
    path leading beyond the mortal world and ascended to
    heaven.[5]

There were warriors who shopped in the great market of   15
    battle and bought universal renown for eternity at the
    cost of their fleeting lives hitherto deposited in their
    bodies.

वीर्योत्सेकश्लाघि कृत्वापदानं
संग्रामाग्रे मानिनां लज्जितानाम् ।
अज्ञातानां शत्रुभिर्युक्तमुच्चैः
श्रीमन्नाम श्रावयन्ति स्म नग्राः ॥

आधावन्तः संमुखं धारिताना-
मन्यैरन्ये तीक्ष्णकौक्षेयकाणाम् ।
वक्षःपीठैरा त्सरोरात्मनैव
क्रोधेनान्धाः प्राविशन्पुष्कराणि ॥

मिश्रीभूते तत्र सैन्यद्वये ऽपि
प्रायेणायं व्यक्त आसीद्विशेषः ।
आत्मीयास्ते ये पराङ्मुः पुरस्ता-
दभ्यावर्ती संमुखो यः परो ऽसौ ॥

सद्द्रंशत्वादङ्गसङ्गिनीत्वं
नीत्वा कामं गौरवेणावबद्धा ।
नीता हस्तं वञ्चयित्वा परेण
द्रोहं चक्रे कस्यचित्स्वा कृपाणी ॥

२० नीते भेदं धौतधारानिपाता-
दम्भोदाभे शात्रवेणापरस्य ।
सासृग्राजिस्तीक्ष्णमार्गस्य मार्गो
विद्युद्दीप्रः कङ्कटे लक्ष्यते स्म ॥

As the hostilities commenced, bards were noisily lauding
the glorious names of proud warriors who, reticent
about a former mighty deed of conspicuous bravery
and enterprise, were unknown to their opponents.

Meanwhile, other soldiers, blinded by fury as they
charged, deliberately skewered their chests up to the
hilt of the sharp swords wielded by their opponents.

Although both armies had come together as one in
battle, as a rule the combatants could clearly be
distinguished: those turning their backs were to
be regarded as friendly and not to be killed,[6] while
anyone advancing and standing his ground face to face
was reckoned a foe.

One warrior had armed himself with a particular sword
because it had a fine long blade, and he had fixed it to
his belt with great care; but when an opponent deftly
grabbed hold of the weapon, it proved treacherous
and wounded him.[7]

A soldier's armor had been pierced by his opponent's   20
clean blade, like a dark monsoon cloud parting when
pure rain pours forth;[8] upon it could be seen the trace
of the sword's blow—a streak of blood like a shaft of
lightning.

आ मूलान्तात्सायकेनायतेन
स्यूते बाहौ मङ्कशिलष्टमुष्टेः ।
प्राप्यासातां वेदनां त्यक्तधैर्या-
दप्यभ्रश्यच्चर्म नान्यस्य पाणेः ॥

भित्त्वा घोणामायसेनाधिवक्षः
स्थूरीपृष्ठो गार्ध्रपक्षेण विद्धः ।
शिक्षाहेतोर्गाढरज्ज्वेव बद्धुं
हर्तुं वक्रं^३ नाशकद्दुर्मुखो ऽपि ॥

कुन्तेनोच्चैः सादिना हन्तुमिष्टा-
न्नाजानेयो दन्तिनस्त्रस्यति स्म ।
कर्मोदारं कीर्तये कर्तुकामा-
न्किं वा जात्याः स्वामिनो ह्रेपयन्ति ॥

जेतुं जैत्राः शेकिरे नारिसैन्यैः
पश्यन्तो ऽधो लोकमस्तेषुजालाः ।
नागारूढाः पर्वतानि श्रयन्तो
दुर्गाणीव त्रासहीनास्त्रसानि ॥

२५ विष्वद्रीचीर्विक्षिपन्सैन्यवीची-
राजावन्तः क्वापि दूरं प्रयातम् ।
बभ्रामैको बन्धुमिष्टं दिदृक्षुः
सिन्धौ वाद्यो मण्डलं गोर्वराहः ॥

Another soldier's arm had been pierced through to the
    armpit by a long arrow; his grip was weakening from
    the agony, but his fist remained tightly clenched and
    he did not release his shield's handle.

A vulture-feathered shaft had penetrated the nostrils of
    a newly broken horse and struck through to its chest;
    although the beast was naturally headstrong, it was
    unable to move its mouth, apparently still controlled
    by a taut rope so it could be trained to the bit.

A thoroughbred stallion showed no fear of an elephant
    that his rider was menacing with spear brandished
    high. When their masters are intent on performing
    a glorious deed to win fame, do retainers with any
    pedigree ever shame them?

Warriors perched on elephants gazed imperturbably
    upon the scene as they dispatched showers of arrows;
    they seemed to be occupying mobile hill-fortresses,
    impregnable by enemy forces.

Aspiring to meet a close comrade in some far-flung part of   25
    the battlefield, one warrior roamed around, parting
    the waves of opponents flooding everywhere; he was
    like Vishnu's Boar incarnation seeking the earth's disc
    sunk in a remote quarter of the ocean.

यावच्चक्रे नाञ्जनं बोधनाय
व्यस्तारज्ञो^४ हस्तिचारी मदस्य ।
सेनास्वानाद्दन्तिनामात्मनैव
स्थूलास्तावत्प्रावहन्दानकुल्याः ॥

क्रुध्यन्गन्धादन्यनागाय दूरा-
दारोढारं धूतमूर्धावमन्य ।
घोरारावध्वानिताशेषदिक्के
धिक्के^५ नागः पर्यणंसीत्स्व एव ॥

प्रत्यासन्ने दन्तिनि प्रातिपक्षे
यन्त्रा नागः प्रास्तवक्त्रच्छदो ऽपि ।
क्रोधाक्रान्तः क्रूरनिर्दारिताक्षः
प्रेक्षांचक्रे नैव किंचिन्मदान्धः ॥

तूर्णं यावन्नापनिन्ये निषादी
वासश्चक्षुर्वारणं वारणस्य ।
तावत्पूगैरन्यनागाधिरोहः
कादम्बानामेकपातैरसीव्यत् ॥

३० आस्थद्दृष्टेराच्छदं च प्रमत्तो^६
याता यातः प्रत्यरीभं द्विपस्य ।
मग्नस्योच्चैर्बर्हभारेण शङ्को-
रावव्राते ईक्षणे च क्षणेन ॥

608

Even before the expert[9] mahouts had slapped their
    elephants to stimulate their enthusiasm, thick ichor
    streams were coursing freely over the beasts' bodies
    when they heard the armies' din.

Enraged by the distant scent of a rival, an elephant tossed
    its head in disregard of its driver and lunged at its calf,
    whose shrill screechings made the sky resound.

When an enemy elephant drew near, a mahout removed
    the blinkers from his own beast; it glared terribly in
    rage, but blinded by ichor could see nothing.

Before another driver could remove the cloth covering his
    elephant's eyes, his opponent quickly stitched it over
    them with a stream of arrows fired in rapid succession.

As an elephant advanced toward the foe, his mahout   30
    carelessly pulled away its cloth blinkers; in an instant
    its eyes were covered by the feathery flight of an arrow
    lodged in its forehead.

यत्तादृक्षन्सुस्थितत्वादनाशं
निश्चिन्तो ऽन्यश्चेतसा भावितेन ।
अन्त्यावस्थाकालयोग्योपयोगं
दध्रे ऽभीष्टं नागमापद्ध्रुवं वा ॥

अन्योन्येषां पुष्करैरामृशन्तो
दानोद्द्रेदानुच्चकैर्भुग्रवालाः ।
उन्मूर्धानः सन्त्रिषद्याअपराभिः
प्रायुध्यन्त स्पष्टदन्तध्वनीभाः ॥

द्राघीयांसः संहताः स्थामभाज-
श्चारूदग्रास्तीक्ष्णतामत्यजन्तः ।
दन्ता दन्तैराहताः सामजानां
भङ्गं प्रापुर्न स्वयं सामजाताः ॥

मातङ्गानां दन्तसंघट्टजन्मा
हेमच्छेदच्छायचञ्चच्छिखाग्रः ।
लग्नो ऽप्यग्निश्चामरेषु प्रकामं
माञ्जिष्ठेषु व्यज्यते न स्म सैन्यैः ॥

३५ ओषामासे मत्सरोत्पातवात-
श्लिष्यद्दन्तक्ष्मारुहाघर्षणोत्थैः ।
यौगान्तैर्वा वह्निभिर्वारणाना-
मुच्चैर्मूर्ध्वोऽग्नि नक्षत्रमाला ॥

Another driver concentrated on restraining his favorite
elephant. Because his beast was so securely
positioned, he had no sense of danger and could
carefully hold it back for deployment in the battle's
final moment of peril—like a reserve of money saved
for use in emergencies.

Scenting each others' ichor flowing, the elephants' tails
curled high in the air and they raised their heads;
then, anchoring themselves on their hindquarters,
they fought amid the din of clashing tusks.

Long, thick, and firm, gleaming, frightening, and sharp—
tusks may have broken when struck by opponents, but
the elephants themselves did not break and run.

When the elephants' tusks clashed, fire sparked up, flames
flashing like shards of gold; it took hold on the yak-tail
banners, so deeply dyed with red madder that the
soldiers were unaware they were ablaze.

A necklace outline was branded on the lofty heads of the   35
elephants by the flames ignited by their tusks' friction;
it was like doomsday when the starry constellation
in the firmament is consumed by a conflagration as
the sudden hurricane winds drive trees against one
another.

सान्द्राम्भोदश्यामले सामजानां
वृन्दे नीताः शोणितैः शोणिमानम् ।
दन्ताः शोभामापुरम्भोनिधीनां
कन्दोद्धेदा वैद्रुमा वारिणीव ॥

आकम्प्राग्रैः केतुभिः सन्निपातं
तारोदीर्णग्रैवनादं व्रजन्तः ।
मग्नानङ्घे गाढमन्यद्द्विपानां
दन्तान्दुःखादुत्खनन्ति स्म नागाः ॥

उत्क्षिप्योच्चैरस्फुरन्तं रदाभ्या-
मीषादन्तः कुञ्जरं शात्रवीयम् ।
शृङ्गप्रोतप्रावृषेण्याम्बुदस्य
स्पष्टं प्रापत्साम्यमुर्वीधरस्य ॥

भग्ने ऽपीभे स्वे परावृत्य देहं
योद्धा सार्धं व्रीडया मुञ्चतेषून् ।
साकं यातुः संमदेनानुबन्धी
दूनो ऽभीक्ष्णं वारणः प्रत्यरोधि ॥

४० व्याप्तं लोकैर्दुःखलभ्याप्यसारं
संरम्भित्वादेत्य धीरो महीयः ।
सेनामध्यं गाहते वारणः स्म
ब्रह्मेव प्रागादिदेवोदरान्तः ॥

612

A troop of elephants, dark as a heavy monsoon cloud,
    turned deep red with blood, their tusks like coral
    branches projecting from the ocean's dark water.

Amid the din of jangling neck chains the elephants
    crashed into the standards with their fluttering
    pennants; they could barely extract their tusks sunk
    deep into the bodies of their foes.

One elephant tossed a lifeless opponent high in the air
    with its tusks long as chariot poles; it looked just like
    a mountain with a monsoon cloud impaled on its peak.

Although his own elephant was fleeing, one warrior
    turned and released his arrows—along with his shame
    in defeat—at a beast in pursuit. Wounded grievously,
    it was held back by its driver—together with his
    exultation at victory.

A valiant elephant charged up and plunged into the midst   40
    of the enemy army, but was so hemmed in by soldiers
    that it could not escape. Thus the seer Markandeya[10]
    at the end of the previous age entered the primal
    deity's stomach, already filled with worlds.[11]

भृङ्गश्रेणिश्यामभासां समूहै-
र्नाराचानां विद्धनीरन्ध्रदेहः ।
निर्भीकत्वादाहवे ऽनाहतेच्छो
हृष्यन्हस्ती हृष्टरोमेव रेजे ॥

आताम्राभा रोषभाजः कटान्ता-
दाशूत्खाते मार्गणे धूर्गतेन ।
निश्श्रोतन्ती नागराजस्य जज्ञे
दानस्याहो लोहितस्योत धारा ॥

क्रामन्दन्तौ दन्तिनः साहसिक्या-
दीषादण्डौ मृत्युशय्यातलस्य ।
सैन्यैरन्यस्तत्क्षणादाशशङ्के
स्वर्गस्योच्चैरर्धमार्गाधिरूढः ॥

कुर्वञ्ज्योत्स्नाविप्रुषां तुल्यरूप-
स्तारस्ताराजालशारामिव द्याम् ।
खड्गाघातैर्दारिताद्दन्तिकुम्भा-
दाभाति स्म प्रोच्छलन्मौक्तिकौघः ॥

४५ दूरोत्क्षिप्तक्षिप्रचक्रावकृत्तं
मत्तो हस्तं हस्तिराजः स्वमेव ।
भीमं भूमौ लोलमानं सरोषः
पादेनासृक्पङ्कपेषं पिपेष ॥

Another elephant, riddled with showers of arrows dark
　　as swarming bees, still trumpeted with joy, fearlessly
　　maintaining its zest for combat; it seemed to be
　　swathed with hair thrilling in excitement.

When a mahout swiftly removed a shaft from his mighty
　　elephant's temple, a copper-colored stream flowed
　　from the enraged beast—but was it ichor or blood?

A foolhardy warrior scrambled onto an elephant's tusks,
　　twin props on death's bed; at that moment he was
　　reckoned by his comrades to have ascended halfway
　　up the high road to heaven.

The pellucid pearl flood pouring like drops of moonlight
　　from an elephant's temple[12] sliced open by slashing
　　swords seemed to cover the sky with a net of stars.

An elephant's trunk, severed by a discus hurled from afar,　　45
　　was rolling on the ground, a terrible sight; maddened
　　with rage, the beast trampled it into the mess of mud
　　and gore.

आपस्काराल्लूनगात्रस्य भूमिं
निःसाधारं गच्छतो ऽवाङ्मुखस्य ।
लब्धायामं दन्तयोर्युगममेव
स्वं नागस्य प्रापदुत्तम्भनत्वम् ॥

लब्धस्पर्शं भूव्यधाद्व्यथेन
स्थित्वा किंचिद्दन्तयोरन्तराले ।
ऊर्ध्वार्धासिक्षुण्णदन्तप्रवेष्टं
जित्वोत्तस्थे नागमन्येन सद्यः ॥

हस्तेनाग्रे वीतभीतिं गृहीत्वा
कंचिद्व्यालः क्षिप्तवानूर्ध्वमुच्चैः ।
आलीनानां व्योम्नि तस्यैव हेतोः
स्वर्गस्त्रीणामर्पयामास नूनम् ॥

कंचिद्दूरादायतेन द्रढीयः-
प्रासप्रोतस्रोतसान्तःक्षतेन ।
हस्ताग्रेण प्राप्तमप्यग्रतो ऽभू-
दानैश्वर्यं वारणस्य ग्रहीतुम् ॥

५० तन्वाः पुंसो नन्दगोपात्मजायाः
कंसेनेव स्फोटितया गजेन ।
दिव्या मूर्तिर्व्योमगैरुत्पतन्ती
वीक्षामासे विस्मितैश्चण्डिकेव ॥

Another elephant's foreleg[13] had been chopped off at
    the base of the knee and it was collapsing helplessly;
    but as the beast's head fell downward, its long tusks
    propped it up.

One warrior remained unscathed when an elephant's tusks
    struck down at him; he squeezed in between them and
    quickly raised himself to cut them from their sockets
    with his sword, finishing off the creature.[14]

As another warrior fearlessly confronted a fierce elephant,
    it seized him with its trunk and hurled him high in the
    air; no doubt it was handing him over to the heavenly
    women thronging the sky to carry him away.[15]

Another elephant, however, could not seize a warrior
    although he had advanced right in front of it; it had
    stretched out its trunk to full length after its nostrils
    had been pierced by a javelin, suffering a grievous
    internal wound.

One soldier had been torn apart by an elephant, and the   50
    gods gazed in wonder at the divine apparition of his
    soul ascending from his body. So Kamsa once beheld
    the goddess Chandika emerging from Yashoda,
    daughter of the cowherd Nanda.[16]

आक्रम्यैकामग्रपादेन जङ्घा-
मन्यामुच्चैराददानः करेण ।
सास्थिस्वानं दारुवद्दारुणात्मा
कंचिन्मध्यात्पाटयामास दन्ती ॥

शोचित्वाग्रे भृत्ययोर्मृत्युभाजो-
रर्यः प्रेम्णा नो तथा वल्लभस्य ।
पूर्वं कृत्वा नेतरस्य प्रसादं
पश्चात्तापादाप दाहं यथान्तः ॥

उत्प्लुत्यारादर्धचन्द्रावलूने
वक्रे ऽन्यस्य क्रोधदष्टौष्ठदन्ते ।
सैन्यैः कण्ठच्छेदलीने कबन्धा-
द्द्वयो बिभ्ये वल्गतः सासिपाणेः ॥

तूर्यारावैराहितोत्तालताले-
र्गायन्तीभिः काहलं काहलाभिः ।
नृत्ते चक्षुःशून्यहस्तप्रयोगं
काये कूजन्कम्बुरुच्चैर्जहास ॥

५५ प्रत्यावृत्तं भङ्गभाजि स्वसैन्ये
तुल्यं मुक्तैराकिरन्ति स्म कंचित् ।
एकौघेन स्वर्णपुङ्खैर्द्विषन्तः
सिद्धा माल्यैः साधुवादैर्द्वये ऽपि ॥

A ferocious elephant pressed down a foe's thigh with
  its forefoot while pulling hard on the other with its
  trunk; then it ripped him in half to the sound of bones
  breaking like wood.

As he grieved for two retainers lying dead before him,
  their lord was consumed with anguish—not from
  affection for his favorite but from regret he had not
  been better disposed toward the other.

A head severed by a half-moon arrow[17] shot high in the
  air, teeth biting its lips in rage, and then plummeted
  back onto its vacant neck; soldiers gaped in terror at
  the corpse dancing in front of them, still clutching its
  sword.

As the cadaver gyrated, sightlessly jerking its hands, a
  conch trumpet brayed with laughter to the applause
  of relentlessly beating drums, while flutes screeched
  raucously.

His comrades broke rank and fled, but one of their   55
  number turned to resist; in a single stream there were
  poured down upon him golden-shafted arrows by his
  enemies, garlands by the heavenly sages, and cries of
  applause from both quarters.

619

बाणक्षिप्तारोहशून्यासनानां
प्रक्रान्तानामन्यसैन्यैर्ग्रहीतुम् ।
संरब्धानां भ्राम्यतामाजिभूमौ
वारी वारैः सस्मरे वारणानाम् ॥

पौनःपुन्यादस्रगन्धेन मत्तो
मृद्नन्कोपाल्लोकमायोधनोर्व्याम् ।
पादे लग्नामन्त्रमालामिभेन्द्रः
पाशीकल्पामायतामाचकर्ष ॥

कश्चिन्मूर्छामेत्य गाढप्रहारः
सिक्तः शीतैः शीकरैर्वारणस्य ।
उच्छ्वास प्रस्थिता तं जिघृक्षु-
र्व्यर्थाकूता नाकनारी मुमूर्छ ॥

लूनग्रीवात्सायकेनापरस्य
घ्रामत्युच्चैराननादुत्पतिष्णोः ।
त्रेसे मुग्धैः सैंहिकेयानुकारा-
त्सभ्रूभङ्गादप्सरोवक्त्रचन्द्रैः ॥

६० वृत्तं युद्धे शूरमाश्लिष्य काचि-
द्रन्तुं तूर्णं मेरुकुञ्जं जगाम ।
त्यक्त्वा नाग्रौ देहमेति स्म याव-
त्पत्नी सद्यस्तद्वियोगासहिष्णुः ॥

Troops of elephants, their seats empty of mahouts killed
by arrows, were about to be captured by enemy
soldiers; as they wandered in distress over the
battlefield, they remembered the forest arbors where
they had first been trapped.

A mighty elephant, maddened by the incessant smell of
blood, dragged a long train of entrails wound round its
foot like a chain, crushing everyone on the battlefield
in its fury.

A soldier fainting from a severe wound was sprinkled with
cool drops of ichor by an elephant; at this the apsaras
who had set out to carry him to heaven also swooned,
her intention frustrated.[18]

The beautiful apsarases with their moon-like faces were
terrified by a grimacing arrow-severed head sent
flying high in the sky—it was just like Rahu, the
bodiless eclipse-demon.

An apsaras gathered into her embrace a heroic warrior   60
slain in battle and quickly made off to a bower on
Mount Meru; she intended to make love with him
before his wife, unable to endure separation, hurried
to give up her life on the funeral pyre and join him.[19]

त्यक्तप्राणं संयुगे हस्तिनीस्था
वीक्ष्य प्रेम्णा तत्क्षणादुद्धतासुः ।
प्राप्याखण्डाद्देवभूयं सतीत्वा-
दाशिश्लेष स्वैव कंचित्पुरन्धरी ॥

स्वर्गे वासं कारयन्त्या चिराय
प्रत्यग्रत्वं प्रत्यहं धारयन्त्या ।
कश्चिद्देजे नाकनार्या परस्मिँ-
ल्लोके लोकं प्रीणयन्त्येह कीर्त्या ॥

गत्वा नूनं वैबुधं सद्म रम्यं
मूर्छाभाजामाजगामान्तरात्मा ।
भूयो दृष्टप्रत्यया प्राप्य संज्ञां
साधीयस्ते यद्रणायाद्रियन्त ॥

कश्चिच्छस्ताबाधमूढो ऽपवोढु-
र्लब्ध्वा भूयश्चेतनामाहवाय ।
व्यावर्तिष्ट क्रोशतः सख्युरुच्चै-
स्त्यक्तक्षात्मा का च लोकानुवृत्तिः ॥

६५ भिन्नोरस्कौ शत्रुणाकृष्य दूरा-
दासन्नत्वात्कौचिदेकेषुणैव ।
अन्योन्यावष्टम्भसामर्थ्ययोगा-
दूर्ध्वावेव स्वर्गतावप्यभूताम् ॥

Another warrior's wife, seated on an elephant, saw he had
died in battle and expired that very moment from
love; in an instant she became a goddess through her
fidelity and embraced him in heaven.

A dead warrior was welcomed by an apsaras in the next
world and by fame in this; both ensured lengthy
residence in heaven, daily rejuvenation, and general
acclaim.

The souls of those fainting from their wounds had clearly
traveled to heaven with all its delights and then
come back; on regaining consciousness, they applied
themselves all the more to battle, convinced they
would return.

A warrior revived after being dazed by a blow and rejoined
the fray, despite the earnest pleas of his comrade
dragging him to the rear. When one has already given
up life, why pay attention to others?

Two warriors had been stationed so close to each other   65
they were pierced through their chests by the same
enemy arrow shot from afar; even in death they stood
bolt upright, propping each other up.

भिन्नाञ्जस्त्रैर्मोहभाजो ऽभिजाता-
न्हन्तुं लोलं[७] वारयन्तः स्ववर्गम् ।
जीवग्राहं ग्राहयामासुरन्ये
योग्येनार्थः कस्य न स्याज्जनेन ॥

भग्नैर्दण्डैरातपत्राणि भूमौ
पर्यस्तानि प्रौढचन्द्रद्युतीनि ।
आहारार्थं प्रेतराजस्य रुप्य-
स्थालानीव स्थापितानि स्म भान्ति ॥

रेजुर्भ्रष्टा वक्षसः कुङ्कुमाङ्का
मुक्ताहाराः पार्थिवानां व्यसूनाम् ।
सैन्यान्सास्थीन्स्वादतो रक्तरक्ता
नष्टा नूनं प्रेतराजस्य दन्ताः[८] ॥

निम्नेष्वोघीभूतमस्त्रक्षताना-
मस्रं भूमौ[९] यच्चकासांचकार ।
रागार्थं तत्किं नु कौसुम्भमम्भः
संव्यानानामन्तकान्तःपुरस्य ॥

७० रामेण त्रिःसप्तकृत्वो ह्रदानां
चित्रं चक्रे पञ्चकं क्षत्रियास्रैः ।
रक्ताम्भोभिस्तत्क्षणादेव तस्मि-
न्संख्ये ऽसंख्याः प्रासरन्द्वीपवत्यः ॥

Some warriors had captured highborn foes fainting from
  sword wounds and were restraining their followers
  bent on killing them. Who would not assist the
  deserving?

Broken-staffed parasols thrown on the ground, white as
  the full moon, looked like silver dishes laid out for a
  feast for the lord of the dead.

Pearl necklaces smeared with saffron gleamed as they fell
  from the breasts of slaughtered kings; most likely
  Yama's bloodstained fangs had been dislodged while
  he gorged on soldiers and their bones.

The blood of the wounded formed glinting coagulations
  in hollows in the ground. Could it not have been red
  safflower juice intended to dye the bodices of the god
  of death's wives?

Twenty-one times Parashurama created five miraculous   70
  lakes with the blood of the warrior class,[20] but
  during that battle endless rivers of gore flowed
  instantaneously.

संदानान्तादस्त्रिभिः शिक्षितास्तै-
राविश्यान्तः^{१०} शातशस्त्रावलूनाः ।
कूर्मौपम्यं व्यक्तमन्तर्नदीना-
मैभाः प्रापन्नद्वयो ऽसृग्ङ्झयीनाम् ॥

पद्माकारैर्योधवक्त्रैरिभानां
कर्णभ्रष्टैश्श्यामरैर्हंसशुभ्रैः ।
सोपस्काराः प्राभवन्नस्रतोय-
स्रोतस्विन्यो वीचिषूच्चैस्तरङ्गिः ॥

उत्क्रान्तानामामिषायोपरिष्टा-
दध्याकाशं बभ्रमुः पत्रवाहाः ।
मूर्ताः प्राणा नूनमद्याप्यपेक्षा-
मासुः कायं त्याजिता दारुणास्तैः ॥

आतन्वद्भिर्दिदिक्षु पक्षाग्रवातं
प्राप्तैर्दूरादाशु तीक्ष्णैर्मुखेषु ।
आदौ रक्तं सैनिकानामजीवै-
र्जीवैः पश्चात्पत्रिपूगैरपायि ॥

७५ तेजोभाजां यद्रणे संस्थिताना-
मादत्तीव्रं सार्धमङ्गेन नूनम् ।
ज्वालाव्याजादुद्धमन्ती तदन्त-
स्तेजस्ताजग्दीप्तजिह्वा ववाशे ॥

Elephants' feet, cut off at the knee joint by crack warriors
striking low with sharp swords, looked just like
tortoises floating on bloody streams.

Torrents of gore sprang up; they were decorated with the
lotus-like heads of warriors bobbing on their billows
and with goose-white yak-tail plumes fallen from the
ears of elephants.

Birds roamed the sky above the dead in search of flesh;
for sure they were reincarnated souls, still seeking
the body that pitiless weapons had forced them to
relinquish.

The soldiers' blood was swiftly drunk, first by inanimate
things—showers of sharp pointed arrows, shot from
a good distance, raising a wind in the sky with their
flights, then by living creatures—flocks of sharp-
beaked birds flying from far off, stirring up the air with
their wings.[21]

A red-tongued jackal suddenly howled; it was vomiting in   75
the guise of flame blazing life energy consumed with
the flesh of heroes killed in battle.[22]

627

नैरन्तर्यच्छन्नदेहान्तरालं
दुर्भक्षस्य ज्वालिना वाशितेन ।
योद्धुर्बाणव्रातमादीप्य मांसं
पाकापूर्वस्वादमादे शिवाभिः ॥

ग्लानिच्छेदि क्षुत्प्रबोधाय पीत्वा
रक्तारिष्टं पाचिताजीर्णशेषम् ।
स्वादुंकारं कालखण्डोपदंशं
क्रोष्टा डिम्बं व्यष्वनद्व्यस्वनच्च ॥

क्रव्यात्पूगैः पुष्कराण्यानकानां[११]
प्रत्याशाभिर्मेदसो दारितानि ।
भुञ्जानो हि प्राणिसङ्घं रणोर्व्यां
नूनं कालो व्याददावाननानि ॥

कीर्णा रेजे साजिभूमिः समन्ता-
दप्राणद्भिः प्राणभाजां प्रतीकैः ।
बह्वारब्धैरर्धसंयोजितैर्वा
रूपैः स्रष्टुः सृष्टये कर्मशाला ॥

८० आयन्तीनामविरतरयं राजकानीकिनीना-
मित्थं सैन्यैः सममलघुभिः श्रीपतेरूर्मिमद्भिः ।
आसीत्तोयैर्मुहुरिव महद्वारिधेरापगानां
दोलायुद्धं कृतगुरुतरध्वानमौद्धत्यभाजाम् ॥

628

Female jackals were ravening a warrior's corpse, but it
　　proved difficult to consume; so with their fiery shrieks
　　they burned away the mass of arrows festooning the
　　torso—this cooking style imparted a grisly savor to
　　their meat!

To revive its appetite, a jackal drank down a refreshing
　　aperitif of blood and digested the remains of its
　　previous meal; then first biting into the liver as a
　　tidbit, it proceeded to devour a corpse, smacking its
　　chops and howling.

Drums, ripped open by vultures hoping for fat within,
　　appeared to be the very maws of death as he
　　consumed mortal creatures on the battlefield.

The arena of conflict was littered with the inert limbs
　　of once living beings; it looked like the creator's
　　workshop, brimful with objects not fully begun or only
　　half completed, waiting to be brought into finished
　　existence.

So, with the din growing ever louder, the great battle　　　　80
　　continued to ebb and flow, as the confident forces of
　　the Chedi kings engaged inexorably with the teeming,
　　surging host of Krishna, the husband of Shri. They
　　were like rivers in flood, their relentless current raging
　　when they merged with the ocean's billowing waters.[23]

CHAPTER 19

The Battle Rages

अथोत्तस्थे रणाटव्यामसुहृद्वेणुदारिणा ।
नृपाङ्घ्रिपौघसंघर्षादग्रिवद्वेणुदारिणा ॥१

आपतन्तममुं दूरादूरीकृतपराक्रमः ।
बलो ऽवलोकयामास मातङ्गमिव केसरी ॥

जजौजोजाजिजिज्जाजी तं ततो ऽतिततातितुत् ।
भाभो ऽभीभाभिभूभाभूरारारिररिरीररः ॥२

भवन्भयाय भूतानामाकम्पितमहीतलः ।
निर्घात इव निर्घोषभीमस्तस्यापतद्रथः ॥

५ रामे रिपुः शरानाजिमहेष्वास विचक्षणे ।
क्रोधादथैनं शितया महेष्वा स विचक्षणे ॥

दिशमर्कमिवावाचीं मूर्छां गतमपावहत् ।
मन्दप्रतापं तं सूतः शीघ्रमाजिविहायसः ॥

As the princes entered the fray, Venudarin,* destroyer
of enemies, also assumed his position in battle, like
fire sparked by the friction of forest trees utterly
consuming bamboo stands.

But Balarama too had already composed himself for
action, and from afar he watched Venudarin
advancing, as a lion does an elephant.[1] Then he moved
against him.

He was relentless in his enmity, always victorious in
battles where warriors showed their mettle, striking
down the arrogant. Blazing like a star as he sped
forward in his chariot, Balarama was full of a vigor
that could overcome any elephant, however fearless.

Balarama's chariot rolled onward to universal
consternation as the earth trembled; it was terrible in
its din, like a falling thunderbolt.

His opponent shot his many arrows at Balarama; but that   5
warrior was skilled in combat, and in his rage he hit
Venudarin with just one strong sharp shaft.

Venudarin's charioteer quickly carried him, fainting and
weakening, away from the battlefield, as if he were
Aruna conveying the sun from the sky when it dims in
the southern region.

---

* Literally "Bamboo-Splitter"; according to M, the son of Bana.

कृत्वा शिनेः साल्वचमूं सप्रभावा चमूर्जिताम् ।
ससर्ज वक्त्रैः फुल्लाब्जसप्रभा वाचमूर्जिताम् ॥

उल्मुकेन द्रुमं प्राप्य संकुचत्पत्रसंपदम् ।
तेजः प्रकिरता दिक्षु सप्रतापमदीप्यत ॥

पृथोरध्यक्षिपदुक्मी यया चापमुदायुधः ।
तयैव वाचापगमं ययाचापमुदा युधः ॥

१० समं समन्ततो राज्ञामापतन्तीररनीकिनीः ।
कार्ष्णिः प्रत्यग्रहीदेकः सरस्वानिव निम्नगाः ॥

दधानैर्घनसादृश्यं लसदायसदंसनैः ।
तत्र काञ्चनसच्छाया ससृजे तैः शराशनिः ॥३

नखांशुमञ्जरीकीर्णामसौ तरुरिवोच्चकैः ।
बभौ बिभ्रद्धनुःशाखामधिरूढशिलीमुखाम् ॥

Shini's mighty host overwhelmed the forces of
    Shishupala's ally Salva, emitting a deep roar of
    exultation, joyful faces like unfolding lotus blossoms.

Ulmuka's* restless energy spread everywhere; when the
    chariots of Druma's† army collided with each other
    in panic, he fell upon that warrior and burnt him to a
    crisp. He was a firebrand, brilliantly illuminating the
    sky as it consumed a forest and shriveled its foliage.[2]

Earlier Rukmin had brandished his weapons and noisily
    mocked Prithu's bow; now equally loud but no longer
    with enthusiasm for battle, he sought leave to retreat.

Krishna's son Pradyumna awaited alone the united forces   10
    of the kings advancing on all sides, as the ocean awaits
    the rivers flowing toward it.

In their tight-fitting armor of gray iron they seemed like
    rain clouds, and like golden lightning the storm of
    arrows they shot.

Pradyumna looked like a lofty tree; his bow wreathed with
    light from his fingernails was its flowering branch, the
    notched shaft was a parade of bees.[3]

---

* Literally, "Torch"; according to V, a son of Krishna.
† Literally, "Tree."

प्राप्य भीममसौ जन्यं सौजन्यं दधदानते ।
विध्यन्नमुमोच न रिपूनरिपूगान्तकः शरैः ॥

कृतस्य सर्वक्षितिपैर्विजयाशंसया पुरः ।
अनेकस्य चकारासौ बाणैर्बाणस्य खण्डनाम् ॥

१५ या बभार कृतानेकमाया सेना ससारताम् ।
धनुः स कर्षन्नहितमायासेनाससार ताम् ॥

ओजो महौजाः कृत्वाधः स क्षणादुत्तमौजसः ।
कुर्वन्नाजावमुख्यत्वमनयन्नाम मुख्यताम् ॥

दूरादेव चमूर्भल्लैः कुमारो हन्ति स स्म याः ।
न पुनः सांयुगीं ताश्च कुमारोहन्ति सस्मयाः ॥

Death to his foes personified, he plunged into the terrible
 battle; he was merciful to anyone who submitted, but
 unsparing as he dispatched his arrows against the
 enemy.

With these shafts he destroyed Bana[4] and his retainers,
 stationed in the vanguard by the other kings in
 expectation of victory.

That army had engaged in many feinting maneuvers   15
 and was most powerful, but drawing back his bow
 Pradyumna could attack it effortlessly.

A hero of massive strength, Pradyumna* in an instant
 proved himself superior in might to Uttamaujas;† in
 the ensuing combat he reduced his enemy's name to
 insignificance and removed the force of its meaning,
 while adding luster to his own already lustrous
 designation.[5]

With his lethal arrows the prince slaughtered the enemy
 armies; for all their bravado they would not enter the
 field again.

―――

* Literally, "Mighty."
† Literally, "Supreme Strength."

निपीड्य तरसा तेन मुक्ताः काममनास्थया ।
उपाययुर्विलक्षत्वं विद्विषो न शिलीमुखाः ॥

तस्यापदानैः समरे सहसा रोमहर्षिभिः ।
सुरैरशंसि व्योमस्थैः सह सारो महर्षिभिः ॥

२० सुगन्धयद्यद्दिशः शुक्लमम्लानि कुसुमं दिवः ।
भूरि तत्रापतत्तस्मादुत्पपात दिवं यशः ॥

सोढुं तस्य द्विषो नालमपयोधरवा रणम् ।
ऊर्णुनाव यशश्च द्यामपयोधरवारणम् ॥

केशप्रचुरलोकस्य पर्यस्कारि विकासिना ।
शेखरेणेव युद्धस्य शिरः कुसुमलक्ष्मणा ॥

सादरं युध्यमानापि तेनान्यनरसादरम् ।
सा दरं पृतना निन्ये हीयमाना रसादरम् ॥

The vanquished enemies he had willingly freed without
concern now felt shame, unlike the arrows he easily
released that did not disgrace themselves by missing
their mark.[6]

Pradyumna's formidable deeds in battle immediately
caused a thrill of excitement; his prowess was extolled
by the gods and great sages in heaven.

A flurry of flowers, perfuming the sky, white and
unfading, fell from heaven upon him, and in response
Pradyumna's fame[7] ascended on high.

20

The enemy no longer bellowed their war cry, for
they could not endure combat with Pradyumna;
meanwhile, his renown ranged over the heavens
unhindered by the clouds.

The epicenter of the battle, choked with combatants, was
ornamented by the bold Pradyumna, like the head of a
thick-haired man by a garland of fresh blossoms.[8]

Although at first fighting with conviction, the Chedi
forces were soon filled with terror by Pradyumna; he
would have reduced any other men to impotence, and
appetite for battle totally deserted them.

इत्यालिङ्गितमालोक्य जयलक्ष्म्या झषध्वजम् ।
क्रुद्धयेव क्रुधा सद्यः प्रपेदे चेदिभूपतिः ॥

२५ अहितानभि वाहिन्या स मानी चतुरङ्गया ।
चचाल वल्गत्कलभसमानीचतुरङ्गया ॥

ततस्ततधनुर्मौर्वीविस्फारस्फारनिःस्वनैः ।
तूर्यैर्युगक्षयक्षुभ्यदकूवारानुकारिणी ॥

सकारनानारकासकायसाददसायका ।
रसाहवा वाहसारनादवाददवादना ॥४

लोलासिकालियकुला यमस्येव स्वसा स्वयम् ।
चिकीर्षुरुल्लसल्लोहवर्मश्यामा सहायताम् ॥

सा सेना गमनारम्भे रसेनासीदनारता ।
तारनादजना मत्तधीरनागमनामया ॥५

Shishupala, king of the Chedis, watched Pradyumna[9]
    being embraced by the goddess of victory in this way
    and was immediately gripped with rage, as if by a
    jealous wife.

In anger he advanced toward his enemies with all four   25
    divisions of his army, its stallions prancing high like
    young elephants.

Then—drums booming like the ocean's thunder when it
    surges up at doomsday, the uproar magnified by the
    thrumming of taut bow strings,[10]

its arrows putting an end to both the maneuvers and the
    lives of exuberant foes of every rank, engaging in
    battle with a genuine passion, its military bands vying
    with the neighing of magnificent cavalry horses,

brandishing swords like black snakes, its iron armor
    glinting darkly like the god of death's sister* intending
    to offer aid herself,

the Chedi army as it commenced its advance was eager,
    full of appetite for battle, its soldiers yelling loudly,
    rutting elephants marching resolutely among them.

---

* The river Yamuna.

३० धौतधारासयः प्रष्ठाः प्रातिष्ठन्त क्षमाभुजाम् ।
शौर्यानुरागनिकषः सा हि वेलानुजीविनाम् ॥

दिवमिच्छन्युधा गन्तुं कोमलामलसंपदम् ।
दधौ दधानो ऽसिलतां को ऽमलामलसं पदम् ॥

कृतोरुवेगं युगपद्ध्वजिगीषन्त सैनिकाः ।
विपक्षं बाहुपरिघैर्जघ्नाभिरितरेतरम् ॥

वाहनाजनि मानासे साराजावनमा ततः ।
मत्तसारगराजेभे भारीहावज्जनध्वनि ॥

निध्वनज्ज्वहारीभा भेजे रागरसात्तमः ।
ततमानवजारासा सेना मानिजनाहवा ॥६

३५ अभग्नवृत्ताः प्रसभादाकृष्टा यौवनोद्धतैः ।
चक्रन्दुरुच्चकैर्मुष्टिग्राह्यमध्या धनुर्लताः ॥

करेणुः प्रास्थितानेको रेणुर्घण्टाः सहस्रशः ।
करे ऽणुः शीकरो जज्ञे रेणुस्तेन शमं ययौ ॥

Their sword blades clean and bright, the outrunners of the   30
    kings advanced for combat. That is the moment when
    servants' heroism and loyalty can be gauged.

What man aspires to battle his way to heaven with its
    abundance of easy comforts and hesitates just when
    he carries his glinting sword into combat?

Putting forth all speed as they ran, the soldiers strove to
    overcome, both at once, their foes with their strong
    arms and their own comrades with their legs.

The army remained undaunted in the ensuing conflict;
    its foes' pride was overthrown when confronted by
    mighty kings like rutting elephants. The battlefield
    was enveloped by the cries of heroic warriors.

The host echoed to the trumpetings of swift elephants,
    and the screams of warriors carried in all directions.
    As its brave soldiers battled it out, intense passion
    caused a dark obsessiveness to take possession of the
    army.

Long bows were gripped tightly by vigorous young   35
    archers, then bending to the full when they were
    drawn back, they sang out loudly.[11]

As the elephants advanced in numbers, their bells jangled
    incessantly, and globules of liquid appeared on their
    trunks, laying the dust to rest.

धृतप्रत्यग्रशृङ्काररसरागैरपि द्विपैः ।
सरोषसंभ्रमैर्बभ्रे रौद्र एव रणे रसः ॥

न तस्थौ भर्तृतः प्राप्तमानसंप्रतिपत्तिषु ।
रणैकसर्गेषु भयं मानसं प्रति पत्तिषु ॥

बाणाहिपूर्णतूणीरकोटरैर्धन्विशाखिभिः ।
गोधाश्लिष्टभुजाशाखैरभूद्द्रीमा बलाटवी ॥

४० नानाजाववजानाना सा जनौघघनौजसा ।
परानिहाहानिराप तान्वियाततयान्विता ॥

विषमं सर्वतो भद्रचक्रगोमूत्रिकादिभिः ।
श्लोकैरिव महाकाव्यं व्यूहैस्तदभवद्बलम् ॥

संहत्या सत्त्वतां चैद्यं प्रति भास्वरसेनया ।
ववले योद्धुमुत्पन्नप्रतिभा स्वरसेन या ॥

The beasts were freshly painted red with liquefied chalk;
in their recent rutting season they had been seized by
an amorous passion, now in their angry excitement for
battle they evinced only terrifying ferocity.[12]

Fear did not enter the minds of the soldiers; they had
received honor and goodwill from their king, and so
their energy was committed solely to fighting.

The battle was appalling, like a fearful forest—archers
were its trees, their arrow-filled quivers holes infested
with snakes, and their arms protected by leather
guards branches crawling with lizards.

The conflict was ever changing, but the Chedi forces felt   40
only contempt as they engaged with their enemies
through their great weight of numbers; feeling
themselves invincible, they were filled with a rash
audacity.

That army, drawn up in its various formations, was
difficult to assault on any front; it was organized
like a complex poem with verses composed in
configurations such as "Correct in Every Direction,"[13]
"The Wheel,"[14] and "Zigzagging like Cow's Urine."[15]

But the massed forces of the Yadavas, a glittering array,
now turned toward Shishupala; their very nature
inspired those heroes to fight.

विस्तीर्णमायामवती लोललोकनिरन्तरा ।
नरेन्द्रमार्गं रथ्येव पपात द्विषतां बलम् ॥

वारणागगभीरा सा साराभीगगणारवा ।
कारितारिवधा सेना नासेधा वारितारिका ॥७

४५ अधिनागं प्रजविनो विकसत्पिञ्छचारवः ।
पेतुर्बर्हिणदेशीयाः शङ्कवः प्राणहारिणः ॥

प्रवृत्ते विलसद्धानां साधने ऽप्यविषादिभिः ।
ववृषे विकसद्धानां युधमाप्य विषाणिभिः ॥८

पुरः प्रयुक्तैर्युद्धं तद्वलितैर्लब्धशुद्धिभिः ।
आलापैरिव गान्धर्वमदीप्यत पदातिभिः ॥

केनचित्स्वामिनान्येषां मण्डलाग्रानवद्यता ।
प्रापे कीर्तिप्लुतमहीमण्डलाग्रानवद्यता ॥

हर्तुं विद्विषतस्तीक्ष्णः सममेव सुसंहतेः ।
परिवारात्पृथक्चक्रे खड्ग आत्मा च केनचित् ॥

The Yadava host, extending far into the distance, was
crowded with seething soldiery; it crashed into the
enemy forces like a chariot[16] racing along a highway.

Packed with mountainous elephants, resounding to the
fearless cries of elite troops, that army in its total
confidence challenged the foe to fight and then dealt
out death.

Swift, lethal arrows descended upon their elephants; as   45
the fine feathers of their flights expanded in the air,
they looked like peacocks swooping down on snakes.[17]

The army advanced amid a crescendo of roaring.
Meanwhile, undismayed, the elephants entered
the fray, shaking off ichor spume with increasing
abandon.

Prominent in the battle were the foot soldiers stationed
in the vanguard, maneuvering in their positions with
undiminished morale.[18]

In shattering the swords of his opponents, one captain
gained unimpeachable renown, and every quarter of
the earth was bathed in his fame.

To better destroy his enemies, a warrior had
simultaneously removed his sharp sword from its
tight scabbard and his own combative person from the
security of massed comrades.

647

५० अन्येन विदधे ऽरीणामतिमात्राविलासिना ।
उद्दूर्णेन चमूस्तूर्णमतिमात्राविलासिना⁹ ॥

सहस्रपूरणः कश्चिल्लूनमूर्धासिना द्विषः ।
तदोर्ध्व एव काबन्धीमभजन्नर्तनक्रियाम् ॥

शस्त्रव्रणमयश्रीमदलंकरणभूषितः ।
दट्टशे ऽन्यो रावणवदलंकरणभूषितः ॥

द्विषद्द्विशसनच्छेदनिरस्तोरुयुगो ऽपरः ।
सिक्तश्वासैरुभयथा बभूवारुणविग्रहः ॥

भीमतामपरो ऽम्भोधिसमे ऽधित महाहवे ।
दाक्षे कोपः शिवस्येव समेधितमहा हवे ॥

५५ दन्तैश्चिच्छिदिरे कोपात्प्रतिपक्षं गजा इव ।
परनिस्त्रिंशनिर्लूनकरवालाः पदातयः ॥

The enemy army, vast in numbers though it was, became   50
    quickly confounded by a single daring warrior
    brandishing a flashing blade.

One soldier decapitated his adversary with his sword,
    gaining his thousandth kill; to celebrate he drew
    himself to his full height and capered in the macabre
    dance of a headless corpse.[19]

Another, gloriously decorated with sword wounds, could
    be taken for the demon king Ravana fighting on a
    battlefield far from his home island of Lanka.[20]

Yet another warrior had lost his legs, severed by enemy
    blades, and was bathed in blood; his body assumed
    a twofold appearance—red all over and similar to
    Aruna, the ruddy dawn, charioteer of the sun.[21]

While the conflict surged like the ocean, one warrior
    assumed a particularly terrible demeanor, seeming to
    be the embodiment of Shiva's anger fiercely blazing
    up at Daksha's sacrifice.[22]

When the infantry's swords were shattered by their   55
    enemies' blades, they tore at them in fury with their
    teeth; so elephants continue to gore their foes with
    their tusks, even after their trunks and tails have been
    severed.

रणे रभसनिर्भिन्नद्विपपाटविकासिनि ।
न तत्र गतभीः कश्चिद्द्विपपाट विकासिनि ॥

यावन्न सत्कृतैर्भर्तुः स्नेहानृण्यं यियासुभिः ।
अमर्षादितरैस्तावत्तत्यजे युधि जीवितम् ॥

अयशोभिदुरा लोके कोपधा मरणादृते ।
अयशोभिदुरालोके कोपधामरणादृते ॥

स्खलन्ती न क्वचित्तैक्ष्ण्यादभ्यग्रफलशालिनी ।
अमोचि शक्तिः शाक्तीकैर्लोहजा न शरीरजा ॥

६० आपदि व्यापृतनया रुषा युयुधिरे नृपाः ।
आप दिव्या पृतनया विस्मयं जनता तया ॥

स्वगुणैरा फलप्राप्तेराकृष्य गणिका इव ।
कामुकानिव नालीकांस्त्रिणताः सहसामुचन् ॥

The battle increased in intensity as seasoned fighters
    strove to cut down elephants with their swords. All
    participants remained steadfast and did not flee.

Some combatants had been honored by their lords and
    wished to discharge their debt of loyalty in battle;
    but before they could lay down their lives, others had
    already done so simply out of fury.

When those favored by fate and beyond the ordinary run
    of men become enraged and bent on combat, how
    can they dispel accusations of cowardice other than
    through their own deaths?

Their weapons, points finely honed, were so sharp that
    they never failed to deal out wounds; when the
    spearmen hurled them, they were only releasing the
    power of the iron, not of their bodies.

Kings who once practiced diplomacy in times of crisis now   60
    took to battle in a state of fury; heavenly onlookers
    were aghast at the forces they deployed.

Arrows were notched, drawn back to their point, and
    then quickly dispatched; the bows could be taken for
    shapely prostitutes, first enticing clients with their
    charms, then immediately throwing them out after
    payment.[23]

वाजिनः शत्रुसैन्यस्य समारब्धनवाजिनः ।
वाजिनश्च शरा मध्यमविशन्द्रुतवाजिनः ॥

पुरस्कृत्य फलं प्राप्तैः सत्पक्षाश्रयशालिभिः ।
कृतपुङ्खतया लेभे लक्ष्मप्याशु मार्गणैः ॥

रक्तसुतिं जपासूनसमरागामिषुव्यधात् ।
कश्चित्परः सपत्नेषु समरागामिषु व्यधात् ॥

६५ रयेन रणकाम्यन्तौ दूरादुपगताविभौ ।
गतासुरन्तरा दन्ती वरण्डक इवाभवत् ॥

भूरिभिर्भारिभिर्भीरा भूभारैरभिरेभिरे ।
भेरीरेभिभिरभ्राभैरभीरुभिरिभैरिभाः ॥१०

निशितासिलतालूनैस्तथा हस्तैर्न दन्तिनः ।
युध्यमाना यथा दन्तैर्भग्नैरापुर्विहस्तताम् ॥

निपीडनादिव मिथो दानतोयमनारतम् ।
वपुषामदयापातादिभानामभितोऽगलत् ॥

Chargers at full gallop and swift-flying feathered shafts[24]
    alike penetrated the ranks of the enemy army
    whenever they entered the fray for the first time.

Accurately aimed arrows, fitted with strong shafts and fine
    feather flights, swiftly pierced their targets.[25]

When the enemy advanced toward him, a warrior struck
    them with his deadly arrows and brought about a
    flood of gore red as rose blossoms.

As two rival tuskers lusting for battle charged at each   65
    other from a distance, a dead elephant lying between
    them seemed to be a separating barrier.[26]

Terrifying elephants engaged with hordes of fearless
    rivals; equipped with every type of military apparel,
    they were strong enough to bear the earth, bellowing
    like booming kettle drums, looking like gray monsoon
    clouds.

It was not the severing of their trunks by sharp swords
    that put the battling elephants' countenances out of
    joint, but having their tusks broken.[27]

The relentless assaults of the elephants led to ichor
    flooding all around, as if their colliding bodies were
    squeezing it out.

रणाङ्गनं सर इव प्लावितं मदवारिभिः ।
गजः पृथुकराकृष्टशतपत्रमलोडयत् ॥

७० शरक्षते गजे भृङ्गैः सुविषादिनिषादिनि ।
रुतव्याजेन रुदितं तत्रासीदतिसीदति ॥

अन्तकस्य पृथौ तत्र शयनीय इवाहवे ।
दशनव्यसनादीयुर्मत्कुणत्वं मतङ्गजाः ॥

अभीकमतिकेनेद्धे भीतानन्दस्य नाशने ।
कनत्सकामसेनाके मन्दकामकमस्यति ॥११

दधतो ऽपि रणे भीममभीक्ष्णं भावमासुरम् ।
हताः परैरभिमुखाः सुरभूयमुपाययुः ॥

येनाङ्गमूहे व्रणवत्सरुचा परतोमरैः ।
समत्वं स ययौ खड्गत्सरुचापरतो ऽमरैः ॥

654

Everywhere was awash with this rut fluid; one elephant
    splashed about in it, overturning squadrons of
    chariots with its long trunk—the battlefield looked
    like a lake being stripped of its lotuses.[28]

Bees settled on another elephant dead from arrow   70
    wounds; as its mahout gave way to grief, they too
    lamented in the guise of humming.

The battle was like death's broad couch; it seemed infested
    with bedbugs, elephants which had lost their tusks
    and been reduced to insignificance.[29]

The struggle caught fire among fearless fighters and
    extinguished the comfort of cowards; triumphant
    warriors basked in its glow, the uncommitted had no
    place there.

Although the combatants had assumed a ghastly demonic
    demeanor throughout the battle, when killed by the
    enemy they headed straight to rebirth as gods in
    heaven.

One glorious hero had been covered with wounds from
    hostile lances, but still tightly gripping his sword and
    looking to his bow, he became equal to the divine
    immortals.

७५ निपातितसुहृत्स्वामिपितृव्यभ्रातृमातुलं ।
पाणिनीयमिवालोचि धीरैस्तत्समराजिरम् ॥

अभावि सिन्ध्वा सांध्याभ्रसट्टग्रुधिरतोयया ।
हृते योद्धुं जनः पांसौ स दृग्रुधि रतो यया ॥

विदलत्पुष्कराकीर्णाः पतच्छङ्खसमाकुलाः ।
तरत्पत्ररथा नद्यः प्रासर्पत्रक्तवारिजाः ॥

असृज्जनो ऽस्त्रक्षतिमानवमज्जवसादनम् ।
रक्षःपिशाचं मुमुदे नवमज्जवसादनम् ॥

चित्रं चापैरपेतज्यैः स्फुरद्रक्तशतह्रदम् ।
पयोदजालमिव तद्द्वैराशंसनमाबभौ ॥

८० बन्धौ विपन्ने ऽनेकेन नरेणेह तदन्तिके ।
अशोचि सैन्ये घण्टाभिर्न रणे हतदन्तिके ॥

Warriors intently scrutinized the battlefield where their 75
    comrades and masters, elderly relatives, brothers, and
    uncles had been slain—it was if they were studying
    rules about special cases in Panini's grammar.[30]

A torrent of gore surged up red as an evening cloud; it
    washed away the dust obscuring the warriors' vision,
    so that the fighting became all the more intense.

Rivers of flowing blood inundated the battlefield. The tips
    of severed elephant trunks floated there like lotus
    blossoms, conch trumpets piled up on each other,
    while wagons and chariots bobbed on the surface like
    birds.

Warriors wounded by missiles vomited blood, causing
    other fighters to lose their footing. Demons and
    ghouls gorged in delight on fresh marrow and fat.

That terrible battlefield was now strewn with unstrung
    bows and dotted with hundreds of lakes of glinting
    gore; it looked like a welter of clouds surrounded by a
    gleaming rainbow while lightning flashed within.[31]

When a comrade died, many soldiers grieved beside his 80
    corpse, while with elephants slain bells no longer
    rang.[32]

कृत्तैः कीर्णा मही रेजे दन्तैर्गात्रैश्च दन्तिनाम् ।
क्षुण्णलोकासुभिर्मृत्योर्मुसलोलूखलैरिव ॥

युधमित्थं विधूतान्यमानवानभियो गतः ।
चैद्यः परान्पराजिग्ये मानावानभियोगतः ॥

अथ वक्षोमणिच्छायाच्छुरितापीतवाससा ।
स्फुरितेन्द्रधनुर्भिन्नतडितेव तडित्वता ॥

नीलेनानालनलिननिलीनोल्ललनालिना ।
ललनाललनेनालं लीलालानेन लालिना ॥१२

अपूर्वयेव तत्कालसमागमसकामया ।
दृष्टेन राजन्वपुषा कटाक्षैर्विजयश्रिया ॥

विभावी विभवी भाभो विभाभावी विवो विभीः ।
भवाभिभावी भावावो भवाभावो भुवो विभुः ॥१३

उपैतुकामैस्तत्पारं निश्रितैर्योगिभिः परैः ।
देहन्यासकृतोद्योगैरदृश्यत परः पुमान् ॥

The earth was littered with the hewn tusks and limbs of
elephants, like death's pestle and mortar for pounding
out the lives of warriors.

Shishupala's enemies had in this way fearlessly
overthrown lesser men than he, but now the haughty
leader of the Chedis aggressively entered the fray and
overcame them.

Then[33]—wearing a yellow robe spangled with light from
his breast jewel, like a rain cloud cleft by lightning
mingling with a sparkling rainbow,

deep blue, flitting bees settling over the dark lotus in
his navel,[34] an alluring tethering post for amorous
delights,

his body eyed meaningfully by the goddess of victory like
a new-wed girl yearning to make love with him there
and then,   85

all pervading, mighty, like the sun bringing light, mounted
on the bird Garuda, fearless, overcoming rebirth on
behalf of his devotees, protecting all living creatures,
not subject to rebirth, the lord of the earth[35]—

the mighty Krishna displayed himself to his foes. For their
part, in eagerness to get the better of him, they at once
resolved on battle still more, bending their efforts to
laying down their lives.[36]

तं श्रिया घनयानस्तरुचा सारतया तया ।
यातया तरसा चारुस्तनयानघयाश्रितम् ॥१४

विद्विषो ऽद्विषुरुद्वीक्ष्य तथाप्यासन्निरेनसः ।
अरुच्यमपि रोगघ्नं निसर्गादिव भेषजम् ॥

विदितं१५ दिवि के ऽनीके तं यातं निजिताजिनि ।
विगदं गवि रोद्धारो योद्धा यो नतिमेति न ॥१६

नियोक्ष्यमाणेन पुनः कर्मण्यतिगरीयसि ।
आरोप्यमाणोरुगुणं भर्त्रा कार्मुकमानमत् ॥

तत्र बाणाः सुपरुषः समधीयन्त चारवः ।
द्विषामभूत्सुपरुषस्तस्याकृष्टस्य चारवः ॥

पश्चात्कृतानामप्यस्य नराणामिव पत्रिणाम् ।
यो यो गुणेन संयुक्तः स स कर्णान्तमागमत् ॥

प्रापे रूपी पुरारेपाः परिपूरी परः परैः ।
रोपैरपारैरुपरि पुपूरे ऽपि पुरः परैः ॥१७

Krishna had been ardently gripped in a tight embrace by
the voluptuous, flawless goddess of good fortune in all
her perfection.

The enemy was possessed by hatred of Krishna, but
beholding him had freed them from sin. Even
unpleasant medicine possesses a natural capacity to
cure.

Who on earth can hinder a warrior renowned in heaven,   90
advancing in full vigor at the head of a victorious
army, never yielding to anyone?

Krishna fixed the long string to his bow and bent it back
strenuously; once again he was about to employ it
together with its many qualities[37] on a vital task.

Fine firm-jointed arrows were nocked on that bow, and the
creak as it was drawn back resounded harshly in the
enemy's ears.

Each arrow from the quiver on his shoulder was quickly
fixed on the bowstring and drawn back as far as his
ear.[38]

Utterly faultless, Krishna had previously incarnated
himself on various occasions while still pervading the
universe. Yet now the supreme being was beset by
enemies; more and more of them showered him on all
sides with countless shafts.

९५ दिङ्मुखव्यापिनस्तीक्ष्णान्ह्लादिनो मर्मभेदिनः ।
चिक्षेपैकक्षणेनैव सायकानहितांश्च सः ॥

शरवर्षी महानादः स्फुरत्कार्मुककेतनः ।
नीलच्छविरसौ रेजे केशवश्छलनीरदः ॥१८

न केवलं जनैस्तस्य लघुसंधायिनो धनुः ।
मण्डलीकृतमेकान्ताद्बलमैक्षि द्विषामपि ॥

लोकालोकी कलो ऽकल्ककलिलो ऽलिकुलालकः ।
कालो ऽकलो ऽकलिः काले कोल्केलिकिलः किल ॥१९

अक्षितारासु विव्याध द्विषतः स तनुत्रिणः ।
दानेषु स्थूललक्षत्वं न हि तस्य शरासने ॥

१०० वररो ऽविवरो वैरिविवारी वारिरारवः ।
विववार वरो वैरं वीरो रविरिवौर्वरः ॥२०

But at one and the same time he dispatched arrows and   95
    opponents—covering the horizon, sharp and bitter,
    loud and lethal.

With flashing bow and banner, shouting his war cry, dark
    skinned Krishna rained arrows; he had disguised
    himself as a black storm cloud, thundering as it
    poured down torrents, a rainbow glistening around
    it.[39]

While he swiftly nocked his shafts, it was not just his bow
    that could be seen drawn back in a full circle, but also
    the cowering enemy forces.

Overseeing the world, softly spoken and without
    deceit, hair dark as a swarm of bees, body deep
    blue, unified,[40] benign, once upon a time playfully
    incarnating himself as a boar, so scripture says—

he pierced his enemies in the very center of their eyes,
    for their bodies were heavily armored. Only when
    bestowing liberality did he take a wider aim, not when
    he was shooting arrows.

Generous-spirited, without any weaknesses, he   100
    summoned his enemies to battle, roaring like a
    thundercloud; the supreme hero, he enveloped his
    foes, like the sun descended to earth.

मुक्तानेकशरं प्राणानहरद्धूयसां द्विषाम् ।
तदीयं धनुरन्यस्य न विषेहे सजीवताम् ॥

राजराजी रुरोजाजेरजिरे ऽजो ऽजरो ऽरजाः ।
रेजारिजूरजोर्जाजीं रराजर्जुरजर्जरः ॥२१॥

उद्वृत्तान्द्विषतस्तस्य निघ्नतो द्वितयं पपुः ।
पानार्थे रुधिरं धातौ रक्षार्थे भुवनं शराः ॥

क्रूरारिकारी कोरेकः कारकः कारिकाकरः ।
कोरकाकारकरकः करीरः कर्करार्करुक् ॥२२॥

१०५ विधातुमवतीर्णो ऽपि लघिमानमसौ भुवः ।
अनेकमरिसंघातमकरोद्भूमिवर्धनम् ॥

दारी दरदरिद्रो ऽरिदारूदारो ऽद्रिदूरदः ।
दूरादरौद्रो ऽददरद्रोदोरुद्दारुरादरी ॥२३॥

His bow shot many arrows and took the lives of a host
    of enemies; it could not endure that any opponent
    should live or that another weapon might still be
    strung.[41]

Experiencing neither birth nor old age, controlled in
    combat, increasingly enlivened by the destruction
    of vigorous enemies, noble and at the height of his
    physical powers—Krishna broke a succession of kings
    on the battlefield as he blazed forth in his glory.

In destroying his arrogant opponents his arrows achieved
    two aims with one action—they drank blood and
    protected the earth.[42]

Scattering fierce enemies, sole creator of the world,
    chastiser of the wicked, hands like lotus buds,
    conqueror of elephants, bright as the blazing sun—

Krishna had descended to the world to lighten its burden,   105
    but he killed so many of the enemy that the weight
    bearing down on it became still greater.[43]

With many wives, completely fearless, noble, hard as a
    mountain but benign, pervading heaven and earth,
    generous and attentive—he split the enemy from afar
    as if they were stumps of wood.

एकेक्षुणा संघतिथान्दि्षो भिन्दन्दुमानिव ।
स जन्मान्तररामस्य चक्रे सदृशमात्मनः ॥

शूरः शौरिरशिशिरैराशाशौराशु राशिशः ।
शरारुः श्रीशरीरेशः शुशूरे ऽरिशिरः शरैः ॥२४

व्यक्तासीदरितारीणां यत्तदीयास्तदा मुहुः ।
मनोहृतो ऽपि हृदये लेगुरेषां न पत्रिणः ॥

१९० नामाक्षराणां मलना मा भूद्धर्तुरिति स्फुटम् ।
अगृह्णन्त पराङ्मानामसूनसं न मार्गणाः ॥

आच्छिद्य योधसार्थस्य प्राणसर्वस्वमाशुगाः ।
ऐकागारिकवद्भूमौ दूराज्जग्मुरदर्शनम् ॥

भीमास्तराजिनस्तस्य बलस्य ध्वजराजिनः ।
कृतघोराजिनश्चक्रे भुवः सरुधिरा जिनः ॥

In cutting down foes in battalions with a single arrow as if
they were saplings, he reprised his deed in a previous
existence when he had been Rama.[44]

At once the heroic Krishna, destroyer of the evil,
complete master of good fortune, repeatedly split
open the heads of his enemies with his blazing arrows
blanketing the sky.

The hostility of Krishna's opponents was time and again
revealed for all to see. While his arrows captivated
with their beauty even as they took lives,[45] they could
not gain a place in his enemies' hearts, since they
rebounded from their breasts as soon as they had
pierced them.

Krishna's arrows did not wish the engraved characters   110
of their owner's name to be smudged; it was obvious
that they removed only his foes' life's breath, not their
blood.

Shafts were dispatched to steal the lives of warriors, and
then dropped all over the battlefield; they were like
thieves going to ground after robbing a merchant of
his wealth.

The enemy army was fully equipped with fearsome
weaponry, and it fought ferociously as its banners
fluttered high, but victorious Krishna covered the
battlefield with its blood.

मांसव्यधोचितमुखैः शून्यतां दधदक्रियम् ।
शकुन्तिभिः शत्रुबलं व्यापि तस्येषुभिर्नभः ॥

दाददो दुद्दुद्दादी दाददो दूददीददोः ।
दुद्दादं दददे दुद्दे ददादददददो ऽददः ॥२५

११५ प्लुतेभकुम्भोरसिजैर्हृदयक्षतिजन्मभिः ।
प्रावर्तयन्नदीरसैर्द्विषां तद्योषितां च सः ॥

सदामदबलप्रायः समुद्धतरसो बभौ ।
प्रतीतविक्रमः श्रीमान्हरिर्हरिरिवापरः ॥

द्विधा त्रिधा चतुर्धा च तमेकमपि शत्रवः ।
पश्यन्तः स्पर्धया सद्यः स्वयं पञ्चत्वमाययुः ॥

Birds of prey descended upon it, now devoid of life and
    still, and deftly pecked at the corpses; in the same way
    Krishna's arrows, crafted to pierce flesh, covered the
    sky, empty and tranquil.[46]

Bounteous with gifts, punishing assailants of the virtuous
    and then offering them protection, destroying with
    his mighty arms the demons oppressing the world,
    liberal toward the generous and the miserly without
    discrimination, but extirpating the greedy—as such a
    hero Krishna had taken up arms against the enemy.

His foes' blood spurted from their chests to wash over the   115
    lobes of their elephants, while the tears coursed over
    the round breasts of their women struck to the heart
    with grief. Thus Krishna set rivers flowing.[47]

Krishna had further intoxicated with delight his brother
    Balarama, who was never sober; incarnated as the
    Boar, he had raised up the earth, while his strides
    through the universe as the Dwarf were known
    to all. As consort of the goddess of victory he was
    unopposed; he was like another Indra.[48]

Krishna was really a single individual, but the enemy
    beheld him manifested in two, three, and four forms;
    so to rival him they immediately divided themselves
    into the five elements—and died![49]

स दैवसंपन्नवपूरणेषु
सदैव संपन्नवपू रणेषु ।
महो दधे ऽस्तारिमहा नितान्तं
महोदधेस्तारि महानितान्तम् ॥

इष्टं कृत्वार्थ पत्रिणः शार्ङ्गपाणे-
रेत्याधोमुख्यं प्राविशन्भूमिमाशु ।
शुद्ध्या युक्तानां वैरिवर्गस्य मध्ये
भर्त्रा क्षिप्तानामेतदेवानुरूपम् ॥

१२० सत्त्वं मानविशिष्टमाजिरभसादालम्ब्य भव्यः पुरो
लब्ध्याघक्षयशुद्धिरुद्दुरतरश्रीवत्सभूमिर्मुदा ।
मुक्त्वा काममपास्तभीः परमृगव्याधः स नादं हरे-
रेकौघैः समकालमभ्रमुदयी रोपैस्तदा तस्तरे ॥२६

Krishna always entered the fray in physically perfect
form, and in combat renewed his abundant good
fortune; as that mighty warrior overthrew the power
of his enemies, he was in full possession of an energy
reaching the very limits of the vast ocean.

After the arrows of the archer Krishna had attained their
desired end of killing enemies, they turned their
tips downward and quickly dropped to the ground.
Wholly appropriate, for when men of high caliber
have become included by their master among his foes,
they immediately cast down their heads.[50]

In the preliminaries to the battle Krishna, worthy of   120
reverence since he had purified himself by the
destruction of sin, had already manifested a bravery
distinguished by total commitment. Now with the
excitement of conflict in full flow, his chest swelling
and utterly without fear, he joyfully emitted a mighty
lion's roar as he hunted his enemy prey; and standing
tall, at one and the same time he filled the sky with a
steady stream of arrows.

CHAPTER 20

The Killing of Shishupala

मुखमुल्लसितत्रिरेखमुच्चै-
र्भिदुरभ्रूयुगभीषणं दधानः ।
समिताविति विक्रमं न मृष्य-
न्नतभीराह्वत चेदिराण्मुरारिम् ॥

शितचक्रनिपातसंप्रतीक्षं
वहतः स्कन्धगतं च तस्य मृत्युम् ।
अभिशौरि रथो ऽथ चोदिताश्वः
प्रययौ सारथिरूपया नियत्या ॥

अभिचैद्यमगाद्रथो ऽपि शौरे-
रवनिं जागुडकुङ्कुमाभिताम्रैः ।
गुरुनेमिनिपीडनावदीर्ण-
व्यसुदेहसुतशोनितैर्विलिम्पन् ॥

स निरायतकेतनांशुकान्तः
कलनिक्काणकरालकिङ्किणीकः ।
विरराज रिपूद्धृतिप्रतिज्ञा-
मुखरो मुक्तशिखः स्वयं नु मृत्युः ॥

५ सजलाम्बुधरारवानुकारी
ध्वनिरापूरितदिङ्मुखो रथस्य ।
प्रगुणीकृतकेकमूर्ध्वकण्ठैः
शितिकण्ठैरुपकर्णयांबभूवे ॥

674

Shishupala, king of the Chedis, could not endure such
    valorous deeds. Head held high, brow furrowed in a
    menacing frown, he boldly challenged Krishna, enemy
    of the demon Mura, in the battle.

With death at his shoulder anticipating a blow from the
    sharp discus,* and fate standing beside him urging on
    his horses, his chariot rolled toward Krishna.

In turn Krishna's chariot headed toward the Chedi lord,
    smearing the earth with blood, dark red as saffron,[1]
    that poured from the corpses crushed under its heavy
    wheels.

With banner billowing behind, bells jangling with a soft,
    sinister noise, it seemed to be the very god of death
    who had untied his topknot in a pledge to destroy the
    enemy.[2]

The chariot's rumble sounded like the thunder of a   5
    monsoon cloud, echoing in all directions; when the
    peacocks heard it, they stretched out their necks and
    redoubled their cries.

---

* Krishna's weapon Sudarshana.

अभिवीक्ष्य विदर्भराजपुत्री-
कुचकश्मीरजचिह्नमच्युतोरः ।
चिरसञ्चितयापि चेदिराजः
सहसावाप रुषा तदैव योगम् ॥

जनिताशनिशब्दशङ्कमुच्चै-
र्धनुरास्फालितमध्वनन्नृपेण ।
चपलानिलबोध्यमानकल्प-
क्षयकालाग्निशिखानिभस्फुरज्ज्यम् ॥

समकालमिवाभिलक्षणीय-
ग्रहसंधानविकर्षणापवर्गैः ।
अथ साभिसरं शरैस्तरस्वी
स तिरस्कर्तुमुपेन्द्रमभ्यवर्षत् ॥

ऋजुताफलयोगशुद्धिभाजा-
मुरुपक्षाश्रयिणां शिलीमुखानाम् ।
गुणिना नतिमागतेन संधिः
सह चापेन समञ्जसो बभूव ॥

१०   अविषह्यतमे कृताधिकारं
वशिना कर्मणि चेदिपार्थिवेन ।
अरसद्धनुरुच्चकैर्हृदार्ति-
प्रसभाकर्षणवेपमानजीवम् ॥

676

As soon as he saw Krishna's chest smeared with saffron
from the breasts of the king of Vidarbha's daughter,*
the Chedi lord rushed to embrace wrath, although he
had long been intimate with it.[3]

Shishupala slapped his bow and the reverberation could be
taken for the crash of a thunderbolt; its string shivered
like flickering flames whipped up by the doomsday
hurricane.

Then that mighty king could be seen seizing, notching,
aiming, and firing his arrows apparently all at once,
raining them down on Krishna and his followers so
they were completely hidden.

These arrows were straight, honed, and true, with
luxuriant feather flights; it was quite fitting for them
to be joined to such a bow so tautly strung and bent.[4]

The mighty Chedi lord had turned his bow to the onerous   10
task of killing Krishna; the string creaked as he
strained to stretch back its tips to their limit and it
sang out loud.[5]

* Rukmini.

अनुसन्ततिपातिनः पटुत्वं
दधतः शुद्धिभृतो गृहीतपक्षाः ।
वदनादिव वादिन ऽथ शब्दाः
क्षितिभर्तुर्धनुषः शराः प्रससुः ॥

गवलासितकान्ति तस्य मध्य-
स्थितघोरायतबाहुदण्डनासम् ।
दद‍ृशे कुपितान्तकोन्नमद्भ्रू-
युगभीमाकृति कार्मुकं जनेन ॥

तडिदुज्ज्वलजातरूपपुङ्खैः
खमयःश्याममुखैरभिध्वनद्भिः ।
जलदैरिव रंहसोत्पतद्भिः
पिदधे संहतिशालिभिः शरौघैः ॥

शितशल्यमुखावभिन्नमेघ-
क्षरदम्भः स्फुटतीव्रवेदनानाम् ।
स्रवदसृततीव चक्रवालं
ककुभामौर्णविषुः सुवर्णपुङ्खाः ॥

१५ अमनोरमतां यती जनस्य
क्षणमालोकपथान्नभःसदां च ।
रुरुधे पिहिताहिमद्युतिद्यौ-
र्विशिखैरन्तरिताच्युता धरित्री ॥

Arrows—sharp, true, and well fletched—then flew from
     the king's bow without pause, like an incessant stream
     of words from the mouth of a debater—pointed, well
     worked, arguing logically in defense of a position.[6]

Shishupala's bow, dark as buffalo horn, gripped in the
     middle by his outstretched arm, seemed to onlookers
     as terrible as the arching eyebrows framing the
     wrathful god of death's imposing nose.

The heavens were overcast with showers of arrows
     speeding everywhere like scudding rain clouds; their
     golden shafts blazed like lightning, their tips were
     iron-dark, and they made a thundering din as they
     clustered together.

Gold-shafted arrows filled the sky; its grievous pain was
     obvious, for with rain pouring from clouds torn open
     by sharp points, it seemed to be shedding streams of
     tears.

The heaven and earth for an instant lost their allure and   15
     became invisible to the army and the gods; both the
     sun and Krishna had been obscured by shafts.

विनिवारितभानुतापमेकं
सकलस्यापि मुरद्विषो बलस्य ।
शरजालमयं समं समन्ता-
दुरु सद्मेव नराधिपेन तेने ॥

इति चेदिमहीभृता तदानीं
तदनीकं दनुसूनुसूदनस्य ।
वयसामिव चक्रमक्रियाकं
परितो ऽरोधि विपाठपञ्जरेण ॥

इषुवर्षमनेकमेकवीर-
स्तदरिप्रस्तुतमच्युतः पृष्ठकैः ।
अथ वादिकृतं प्रमाणमन्यैः
प्रणिरास प्रतिवादिवत्प्रमाणैः१ ॥

परिकुञ्चितकुपरेण तेन
श्रवणोपान्तिकनीयमानगव्यम् ।
ध्वनति स्म धनुर्धनान्तमत्त-
प्रचुरक्रौञ्चरवानुकारमुच्चैः ॥

२० उरसा विततेन पातितांसः
स मयूराञ्चितमस्तकस्तदानीम् ।
क्षणमालिखितो नु सौष्ठवेन
स्थिरपूर्वापरमुष्टिराबभासे ॥

Shishupala at the same time was conjuring up what
     seemed to be a miraculous overarching tent of arrows
     holding back the sunlight from the entire army of
     Mura's enemy.

In this way the king of the Chedis enclosed within an
     arrow cage the host of Krishna, destroyer of the sons
     of Danu, immobilizing it like a flock of birds.

But Krishna, in his singular heroism, repulsed with his
     own arrows that heavy monsoon of shafts shot by the
     enemy, as a respondent in a debate disposes of his
     opponent's position by adducing other arguments.

He bent his elbow to draw the string back to his ear; the
     bow twanged loudly, sounding like the cry of curlews
     excited at the rainy season's end.

His chest was expanded and shoulders tensed, his head   20
     cocked like a peacock's with both fists motionless on
     his bow. In this practiced posture Krishna appeared
     for an instant to be painted in a picture.

स्तनतो नितरां रयेण गुर्व्य-
स्तडिदाकारचलद्गुणादसंख्याः ।
इषवो धनुषः सशब्दमाशु
न्यपतन्नम्बुधरादिवाम्बुधाराः ॥

शिखरोन्नतनिष्ठुरांसपीठः
स्थगयन्नेकदिगन्तमायतान्तः ।
निरवर्णि सकृत्प्रसारितो ऽस्य
क्षितिभर्तेव चमूभिरेकबाहुः ॥

तमकुन्ठमुखाः सुपर्णकेतो-
रिषवः क्षिप्तमिषुव्रजं परेण ।
विभिदामनयन्त कृत्यपक्षं
नृपतेर्नेतुरिवायथार्थवर्णाः ॥

दयितैरिव खण्डिता मुरारे-
र्विशिखैः संमुखमुज्ज्वलाङ्गलेखैः ।
लघिमानमुपेयुषी पृथिव्यां
विफला शत्रुशरावलिः पपात ॥

२५ प्रमुखे ऽभिहताश्च पत्रवाहाः
प्रसभं माधवमुक्तवत्सदन्तैः ।
परिपूर्णतरं भुवो गतायाः
परतः कातरवत्प्रतीपमीयुः ॥

Whirring arrows, formidable, numberless, flowed swiftly
from that bow as rain pours in roaring torrents from a
cloud; its string flickered like lightning and thundered
aloud.

Krishna had only to extend his long arm once to wield his
bow and the soldiers fancied they were looking at a
mountain, stretching into the distance and concealing
part of the sky, with muscular shoulders its lofty peak.

The sharp-pointed arrows of Krishna of the Garuda
banner destroyed the storm of shafts dispatched by
his enemy, just as the eloquently dissembling agents
of an aggressive monarch can detach a neighboring
ruler's disaffected followers.

The enemy's arrows were split by Krishna's splendidly
ornate shafts, and shorn of their points, they drifted
ineffectually to the ground; so a woman spurned by
a lover sporting another's love-marks becomes faint
and sinks down hopelessly.

Others of Shishupala's shafts were violently struck   25
head-on by the razor arrows energetically dispatched
by Krishna; spinning round, they returned like
cowards over the ground they had just traversed.

इतरेतरसन्निकर्षजन्मा
फलसंघट्टविकीर्णविस्फुलिङ्गः ।
पटलानि लिहन्बलाहकाना-
मपरेषु क्षणमज्वलत्कृशानुः ॥

शरदेव² शरश्रिया विभिन्ने
विभुना शत्रुशिलीमुखाभ्रजाले ।
विकसन्मुखवारिजाः प्रकाशं
बभुराशा इव यादवध्वजिन्यः ॥

स दिवं समचिच्छदच्छरौघैः
कृततिग्मद्युतिमण्डलापलापाम् ।
दददृशे ऽथ च तस्य चापयष्टया-³
मिषुरेकैव जनैः सकृद्विकृष्टा ॥

भवति स्फुटमागतो विपक्षा-
न्न सपक्षो ऽपि हि निर्वृतेर्विधाता ।
शिशुपालबलानि कृष्णमुक्तः
सुतरां तेन तताप तोमरौघैः ॥

३० गुरुवेगविराविभिः पतत्रै-
रिषवः काञ्चनपिङ्गलाङ्गभासः ।
विनतासुतवत्तलं भुवः स्म
व्यथितभ्रान्तभुजङ्गमं विशन्ति ॥

Sparks scattered when arrowpoints clashed, and fire was
kindled from the friction of their shafts; licking the
clouds above, it blazed up among the other arrows.

The foe's arrows were dispelled by Krishna's shafts, like
clouds by the beauty of early autumn, and the Yadava
forces glowed like the sky after the rains, as their
lotus-like faces opened wide in delight.

Krishna covered the sky with a cloud of shafts concealing
the sun's disc, but all that could be seen was just a
single arrow drawn back once on his bow.

Clearly an ally come over from an enemy's camp does not
necessarily bring any advantage, nor does a feathered
shaft dispatched from a featherless bow;[7] but the
shower of arrows released by Krishna certainly
tormented the armies of Shishupala.

Flights whirring as they raced through the air, shafts   30
yellow as gold, the arrows pierced the earth like
Garuda, terrorizing and confusing the serpents in the
underworld.

शतशः परुषाः पुरो ऽपशङ्कं
शिशुपालेन शिलीमुखाः प्रयुक्ताः ।
परमर्मभिदो ऽपि दानवारे-
रपराधा इव न व्यथां वितेनुः ॥

विहिताद्भुतलोकसृष्टिमाये
जयमिच्छन्किल मायया मुरारौ ।
भुवनक्षयकालयोग्यनिद्रे४
नृपतिः स्वापनमस्त्रमाजहार ॥

सलिलार्द्रवराहदेहनीलो
विदधद्भास्करमर्थशून्यसंज्ञम् ।
प्रचलायतलोचनारविन्दं
विदधे तद्बलमन्धमन्धकारः ॥

गुरवो ऽपि निषद्य यन्निदद्धु-
र्धनुषि क्षमापतयो न वाच्यमेतत् ।
क्षपितापदि जाग्रतो ऽपि नित्यं
ननु तत्रैव हि ते ऽभवन्निषण्णाः ॥

३५ श्लथतां व्रजतस्तथा परेषा-
मगलद्धारणशक्तिमुज्झतः स्वाम् ।
सुगृहीतमपि प्रमादभाजां
मनसः शास्त्रमिवास्त्रमग्रपाणेः ॥

686

Undaunted, Shishupala continued to dispatch hundreds
of hard shafts against the enemy of the demons;
but deadly though they were, they gained no more
purchase on him than moral faults.

Mura's enemy had deployed his own extraordinary magic
power to create the world and taken a deserved repose
only at doomsday; now it seemed that Shishupala
wished to gain the victory through deceiving sorcery
and so dispatched a sleep-inducing weapon.

Darkness, black as the body of Vishnu's Boar incarnation
emerging dripping from the primeval ocean, made
the sun's epithet, "blazing one," bereft of meaning; it
blinded Krishna's soldiers, and their lotus-like eyes
rolled with drowsiness.

But it should be no surprise that even resolute kings now
sat dozing by their bows; when wide awake they had
always stationed themselves there to keep danger at
bay.

The fingers of the bewitched kings relaxed and lost their   35
power to hold anything; their weapons, though tightly
gripped, fell from their hands, just as knowledge, even
when properly mastered, quits the lazy unretentive
minds of the negligent.

उचितस्वपनो ऽपि नीरराशौ
बलयादोनिधिमध्यगस्तदानीम् ।
भुवनत्रयकार्यजागरूकः
स परं तत्र परः पुमानजागः ॥

अथ सूर्यरुचीव तस्य दृष्टा-
वुदभूत्कौस्तुभदर्पणं गतायाम् ।
पटु धाम ततो न चाद्धुतं त-
द्विभुरर्केन्दुविलोचनः किलासौ ॥

महतः प्रणतेष्विव प्रसादः
स मणेरंशुचयः ककुब्मुखेषु ।
व्यकसद्द्विकसद्द्विलोचनेभ्यो
दददालोकमनाबिलं बलेभ्यः ॥

प्रकृतिं प्रतिपादुकैश्च पादै-
श्चकूपे भानुमतः पुनः प्रसर्तुम् ।
तमसो ऽभिभवादवाप्य मूर्छा-
मुदजीवत्सहसैव जीवलोकः ॥

४०   गतसन्तमसैर्जवेन भूयो
यदुयोधैर्युधि रेधिरे द्विषन्तः ।
ननु वारिधरौघरोधमुक्तः
सुतरामुत्तपते पतिः प्रभाणाम् ॥

However, although accustomed to sleeping on the
primeval waters, at that moment in the battle the
supreme being was very much awake within his ocean-
like army, watchful over the affairs of the universe.

His gaze was reflected in his jewel Kaustubha, whereupon
a fierce light, bright as the sun, emerged from it. No
wonder—all know that god has the sun and moon for
eyes.

Like the favor of a great ruler toward his subjects, the
mass of rays streaming from that jewel spread over the
skies, clarifying the vision of Krishna's forces as their
eyes reopened.

The sun's rays returned to their normal state and began
to shine again, while the living world at once revived
from the swoon induced by the overwhelming
darkness.

The Yadava warriors now liberated from the murk   40
engaged at once with the enemy again. The sun, lord
of light, shines all the more when freed from its cloud
canopy.

व्यवहार इवानृताभियोगं
तिमिरं निर्जितवत्यथ प्रकाशे ।
रिपुरुत्फणभीमभोगभाजां
भुजगानां जननीं जजाप विद्याम् ॥

पृथुदर्विभृतस्ततः फणीन्द्रा
विषमाशीभिरनारतं वमन्तः ।
अभवन्युगपद्विलोलजिह्वा-
द्वयलीढोभयसृग्विभागमाविः ॥

कृतकेशविडम्बनैर्विहायो
विजयं तत्क्षणमिच्छुभिश्छलेन ।
अमृताग्रभुवः पुरेव पुच्छं
वडवाभर्तुरवारि काद्रवेयैः ॥

दधतस्तनिमानमानुपूर्व्या
बभुरक्षिश्रवसो मुखे विशालाः ।
भरतज्ञकविप्रणीतकाव्य-
ग्रथिताङ्का इव नाटकप्रपञ्चाः ॥

४५   सविषश्वसनोद्धतोरुधूम-
व्यवधिम्लानमरीचि पन्नगानाम् ।
उपरागवतेव तिग्मभासा
वपुरौदुम्बरमण्डलाभमूहे ॥

So light overcame darkness, just as proper legal
    proceeding prevails over false testimony. But then
    Shishupala intoned a spell to conjure up snakes with
    hoods expanded and terrible coils.

Mighty serpents with huge hoods appeared, incessantly
    spitting out venom through their fangs while licking
    the corners of their maws with their flickering forked
    tongues.

In an instant the sons of Kadru,* intent on victory through
    false enchantment, had filled the sky as if they were
    strands of black hair. So, once upon a time, they had
    covered the tail of the divine horse Ucchaihshravas,
    the elder brother of Amrita,[8] completely transforming
    its color.[9]

The serpents were broad in the head and gradually
    tapered in size; they were like the phases of elaborate
    dramas—detailed in the prologue but more compact
    as the plot develops[10]—assembled into poetic form
    by an author familiar with Bharata's dramaturgical
    prescriptions.†

The sun's disc, apparently eclipsed, looked like a copper   45
    wheel; its rays had faded, hidden by the thick
    poisonous vapor of the serpents' hissing.

———

* The mother of snakes.
† Expressed in the *Nāṭyaśāstra* (Treatise on Drama).

शिखपिच्छकृतध्वजावचूल-
क्षणसाशङ्कविवर्तमानभोगाः ।
यमपाशवदाशु बन्धनाय
न्यपतन्वृष्णिबलेषु लेलिहानाः ॥

पृथुवारिधिवीचिमण्डलान्त-
र्विलसत्फेनवितानपाण्डुराणि ।
दधति स्म भुजङ्गमाङ्गमध्ये
नवनिर्मोकरुचं ध्वजांशुकानि ॥

कृतमण्डलिबन्धुमुल्लसद्भिः
शिरसि प्रत्युरसं विलम्बमानैः ।
व्यरुचज्जनता भुजङ्गभोगै-
र्दलितेन्दीवरमालभारिणीव ॥

परिवेष्टितमूर्तयश्च मूला-
दुरगैरा शिरसः सरत्नपुष्पैः ।
दधुरायतवल्लिवेल्लिताना-
मुपमानं मनुजा महीरुहाणाम् ॥

५० बहलाञ्जनपङ्कपट्टनील-
द्युतयो देहमितस्ततः श्रयन्तः ।
दधिरे फणिनस्तुरङ्गमेषु
स्फुटपर्याणनिबद्धवध्रलीलाम् ॥

The snakes turned away, for a moment apparently startled
    by the peacock-feather pendants on the banners,[11]
    and then immediately fell upon the Vrishni forces as if
    to bind them with the fetters of the god of death.

Surrounded by these serpents, the cloth of the banners,
    white as foamy spume playing on the wide ocean's
    rolling waves, appeared like freshly sloughed skin.

The soldiery could now be seen with writhing serpentine
    coils tightly twined round their heads and hanging
    down on their chests, as if garlanded[12] with
    blossoming water lilies.

Men encoiled from top to toe by snakes with gems in their
    heads bore comparison to trees festooned with long
    flowering vines.

For their part, as they twisted around bodies everywhere,   50
    the serpents, black as thick strands of congealed
    unguent, looked like broad cords tied to the saddles of
    horses.

प्रसृतं रभसादयोभिनीला
प्रतिपादं परितो ऽभिवेष्टयन्ती ।
तनुरायतिशालिनी महाहे-
र्गजमन्दूरिव निश्चलं चकार ॥

अथ सस्मितमीक्षितादवज्ञा-
ललितैकोन्नमितभ्रु माधवेन ।
निजकेतुशिरःश्रितः सुपर्णा-
दुदपप्तन्नयुतानि पक्षिराजाम् ॥

द्रुतहेमरुचः खगाः खगेन्द्रा-
दलघूदीरितनादमुत्पतन्तः ।
क्षणमैक्षिषतोच्चकैश्चमूभि-
र्ज्वलतः सप्तरुचेरिव स्फुलिङ्गाः ॥

उपमानमलाभि लोलपक्ष-
क्षणविक्षिप्तमहाम्बुवाहमत्स्यैः ।
गगनार्णवमन्तरा सुमेरोः
कुलजानां गरुडैरिलाधरानाम् ॥

पततां परितः परिस्फुरद्भिः
परिपिञ्जीकृतदिङ्मुखैर्मयूरवैः ।
सुतरामभवद्दुरीक्षबिम्ब-
स्तपनस्तत्किरणैरिवात्मदर्शः ॥

694

As an elephant charged forward, one huge snake coiled its
    long iron-dark body around its feet like a fetter and
    brought it to a halt.

But then Krishna, nonchalantly raising an eyebrow in
    disdain, glanced smilingly at Garuda perched on top
    of his standard, whereupon flocks of great birds flew
    up from him.

Blazing like molten gold, they ascended from Garuda with
    a shrill screech, and for an instant the armies saw what
    seemed to be glowing sparks of fire in the heavens.

With their beating wings the birds instantaneously
    dispelled the fish-like clouds throughout the ocean-
    like sky; they could be compared with the mountains
    born from the lineage of Meru the golden.[13]

The rays of light flashing from the birds turned the   55
    heavens all yellow: the sun's orb was impossible to see,
    like a mirror when a fierce glare falls on it.

दधुरम्बुधिमन्थनाद्रिमन्थ-
भ्रमणायस्तफणीन्द्रपित्तजानाम् ।
रुचमुल्लसमानवैनतेय-
द्युतिभिन्नाः फणभारिणो मणीनाम् ॥

अभितः क्षुभिताम्बुराशिधीर-
ध्वनिराकृष्टसमूलपादपौघः ।
जनयन्नभवद्युगान्तशङ्का-
मनिलो नागविपक्षपक्षजन्मा ॥

प्रचलत्पतगेन्द्रपत्रवात-
प्रसभोन्मूलितशैलदत्तमार्गैः ।
भयविह्वलमाशु दन्दशूकै-
र्विवरैराविविशे स्वमेव धाम ॥

खचरैः क्षयमक्षये ऽहिसैन्ये
सुकृतैर्दुष्कृतवत्तदोपनीते ।
अयुगार्चिरिव ज्वलन्नृषाथो
रिपुरौदर्चिषमाजुहाव मन्त्रम् ॥

६० सहसा दधदुद्धताट्टहास-
श्रियमुत्त्रासितजन्तुना स्वनेन ।
विततायतहेतिबाहुरुच्चै-
रथ वेताल इवोत्पपात वह्निः ॥

The serpents were now saturated with the light from the
    resplendent birds; they had become dark green as
    emeralds sprouting from the bile vomited by Vasuki
    the snake-king, exhausted by the whirling of the
    mountain at the ocean's churning.[14]

Thundering deeply like the ocean when it inundates the
    shore, a wind sprang up from the booming of Garuda's
    wings, uprooting forests, inspiring apprehension that
    doomsday had arrived.

Trembling with terror, the snakes quickly slithered back,
    baffled, to their nether abode. A route was provided
    through the mountains torn down by the hurricane
    from Garuda's beating wings.

So the serpent host, although numberless, was destroyed
    by the birds, like an evil action by good deeds. At
    that, Krishna's enemy, burning with anger like a
    conflagration, invoked the mantra that conjures up
    flame.

Fire suddenly soared into the air as if it were a ghoul; with   60
    a terrifying roar it seemed to be cackling aloud, its
    flames groping into the distance like arms.

चलितोद्धतधूमकेतनो ऽसौ
रभसादम्बररोहिरोहिदश्वः ।
द्रुतमारुतसारथिः शिखावा-
न्कनकस्यन्दनसुन्दरश्चचाल ॥

ज्वलदम्बरकोटरान्तरालं
बहलार्द्राम्बुदपत्रबद्धधूमम् ।
परिदीपितदीर्घकाष्ठमुच्चै-
र्वनवद्द्विश्वमुवोष जातवेदाः ॥

गुरुतापविशुष्यदम्बुशुभ्राः
क्षणमालग्नकृशानुताम्रभासः ।
स्वमसारतया मषीभवन्तः
पुनराकारमवापुरम्बुवाहाः ॥

ज्वलितानललोलपल्लवान्ताः
स्फुरदष्टापदपत्रपीतभासः ।
क्षणमात्रभुवामभावकाले
सुतरामापुरिवायतिं पताकाः ॥

६५ निखिलमिति कुर्वतश्चिराय
द्रुतचामीकरशारितामिव द्याम् ।
प्रतिघातसमर्थमस्तमग्रे-
रथ मेघङ्करमस्मरन्मुरारिः ॥

The conflagration's banner was smoke billowing high in
the air; flames raced onward, dazzling as the golden
chariot of the sun driven by the swift wind with its
roan horses galloping through the sky.

The heavens were now alight, the smoke thick as rain
clouds and the furthest reaches of the firmament
illuminated; the fire burned everything as if it were
a forest, blazing up inside the clefts of trees while
their foliage smoked and their long branches were
consumed within the blaze.[15]

The clouds turned white as their water dried up in the
intense heat, then reddened for an instant with flames
licking around them; finally, completely empty, they
became black as soot and regained their original hue.

The pennants on the standards flapped in the fire, turning
yellow as leaves of bright gold; then, as they were
consumed, they flared up like streaks of flickering
lightning.

But Krishna, Mura's enemy, now invoked a magic weapon   65
to conjure up rain clouds; this had the power to
combat the fiery spell that for a moment had made the
sky look flecked with molten gold.

चतुरम्बुधिगर्भधीरकुक्षे-
र्वपुषः संधिषु लीनसर्वसिन्धोः ।
उदगुः सलिलात्मनस्तिधाम्नो
जलवाहावलयः शिरोरुहेभ्यः ॥

ककुभः कृतनादमास्तृणन्त-
स्तिरयन्तः पटलानि भानुभासाम् ।
उदनंसिषुरभ्रमभ्रसंघाः
सपदि श्यामलिमानमानयन्तः ॥

तपनीयनिकाषराजिगौर-
स्फुरदुत्तालतडिच्छटाट्टृहासम् ।
अवबद्धसमुद्धताम्बुवाह-
ध्वनिताडम्बरमम्बरं बभूव ॥

सवितुः परिभावुकैर्मरीची-
रचिताभ्यङ्गमतङ्गजाङ्गभाभिः ।
जलदैरतिविस्फुरद्भिरुच्चै-५
र्विदधे केतनतेव धूमकेतोः ॥

७० ज्वलतः शमनाय चित्रभानोः
प्रलयाप्लावमिवाभिदर्शयन्तः ।
ववृषुर्वृषनादिनो नदीना-
मतटारोपितवारि वारिवाहाः ॥

A stream of clouds emerged from Krishna's hair; for that
all-pervading deity[16] is of the very nature of water—
his capacious stomach holds the four oceans, while all
the rivers are contained within his body's inner parts.

These clouds quickly clustered in the sky, blanketing the
horizons amid a thundering roar, obscuring the rays of
the sun, and bringing on gloom.

The heavens laughed aloud, huge streaks of lightning
flashing bright yellow as veins of gold on a touchstone,
echoing with the booming of the lofty storm clouds as
they thundered.

The clouds lowered everywhere, subduing the sun's rays;
dark as a freshly decorated elephant, they took on the
appearance of smoke, fire's banner.

Roaring like bulls, the clouds poured down rain to   70
extinguish the blazing fire; as water flooded over
the steep riverbanks, it seemed to be enacting the
inundation at doomsday.

मधुरैरपि भूयसा स मेघ्यैः
प्रथमं प्रत्युत वारिभिर्दिदीपे ।
पवमानसखस्ततः क्रमेण
प्रणयक्रोध इवाशमीन्निनादैः ॥

परितः प्रसभेन नीयमानः
शरवर्षैरवसायमाश्रयाशः ।
प्रबलेषु कृती चकार विद्यु-
द्व्यपदेशेन घनेष्वनुप्रवेशम् ॥

प्रयतः प्रशमं[६] हुताशनस्य
क्वचिदालक्ष्यत मुक्तमूलमर्चिः ।
बलभित्प्रहितायुधाभिघात-
त्रुटितं पक्षिपतेरिवैकपत्रम् ॥

व्यगमन्सहसा दिशां मुखेभ्यः
शमयित्वा शिखिनं घनाघनौघाः ।
उपकृत्य निसर्गतः परेषा-
मुपरोधं न हि कुर्वते महान्तः ॥

७५   कृतदाहमुदर्चिषः शिखाभिः
परिषिक्तं मुहुरम्भसा नवेन ।
विगताम्बुधरव्रणं प्रपेदे
गगनं तापितपायितासिलक्ष्मीम् ॥

The fire, friend of the wind, contrived to blaze up strongly,
	for the downpour was initially gentle; but then it was
	gradually extinguished, like a love quarrel flaring up
	only to subside after affectionate words.

The fire was momentarily cunning; extinguished by the
	pouring rain, it disguised itself as lightning and took
	refuge in the huge clouds.

As the conflagration was quenched, a flame could be seen
	broken free in one place, looking like Garuda's golden
	wing severed by a blow from the mace wielded by
	Indra.

After the thick rain clouds had doused the blaze, they
	immediately disappeared from the face of the sky.
	When the mighty have assisted others from natural
	goodwill, they do not involve themselves further.

After being scorched by the flames, the sky was laved   75
	repeatedly by fresh rain so that it lost its blemishes,
	the clouds; it became bright as a sword blade forged in
	fire and tempered with water.

इति नरपतिरस्खं यद्यदाविश्चकार
प्रकुपित इव रोगः क्षिप्रकारी विकारम् ।
भिषगिव गुरुदोषच्छेदिनोपक्रमेण
क्रमविदथ मुरारिः प्रत्यहंस्तत्तदेव ॥

शुद्धिं गतैरपि परामृजुभिर्विदित्वा
बाणैरजय्यमविघट्टितमर्मभिस्तम् ।
मर्मातिगैरनृजुभिर्नितरामशुद्धै-
र्वाक्सायकैरथ तुतोद तदा विपक्षः ॥

राहुस्त्रीस्तनयोरकारि सहसा येनाश्लथालिङ्गन-
व्यापारैकविनोददुर्ललितयोः कार्कश्यलक्ष्मीर्वृथा ।
तेनाक्रोशत एव तस्य मुरजित्तत्काललोलानल-
ज्वालापल्लवितेन मूर्धविकलं चक्रेण चक्रे वपुः ॥

श्रिया जुष्टं दिव्यैः सपटहरवैरन्वितं पुष्पवर्षै-
र्वपुष्टश्चैद्यस्य क्षणमृषिगणैर्नूयमानं निरीय ।
प्रकाशेनाकाशे दिनकरकरान्विक्षिपद्भिस्मिताक्षै-
नरेन्द्रैरौपेन्द्रं वपुरथ विशद्धाम वीक्षांबभूवे ॥

So the Chedi king in his wrath had craftily deployed
 various modes of weaponry, but Mura's enemy
 was equal to each of them in succession, and he
 immediately repelled them with his own powers,
 putting an end to their evil influence. In a similar
 manner a doctor familiar with the sequence of
 symptoms can prescribe a regime removing malignity
 and quickly cure a virulent debilitating disease.[17]

Krishna's enemy now knew his foe was immune to his
 arrows, for though straight and true, they were not
 deadly. So he struck at him with the shafts of his
 words, wounding to the core, crooked and false.

The breasts of Rahu's wives had once been eager for no
 other pleasure than experiencing his close embraces,
 but Vishnu had speedily made fruitless their exquisite
 firmness.[18] Now with the same discus,[19] at that
 moment edged with flickering flame, Krishna struck
 off Shishupala's head as he was in the very act of
 cursing him.

Then, wide-eyed in astonishment, the princes beheld
 the vital energy, tinged with beauty, emerging from
 Shishupala's body. To the beating of heavenly drums,
 as flowers rained down and choirs of seers sang
 praises, for an instant it surpassed in brilliance the
 blazing sun in the sky and then merged into Krishna's
 body.[20]

Description of the Poet's Lineage

सर्वाधिकारी सुकृताधिकारः श्रीवर्मलाख्यस्य⁹ बभूव राझः ।
असक्तदृष्टिर्विरजाः सदैव देवो ऽपरः सुप्रभदेवनामा ॥

काले मितं तथ्यमुदर्कपथ्यं तथागतस्येव जनः सचेताः ।
विनानुरोधात्स्वहितेच्छयैव महीपतिर्यस्य वचश्चकार ॥

तस्याभवद्वृत्तक इत्युदात्तः क्षमी मृदुर्धर्मपरस्तनूजः ।
यं वीक्ष्य वैयासमजातशत्रोर्वचो गुणग्राहि जनैः प्रतीये ॥

सर्वेण सर्वाश्रय इत्यनिन्द्यमानन्दभाजा जनितं जनेन ।
यश्च द्वितीयं स्वयमद्वितीयो मुख्यः सतां गौणमवाप नाम ॥

५ श्रीशब्दरम्यकृतसर्गसमाप्तिलक्ष्म
लक्ष्मीपतेश्वरितकीर्तनमात्रचारु ।
तस्यात्मजः सुकविकीर्तिदुराशयादः
काव्यं व्यधत्त शिशुपालवधाभिधानम् ॥

There was a chief minister, fully intent on good works,
    who served King Varmala.[1] His gaze was always steady
    and unblinking; free from passion, like another of the
    gods, he was called Suprabhadeva.

In the same manner as intelligent people adopted the
    teaching of the Buddha, the king, without being
    pressed but simply desiring what was beneficial to
    himself, followed his advice. For it was appropriate to
    the occasion, sensible, and had a positive result.

Suprabhadeva had a son called Dattaka—distinguished,
    patient, of a gentle nature, and concerned to do
    what was right. When people saw him, they could
    understand what Vyasa meant when he described
    Yudhishthira's virtues.[2]

The whole world took such delight in Dattaka that he,
    first among the virtuous, second to none, gained for
    himself the splendid sobriquet—metaphorically
    alluding to his principal quality[3]—of "Everyone's
    Refuge."

His son, with the forlorn ambition of gaining the renown   5
    of an eminent poet, composed this poem *The Killing
    of Shishupala.* If the work has any distinguishing
    feature, it is that each chapter concludes with the
    excellent word "shri," while its charm derives simply
    from recounting the deeds of Krishna.

ABBREVIATIONS

M   Durgāprasād and Śivadatta's edition of *Śiśupālavadha* with
         Mallinātha's commentary
Musalgāonkara
         Musalgāonkara's edition of *Śiśupālavadha* with Mallinātha's
         commentary
V   Kāk and Śāstrī's edition of *Śiśupālavadha* with Vallabhadeva's
         commentary

NOTES TO THE TEXT

सर्ग १

१ पतन्पतङ्ग-] पततपतङ्ग- M.
२ जिगाय] M; जिघाय V.
३ निबृंहितांहसा] निबर्हितांहसा M.
४ हेलयोद्धृतं] M; हेलयोद्धतं V.
५ 63–66 = M 64, 63, 66, and 65.
६ आविद्ध-] आबद्ध- M.
७ सुनिश्चिता] सुनिश्चला M.

सर्ग २

१ M transposes lines.
२ 24–28 = M 25, 24, 28, 26, and 27.
३ कल्पितैरपि] संवृतैरपि M.
४ 82–89 = M 88-89 and 82-87.
५ M transposes lines.
६ तीर्थैरतः] तीर्थेष्वन्तः M.

सर्ग ३

१ कर्चूर-] M; कर्पूर- V.
२ V commentary refers to a verse that occurs in M as 3.13.
३ विवक्षन्निव] M 22; विविक्षुरिव V.
४ ईयुर्] M 31; आययुर् V.
५ अनल्पा M 31; अनल्पा- V.
६ काञ्चनवप्र-] M 32; काञ्चनभूमि- V.
७ यस्या] M 41; यस्यां V.
८ सावर्ण्यभाजः प्रतिमागताया
   लक्ष्यैः स्मरापाण्डुतया तरुण्याः]
   सावर्ण्यभाजां प्रतिमागतानां
   लक्ष्यैः स्मरापाण्डुतयाङ्गनानाम् M 47.

सर्ग ४

१ Every third verse of this sarga employs a *yamaka*, or rhyming
   assonance. For the overall figurative structure of the sarga, see
   Tubb 2014: 173–189.
२ संक्रान्तिराक्रान्तगुणान्तरेति] संक्रान्तिमाक्रान्तगुणातिरेकाम् M.

३ नितम्बशोभा-] निकुञ्जशोभा- M.
४ स्वानमा] M; [ऽ]स्वानमा V.
५ निस्यन्दि-] M; निष्यण्ण- V.

सर्ग ५

१ जवेन] निरीक्ष्य M.
२ अतितूर्णमन्य-] अभिहन्तुमन्य- M.
Uncertainty about the transmission of this verse may be the result of M's "corrections." M's reading निरीक्ष्य for V's जवेन may have been prompted by the judgment that अधावत् renders जवेन tautologous. M reads अभिहन्तुम् for V's अतितूर्णम्, another expression for "quickly," but the printed versions of his commentary refer only to the reading अतितूर्णम्. While both V and M read जलधेः (glossed as अब्धेः and जलाशयस्य respectively), this requires taking जलधि in the unusual sense of "river" (so translated here), rather than its normal sense of "ocean."
३ विधानपिण्ड-] M; विधान्नपिण्ड- V.

सर्ग ६

१ अववादकरैरिव] अपवादकरैरिव M and V commentary.
२ वदन-] M; कुसुम- V.
३ ऽङ्गतां] M; ऽङ्गतां V.
४ V commentary quotes M 59 as an alternative verse, but it is not otherwise included in V's recension.
५ घनमतो नमतो] M 65; घनमतो ऽनमतो V.

सर्ग ७

१ भवतु] भवति M.
२ -निरन्तरावलग्न-] M; -निरन्तरावमग्न-V.
३ प्राप्योरुत्वं स्तनटभुवि] उल्लङ्घ्योच्चैः कुचतटभुवं M.

सर्ग ८

१ चुम्बितायाः] M; चुम्बितस्य V.
२ जलैर्निरासि] M; जनैर्निरासि V, तोयैर्निरासि V commentary.

सर्ग ९

१ तया] M; यया V.
२ किमु चोदिताः प्रियहितार्थकृतः
कृतिनो भवन्ति सुहृदः सुहृदाम् ॥] M;

किमचोदितप्रियहितार्थकृतः
कृतिनो भवन्ति सुहृदो ऽसुकृताम् ॥ V.

सर्ग १०

१ परिरक्तयात्मा] M; परितिक्ततयात्मा V.
M's परिरक्तया is conventional and slightly easier than V's परितिक्ततया: the girl's lip loses the redness of the lac through drinking but regains it because of the pressure of her lover's teeth; cf. 10.26. However, as V points out, the taste of lac is astringent (परितिक्त), as opposed to the sweet wine, and a bite would restore a sharp sensation to the lip.

२ पीतशीधुमधुरैर्मिथुनानाम्] M; पीतशीधुमदिरैर्मिथुनानाम् V.
३ पिहितैकतमोरु] M; पिहितैकतमोरूः V.

सर्ग ११

१ -अकाकि-] -अकाकु- M.
२ न्यङ्क्तितैकेक्षणेव] व्यङ्क्तितैकेक्षणेव M.

सर्ग १२

१ भूभृद्धिरप्यस्खलिता] Musalgāonkara; भूभृद्धिरप्यस्खलिताः V and M. Hultzsch 1926: 123, n. 4, attributes the reading अस्खलिता to V on the basis of his *śāradā*-script manuscript.
२ 29–32 = M 31, 32, 29, and 30.
३ घण्टयोः] M; गण्डयोः V.
४ -गवलावलिद्युतिः] -गवलासितद्युतिः M.

सर्ग १३

१ -कुरुचक्र-] M; -गुरुचक्र- V.
२ नृपतेः] M; नृपतिः V.
३ हरि-र्विनयं] हरे-र्विनयं M.
४ सुरारिबन्धन-च्छलवामनं] Musalgāonkara note; सुरारिबन्धन-श्छलवामनं V; सुरारिबन्धने छलवामनं M.
५ जनसभाजनोचितः] M; जनसभाजनोचितान् V.
६ त्रपाभरपराङ्मुखैरपि] M; त्रपाभरपराङ्मुखैरिव V, अपिर्विरोधे V commentary.
७ नूतनत्वमतिरिक्ततयानुपदं] M; नूतनत्वमविरक्ततयानुपदं V.

सर्ग १४

१ स्थिरा] M; स्थिरे V.
२ ववल्मिरे] ववल्गिरे M.

715

३   निरवापयन्नखैः] निरदारयन्नखैः M.

सर्ग १५

१   अभितर्जयन्निव] M; अभितेजयन्निव V.
२   The text follows M 14–39. M holds that V 14–47 are interpolated and accordingly reproduces these verses without commentary after 39. The verses are omitted here. See Note on the Text and Translation.
३   This verse = V 48.
४   V omits this verse, while M comments that it reprises 44 in order to establish Bhishma's state of mind. Shishupala has insulted Bhishma specifically at 19–21 whereas he only alludes to him indirectly at V 31, and so 45 can be held to be appropriate to the narrative structure. However, the repetition वचः स्माह (44) and प्राह ...स्म वाचम् (45) does involve an awkwardness that has been smoothed out in translation.
५   मुदमाहृतिः] मुदमाहुकिः M.

सर्ग १६

१   Verses 2-15 of the deliberately ambiguous Sanskrit text are repeated in this edition.
२   मधुद्विषो] महीपतिर् M.
३   चेदिपः] शार्ङ्गिणः M.
४   I omit V 82. This verse is not commented on by V on the grounds that it reprises 62 and occurs in few recensions. It is also omitted by M.

सर्ग १७

१   शिनिर्-] M; शनिर्- V.
२   विड्रथः] विदूरथः M.
३   निषादिभिर्विदितयताङ्कुशक्रियैः] M; निषादिभिर्विदितमताङ्कुशक्रियैः V.
४   हता मुहुः प्रणदितघण्टमाययुः] M; हतासकृत्वप्रणदितघण्टमाययुः V. Establishing a text for this difficult verse is not assisted by the absence of part of V's commentary. I have adopted M's reading of the compound in the second part of the first line on the grounds that यत in the technical sense of "guidance of an elephant with the foot" (Edgerton 1985: 122 s.v.) seems to make slightly better sense than V's मत. In the second line I have resisted M's नालिका, "vein, artery (on an elephant's trunk)" in favor of V's लालिका,

"coaxing," but have reluctantly incorporated M's मुहुः. M's version has the appearance of an attempt to rework an already awkwardly transmitted text.

५ तूर्यमाननैः] M; तूर्यमानकैः V.

६ क्वचिच्छरच्छशधरखण्डपाण्डुरः] M; क्वचिच्छरज्जलधरपिण्डपाण्डुरः V.

सर्ग १८

१ -कक्ष्याम्] -कक्षा M.

२ उद्गम्याराद्] उद्गम्याराम् M.

३ वक्रं] M; वक्षो V.

४ व्यस्तारज्ञो] व्युत्थानज्ञो M.

५ धिक्के] विष्के M.

६ च प्रमत्तो] M; चाप्रमत्तो V.

७ लोलं] M; लोकं V.

८ सैन्यान्सास्थीन्खादतो रक्तरक्ता
  नष्टा नूनं प्रेतराजस्य दन्ताः]
  हासालक्ष्याः पूर्णकामस्य मन्ये
  मृत्योर्दन्ताः पीतरक्तासवस्य M (cited by V as a variant).

९ भूमौ] M; भूयो V.

१० आविश्यान्तः] आविश्याधः M.

११ पुष्कराण्यानकानां] M and V commentary; पुष्करैरानकानां V.

सर्ग १९

१ For a conspectus of the various examples of rhyming assonance (*yamaka*) and "brilliant poetry" (*citrakāvya*) deployed in this chapter, see Tubb 2014b: 190–192.

२ This verse employs only the consonantal phonemes *j*, *t*, *bh*, and *r*.

३ This verse employs no labial phonemes.

४ This verse is an example of the figurative structure "correct in every direction" (*sarvatobhadra*), a double palindrome, in which the Sanskrit can be read backward and forward both horizontally and vertically. See Lienhard 2007: 143 for a schematic representation of this verse.

५ This verse is an example of the figurative structure "binding of a drum" (*murajabandha*), in which the Sanskrit can be read both regularly and in a crisscross fashion. See Lienhard 2007: 146 and Tubb 2014b:154 for schematic representations of this verse.

६ This verse is an example of *pratilomayamaka* whereby it represents the previous verse read backward.

७ This verse is an example of the palindromic *pratilomānulomapada*.

८ This verse is an example of the figurative structure *gomūtrikā*, "cow urine," in which the Sanskrit can be read in a regular or zigzag fashion. See Tubb 2014b: 152 for a schematic representation of this verse.

९ चमूस्तूर्णमतिमात्राविलासिना] M; चमूस्तूर्णं मतिमात्रा विलासिना V.

१० This verse employs only two consonantal phonemes, *bh* and *r*.

११ This verse is an example of the figurative structure "half turner" (*ardhabhramaka*), similar in form to "cow urine." See Lienhard 2007: 145.

१२ This verse employs only two consonantal phonemes, *l* and *n*.

१३ This verse employs only two consonantal phonemes, *bh* and *v*.

१४ This verse is palindromic.

१५ विदितं] M; विदिते V.

१६ This verse, which is syntactically linked to 19.89, is palindromic.

१७ This verse employs only two consonantal phonemes, *p* and *r*.

१८ V and M commentaries identify this verse as "having the final quarter concealed" (*gūḍhārthacaturtha*), that is, with the syllables of the fourth quarter included in the preceding three. See Lienhard 2007: 178.

१९ This verse employs only two consonantal phonemes, *k* and *l*.

२० This verse employs only two consonantal phonemes, *v* and *r*.

२१ This verse employs only two consonantal phonemes, *r* and *j*.

२२ This verse employs only two consonantal phonemes, *k* and *r*.

२३ This verse employs only two consonantal phonemes, *d* and *r*.

२४ This verse employs only two consonantal phonemes, *ś* and *r*.

२५ This verse employs only one consonantal phoneme, *d*.

२६ This verse is an example of the figurative structure called "the wheel" (*cakra*). When the syllables of the Sanskrit are deployed in a particular order on a six-spoked wheel, they represent the words *Māghakāvyam idam* (This is Magha's poem) and *Śiśupālavadha* (The killing of Shishupala). A schematic representation of the verse is given by V. See also Lienhard 2007:151.

सर्ग २०

१ प्रणिरास प्रतिवादिवत्प्रमाणैः] प्रतिवादीव निराकरोत्प्रमाणैः M.

२ शरदेव] शरदीव M.

३ चापयष्ट्याम्] M; चापयष्ट्या V.

४ -योग्यनिद्रे] -योगनिद्रे M.

५ जलदैरतिविस्फुरद्भिरुद्यैर्] conjecture; जलदैरिति विस्फुरद्भिरुद्यैर् V, जलदैरभितः
स्फुरद्भिरुद्यैर् M.

६ प्रशमं] M; प्रथमं V.

Description of the Poet's Lineage

१ श्रीवर्मलाख्यस्य] M; श्रीधर्मलाभस्य V.

NOTES TO THE TRANSLATION

1 Narada's Message

1   The subject of this verse is Hari, a name that can denote both the god Vishnu, whose wife is Shri, the goddess of royal majesty, prosperity, and auspiciousness, and his incarnation Krishna, the son of Vasudeva and his wife Devaki, who is the courtly and martial hero of *The Killing of Shishupala*. In the course of this chapter Krishna, who is generally referred to by epithets, is variously portrayed as an earthly ruler, in cosmic terms as the supreme or primal being, and as Vishnu and three of that deity's world-protecting and demon-destroying incarnations (*avatāras*), namely the Boar (34), the Man-Lion (47), and Rama (67–69), respectively the third, fourth, and seventh of what became a standard list of ten such *avatāras*, with Krishna himself as the eighth. On the structure of chapter 1 of *The Killing of Shishupala*, see Trynkowska 2004a.

2   The god Shiva, whose *tāṇḍava* dance is an instrument of the destruction of the universe prior to its re-creation, is typically portrayed as an ascetic who frequents cemeteries and smears his body with the ashes of the cremated dead.

3   In contrast to his brother Krishna, who is dark, Balarama has a white complexion.

4   The ritual thread thrown over the shoulder is worn in token of a childhood initiation as a member of the Brahman class.

5   The discus named Sudarshana (literally, "Beautiful"), both a sharp-edged missile and a symbol of kingship, is the weapon borne by Vishnu in combat with the demons and later wielded by Krishna.

6   In a previous incarnation as the god Narayana.

7   The killing of their malign uncle Kamsa, king of Mathura and incarnation of the demon Kalanemi, was the climax of the youthful careers of Krishna and Balarama. See Couture 1991: 313–316.

8   In ancient Indian cosmology a black plum (*jambū*) tree is envisaged as growing on or beside the axis mundi, Mount Meru.

9   The mark on the moon is envisaged as having the shape of a deer or a hare.

10   The sage Aurva cast his anger into the depths of the sea, where it took the form of a fire with the head of a mare. See *Mahābhārata* 1973: 341–342 and also 8.49 and 11.43 and 45.

11 An epithet of Vishnu.
12 "(White-)lotus-eyed" is a conventional term denoting facial beauty.
13 The reference is to the revealed, authorless texts of the Veda.
14 The verse plays on *sadopayoga,* "continually used" and *akṣati,* "unfailing."
15 Narada describes Krishna in terms of the self as envisaged in the dualist Samkhya philosophy. See chapter 14 n. 10.
16 The cosmic snake Shesha supports the earth. See 3.24.
17 The verse plays on *hari,* "lion" and a name of Vishnu. According to poetic convention the lion always defeats the elephant. For Hiranyakashipu, see 42–47.
18 The relationship derives from Indra and Vishnu's role as companions in destroying demons. See 14.74 and 16.12 (alternative translation).
19 The word *indra* denotes the god of that name and "strength."
20 See 71.
21 The name of this paragon of stallions can be translated as Long Ears, Loud Neigher, or Far-famed.
22 The verse plays on *kauśika,* a name of Indra and "owl."
23 The verse plays here on *mada,* "arrogance" and "ichor," the sweet, sticky secretion, also known as rut fluid or must, discharged from an elephant's forehead lobes.
24 Ravana is compared through wordplay to Indra's elephant.
25 The verse plays on *kalā,* "art" and "phase of the moon." There may also be wordplay on *gṛha,* "palace" and "lunar mansion."
26 Divine protectors of the world, located at each of the cardinal directions.
27 Snakes were believed to use their eyes to hear.
28 Rama, the hero of Valmiki's epic poem the *Rāmāyaṇa* (The Career of Rama), whose origins lie in the second half of the first millennium B.C.E., was to become, along with Krishna, Vishnu's most celebrated incarnation.
29 The Mahabharata describes how two of the young Shishupala's four arms and his third eye were predicted to disappear when he sat on the knee of the one destined to kill him. This duly occurred when the young Shishupala was placed on Krishna's lap. Krishna then granted a boon to his aunt, Shishupala's mother, that he would subsequently pardon him for any offenses one hundred times. See Introduction.

30   The verse plays on *mahībhṛt,* "king" and "mountain," and *kara,*
     "tax" and "sunray." The reference to the sun presages Shishupala's
     fate as described in the final verse of the poem.

2 The Discussion in the Council Chamber

1   Strictly speaking, Yudhishthira is the son of Dharma, approx-
     imately "Righteousness" or "Duty," of which religious austerity
     can be regarded as a component. Fasting undertaken by the ritual's
     sponsor is the necessary preliminary to any significant sacrifice.

2   The sacrifice called *rājasūya,* literally "bringing forth a king," is to
     confirm Yudhishthira as a universal monarch. See chapter 14.

3   The bees have been attracted by the scent of the wine of which
     Balarama is habitually fond. This predilection may explain why
     Balarama's advice to Krishna is at times slightly inconsistent.
     Compare 60 and 61.

4   In this and the following verses, Balarama's perspective conforms
     to the analysis of political policy found in the celebrated *Artha-*
     śāstra of Kautilya (c. second–third centuries C.E.). See Olivelle
     2013. The five principles of statecraft are: preparing the ground
     for action, securing access to resources, identifying the appropriate
     place and time, having the ability to respond to setbacks, and
     successfully concluding any undertaking.

5   Buddhism identifies selfhood as a construction involving five
     impermanent and conditioned processes: name and form, latent
     traces, feeling, ideation, and consciousness. For other references
     to Buddhism, see 15.58 and the second verse of *Description of the*
     Poet's Lineage. See also Mejor 2007.

6   The six modes of strategy are negotiating peace, initiating
     hostilities, remaining stationary, marching into battle, seeking
     refuge, and dissembling. The three types of power are power
     from financial and military resources, power from diplomacy, and
     power from resourcefulness. The three successes arise from power,
     diplomacy, and resourcefulness. The three phases of action are
     progress, decline, and stasis.

7   The verse plays on *aṅga* "component part" and "body"; *kalpita,*
     "arranged" and "armored"; and *bheda,* "revealing" and "injury."

8   A slightly condensed verse about whose structure V and M differ.
     A natural enemy is defined as such by immediate geographical
     proximity. Balarama is suggesting that Shishupala, a natural ally

of Krishna and his clan, has been turned into an enemy. Compare 41. This ignores Shishupala's demonic background, described by Narada in the previous chapter.

9   The story of Rukmini's abduction by Krishna is incidental in the Mahabharata. See *Mahābhārata* 1978: 473. However, the *Harivaṃśa* portrays it as a major cause of the enmity between Krishna and Shishupala. See Austin 2014. The episode is mentioned only in passing in *The Killing of Shishupala*. See 38 and 41, 15.53, 16.48, and 20.6.

10   The verse plays on *jāti*, "birth" and "class"; *kriyā*, "act" and "agency"; and *guṇa*, "quality," "talent," and "attribute."

11   Compare 35.

12   This ascetic practice involves sitting within a circle of four fires during the hot season when the sun, regarded as the fifth fire, is at its most intense.

13   See chapter 1 n.9.

14   The other three political expedients are conciliation, generosity, and sowing dissension.

15   Krishna is compared through wordplay to the self as conceived in the Samkhya philosophical system. Compare 14.39.

16   Jarasandha, king of Magadha and Shishupala's closest ally, was simultaneously born as the separate halves of a child of two wives of Brihadratha and then joined together. See Brockington 2002.

17   The parallel, drawn through wordplay, between the blockaded city of Mahishmati and penned cattle is not mentioned by V.

18   Eloquence is compared through wordplay to the weaving of cloth.

19   Uddhava is referring to the typology of rulers described in Kautilya's *Arthaśāstra*. See Olivelle 2013: 274. Those rulers whose kingdoms are located next to the "aggressive" (*jigīṣu*) king are deemed to be natural enemies, those adjacent to them are in turn their enemies and the expansive king's allies, and so on.

20   The political activity of the king is compared through wordplay to a snake charmer's skills.

21   The behavior of the king is compared through wordplay to an illness. The secondary meaning here is: "Illness, even when treated by doctors, may not clearly manifest its symptoms at the outset, only later to become incurable and infect the body virulently."

22   A reference to the explanation given in the manual of dramaturgy, the *Nāṭyaśāstra*, to the manner in which *rasa*, the "flavor" of

aesthetic experience, emerges during the performance of a play.

23 See n. 6.

24 Vedic Sanskrit was pronounced with a pitch accent system not found in classical Sanskrit.

25 The attributes of Bana are compared through wordplay to a bow (*bāṇa*).

26 The verse plays on *pradoṣa,* "fault" and "first part of the night."

27 The churning of the ocean of milk by the gods and demons brought forth various precious objects and substances, including the goddess Shri, a great horse, the Kaustubha jewel, and ambrosia. See *Mahabhārata* 1973:73–74 and *Viṣṇupurāṇa* 1.9.90–98. Other versions of the myth name the horse as Ucchaihshravas. See chapter 1 n.21.

28 See chapter 1 n.29.

29 The translation derives from a conflation of V and M's interpretations. The verse plays on *tīrtha,* "disguise" (V) or "stratagem" (M) and "ford."

30 Political policy is compared through wordplay to grammar. This complex verse turns around the word *paspaśa,* literally "spying," which (in the feminine gender) is the title of the introduction to the commentary by Patanjali (c. first century B.C.E.) on Panini's grammar of Sanskrit (c. fourth century B.C.E.). My translation derives from a conflation of V and M's interpretations. M identifies a further layer of meaning relating to financial subvention. See also Kielhorn 1908.

31 An anthropomorphizing of the auspicious *śrīvatsa* mark on the chest of Vishnu-Krishna. See Introduction.

3 Departure for Indraprastha

1 The Ganga originates from Vishnu's left foot, whence its white stream flows across the heavens and then descends to earth. Compare 10.

2 See 13 and 1.47.

3 See n. 1.

4 The Yamuna is regarded as being dark. In Hindu mythology there is a close relationship between this river and Krishna.

5 The verse plays on *śrī,* "beauty" and the name of the goddess Shri. Compare 2.118.

6 Both V and M identify alternative layers of meaning in this verse

relating respectively to a poor man and his patron and an aggressive king and his weak enemy.

7   The verse plays on the literal meaning of the sword's name.

8   The verse plays on *nati*, "bending" and "bowing"; *karṇāntika*, "to the ear" and "loyal"; and *guṇa*, "string" and "attribute."

9   The verse plays on *puṣya*, "splendid" and the name of a constellation.

10 Garuda, king of the birds, is the enemy of snakes.

11 The rising dust is compared through wordplay to dignified behavior. The secondary meaning here is: "Everyone should act with due gravity, not disrespecting the distinguished or behaving arrogantly toward them."

12 See chapter 1 n. 10.

13 Dvaraka was founded by Krishna as the Yadava capital in the wake of Jarasandha's attack on Mathura.

14 The sea is compared through wordplay to a father.

15 "Mine of jewels" is a standard epithet for the ocean.

16 The apsarases are divine courtesans and dancers; like the gods and goddesses, they do not blink or perspire.

17 The mansion roofs are compared through wordplay to the women.

18 The verse plays on *ambara*, "garment" and "air."

19 The verse plays on *vinītamārgāḥ*, "well-constructed roads" and "the paths of good conduct," and the adjectives describing the compound.

20 The verse plays on *kalā*, "art" and "phase of the moon."

21 Kamadeva, the god of love, was reduced to ashes by flame emanating from Shiva's forehead eye. Bana, the son of Bali, had received the boon of a thousand arms from Shiva, but they were cut off by Krishna. See Couture 1991: 404.

22 Dvaraka is compared through wordplay to Amaravati.

23 Krishna is compared through wordplay to a dark collyrium mark.

24 The royal thoroughfare is compared through wordplay to the army of the gods. Indra's mace (*vajra*) is frequently understood to be a thunderbolt.

25 After emerging from Vishnu's foot, the fierce surge of the Ganga was diminished in force by flowing through Shiva's matted hair.

26 A standard trope for amorous pining resulting from separation from the beloved.

27 The verse plays on *dvāravatī*, "Dvaraka" and "possessing gates."

28 The verse plays on *lakṣmībhṛt*, "majestic" and "bearing the goddess Shri."

29 A statement of the principle of *vedasarvamūlatva*—that is, every form of knowledge originates in and is encompassed by the Veda.

30 The reference is to Vishnu's cosmic role at the transition of world ages.

31 The churning of the ocean by the gods and demons had brought forth precious objects and substances, including the goddess Shri; see chapter 2 n. 27.

4 Mount Raivataka

1 In 1.1 this deity has the alternative name Golden Embryo. V quotes *Ṛg Veda* 10.90, which describes the "Man" (*puruṣa*) of a thousand heads, eyes, and feet from which the universe originates.

2 The verse plays on the compound *sādhuhiraṇyagarbha*, "containing finest gold" and "the god Golden Germ," and the expressions describing it.

3 The deadly *kālakūṭa* poison was churned out of the depths of the ocean by the gods and demons and swallowed by Shiva in an act of compassion.

4 The trees are compared through wordplay to imagined Shivas.

5 Raivataka had been recognized since the time of the Mahabharata as a site of comfort and pleasure. See *Mahābhārata* 1973: 405–407. It also became associated with wonder-working and activities such as treasure hunting and alchemy. See also n. 55. Magha's description of the delights of Mount Raivataka is undoubtedly intended to surpass Bharavi's depiction of Mount Himalaya in *Arjuna and the Hunter.* See Bharavi 2016, chap. 5.

6 The opening flowers are implicitly compared to the thousand vulva marks that Indra was cursed to bear because of a sexual misdemeanor.

7 The horses of the sun's chariot are frequently depicted as green in color.

8 My translation of the second line of this verse is tentative, reflecting the slight uncertainty of the text. Magha may be wittily alluding to the view, attributed to the Pashupata Shaivas, that God's qualities could be transferred to a soul. For the Pashupata teaching of *saṃkrānti*, see Watson, Goodall, and Sarma 2013: 41–51.

9 Daruka's eloquence is signaled by his use of a variety of meters. See Tubb 2014b: 184.

10 Mount Raivataka is compared through wordplay to Shiva.

11 This verse is the source of a well-known epithet of the author of *The Killing of Shishupala*, "Bell-Magha" (*ghaṇṭāmāgha*).

12 See chapter 1 n. 9.

13 The *cātaka*, or crested cuckoo, mates during the rainy season.

14 This verse employs wordplay to make an unlikely comparison. The secondary meaning here is: "The rock crags are bent old women, decrepit and obese, with drooping breasts, invariably shunned by virile young men."

15 Raivataka and its hidden treasure are compared through wordplay to a Brahman who has amassed wealth by his performance of ritual. The secondary meaning here is: "This Brahman is master of a repertoire of mantras that can dispel all evil but whose precise meaning is arcane; they can only be interpreted by learned exegetes and are impossible for novices to understand even after hearing them intoned."

16 The class of semidivine beings possessing a human head and a horse's body, akin to the centaur, is called *kiṃnara*, "what sort of man?" or "half-man." Because of his physique a *kiṃnara* can kiss but not embrace, while a horse-headed creature can embrace but not kiss. See Parpola 2015: 171–172.

17 Raivataka's plateaus are compared through wordplay to young women.

18 This verse employs a range of technical vocabulary relating to yogic practice, with which Mount Raivataka became increasingly associated from around the sixth century C.E. Magha's diction reflects his easy familiarity with traditional modes of learning playfully deployed throughout his poem.

19 The expression *kṛtābhiṣeka*, "anointed," can also have the sense of being initiated into a religious vow or path.

20 See chapter 1 n. 28. Valmiki's epic poem the *Rāmāyaṇa* describes the attack on the demon stronghold of Lanka by the half brothers Rama and Lakshmana to rescue the kidnapped Sita. Their monkey ally, Hanuman, flew there beforehand to spy out the land. The mountain lakes are compared through wordplay to the plot and effect of the Ramayana. The second meaning here is: "The Ramayana is full of stories about monkeys (not forgetting the exploits of Rama and Lakshmana themselves!) and stirs its audience with its account of Hanuman flying to Lanka."

5 On the March

1 The verse plays on *kara*, "ray of light" and "hand," and *ambara*, "sky" and "garment."

2 On the hair whorls, called *āvarta*, on horses' coats, see Caland 2010. I have condensed the verse's references to these.

3 The horses are compared through wordplay to the ocean. The secondary meaning here is: "Glistening, whirling, rich in corals bestowing flawless pearls, the ocean is the source of the divine Kaustubha jewel, all the while harboring deep chasms." For Vishnu-Krishna's Kaustubha jewel, see 3.9.

4 Elephants secrete a pearl-like substance from their forehead lobes. Lions are still to be found in the Saurashtra region, where the first half of the poem is set.

5 From the time of the Gupta dynasty (fourth and fifth centuries C.E.) the divine bird Garuda, Vishnu's mount, was depicted on coinage and banners as a symbol of royal authority. See Raven 1994 and also 3.22. At the climax of the poem Garuda assists Krishna in vanquishing Shishupala.

6 The chariots are compared through wordplay to the foothills.

7 A slightly obscure verse that may turn on a contrast between *alpa*, "little," and *analpa*, "much." V mentions an alternative explanation, with *avan* taken in the sense of "killing" (*mārayan*), referring to a popular custom (*lokācāra*) requiring that a hare running through a royal encampment (*kaṭaka*) be killed (*sarvathāvadhya*), presumably on the grounds that it is an ill omen.

8 I translate against the commentators in taking *maṇḍuka* as a variant of *maṇḍūka*, "frog" (compare Prakrit *maṃḍuka*, "frog"). M reads *madduka* (occurring in the sense of "handle" at 18.21, where M reads *maṇḍuka*) and states that "it is commonly known that water stirred up up with one hand and slapped with the other makes a noise like a *madduka*" (*jalam ekena pāṇinotthāpitam apareṇa tāḍitaṃ maddukavad dhvanatīti prasiddham*). This suggests that the word may mean "drum." However, the existence of the phonetically similar Prakrit word *madduya*, which is the equivalent of Sanskrit *madguka*, the avian Darter (see Dave 2005: 372 and 505 s.v. *madgu*), allows for the possibility that the verse is referring to the noise made by this bird thrusting its bill into water.

9 See n. 4.

10 According to a Vedic myth, Indra cut off the wings of the mountains,

as they had ceased to anchor the earth because of their continual flying back and forth. The story has epic and puranic variants connected with Vishnu and Krishna. See Couture 2015: 277–300.

11 Bees are attracted by the sweet ichor exudations of rutting elephants. The verse plays on *dāna*, "liberality" and "ichor," and *jala*, "fool" and "water."

12 The verse uses the verbal form *abhāji* twice in its differing senses of "possessed" and "broken."

13 The verse plays on *mada*, "pride" and "ichor." Compare chapter 1 n. 23.

14 The verse plays on *nāga*, "elephant" and "snake," with adjectival forms describing both creatures. Compare 4.63.

15 The behavior of an elephant is compared through wordplay to the attributes of a king. The secondary meaning here is: "When resolved to abandon his habitual pride, he can exercise a wonderful spontaneity, giving generously to Brahmans (after purifying his hands, of course) and declaring a total amnesty for imprisoned enemies."

16 Balkh, in the ancient region of Bactria, now northern Afghanistan, was renowned for the quality of its horses.

17 See 3.81.

18 According to the Mahabharata, the ravenous Garuda was instructed by his mother to devour the outcast tribesmen known as *niṣāda* but to spare Brahmans. Garuda subsequently spat out a Brahman who had a *niṣāda* wife. See *Mahābhārata* 1973: 81–82.

19 Krishna's lifting of Mount Govardhana with one hand to shelter his fellow cowherds from a rainstorm sent by Indra is one of his most celebrated childhood exploits. See Couture 1991: 244–249.

6 The Seasons on Mount Raivataka

1 The seasons are depicted as occurring simultaneously on various parts of Mount Raivataka. The appearance of wintry blizzards on a mountain in the Saurashtra Peninsula (55–64) might be explained by the fact that Raivataka is the son of Himalaya.

2 The *kiṃśuka* tree has brilliant red flowers.

3 The *kurabaka*, or amaranth, normally has red blossoms, but V describes them as white, necessary for the comparison being made.

4 Compare 4.16 and 5.38 for similar mock-philosophical usage.

5 The melancholy state of the traveler absent from his wife or the

woman separated from her lover at an erotically charged time of the year, such as spring or the rainy season, is a common theme in Indian poetry.

6   A slightly awkward verse. As V and M point out, the gender of *pādapa,* "tree," is normally neuter but in this verse is masculine. M further points out that a tree cannot appropriately be envisaged as the equivalent of a sophisticated man.

7   Lightning in the clouds is compared through wordplay to a woman who, according to the secondary meaning here, "has firm, full breasts and darting, tremulous, lightning-like eyes."

8   Peacocks are conventionally depicted as stimulated by the rainy season.

9   See chapter 1 n. 9.

10   Against V, I take *paṭavāsa* as denoting the illustrated cloth tableaux or screens employed to this day by itinerant bards to enhance their storytelling.

11   The name of the plant *asana* is given a folk etymology derived from the verbal root *as,* "throw."

12   The verse plays on *kṛtamada,* "rutting" and "enflaming lust."

13   The expression *sahasā* occurs in this verse four times with four different meanings: as an adjectival compound in the sense of "smiling," as the instrumental case of the noun *sahas,* which can mean both "force" and "the month of Mārgaśīrṣa" (November–December), and as two separate words, *saha,* "with" and *sā,* "she."

14   This verse can be taken to be alluding to Magha's sense of superiority over his literary predecessor, Bharavi, the author of *Arjuna and the Hunter* (see Introduction), the components of whose name are *bhā,* "light" and *ravi,* "sun."

15   V takes the jasmine as laughing at the bee, which had formerly been its lover. M sees a play on *rajasā,* which can mean both "by pollen" and "by menstruation," and suggests that the subtext of the verse is a warning that a man's wives will laugh at him if he tries to make love to one of their number while she is menstruating.

16   This is taken by M (on 67 of his recension) to be a wishing tree (*kalpavṛkṣa*).

17   That is, instead of visiting him in the darkness of night.

18   The meter of this verse is *kuṭajā.*

7 Forest Flirtations

1   Compare 10.72.
2   Lac was applied as decoration on women's hands and feet, and as gloss on lips.
3   I follow M in taking the vocative *guṇagauri* as meaning literally "you (goddess) Parvati in your attributes."
4   The verse plays on *sumanas,* "cheerful" and "flower."
5   The secondary meaning here is: "A spry young man, ardent and full of passion, had received amorous scratches from a girl; later pitilessly cut by her, he quickly lost his enthusiasm."
6   V and M understand the leaf fragments to be used to cool bodies suffering the pain of separation.
7   Bitten by her lover.
8   According to V, this quartet of verses is a *kalāpaka,* "bundle," an identification possibly linked to the occurrence of the phonetically approximate forms *kalikā* and *kali* in 55. M explains the context as involving a woman who has been cheated on (*khaṇḍitā*) rebuking her erring lover when he attempts to mollify her with the gift of a branch (*pallava*).
9   I translate against V and M, taking *kali,* "fourth (and unlucky) throw of the dice," as following on from *kitava,* literally "gambler," here verging on "chancer," in 54, and as being mockingly contrasted with *kalikā,* "twig" in the first line of this verse. V glosses *kalikā* with *koraka,* "bud."
10 The expensive gift is insignificant compared with a simple one sincerely given.
11 The verse plays on *malina,* "soiled, dark" and "morally impure."
12 Verses 62–68 form a syntactic unit (*kulaka*).
13 The verse plays on *vipulaka,* "expansive" and "smooth," and *parimalita,* "fondled" and "darkened."
14 The upward flow of the women's sweat parallels the flow of the Ganga from Vishnu's foot.

8 Water Games

1   The verse plays on *chāyā,* "shade" and "beauty."
2   The gender in the second line of the verse is masculine.
3   Sheldrakes (*cakravākas*) are proverbial for their loyalty and attentiveness toward their mate, but they have been cursed by Rama to be separated at night.

4   Shri is iconographically depicted as sitting or standing on a lotus as well as being located on Vishnu's chest.

5   The verse plays on *nirāsire*, "expelled" and "surpassed," and *rāga*, "jealousy" (V) and "redness."

6   The verse plays on *anurañjayāṃ babhūvuḥ*, "reddened" and "roused to passion." Krishna's wives have lac-reddened hands.

7   The verse plays on *udvṛtta*, "swollen" and "arrogant."

8   A condensed verse in which the lake and the ocean, along with the adjectival compounds describing them, are correlated in the form of a metaphor. For the winged mountains, see 5.31.

9   The verse plays on *gāmbhīrya*, "depth" and "calmness"; *saṃkṣobha*, "swelling" and "emotionally stirred"; and *maryādā*, "shore" and "propriety."

10   The verse plays on *yuktānāṃ vimalatayā*, "bright" and "pure, intelligent"; *tiraskriyā*, "hiding" and "overcoming"; *ākramaṇa*, "flowing" and "insulting"; and *jala*, "water" and "fool."

11   Herons are typically portrayed as standing on lotus leaves.

12   According to the *Kāmasūtra* (1.3.15) of Vatsyayana (c. third century C.E.), the standard treatise on sexual etiquette in ancient India, splashing with water (*udakāghāta*) is one of the sixty-four forms of sophisticated activity (*kalā*) to be mastered by a woman.

13   A lustration or consecration (*mahābhiṣeka*) is performed on a prince when he succeeds to the throne after the king's death.

14   Cupped hands (*añjali*) signify both greeting and beseeching.

15   The verse plays on *jala*, "water" and "fool," and *guṇa*, "string" and "quality."

16   The verse plays on *kaluṣa*, "dark" and "excited," and *āśayo jalānām*, "lake" and "mind of fools."

17   The verse appears to play on *cakṣuṣya*, "pleasing to the eyes" and "within the range of vision."

18   The verse plays on *rāga*, "redness" and "passion."

19   When he had been Vishnu. See 2.107 and 3.81.

20   According to V the secondary meaning here is: "Young men in the grip of erotic passion for the very first time, and driven by their ardor to deep infatuation, only with difficulty give up on good-looking girls, even though rejected time and again."

9 Romantic Encounters After Sunset

1   The western mountain behind which the sun is believed to set.

See 26 and 5.56 for the eastern sunrise mountain.

2   The verse plays on *payodhara,* "cloud" and "breast"; *kara,* "ray" and "hand"; *ambara,* "sky" and "garment"; and *anvarajyat,* "reddened" and "became infatuated."

3   The primeval egg contains the three worlds of heaven, earth, and the intermediate space.

4   The humorous metaphor *aparadiggaṇikā,* linking "western region" and "prostitute," is amplified through wordplay on *anurāgavat,* "reddened" and "infatuated"; *atāpakara,* "with rays cooled" and "lacking energy"; and *apetavasu,* "without luster" and "without money."

5   Lotuses close as the moon rises.

6   The sun's rays are like the "virtuous woman" (*satī;* anglicized as "suttee") who loyally immolates herself on her husband's funeral pyre. Compare 15.92 and 18.60.

7   Brahma, iconographically depicted as red, (the color associated with *rajas,* "vigorous creative power") assumed a variety of embodiments as he engaged in succeeding phases of creation. Twilights, both morning and evening, are important times for worship. Strictly speaking, the safflower (*kusumbha*) is orange-yellow in color.

8   Compare 8.13.

9   Compare 8.15. Shri here may also be taken as equivalent to "good fortune."

10   The verse plays on *mitra,* "friend" and "sun."

11   The verse plays on *malina,* "dark" and "tarnished."

12   The ether constitutes one of Shiva's eight bodies, along with earth, water, fire, air, sun, moon, and soul. Shiva is typically envisaged as an ascetic with matted hair.

13   See 3.81.

14   See 2.53.

15   The metaphors *śaśidāśarathi,* "moon-Rama," and *timiraugha-rākṣasabala,* "darkness-demon army," are expanded through wordplay on *lakṣmaṇa,* "mark" and the name of Rama's brother, and *ṛkṣa,* "planet" and "monkey."

16   The bathetic, presumably humorous simile is expanded through wordplay on *parimugdhatā,* "beauty" and "innocence"; *vīthi,* "path" and "market"; and *kalā,* "phase of the moon'" and "financial gain" (V).

17 The verse plays on *kara,* "ray of light" and "hand." The water lily blossoms at night.

18 The moon's cool rays are beneficial to plants.

19 The verse plays on *kara,* "ray of light" and "hand."

20 The verse plays on *śilīmukha,* "bee" and "arrow."

21 See chapter 3 n. 21. The verse plays on *rati,* "intercourse", "sexual pleasure" and the name of the love god's wife, and *atrinaya-naprabhava,* "arising from Atri's eye" (*atri-nayana-prabhava*) and "not originating with Shiva" (*a-trinayana-prabhava*).

22 According to V, the belt string on the girl's buttocks stimulates lust.

23 Singular in the Sanskrit.

24 The verse plays on *avalepa,* "cosmetic cream" and "pride."

25 Typically made from perfumed seeds or aromatic nuts. See Zumbroich 2012.

26 The god of love is bodiless through having been burnt by the fire from Shiva's forehead eye. Compare 42.

27 I translate against V and M, who seem to envisage the girl as closing her ear, perhaps to concentrate on the accounts of her lover's qualities already within.

28 The expression *adhiveśma* does not convey with any precision where the women are residing.

29 The verse plays on *gotra,* "name" and "mountain." The young man has confused his lover's name with that of another woman. Indra was cursed to be covered with a thousand vulva marks; see chapter 4 n. 6. He was eventually freed from the curse, and the marks were transformed into eyes. Indra's destruction of a mountain relates to his smashing open a cave in which cows representing the dawns had been penned.

30 The verse plays on *akṣigata,* "within sight" and "detestable" (M).

31 Urvashi was a celestial nymph who came to earth to live with King Pururavas for a period and then returned to heaven. Menaka was the wife of Himalaya and mother of Parvati.

10 Wine and Women

1 While the Sanskrit literary tradition as represented by poets such as Magha shows no serious interest in describing the pleasures of food, drunken parties that verge on orgies, involving the enthusiastic consumption of intoxicating drink, are a stock subject

of the post-Kalidasa *mahākāvya*. The subject is not inappropriate in *The Killing of Shishupala*, with its pronounced Vaishnava theme, since according to *Viṣṇupurāṇa* 1.9.92 the churning of the ocean presided over by Vishnu produced Varuni, the goddess of intoxicating drink, who was already manifesting the effects of drunkenness.

Early India had no familiarity with a generic substance equivalent to "alcohol." Instead, a variety of drinks was accepted as possessing the capacity to induce intoxication. See McHugh 2013: 30. It is not entirely clear what forms of beverage are being taken by the revelers described in the first half of this chapter, and the translation accordingly varies in identifying them. Although wine in the sense of fermented grape juice was imported as a luxury item from the far northwest of the subcontinent during the first millennium C.E. (compare *kāpiśāyana* mentioned in 4) and was also produced more locally (*madhu*), other terms used by Magha (e.g., *āsava, hālā, maireya, madirā, saraka, surā, sīdhu,* and *vāruṇī*) seem to refer to varieties of spiced rice wine, or liquor based on fermented sugarcane (the latter sometimes mixed with honey or garnished with types of flowers, such as lotuses or water lilies).

2   The verse plays on *sajjita,* "made up" and "garnished"; *ullasannayanavāriruha,* "with lotus-like eyes flashing" and "with eye-like lotuses gleaming"; and *sughaṭita,* "symmetrical" and "well-made." I translate *vadanāni* as both "faces" and "mouths" to make the description smoother.

3   The verse plays on *pīta,* "yellow" and "drunk."

4   An example of Magha's penchant for a wittily learned reference, on this occasion prefigured by Kalidasa (*Raghuvaṃśa* 15.9), albeit in slightly less complex form. The secondary meaning here is: "While latent within a basic linguistic unit (*santam eva*), semantic significance does not manifest itself directly (*aprakāśitam*) if inoperative in a specific grammatical context (*aprakṛtatvāt*)." M cites Panini, *Aṣṭādhyāyī* 1.4.13, to explain the allusion.

5   The verse plays on *rāga,* "passion" and "redness."

6   The verse plays on a derivation of *pramadā,* "woman," from *mad,* "become intoxicated."

7   The verse plays on *rāga,* "passion" and "redness."

8   The verse uses the term *vallabha,* "beloved." The women described

here are apparently not the same as those in the previous verse.

9   The verse plays on *lāvaṇika*, "delightful" and "salt merchant." The secondary meaning here is: "As a salt dealer cunningly gives false measure, weighing and selling a consignment in a trice, while concealing its actual weight."

10   Literally, "did not go beyond their ears endowed with the power of hearing," with wordplay on *śruti*, "hearing" and "the Veda." The secondary meaning here is: "Even experienced men may give way to passion and go astray, but they never express contempt for a scholar familiar with the virtuous precepts of the Veda."

11   According to V this woman is newly wed.

12   The verse plays on *harṣa*, "joy" and "thrilling of body hair."

13   This verse plays on *nīvī*, "dress" and "hostage." The secondary meaning here is: "Like prisoners who jump for joy on being amnestied from captivity on the birth of a royal heir."

14   The opening of this verse is couched in what seems to be a mock-learned idiom.

15   I follow M's explanation. Whether this is a generalized pleasure pavilion or some structure in the Yadava encampment is unclear.

16   The secondary meaning here is: "The hands were sweating men diving from rocky sun-scorched promontories into deep pools where delightful lotuses floated."

17   Conventionally, flowers rain down from heaven in celebration of heroism in battle. According to V the verse describes the sexual position of *puruṣāyita*, when the woman sits astride her partner.

18   Plural in the Sanskrit.

19   The verse plays on *guṇa*, "string" and "virtue."

20   The verse plays on *paryastahasta*, "with the constellation Hasta disappeared" and "with hands thrown over."

11   The Court Bards Welcome the Dawn

1   I follow V's explanation of *akāki*, an expression not found in the standard Sanskrit dictionaries, as meaning "without any flaw in singing" (*geyadoṣavarjita*). There are seven main notes in the Indian musical scale. According to M, the fifth note is like the call of the cuckoo, while the bull note is like the bellow of a bull. The former is associated with the erotic flavor in Indian music. The bards' song continues until the end of the chapter.

2   A demon who took the form of a wagon, or possibly a chariot,

under which the child Krishna slept, later awaking to destroy the vehicle with a kick. Compare 15.37 and see also Couture 1991: 200–201 and 362. The designation "the Wagon" (*śakaṭa*) was also used of the constellation Rohini.

3   The kings are compared through wordplay to poets.

4   The gods are compared through wordplay to the cowherds.

5   The night is compared through wordplay to a woman.

6   The verse plays on *srastahasta,* "with rays disappeared" and "with hands fallen."

7   The verse plays on *aruṇa,* "red" and the name of the charioteer of the sun.

8   See chapter 8 n. 3.

9   The verse plays on *varṇaka,* "sandalwood makeup" and "describing."

10   The verse plays on *lakṣman,* "mark" and "sign."

11   According to M, 31–35 form a thematic unit (*kulaka*) in which a woman rebukes her inconstant husband, who has returned to her after spending the night with her cowife.

12   The mark from the lac-covered foot indicates energetic lovemaking.

13   The man has inadvertently put on his beloved's garment in the morning.

14   Or: "It is pointless for their friends to urge restraint upon them." M understands these women to be affectionate attendants.

15   According to V, the speaker is a newly married woman.

16   Because the time is between night and morning, both (day) lotuses and (night) water lilies are blossoming.

17   The morning twilight is compared through wordplay to a child.

18   The *adhvaryu* priest is responsible for the practical aspects of a Vedic sacrifice, including chanting the liturgical formulas.

19   The *sāṃnāyya* offering of milk and curds.

20   Literally, "ascetics" (*niyamabhāj*).

21   This plant blossoms red at midday and then fades the next morning.

22   The subject of this verse is a metaphor, *bālasūrya,* literally "the boy-sun." The secondary meaning here is: "In the same way, a little boy crawling in the courtyard, smilingly admired by pretty women, stretches out his soft fingers and falls playfully onto his mother's lap when she calls him."

23   The rising of the sun is compared through wordplay to the actions

of a king. The secondary meaning here is: "A king sits for a while on his throne with feet firmly planted while attending to his loyal vassal bent in obeisance, and then gets up with a view to govern the world."

24 The secondary meaning here is: "So Indra with his ray-like eyes, myriad and all-seeing, fair as lotus clusters, intrepidly overcame the demon Vritra, oppressor of the universe."

25 In observing that this verse reprises 4.67, V comments that there is nothing wrong with a poet reworking his own material.

26 M, comparing 5.48, interprets the sun as being like a king who has regained his lost kingdom and as his first command issues a general amnesty.

27 An allusion to Shri dwelling in the lotus in Vishnu's navel.

28 According to V, the verse plays on *rāga*, "redness" and "anger."

29 See chapter 8 n. 3.

30 The waning moon is compared through wordplay to a fleeing lover.

31 The verse plays on *anatiśayaśrī*, "unrivaled in glory" and "in supreme majesty," and *sānurāga*, "red" and "beloved."

12 The Yadava Army on the March Again

1 Vishnu's vehicle Garuda is compared through wordplay to Krishna's chariot. Krishna's identity as Vishnu is increasingly signaled in the second half of the poem.

2 The kings are compared through wordplay to Krishna, with *dvijendrakānta* also meaning "beloved of Garuda, king of birds" (or, according to M, "fair as the moon") and *narakasya jiṣṇavo guṇaiḥ* also meaning "conquerors of the demon Naraka with their bow-strings" (Naraka was killed by Krishna and his allies when he assumed control of Dvaraka; see chapter 15 n. 21). V and M claim that these epithets can here apply grammatically to Krishna.

3 Krishna was also, according to V and M, "devoted to his wife Satyabhama," with wordplay on *satya*, "true."

4 The verse plays on *satāra*, "with stars" and "with ropes," and *mukulīkṛta*, "folded" and "closed."

5 The chariot is compared through wordplay to a wife. The secondary meaning here is: "A man with many friends desired a still more agreeable life, so he married a pert, bright-cheeked young wife with a delightfully round navel and svelte stomach." V, after

commenting on the components of the chariot to which the verse refers, adds: "We Kashmiris are ignorant of chariots and know nothing of their individual parts."

6 The army is compared through wordplay to the Sama Veda. The secondary meaning here is: "Its tones sound out within melodies in a variety of styles. While these hymns have a thousand schools of transmission, they are still difficult for the unmotivated to master since, above all, vocal skill is required."

7 The verse plays on *sattva*, "living creature", "entity", and "bravery", and *mahībhṛt*, "mountain" and "ruler".

8 Both V and M state that horses were formerly winged, with the latter adding that, according to tradition, the gods cut off their wings for some unspecified reason.

9 The verse plays on *bhūbhṛt*, "mountain" and "king."

10 The Ganga is regarded as flowing through heaven, earth, and the underworld. Its course is also linked to the three gods Brahma, Shiva, and Vishnu. This verse interrupts a series of descriptions of chaotic occurrences as Krishna's army proceeds on the march. However, the fact that the occurrence of *unnata*, "high", in 23 echoes the same form in 21 in a manner found elsewhere in the poem (see Trynkowska 2004b: 188) suggests that this verse is not an interpolation.

11 I follow M. V reads *karabhau* in the sense of "camels."

12 The activities of the carpenter are compared through wordplay to the ministrations of a doctor. The secondary meaning here is: "An experienced doctor treating an illness prescribes a regime involving fasting for an invalid with feeble joints and failing senses."

13 The qualities of Krishna are compared through wordplay to the compositions of poets. The elaborate poetic style referred to in the verse would not normally be associated with the quality of lucidity or clarity (*prasāda*).

14 V states that the village women were not noticed because their pale faces were like *kauśātakī* blossoms, but provides as an equivalent for this plant the *dhātakī*, or fire flame bush, whose blossoms are usually red. M gives *paṭolī* as an equivalent of the plant he names as *kośātakī*, which I take to be the same as *paṭolā*, the bitter snake gourd, whose flowers are white.

15 I follow M. Compare 6.42. V interprets *svagotrasaṃkīrtana* as "boasting about their families."

16 Krishna's exploits as a youthful cowherd were described for the first time in the *Harivaṃśa*. See Couture 2015: 180–213.

17 The rope is to hobble the cow.

18 The verse plays on *mahībhṛt*, "mountain" and "king."

19 The verse plays on *nāga*, "elephant" and "mountain."

20 According to M the secondary meaning here is: "In the same way teachers are, occasionally obsequious to their employer and at other times haughty, sometimes well disposed toward a pupil, then again angry."

21 M interprets this verse as referring to the humiliation of the women of a defeated king.

22 The expression *vanecara* could also refer to monkeys.

23 Of the major Indian philosophical systems, only the Vaisheshika school omits verbal and scriptural testimony in favor of direct experience and inference as valid sources of authoritative knowledge. V refers to the tradition that the sage Agastya drank the ocean, whereupon the Ganga refilled it.

24 Shiva's throat is stained black from swallowing the poison churned up from the depths of the ocean. See 4.7.

25 The verse plays on *tīrtvā*, "crossed" and "honored"; *dustara*, "difficult to ford" and "difficult to fulfill"; and *garīyāṃs*, "mighty" and "solemn."

13 Arrival at Indraprastha

1 See chapter 2 n. 1.

2 The Pandava brothers were descended from the Kuru royal house. Compare 13 and 16.

3 See chapter 6 n. 8.

4 The verse plays on *mada*, "passion" and "ichor."

5 See 1.31–36 and 14.59–62.

6 The verse plays on *śrī*, the name of the goddess and "beauty." See also chapter 8 n. 4.

7 A reference to one of Vishnu's major incarnations. See 14.74–77.

8 Krishna stole the divine coral tree (*pārijāta*) from Indra's heaven as a gift for his wife Satyabhama. See chapter 14 n. 53.

9 The verse plays on *pakṣa*, "alliance" and "wing." For the winged mountains, see 5.31.

10 The verse plays on *prajāpati*, "king" and a name of Brahma, and *sānurāga*, "affectionately" and "red." Shiva destroyed the demons

in their strongholds in heaven, earth, and the intermediate region. For Brahma as red, see 9.14.

11   The verse plays on *nava*, "new" and "nine"; *puruṣa*, "being" and "soul"; and *pura*, "city" and "body." The mind is included among the senses. The nine bodily orifices are the two eyes, two ears, two nostrils, and the mouth, urethra, and anus.

12   Krishna's epithet *mādhava*, "killer of the demon Madhu," can also mean "spring."

13   The secondary meaning here is: "Fair as the moon emerging from mist, Krishna possessed the auspicious mark of Shri on his chest; a source of deep satisfaction to Brahmans, he had brought the god of love into being once again as his son Pradyumna, enrapturing the gods." V and M take this as the primary meaning

14   Compare 3.60.

15   In the form of Vishnu.

16   According to V the woman does this to display her breasts to Krishna. However, the gesture itself may be erotically coded. Compare also 9.64.

17   M explains this as the woman's naively spontaneous reaction on seeing the object of her desires.

18   See chapter 3 n. 16.

19   The verse plays on *mādhava*, "wine" and an epithet of Krishna. Compare n. 12.

20   The construction of the magnificent Pandava hall (*saṃsad, sabhā*) is described in book 2 of the Mahabharata. See *Mahābhārata* 1975: 33–39. Maya, a demon who was gifted as an architect, built the hall in gratitude to Arjuna for saving him from a forest conflagration. Magha presents the building in lavish terms as the equivalent of a palatial residential compound replete with mansions, parks, and lakes.

21   Vishnu's sixth incarnation (in the standard list of ten); Parashurama destroyed twenty-one generations of Brahmans to avenge his father.

22   The verse plays on *atrasat*, "brilliant" and "bold," and *gaurava*, "intensity" and "honor." The lotuses have closed at night with the rising of the moon, but its light is then nullified by the sapphires' brilliance. V states that an honor (*gauravarakṣārtham*) killing carried out secretly is justified when a wife has been publicly treated with disrespect. The Kashmiri commentator accordingly takes

vadhū in the sense of "wife," but the lotuses are not figuratively married to the emeralds, and so I take *vadhū* as referring to women in general. M regards those killed to protect honor as being violators of the women of a harem.

23 V and M invoke popular lore for clouds thundering in the vicinity of the jeweled hoods of cobra princes and beryls emitting slivers at the sound of thunder.

24 Duryodhana's resentment at his humiliation in Indraprastha (in the Mahabharata account he is also mocked by Krishna; see *Mahābhārata* 1975: 116) in part led to the enmity toward his cousins, the Pandava brothers, that culminated in the slaughter of the battle of Kurukshetra.

25 The verse plays on *śrī*, "good fortune" and the name of the goddess.

14 Yudhishthira's Sacrifice

1 The *rājasūya* ceremony in which a king is consecrated and his power, along with that of the Brahman class, is validated. See Heesterman 1957. In the manuals, this collection of rituals is envisaged as requiring at least one year to perform. Magha presents an encapsulated version with narratively significant events occurring at the conclusion of the sacrifice.

2 The verse plays on *upakaraṇa*, "material" and "tool."

3 The name of both a plant and the juice squeezed from its stalk, *soma* played a central role in the most elaborate Vedic sacrifices.

4 The Boar, the third in the standard list of Vishnu's incarnations, lifted up the earth, sunk in the ocean, on the tip of its horn. See 43, 71, and 86, and also 1.34, 15.5, 16.81, 18.25, 19.98 and 116, and 20.33.

5 Krishna is not a king in the sense of being a fully consecrated ruler, since the Yadavas had been cursed by their ancestor Yayati never to possess regal power. See Mahabharata 1973: 191–192 and 15.15 and 27.

6 A promise fulfilled at the end of the poem.

7 He has grown pale through the fasting obligatory for the *yajamāna*, the sponsor of the sacrifice.

8 V defines the eight forms as earth, water, wind, fire, moon, sun, air, and the sponsor of the sacrifice.

9 Yudhishthira is compared through wordplay to the god Shiva.

10 The sponsor of the sacrifice does not engage in any formal

sacrificial activity. Samkhya, "Enumeration," is a dualist system providing both an analysis of reality and, in conjunction with Yoga, a means of enabling the self to distentangle itself from nature, of which consciousness (*buddhi*) is one of the twenty-five evolved entities. Compare 2.59.

11   The verse plays on *vṛttibhāj*, "carrying out procedures," or "receiving the fee" (V), and "undergoing transformations."

12   The reference is to the ritual called *praṇayana* in which, as V describes it, a kindled fire is taken from the household hearth and deposited on the northern altar of the sacrificial enclosure.

13   The technical expression *ūha*, "semantic adjustment," denotes the modification of Vedic mantras to render them appropriate to different ritual contexts.

14   See chapter 2 n. 24.

15   Uttered by the main priest (*hotṛ*) in the ritual who thereby prompts the *adhvaryu* priest involved in the actual performance of the ritual to make the offering.

16   The literal sense of the epithet *havirbhuj*. Compare 1.2.

17   The goddesses pay no attention to beautifying themselves when their husbands are absent.

18   According to V, the gods gained only partial immortality when they consumed the ambrosia churned from the ocean.

19   The adjective *dakṣiṇa*, which can also mean "honest" and "noble," is echoed in the verse by *dakṣiṇīya*, "worthy of recompense" and *dakṣiṇā*, "sacrificial fee." On *dākṣiṇya*, the abstract noun deriving from *dakṣiṇa*, as a salient virtue in ancient Indian aristocratic interaction, with a sense akin to "courtesy," see Ali 2004: 135–137.

20   The temporary shed-like structure called *sadas*. The giving of a fee (*dakṣiṇā*) to the Brahman officiants and the ensuing honor offering form part of the ritual.

21   The conclusion of this verse is a variant of a legalistic formula found in many ancient Indian inscriptions.

22   Literally "by means of books" (*pustakaiḥ samam*), that is to say, manuscripts. Brahman intellectual culture was characteristically oral, but M comments that preserving orally transmitted knowledge in manuscripts can be judged to be unexceptional.

23   The verse plays on *śuddha*, "pure" and "correct"; *śruti*, "hearing" and "the Veda"; and *avarṇasaṃkara*, "clearly formulated" and "orthodox" (literally, "not bringing about mixture of the four

social classes"). The Brahman philosophical school par excellence is Mimamsa, "Enquiry," which argues for the centrality of the Veda as a noncreated, authorless system of injunctions.

24   The idealized states of student, householder, forest dweller, and full renunciant. Originally differing options for modes of life, they were eventually envisaged as forming a gradualist path.

25   The verse plays on *laghu,* "light, minor"; *laghūkṛta,* "made light, diminished"; and *gaurava,* "heaviness, respect."

26   See n. 4.

27   The verse plays on *āhava,* "sacrifice" and "battle."

28   The *rājasūya* ceremony necessarily concludes with the distribution of food and honors. I follow V, who explains *bhāvaśuddhivihita* as "given with a pure mind." M further suggests "made with pure ingredients."

29   The verse plays on *rasa,* literally "flavor," which has a primary culinary sense but also denotes the eight (sometimes nine) emotional moods that can be aroused in a drama. The secondary meaning here is: "As if in dramas in which emotions were precisely conveyed and actors speaking Sanskrit and Prakrit took clearly defined roles."

30   According to V, the *yūpa,* the stake of wood serving as a tethering post for sacrificial animals and a boundary marker of sacred space, is fixed in the ground at the conclusion of the ritual, although most naturally this would have taken place at the beginning.

31   Compare 1.17.

32   This offering (not described by Magha) typically consisted of water, rice, sacred grass, and flowers.

33   According to *Ṛg Veda* 10.90, the Brahmans constituted the mouth of a cosmic giant sacrificed by the gods.

34   The kings are compared through wordplay to Brahmans.

35   Bhishma equates Krishna with the three constituent "elements" or "powers of nature" (*guṇa*) as identified by Samkhya philosophy, and with the three main gods of Hinduism.

36   According to Jain tradition, Magha was a cousin of the Jain monk Siddharshi, whose great Sanskrit novel allegorizing Jainism, *Upamitibhavaprapañcakathā* (The Story of an Extensive Series of Existences Explained by Comparison), was written in Sirohi in 905. See Note on the Text and Translation, n. 5. This claim of a Jain connection for Magha may have been prompted in part by

the trope of the drama of rebirth, employed in this verse, which was the master-theme of Siddharshi's novel.

37 The expression *durgam,* "remote, inaccessible," is slightly awkward, given that Krishna's accessibility to his devotees is being stressed. This may support V's contention (not followed by M) that Magha is employing wordplay on *durga* and *grāmyabhāva,* "sensory world," to give the alternative meaning: "Just as someone leaves village life (*grāmyabhāva*) and seeks a walled city (*durga*)."

38 Krishna-Vishnu is both immanent and transcendent.

39 M quotes *Manusmṛti* 1.8–9: "It was the waters that he first brought forth; and into them he poured forth his semen. That became a golden egg, as bright as the sun; and in it he himself took birth as Brahmā, the grandfather of all the worlds" (Olivelle 2005: 87). In addressing the issue of whether Brahma or Vishnu brought the world into being, V paraphrases the *Manusmṛti* verses (where the agent is the Vedic creator god Prajapati) in more overtly theistic terms, ascribing the act of creation to the "lord" (*bhagavān*)—that is, Vishnu.

40 The verse plays on *śrautamārga,* "hearing" and "Veda."

41 The lotus closes when the moon rises. For Vishnu as creator, see n. 39.

42 V and M refer to the sleep of yoga.

43 See n. 4.

44 See 1.48.

45 See 1.63 and 5.12.

46 The Dwarf is the fifth in the standard list of Vishnu's incarnations. He secured a promise from the demon Bali to grant him land encompassed by three strides, whereupon he took two steps over the earth and sky. Bali was forced to offer his head for the Dwarf's third step.

47 The Ganga was said to originate from Vishnu's left foot; see 3.10.

48 Dattatreya was regarded from the time of the *Harivaṃśa* as an incarnation of Vishnu, although he is not included in the standard list of ten incarnations. In some more developed enumerations, Dattatreya is the sixth of twenty-two incarnations.

49 A king who received the boon of a thousand arms from the god Brahma but used them to oppress the earth. For Parashurama, see 13.52 and 18.70.

50 The verse plays on *patra,* "leaf" and "vehicle"; *chāyā,* "shade" and

"beauty"; and *arjuna,* the name of a king and a type of tree.

51 See chapter 1 n. 28 and chapter 4 n. 20. The verse plays on *vibhī-ṣaṇa,* "terrible" and the name of a demon who attempted to dissuade Ravana from abducting Rama's wife Sita.

52 Bhishma combines two idioms of Krishna's divinity: the mighty god Vishnu and the playful cowherd boy. Compare 86. The verse plays on *tāta,* a term of affectionate address for both elders and juniors, and *nodadhivilodana,* "not churning the ocean" (*na udadhivilodana*) and "not churning milk" (*no dadhivilodana*). See chapter 2 n. 27. The reference by the cowherds to Krishna's absence may relate to his resolve, described in the *Harivaṃśa,* to leave the forest where he and his brother were guarding cattle and move to the more pleasant environment of Vrindavana. See Couture 2015: 165.

53 The coral tree (*pārijāta*) had been churned up from the ocean with other precious objects. The episode of the seizing of this tree from heaven, incidental in the earliest stratum of Krishna mythology but increasingly significant from the fifth century, exemplifies the god's often uproarious behavior. See 13.12 and Austin 2013.

54 The coral tree is compared through wordplay to Indra's self-esteem.

55 See 1.70.

56 See chapter 5 n. 18. The actions of Vishnu's Boar incarnation are compared through wordplay to Krishna's rescuing of the cows.

57 V specifically identifies Krishna as Vishnu.

15 Shishupala's Anger

1 The comparison is facilitated by *kara* meaning both "hand" and "elephant's trunk."

2 See 1.70.

3 Shishupala is compared through wordplay to a woman.

4 M points out that Krishna never received formal consecration as a king. See chapter 14 n. 5.

5 Tuesday is associated with the maleficent planet Mars, both being euphemistically called "auspicious" (*maṅgala*).

6 See 14.55.

7 Bhishma is compared through wordplay to a river.

8 A sarcastic gloss on Krishna's epithet Madhusudana, which derived from Vishnu's killing of the demon Madhu, "Honey."

9   A typically distorted allusion. Krishna, pursued by Kalayavana, entered the cave of Muchukunda, who had been given the boon of sleep by Indra after his strenuous exploits against the demons. Kalayavana attacked Muchukunda, taking him for Krishna, and was summarily destroyed. Muchukunda then acknowledged Krishna to be a "portion" (*aṃśa*) of Vishnu. This event is described at *Viṣṇupurāṇa* 5.23.15–25.

10   Krishna and the Yadavas prudently left Mathura in the wake of conflict with Jarasandha. See Brockington 2002.

11   Krishna was assisted by Balarama in killing Kamsa, the tyrannical king of Mathura.

12   A play on *satya,* "true," and Satya, one of eight wives of Krishna named at *Viṣṇupurāṇa* 5.28.1–5.

13   The word *cakra,* whose meanings include "circle," "wheel," "discus," and "army," is used three times in this verse. Shishupala is playing on *cakradhara,* in the senses of "discus holder" (a common epithet of Krishna) and "general," or possibly "emperor."

14   Literally, *śrī.* See chapter 14 n. 5.

15   The goddess Shri, or Lakshmi, had emerged from the ocean when it was churned by the gods and demons. See 3.81.

16   See 1.1 and 2.118.

17   A sarcastic interpretation of Vishnu's Dwarf incarnation. See 14.75. The word *vikramin* can mean "brave" and "striding."

18   Ancient Indian kings were conventionally known as "earth-bearer" and could thus be assimilated to Vishnu in his Boar incarnation.

19   See 24.

20   See n. 18. The verse plays on *tulita,* "overcome" and "lifted up," and *bhūbhṛt,* "mountain" and "king."

21   Naraka was killed by Krishna when he assumed control of Dvaraka. See Brinkhaus 2011–12. The verse puns on Naraka's name, which can mean "hell." See 12. 3 and also Note on the Text and Translation, n. 5.

22   The verse plays on *guṇa,* "moral quality" and the "powers of nature" (energy, brightness, and darkness) that evolve within phenomenal existence. Samkhya philosophy in its developed form regards abandonment of the latter as constituting deliverance.

23   The demon Arishta took the form of a bull to assault the cows guarded by Krishna. See Couture 1991: 263–264. Shishupala is accusing Krishna of effectively being guilty of the heinous crime

of killing a cow. The verse plays on *vṛṣa,* "bull" and "morality."

24 Putana, daughter of the demon Bali and nurse of Kamsa, had poisoned her breast milk in order to murder the baby Krishna. See Couture 2015: 242–244. Shishupala is implying that in killing the demoness as he did (by draining her life through her breast), the child Krishna had murdered his foster mother and was therefore guilty of matricide.

25 The boisterous child Krishna was tethered by his mother to a mortar. In trying to escape he dragged it between two huge trees and uprooted them. See Couture 1991: 204–206. For Krishna and the wagon, see 11.3, and for his lifting the mountain, see 30.

26 Or "king." Kamsa, ruler of Mathura and incarnation of the demon Kalanemi, was owner of the forest where the cows Krishna was guarding were pastured. Shishupala could also have pointed out that Kamsa was related to Krishna through his mother, Devaki.

27 See 2.108 and 110.

28 See n. 21.

29 Druma means "Tree." Cf. 19.8. The poison tree, of a type unspecified by V and M, is a regular trope in Sanskrit poetry, reflecting the existence on the subcontinent of at least two varieties of trees that produce toxic substances. See Meulenbeld 2007–2008.

30 Rukmini had been promised in marriage to Shishupala but was forcibly taken by Krishna. See 2.38.

31 As M points out, an ill omen.

32 The Buddhist god of death, who was also identified with the god of love, as confirmed by V and M (at 58 in M's recension).

33 The kings are compared through wordplay to Mara's army.

34 Shishupala is successively alluding to Krishna's role as Pandava counselor, the irregularity of the Pandava brothers' origins (Pandu was only nominally their father, since a curse had prevented him siring children), and Bhishma's celibacy.

35 After being allowed to roam free for a year, the sacrificial horse is killed at the conclusion of the royal *aśvamedha* ceremony.

36 Horses are aspects of the auspiciousness associated with Lakshmi, goddess of prosperity.

37 See chapter 1 n. 9.

38 A series of inauspicious actions and ill omens is described in 80–91.

39 Weeping is particularly inappropriate for the wives of warriors. Compare 6.17 for a different context.

40 An ill omen, since a wife's armlets should only be removed with the death of her husband.

41 The term *rana* can mean both "joy" and "battle." The ancient Indo-European belief that a glorious death in battle leads to eternal lovemaking in heaven continued to inform the ideology of warfare in early India. See Hara 2001 and chapter 18 n. 15.

42 See n. 40.

43 An ill omen.

44 An inauspicious act of lamentation. The term *rajas,* "dust," can also punningly signify "menstruation," a highly inauspicious state.

45 In the first half of the verse the women's emotional states are compared through wordplay to natural phenomena.

16 The Emissary from Shishupala

1 The emissary's message contains a double meaning in which ostensible praise of Krishna simultaneously signifies denigration of him. See 16.42. Verses 2–15 are accordingly given two different translations. This is a classic example of "extreme poetry" (Bronner 2010), deploying the regrouping of grammatical forms and sequences of phonemes, the exploitation of the structural ambiguity of nominal compounds, and the assigning of alternative or secondary meanings to words. Although shorter in length, this speech amplifies Shishupala's mockery of Krishna in chapter 15. The emissary is described as possessing *pratibhāna,* a term equivalent to both "shrewdness" and "inspiration." Magha may here be regarded as paying oblique homage to the rich capacities of the Sanskrit language, of which he was a master manipulator. See also Brocquet 2010 441–446.

2 See chapter 15 n. 23.

3 See chapter 15 n. 21.

4 An allusion to Krishna's youthful connection with cowherds.

5 A possible reference to Krishna's flight from Kalayavana. See chapter 15 n. 9.

6 See Note on the Text and Translation, n. 5, and also chapter 15 n. 23.

7 See 1.41.

8 A possible reference to Jarasandha's expulsion of Krishna from Mathura. See 15.24.

9 I follow V, who interprets the verse as having a secondary sense relating to unpalatable food.

10 Wicked behavior is compared through wordplay to barren ground.

11 The verse plays on *hari*, "lion" and a name of Krishna.

12 See 2.108 and 110.

13 The emissary employs epistemological terminology typical of the Mimamsa school of ritual hermeneutics.

14 See chapter 5 n. 4.

15 See chapter 3 n. 1. The verse plays on *dhavala*, "white" and "good," and *sitetara*, "black" and "'evil." Krishna's name literally means "dark."

16 See 2.38.

17 Krishna is here accused of not being a proper ruler, in that he does not hold in equilibrium the three aims of man (maintaining social norms, gaining wealth, and sensual enjoyment). The emissary also refers to the fact that Shishupala is Krishna's cousin, his mother's sister's son. V sees wordplay on *janārdana*, the epithet (possibly signifying "enlivening mankind") used for Krishna in this verse, in an alternative sense of "oppressor of the people," and also takes the emissary as alluding to Krishna's being the father of Pradyumna, the human form in which the god of love has taken birth.

18 See n. 15. The Indian cuckoo is gray-black in color.

19 Krishna is compared through wordplay to darkness.

20 The name Shishupala means "protecting the young." See 85.

21 The emissary would appear to be contradicting the claims he made in his earlier hostile message. See 15 (alternative translation).

22 Shishupala is compared through wordplay to Shiva.

23 A contemptuous reply to 15.34. The verse plays on *hari*, "tawny" and "lion," and a name of Krishna.

24 The emissary is alluding to Vishnu's Dwarf incarnation and the young Krishna's killing of an elephant named Kuvalayapida that had been set on him by Kamsa. See Couture 1991: 304–308. Krishna is further mocked by the implication that it is more difficult to kill a lion than an elephant. The verse plays on *kramārjita*, "gradually won" and "taking a step," and *vṛṣṇi*, "bull" and the name of Krishna's clan.

25 Clouds are compared through wordplay to Shishupala's enemies.

26 Shishupala's enemies are compared through wordplay to his bow.

27 Shishupala's enemies are compared through wordplay to the gods.

28 The Hindu gods are often depicted as behaving with unrestrained spontaneity.

29 The verse plays on *akṣaya*, "indestructible" and "homeless," and *kṣaya*, "destruction" and "realm."

30 The verse plays on *kabandha*, "headless corpse" and "water," and *makaravyūha*, "shoal of sea monsters" and a type of military formation.

31 V points out that a "four-tusked" battle would normally take place between two rival forces containing elephants. However, Shishupala's prowess is such, it is claimed by his emissary, that he can fight with Indra, king of the gods, whose elephant is conventionally represented as having four tusks. A "four-limbed" army consists of chariots, elephants, infantry, and cavalry. See 1.51–53 for Shishupala in his manifestation as the demon Hiranyakashipu overcoming Indra.

32 The verse plays on *cakra*, "discus" and "kingdom."

33 See 1.41.

34 See 13.19.

35 Shishupala's superiority to Shiva is pointed to through wordplay.

36 Verses 72–75 are to be taken together as a unit, called by V *caṅka-laka* (with reference to the verse cluster 19.26–29 the designation is spelt *cakkalaka*) and by M *kalāpaka*.

37 Verses 73 and 74 employ wordplay to compare Shishupala to a surging river.

38 The unhappy fate of the wives of conquered kings is a common theme of Sanskrit panegyric. Verses 76 and 77 play on *upala*, "jewel" and "rock"; *ambara*, "garment" and "sky"; *nitambabhūmi*, "buttocks" and "escarpment"; *mekhalā*, "belt" and "mountain slope"; *kaṭaka*, "bracelet" and "ridge"; *muktāphalabhūṣaṇa*, "pearl ornament" and "ornament abandoned as useless"; *citraka*, "makeup" and "dappled deer"; and *gaṇḍaśaila*, "high cheek" and "stony moor." This extended wordplay serves to contrast the state of the royal women before and after their husband's defeat, with 78 providing a sardonic conclusion. Compare 84 for a similar ironic contrast.

39 The emissary plays on *akṛṣṇa*, "without Krishna" and "without black ashes."

40 The comparison, conveyed through wordplay, of Shishupala's command with the metarules (*paribhāṣā*) that structure Panini's grammar would have been appreciated by all knowing Sanskrit.

41 The verse employs wordplay based on *varāha*, "boar" and

"marriage day" (*vara-aha*). The secondary meaning here is: "The earth is a young widow, only briefly married when her aged husband dropped dead on their nuptial day—as her virginity is intact, there is nothing to prevent a more youthful man wedding her!"

42   The verse plays on *pāra,* "shore" and "limit."

43   This mountain range, bright on one side and dark on the other, represents the juncture between the human and nonhuman realms. The verse plays on *bhūbhṛt,* "mountain," and "king."

44   The verse plays on *vicchitti,* "decoration" and "removal"; *bhinna,* "distinguished" and "separated"; and *patitāñjana,* "covered with kohl" and "with kohl removed," while also exploiting ambiguous word junctures to give a second contradictory meaning, pointing to a mordantly ironic contrast. Compare 76–78.

45   The emissary may be implying either that Krishna's wives are very young or that Shishupala will protect his abandoned children.

17 The Yadavas Prepare for War

1   The verse plays on *sarāga,* "reddened" and "passionate."

2   The expression *prajāpati* could refer to Yudhishthira, but Magha is no doubt also alluding to the celebrated myth of the destruction of Daksha's sacrifice by Shiva in his fierce Virabhadra form. Compare 19.54.

3   See chapter 3 n. 21 and chapter 16 n. 17.

4   Prasenajit is compared through wordplay to a rutting elephant.

5   The primary sense of *nīrājayati* is "illuminate," but the verb can also denote the ceremony for the purification of weapons, horses, elephants, and soldiers, performed by a king at the beginning of the campaigning season.

6   The secondary meaning here is: "A mighty warrior, fully prepared for combat with his enemies, is lauded by sweet singing bards as he washes his hands before lavishing gifts on his followers."

7   The secondary meaning here is: "The swords were like their lovers—exquisitely girdled, their teeth sparkling delightfully, and their dresses of a particular elegance; as they clung to their men in embrace, their body hair thrilled in excitement."

8   In the rainy season geese must make the arduous journey to Lake Manasa in the Himalayas.

9   See chapter 15 n. 41. V explains *suragaṇikāḥ* as referring to apsarases.

10   This verse may be an interpolation. It interrupts a cluster of verses describing military elephants and reprises 5.6. However, see chapter 11 n. 25.

11   V and M interpret the actions of the elephants as equivalent to women's behavior.

12   Freshly filled pots of water are redolent of auspiciousness.

13   A reference to Vishnu-Krishna as primal deity. Compare 13.8, 18.40, and 20.66.

14   The secondary meaning here is: "When mighty four-headed Brahma, the red one, was intending to create living creatures, the power of energy became predominant and outweighed the power of brightness." For Brahma, see chapter 9 n. 7; for the three creative powers of Samkhya philosophy, see chapter 15 n. 22.

15   Compare 64 and also 1.63.

16   The dust has the appearance of rut fluid. Alternatively, as the elephants of the quarters live high in the sky, the unaccustomed pleasure of bathing in dust causes them to become excited. See 64. M quotes a verse ascribed to the Mahabharata: "Women take delight in a lover, cows in wandering free, elephants in a rain of dust, and Brahmans in reviling others."

17   See chapter 16 n. 18.

18   The verse employs wordplay based on *rajasvala,* "dusty" and "menstruating." The secondary meaning here is: "Women when menstruating lose their attractiveness for a brief time; their faces become wan, they must wear drab clothes, and men cannot associate with them."

19   See chapter 3 n. 16.

20   Compare 57.

21   The expression *nabhaḥsad,* literally "sky dweller," normally denotes a god. V and M interpret it as referring to the *vidyādhara,* or wizard, a type of semidivine being possessed of the power of flight and skilled in magical arts who is frequently portrayed in Sanskrit literature as embroiled in amorous adventures.

22   V identifies the seven areas from which rut fluid emerges as being the elephant's two temples, two forehead lobes, tongue (*tālu*), chest, and trunk.

18 *The Battle Begins*

1   See chapter 5 n. 10.

2   V understands the reference as being to *śabdabrahman,* ultimate reality envisaged as sacral sound.

3   A playful, quasi-technical observation to be taken in conjunction with the following verse.

4   The verse plays on *vājin,* "feathered" and "horse."

5   The secondary meaning here is: "Acrobats jumped from the ground onto their partners' shoulders, then nimbly clambered upon their heads and made a superhuman leap, somersaulting in the air with ease."

6   An allusion to the rules of engagement in battle described at *Manusmṛti* 7.91–95. See Olivelle 2005: 159.

7   The secondary meaning here is: "A man married a woman because she was of good birth; despite being treated with consideration, she turned out to be unfaithful, for another man had craftily seduced her."

8   The verse plays on *bheda,* "piercing" and "parting," and *dhautadhārā,* "clean blade" and "fresh rain-shower."

9   Literally, "knowledgeable about stimulating excitement" (V) or "knowledgeable about getting elephants to their feet" (M).

10   Literally, "the Brahman." The Mahabharata describes how at the end of a world age Markandeya entered the child Krishna's mouth and saw the universe within him. See *Mahābhārata* 1975: 589–590. M refers to a puranic story in which Brahma, about to engage in the act of creation, entered the stomach of Vishnu in desire to see the previous creation.

11   The verse plays on *vyāptaṃ lokaiḥ,* "hemmed in by soldiers" and "filled with worlds."

12   Compare 5.12.

13   V takes *gātra* in its technical sense of "forequarters of an elephant" (compare Edgerton 1985: 117–118 s.v.), referring to an alternative explanation of the term as "trunk," but neither gloss fully fits the context.

14   The translation is tentative.

15   Compare 15.87 and 18.58–63 for dead warriors being carried away by apsarases, who live in Indra's heaven. Unlike the Valkyries, their counterparts in Nordic mythology, the apsarases, who are frequently associated with clouds, do not ride above battlefields dressed in armor.

16   A condensed reference to a complicated mythological episode.

Chandika, also known variously as Ekanamsha, Kalika, and Nidra (the personification of sleep), was substituted in the womb of Yashoda to protect the unborn Krishna from the murderous Kamsa. See Couture 2015: 93–97. The translation smoothes over the grammar, which would suggest that Yashoda was killed by Kamsa (understood so by V, but not by M), although the puranic versions of the story are clear that it was Chandika who suffered that fate.

17   An arrow with a semicircular tip.

18   See n. 15.

19   The woman would thus become a "true wife" (*satī*). This embodiment of marital loyalty was idealized in Indian warrior society. See chapter 9 n. 6.

20   Compare 13.52.

21   Arrows are compared through wordplay to birds.

22   Jackals were believed to emit fire when they howled.

23   The armies are compared through wordplay to rivers.

19   The Battle Rages

1   See chapter 1 n. 17.

2   The verse plays on the literal sense of the two warriors' names.

3   The verse plays on *śilīmukha,* "arrow" and "bee."

4   The verse plays on *bāṇa,* "arrow" and the name of a warrior.

5   The verse plays on *ojas,* which can variously mean "force," "luster," and "energy."

6   The verse plays on *mukta,* "released" and "set free," and *vilakṣa,* "missing the mark" and "embarrassed."

7   Fame was imagined as being of a lustrous white color.

8   The verse plays on *śiras,* "head" and "forefront, epicenter"; *vikāsin,* "blossoming" and "bold"; and *kusumalakṣman,* "flowery" and an epithet for Pradyumna.

9   Literally, "he of the fish ensign," an epithet connecting Pradyumna with the god of love, of whom he is the incarnation.

10   V identifies 26–29 as a unit of syntactically linked verses called *cakkalaka* (and by M, *kalāpaka*).

11   The secondary meaning here is: "Demure, ever so slender girls shrieked when impudent youths roughly tugged their hair."

12   The verse plays on *rāga,* "redness" and "passion." According to Indian aesthetic theory the amorous (*śṛṅgāra*) and fierce (*raudra*)

flavors (*rasa*) should not be used in conjunction. However, in this verse they are simply designated by name rather than evoked.

13 See n. 4 to the Sanskrit text of chapter 19. Elaborate patterned verse types such as the three mentioned here were generally employed in *mahākāvyas* when the subject was violent battlefield activity.

14 See n. 26 to the Sanskrit text of chapter 19.

15 See n. 8 to the Sanskrit text of chapter 19.

16 I take *rathyā* in the sense of "chariot" rather than the more normal "road."

17 The verse plays on *nāga*, "elephant" and "snake."

18 The secondary meaning here is: "The character of a musical work is established at the outset when the tones of its melody are enunciated successively in their basic configuration."

19 A convention of warfare as imaginatively envisaged in the *mahākāvya* genre and elsewhere is that when the thousandth warrior falls in combat, his corpse dances in celebration. See Kālidāsa, *Raghuvaṃśa* 7.51 and Pravarasena, *Setubandha* 13.64. I follow V in taking this verse to be describing the killer of a thousand opponents imitating this action.

20 The point of this verse derives from wordplay on *alaṃkara-ṇabhūṣita*, "decorated with ornaments" (*alaṃkaraṇa-bhūṣita*) and "fighting on a battlefield that was not Lanka" (*alaṃka-raṇabhū-uṣita*).

21 The verse plays on *aruṇa*, "red" and the name of the charioteer of the sun. Aruna was also known as Anuru, "Legless" (*anūru* literally denotes "thighless"), because when he was born, the lower part of his body was deformed. See *Mahābhārata* 1973: 71–72.

22 See chapter 17 n. 2.

23 Arrows are compared through wordplay to prostitutes.

24 The verse plays on *vājin*, "feathered" and "horse."

25 The secondary meaning here is: "Suppliants with reward in the forefront of their minds quickly thronged around the generous and through importuning received much money."

26 I follow V and M, who refer to elephant fighting as a spectator sport in which the beasts are separated by some sort of barrier or dais (*varaṇḍaka*).

27 The verse plays on *vihasta*, "agitated" and "without a trunk."

28 The verse plays on *śatapatra*, "a hundred chariots" and "lotus."

29   The verse plays on *matkuṇa,* "bug" and "tuskless elephant."

30   The verse plays on *nipātita,* "killed" and "representing a special case." Panini's grammar prescribes that words designating the relationships mentioned in the verse can be treated as special cases in particular rules. Compare 10.15 for a similar allusion.

31   The verse plays on *cāpa,* "bow" and "rainbow," and *sphuradraktaśatahrada,* "with hundreds of lakes of glinting gore" and "with brightly flashing lightning."

32   For elephants and bells, see 36 and also 4.20, 17.35, and 18.10.

33   Verses 83–87 form a syntactic unit (*kulaka*) describing Krishna.

34   Krishna is here envisaged as Vishnu.

35   Krishna is again envisaged as Vishnu.

36   The secondary meaning here is appropriate to Krishna's divine status: "The supreme being appears to advanced yogis confidently aspiring to liberation and to that end devoted to abandoning their physical bodies."

37   The verse plays on *guṇa,* "string" and "quality."

38   The secondary meaning here is: "Any man, however obscure, can gain a hearing if he is possessed of some talent."

39   Krishna is compared through wordplay to a rain cloud.

40   Literally, "without any parts" (*akala*), a characteristic of divinity.

41   The verse plays on *jīva,* "life" and "bowstring."

42   The verse plays on the verbal root *pā,* "protect" and "drink."

43   The overburdened earth is an epic motif that can be traced back into Indo-European antiquity. However, Vishnu-Krishna descends to earth to eliminate evil rather than overpopulation. Compare 1.36.

44   According to the Ramayana, Rāma pierced seven plane trees with one arrow to impress the monkey king Sugriva. See *Rāmāyaṇa* 1984: 77–78.

45   The verse plays on *manohṛtaḥ,* "captivating" and "taking life."

46   Krishna's arrows are compared through wordplay to birds of prey.

47   The verse plays on *hṛdaya,* "chest" and "heart," and *asra,* "blood" and "tears." At 109 and 110 Magha has fancifully implied a disconnection between the impact of Krishna's deadly arrows and his enemies' blood flowing on the battlefield described at 112 and 115.

48   This by no means linguistically sophisticated verse employs wordplay centering on the various possible referents of the

designation *hari* by which (following M) Krishna's attributes are compared to those of the gods Indra and Surya. These alternative meanings are: "Indra, destroyer of demonic Bali, tormenter of the virtuous, the god who had comfortably neutralized poison through drinking ambrosia, heroic in the face of every opponent, majestic lord of heaven, elder brother of Vishnu. He was like another Surya—Surya, the sun god, who destroys disease and grants strength to his devotees, drying up water in high summer, resplendent as he flies like a bird in the sky." After identifying a total of six layers of meaning in the verse (relating successively to Vishnu, Indra, Krishna, a lion, Krishna again, and Surya), V admits disarmingly that while his virtuoso exegesis does not necessarily reflect what Magha intended, it is nonetheless in keeping with the overall tenor of the verse.

49 "Enter the five elements" is a Sanskrit idiom for dying.

50 The verse plays on *ādhomukhya,* "turning downward."

20 The Killing of Shishupala

1 More precisely, saffron from Jaguḍa, in the region of what is now Afghanistan.

2 M explains that Yama has pledged not to tie up his hair until he has killed the enemy.

3 This verse encapsulates Shishupala's ostensible grievance against Krishna.

4 The secondary meaning here is: "Honest, successful, and plain-dealing kings with reliable allies may make a treaty with a vanquished foe if he is worthy."

5 The secondary meaning here is: "A servant employed by his master on a delicate mission cried out when through some mistake he was dragged into court and his life put in jeopardy." I follow V's explanation of *dṛḍhārti* as meaning "the ends of whose bow are tight" (*dṛḍha-arti*) and "in intense agony" (*dṛḍha-ārti*).

6 The arrows are compared through wordplay to a debater's words.

7 V and M are unclear about the point of the first line of this verse, which plays on *sapakṣa* in the senses of "ally" and "feathered." M explains: "A bird such as a heron and a friend come from an enemy do not bring cheer."

8 Ucchaihshravas was churned from the ocean before ambrosia (*amṛta*) emerged. See 2.107, 3.81, and 5.57.

9   V recounts a version of a story found in the Mahabharata. "Kadru
    and Vinata, daughters of the seer Daksha and wives of the sage
    Kashyapa, started a quarrel. The former said that the tail of the
    divine horse Ucchaihshravas was black, while the other said it was
    white. They had a wager about it, with the loser to become the
    winner's slave. Kadru was anxious and said to the snakes, 'Sons,
    you should know that I am in danger of being enslaved. The king
    of horses is white. Think of a plan and save your mother.' The five
    hundred snakes, Shesha, Vasuki, and the rest, were full of pride and
    said to her, 'You have made a rash promise! You are our mother,
    but Vinata is also our maternal aunt. What can we do?' Another
    snake, Takshaka, took pity on her and said, 'Be brave, Mother! I
    and the snakes will turn the king of the horses' tail black.' And
    they all covered his tail." In the Mahabharata version of this story
    (*Mahābhārata* 1973: 76–78) the sisters inspect Ucchaihshravas
    and see that there are in fact black hairs in his tail, whereupon
    Vinata becomes Kadru's slave. However, in a short interpolation
    in the story, the snakes are presented as changing their minds and
    carrying out Kadru's wishes. Magha seems to be following this
    version.

10 The snakes are compared through wordplay to dramas.

11 Peacocks are the traditional enemies of snakes. Compare 19.45.

12 The adjective *mālabhāriṇī,* "garlanded" is the name of the meter
    in which this verse is composed. This is a variety of the syllable-
    based *aupacchandasika* meter exemplified by 1–75 of this chapter.
    See Morgan 2011: 188–189.

13 Mountains originally possessed wings. See chapter 5 n. 10.

14 Vasuki was used as the rope when the gods churned the ocean.

15 The blazing heavens are compared through wordplay to a forest
    fire.

16 Krishna is referred to as *tridhāman,* a universalizing designation
    of Vishnu signifying "Of the Three Abodes." V and M take this as
    referring to the earth, the intermediate space, and the heavens.

17 Krishna is compared through wordplay to a doctor.

18 In decapitating Rahu, Vishnu reduced him to a mere bodiless head
    incapable of giving an embrace.

19 Thus emphatically confirming the identity of Krishna and Vishnu.

20 The opening words of the verse, *śriyā juṣṭam,* "tinged with beauty"
    or, alternatively, "conjoined with the goddess Shri," could be

taken either with *dhāma,* the undying subtle body, or with *vapus,* Krishna's physical body, which is literally and figuratively embraced by Shri. V quotes *Mahābhārata* 2.42.22–24 (*Mahābhārata* 1975: 104), which Magha follows closely in this verse. See Brockington 2010, and also Hudson 2008: 286 for an eighth-century sculpture panel from a temple in Kanchipuram depicting Shishupala's end.

Description of the Poet's Lineage

1   V provides an alternative name, Dharmalabha, slightly improbable for an early Indian ruler, that recalls the greeting *dharmalābhaḥ,* "May you fully attain the teachings of Jainism," given by a Jain monk to a lay follower. For the various names of Suprabhadeva's master found in the manuscripts, see Klatt 1890: 62.

2   Yudhishthira is the paragon of dutiful behavior in the Mahabharata.

3   The verse plays on *gauṇa,* "secondary meaning" and "relating to qualities."

GLOSSARY

Full descriptions and images of many of the plants and trees mentioned in *The Killing of Shishupala* can be found in the online Pandanus Database of Plants (iu.ff.cuni.cz/pandanus/database/).

AIRAVATA (*airāvata*) The elephant mount of the god Indra

AMARAVATI (*amarāvatī*) The city of the god Indra

ANDHAKA Name of a demon; also a name of the Yadava clan

APSARAS A type of semidivine dancer and courtesan living in the god Indra's heaven

ARJUNA One of the five Pandava brothers, known by the epithet "wealth-winner"

ARUNA (*aruṇa*) The dawn, charioteer of the sun

BANA (*bāṇa*) "Arrow," the son of the demon Bali

BALI A demon overcome by Vishnu in his Dwarf incarnation

BALARAMA (*balarāma*) Krishna's half brother

BHISHMA (*bhīṣma*) The son of Ganga and celibate great-uncle of the Pandavas

BRAHMA (*brahmā*) The god involved in cosmic creation at the beginning of each aeon

BRAHMAN (*brāhmaṇa*) A member of the learned priestly class

CHEDI (*cedi*) Name of the kingdom and the people ruled by Shishupala

DANU Mother of the demons

DARUKA (*dāruka*) Krishna's charioteer

DATTATREYA (*dattātreya*) An incarnation of Vishnu

DEVAKI (*devakī*) Krishna's mother

DHARMA Righteousness, duty

DRAUPADI (*draupadī*) Wife of the five Pandava brothers

DURYODHANA Prince of the Kaurava clan whose enmity toward the Pandavas precipitated a cataclysmic war

DVARAKA (*dvārakā*) The city of Krishna and the Yadava clan

GANESHA (*gaṇeśa*) The elephant-headed son of the god Shiva

GADA Krishna's younger brother

GANGA (*gaṅgā*) The heavenly and earthly river (Anglicized as "Ganges"), daughter of the sage Jahnu

GARUDA (*garuḍa*) Vishnu's vehicle; in appearance, half man and half bird

HIRANYAKASHIPU (*hiraṇya-kaśipu*) "Golden Robe," an earlier demonic incarnation of Shishupala killed by Vishnu in his Man-Lion incarnation

HANUMAN (*hanumat*) The

monkey companion of the hero-god Rama

HIMALAYA (*himālaya*) "The Snowy Place," the name of a mountain, personified as the father of Parvati

INDRA The king of the gods

INDRAPRASTHA The city of Yudhishthira and the Pandava brothers

JARASANDHA (*jarāsandha*) The king of Magadha and an ally of Shishupala

KAILASA (*kailāsa*) The name of a mountain in the Himalayas, the abode of the god Shiva

KAITABHA (*kaiṭabha*) A demon killed by Vishnu

KAMA (*kāma*) The god of love, armed with flowery arrows, who was incinerated by a blast of flame from the god Shiva's forehead eye

KAMA SUTRA (*kāmasūtra*) Sanskrit treatise on sexual etiquette written by Vatsyayana

KAMSA (*kaṃsa*) The incarnation of the demon Kalanemi; when king of Mathura, he was killed by his nephew Krishna

KAUSTUBHA The breast jewel worn by Vishnu and Krishna

KRISHNA (*kṛṣṇa*) The incarnation of Vishnu, ruler of Dvaraka, and counselor of the Pandava brothers

KUBERA The god of wealth

KUNTI (*kuntī*) The mother of the Pandava brothers; also called Pritha

KURU An ancestor of the Pandavas

LAKSHMANA (*lakṣmaṇa*) Half brother of Rama

LAKSHMI (*lakṣmī*) The goddess of prosperity; another name of Shri

MADHU Name of a demon killed by Vishnu

MAHABHARATA (*mahābhārata*) One of the two main Sanskrit epic poems

MAHAKAVYA (*mahākāvya*) "Great poem," the literary genre to which *The Killing of Shishupala* belongs

MANDARA Name of the cosmic mountain used by the gods and demons to churn the ocean and gain treasures such as the goddess Shri, the horse Ucchaih-shravas, the moon, and ambrosia

MAHISHMATI (*māhiṣmatī*) The city of Shishupala

MANASA (*mānasa*) Name of a lake in the Himalayas

MATHURA (*mathurā*) The city of Kamsa and former home of Krishna and the Yadavas

MAYA A demon who constructed the assembly hall of the Pandavas

MERU Name of the mountain located at the center of the world, around which the sun and moon revolve

MURA Name of a demon killed by Vishnu

NARADA (*nārada*) A brahman sage who, as the son of Brahma, is the intermediary between gods and men

NARAKA Name of a demon killed by Krishna

NATYASHASTRA (*nāṭyaśāstra*) Treatise on dramaturgy attributed to Bharata and dating from about the third century C.E.

PANDAVA (*pāṇḍava*) Family name of Yudhishthira, Bhima, Arjuna, Nakula, and Sahadeva, the five sons of Pandu with whom Krishna is allied

PANINI (*pāṇini*) The preeminent grammarian of the Sanskrit language

PARASHURAMA (*paraśurāma*) "Rama with the Axe," an incarnation of Vishnu; exterminated the warrior class after his father was killed by King Arjuna Kartavirya

PARVATI (*pārvatī*) "Daughter of the Mountain," the divine consort of the god Shiva; also known as Uma

PRADYUMNA The incarnation of the god of love; son of Krishna

PRITHA (*pṛthā*) Mother of the Pandava brothers; also known as Kunti

PURANA (*purāṇa*) A Sanskrit compendium of Hindu mythological tradition

PUTANA (*pūtanā*) Daughter of the demon Bali; nurse of Kamsa

RAHU (*rāhu*) The demon of the eclipse; possesses only a head

RAIVATAKA "Opulence," the name of a mountain in the Saurashtra

region of what is now Gujarat

RAMA (*rāma*) An incarnation of Vishnu; defeated Ravana, the demon king of Lanka, who had abducted his wife, Sita

RAMAYANA (*rāmāyaṇa*) One of the two main Sanskrit epic poems

RATI "Sexual Pleasure," the wife of Kama

RAVANA (*rāvaṇa*) An earlier demonic incarnation of Shishupala who, as the demon king of Lanka, was defeated by Rama

REVATI (*revatī*) The wife of Balarama

RUKMINI (*rukmiṇī*) Shishupala's betrothed, who was abducted and married by Krishna

SAMKHYA (*sāṃkhya*) "Enumeration," a dualist philosophical system

SATYA (*satyā*) A wife of Krishna

SATYABHAMA (*satyabhāmā*) A wife of Krishna

SATYAKI (*sātyaki*) An ally of the Pandava brothers

SHAIVA (*śaiva*) A follower of the god Shiva

SHESHA (*śeṣa*) The cosmic serpent who encircles the world and on whom Vishnu sleeps

SHISHUPALA (*śiśupāla*) "Child-protector"; a demonic figure, overcome by Vishnu in previous incarnations, reborn as king of the Chedis and enemy of Krishna

SHIVA (*śiva*) The god living on Mount Kailasa; rides the bull

Nandin, has the crescent moon in his matted hair, and is smeared with cemetery ashes in token of his ascetic practices

SHRI (*śrī*) The consort of Vishnu-Krishna and embodiment of royal majesty and prosperity; also called Lakshmi

SITA (*sītā*) The wife of Rama

UCCHAIHSHRAVAS (*uccaiḥśravas*) "Long Ears", "Loud Neigher," or "Far-famed," the divine stallion churned from the ocean by the gods and demons

UDDHAVA Name of an adviser to Krishna

UMA (*umā*) The consort of the god Shiva; also known as Parvati

VAISHNAVA (*vaiṣṇava*) Relating to Vishnu

VASUKI The king of the snakes

VEDA "Knowledge," the authorless and eternal body of texts regarded as the foundation of Hinduism

VINDHYA Name of a mountain and a range of mountains traditionally regarded as marking the boundary between northern and southern India

VISHNU (*viṣṇu*) The god who presides over cosmic transition and incarnates himself periodically to protect the world

VRISHNI (*vṛṣṇi*) Krishna's clan within the wider Yadava family

YADAVA (*yādava*) "Descendants of Yadu," the family lineage to which Krishna belongs

YAMA The ruler of the realm of the dead

YAMUNA (*yamunā*) Name of an earthly river whose water is black, and a goddess (Anglicized as "Jumna")

YUDHISHTHIRA (*yudhiṣṭhira*) The king and senior member of the Pandava family

BIBLIOGRAPHY

Editions and Translations

Durgāprasād, Paṇḍit, and Paṇḍit Śivadatta. 1927. Māgha. *Śiśupālavadha* with the commentary *Sarvaṅkaṣā* of Mallinātha. 9th edition, revised by Wāsudev Laxman Śāstrī Paṇśīkar. Bombay: Nirṇaya Sāgar Press.

Kāk, Rām Candra, and Harābhaṭṭ Śāstrī. 1990. Māgha. *Śiśupālavadha* with the commentary *Viṣauṣadhi* of Vallabhadeva. Dillī: Bhāratīya Buk Kārporeśan. Reprint of 1935 edition.

Musalgāonkara, Gajānanaśāstrī. 2006. Māgha. *Śiśupālavadha* with the commentary *Sarvaṅkaṣā* of Mallinātha. 2nd edition. Vārāṇasī: Caukhambā Saṃskṛt Bhavan. Original edition 1998.

Sutherland, J. C. C. 1839. "Sisupála Bad'ha, or Death of Sisupála by Mágha." *Journal of the Asiatic Society of Bengal* 8: 16–21.

Fauche, Hippolyte. 1863. *Une Tétrade, ou Drame, hymne, roman et poème.* Vol. 3: *Le Çiçoupâla-Badha: Poème en 20 chants par Mâgha.* Paris: Librairie de A. Durand et Librairie de Benjamin Duprat.

Cappeller, Carl. 1915. *Bālamāgha: Māgha's Śiśupālavadha im Auszuge.* Stuttgart: W. Kohlhammer.

Hultzsch, E. 1926. *Māgha's Śiśupālavadha nach den kommentaren des Vallabhadeva und des Mallināthasūri ins deutsch übertragen.* Leipzig: Verlag der Asia Major.

Bhandare, M.S.,ed. and trans.2010. *Śiśupālavadha of Māgha, Cantos I–IV.* Reprint edition. Varanasi: Chowkhamba Krishnadas Academy.

Other Sources

Ali, Daud. 2004. *Courtly Culture and Political Life in Early Medieval India.* Cambridge: Cambridge University Press.

Austin, Christopher. 2013. "The Fructification of the Tale of a Tree: The Pārijātaharaṇa in the *Harivaṃśa* and Its Appendices." *Journal of the American Oriental Society* 133: 249–268.

———. 2014. "The Abduction of Śrī-Rukmiṇī: Politics, Genealogy and Theology in *Harivaṃśa* 87–90." *Religious Studies and Theology* 33: 23–46.

Bakker, Hans. 2014. *The World of the Skandapurāṇa.* Leiden: Brill.

Bhāmaha. 1970. *Kāvyālaṅkāra*. 2nd ed. Edited and translated by P. V. Naganatha Sastry. Delhi: Motilal Banarsidass.

Bharavi. 2016. *Arjuna and the Hunter.* Edited and translated by Indira Viswanathan Peterson. Murty Classical Library of India 9. Cambridge, Mass.: Harvard University Press.

Brinkhaus, Horst. 2011–12. "Die Narakavadha-Episode in der epischpurāṇischen Sanskrit-Literatur—eine textgeschichtliche Studie." *Wiener Zeitschrift für die Kunde Südasiens* 54: 35–83.

Brockington, John. 2002. "Jarāsaṃdha of Magadha (MBH 2,15–22)." In *Stages and Transitions: Temporal and Historical Frameworks in Epic and Purāṇic Literature*, ed. Mary Brockington. Zagreb: Croatian Academy of Sciences and Arts, pp. 73–88.

———. 2010. "*sūrya ivāparaḥ*: Exemplary Deaths in the Mahābhārata." In *Release from Life–Release in Life: Indian Perspectives on Individual Liberation,* ed. Andreas Bigger et al. Bern: Peter Lang, pp. 21–32.

Brocquet, Sylvain. 2010. *La geste de Rāma: Poème à double sens de Sandhyākaranandin*. Pondicherry: Institut Français de Pondichéry.

Bronner, Yigal. 2010. *Extreme Poetry: The South Asian Movement of Simultaneous Narration.* New York: Columbia University Press.

Bronner, Yigal, and Lawrence McCrea. 2012. "To Be or Not to Be Śiśupāla: Which Version of the Key Speech in Māgha's Great Poem Did He Really Write?" *Journal of the American Oriental Society* 132: 427–455.

Bronner, Yigal, David Shulman, and Gary Tubb. 2014. *Innovations and Turning Points: Toward a History of Kāvya Literature.* New Delhi: Oxford University Press.

Caland, Willem. 2010 [1911]. "Über den Aberglauben betreffend die Haarwirbel des Pferdes." Translation by W. B. Bollée. *Studia Indologiczne* 17: 9–17.

Couture, André. 1991. *L'enfance de Krishna.* Quebec: Presses de l'Université Laval.

———. 2015. *Kṛṣṇa in the Harivaṃśa. Vol. 1: The Wonderful Play of a Cosmic Child.* New Delhi: D. K. Printworld.

Couture, André, and Christine Chojnacki. 2014. *Krishna et ses metamorphoses dans les traditions indiennes: Récits d'enfance autour du Harivamsha.* Paris: Presses de l'université Paris-Sorbonne.

Dandin. 1924. *Kāvyādarśa.* Edited and translated by S. K. Belvalkar. Poona: Oriental Book Supplying Agency.

Dave, K.N. 2005. *Birds in Sanskrit Literature.* Delhi: Motilal Banarsidass.

Dumézil, Georges. 1983. *The Stakes of the Warrior.* Berkeley: University of California Press.

Dundas, Paul. 2000. "The Meat at the Wedding Feasts: Kṛṣṇa, Vegetarianism and a Jain Dispute." In Joseph T. O'Connell (ed.), *Jain Doctrine and Practice: Academic Perspectives.* University of Toronto: Centre for South Asian Studies, pp. 95–112.

Edgerton, Franklin. 1985. *The Elephant-Lore of the Hindus: The Elephant-Sport (Matanga-Lila) of Nilakantha.* Reprint edition. New Delhi: Motilal Banarsidass.

Gerow, Edwin. 1971. *A Glossary of Indian Figures of Speech.* The Hague: Mouton.

Goodall, Dominic. 2001. "*Bhūte 'āha' iti pramādāt*: Firm Evidence for the Direction of Change Where Certain Verses of the *Raghuvaṃśa* Are Variously Transmitted." *Zeitschrift der Deutschen Morgenländischen Gesellschaft* 151: 103–124.

Goodall, Dominic, and Harunaga Isaacson. 2003. *The Raghupañcikā of Vallabhadeva.* Vol. 1. Groningen: Egbert Forsten.

Hahn, Michael. 2007. "Unnütze Spielereien? Zur Frage des Sinnes der figurativen Dichtung in der Sanskritliteratur." *Studien zur Indologie und Iranistik* 24: 67–89.

———, ed. 2013. *Śivasvāmin's Kapphiṇābhyudaya.* New Delhi: Aditya Prakashan.

Hara, Minoru. 1996–1997. "Śrī-Mistress of a King." *Orientalia Suecana* 45-46: 33–61.

———. 2001. "Apsaras and Hero." *Journal of Indian Philosophy* 29: 135–153.

Heesterman, J. C. 1957. *The ancient Indian royal consecration: the rājasūya.* 's-Gravenhage: Mouton.

Hudson, D. Dennis. 2008. *The Body of God: An Emperor's Palace for Krishna in Eighth-Century Kanchipuram.* New York: Oxford University Press.

Jacobi, Hermann. 1970 [1889]. "On Bhāravi and Māgha." In Hermann Jacobi, *Kleine Schriften.* Wiesbaden: Harrassowitz, pp. 447–471.

Kālidāsa. 1971. *Raghuvaṃśa.* 4th edition. Edited by Gopal Raghunatha Nandargikar. Delhi: Motilal Banarsidass.

Kielhorn, Franz. 1908. "On Śiśupālavadha II, 112." *Journal of the Royal Asiatic Society,* n.s., 34: 409–502.

Klatt, Johannes. 1890. "The Date of the Poet Māgha." *Wiener Zeitschrift für die Kunde des Morgenlandes* 4: 61–71.

Krümpelmann, Kornelius. 2000. *Das Dhuttakkhāṇa: Eine jinistische Satire.* Frankfurt: P. Lang.

Kuntaka. 1977. *Vakroktijīvita.* Edited and translated by K. Krishnamoorthy. Dharwad: Karnataka University.

Lienhard, Siegfried. 1984. *A History of Classical Poetry: Sanskrit-Pali-Prakrit.* Wiesbaden: Harrassowitz.

———. 2007. *Kleine Schriften.* Wiesbaden: Harrassowitz.

Mahābhārata. 1973. *The Mahābhārata,* vol. 1: *1. The Book of the Beginning.* Translated and edited by J. A. B. van Buitenen. Chicago: University of Chicago Press.

———. 1975. *The Mahābhārata,* vol. 2: *2. The Book of the Assembly Hall; 3. The Book of the Forest.* Translated and edited by J. A. B. van Buitenen. Chicago: University of Chicago Press.

———. 1978. *The Mahābhārata,* vol. 3: *4. The Book of Virāṭa; 5. The Book of the Effort.* Translated and edited by J. A. B. van Buitenen. Chicago: University of Chicago Press.

Matchett, Freda. 2001. *Kṛṣṇa: Lord or Avatāra? The Relationship between Kṛṣṇa and Viṣṇu.* London: Routledge.

McCrea, Lawrence. 2014. "The Conquest of Cool: Theology and Aesthetics in Māgha's *Śiśupālavadha.*" In *Innovations and Turning Points: Towards a History of Kāvya Literature,* ed. Yigal Bronner, David Shulman, and Gary Tubb. New Delhi: Oxford University Press, pp. 123–141.

McHugh, James. 2013. "Alcohol in Pre-modern South Asia." In *A History of Alcohol and Drugs in Modern South Asia,* ed. Harold Fischer-Tine and Jana Tschuranev. London: Routledge, pp. 29–44.

Mejer, Marek. 2007. "Buddhist Echoes in Māgha's *Śiśupāla-vadha.*" *Rocznik Orientalistyczny* 60:24.

Merutuṅga. 1901. *The Prabandhacintāmaṇi or Wishing-Stone of Narratives.* Translated by C. H. Tawney. Calcutta: Asiatic Society.

Meulenbeld, G. Jan. 2007–2008. "A Quest for Poison Trees in Indian Literature, Along with Notes on Some Plants and Animals of the Kauṭilīya Arthaśāstra." *Wiener Zeitschrift für die Kunde Südasiens* 51: 5–75.

Minkowski, Christopher Z. 2001. "The Interrupted Sacrifice and the Sanskrit Epics." *Journal of Indian Philosophy* 29: 169–186.

Morgan, Les. 2011. *Croaking Frogs: A Guide to Sanskrit Metrics and Figures of Speech.* Mahodara Press.

Olivelle, Patrick. 2005. *Manu's Code of Law: A Critical Edition and*

Translation of the Mānava-Dharmaśāstra. New York: Oxford University Press.

————. 2013. *King, Governance, and Law in Ancient India: Kauṭilya's Arthaśāstra.* New York: Oxford University Press.

Pāṇini. 1989. *Aṣṭādhyāyī.* Edited by Sumitra M. Katre. Delhi: Motilal Banarsidass.

Parpola, Asko. 2015. *The Roots of Hinduism: The Early Aryans and the Indus Civilization.* New York: Oxford University Press.

Patel, Deven M. 2014. *Text to Tradition: The Naiṣadhīyacarita and Literary Community in South Asia.* New York: Columbia University Press.

Peterson, Indira Viswanathan. 2003. *Design and Rhetoric in a Sanskrit Court Epic: The Kirātārjunīya of Bhāravi.* Albany: State University of New York Press.

Pollock, Sheldon. 2006. *The Language of the Gods in the World of Men: Sanskrit, Culture, and Power in Premodern India.* Berkeley: University of California Press.

Pravarasena. 2002. *Setubandha.* Edited by Ramnath Tripathi Shastri. Varanasi: Krishnadas Academy.

Rāmāyaṇa. The Rāmāyaṇa of Vālmīki: An Epic of Ancient India, vol. 4: *Kiṣkindhākāṇḍa.* 1984. Introduction, translation, and annotation by Rosalind Lefeber. Princeton: Princeton University Press.

Rau, Wilhelm. 2012 [1949]. "Vallabhadeva's Kommentar zu Māghas Śiśupālavadha: Ein Beitrag zur Textgeschichte des Māghakāvya." In *Kleine Schriften.* Wiesbaden: Harrassowitz, pp. 1–204.

Raven, Ellen M. 1994. *Gupta Gold Coins with a Garuḍa-Banner.* 2 vols. Groningen: Egbert Forsten.

Ṛg Veda. The Rigveda: The Earliest Religious Poetry of India. 2014. Translated by Stephanie W. Jamison and Joel P. Brereton. New York: Oxford University Press.

Saindon, Marcelle. 2009. *Trois manifestations de Vishnu: le Sanglier, l'Homme-Lion, le Nain: Les récits du Harivamsha.* Paris: Presses de l'université Paris-Sorbonne.

Salomon, Richard. 2014. "Māgha, Mahābhārata, and Bhāgavata: The Source and Legacy of the *Śiśupālavadha.*" *Journal of the American Oriental Society* 134: 225–240.

Schmid, Charlotte. 2010. *Le Don de voir: Premières représentations krishnaites de la région de Mathurā.* Paris: École française d'Extreme-Orient.

Sheth, Noel. 1999. "Salvation through Hatred." *Annals of the Bhandarkar Oriental Institute* 80: 167–181.

Siddharṣi. 1999. *Upamitibhavaprapañcakathā.* Edited by Vijayajinendrasūri. Śāṃtipurī: Harṣapuṣpāmṛta Jain Granthamālā.

Smith, David. 1985. *Ratnākara's Haravijaya: An Introduction to the Sanskrit Court Epic.* Delhi: Oxford University Press.

Sudyka, Lidia. 2002–2003. "From Aśvaghoṣa to Bhaṭṭi: The Development of the *Mahākāvya* Genre." *Cracow Indological Studies* 4–5: 527–545.

Tenshe, S. A. 1972. *Contribution of Māgha to Sanskrit Literature, with Special Reference to His Vocabulary.* Poona: Venus Prakashan.

Trautmann, Thomas. 2015. *Elephants and Kings: An Environmental History.* Chicago: University of Chicago Press.

Trynkowska, Anna. 2002–2003. "The Description of Kṛṣṇa in Māgha's *Śiśupālavadha.*" *Cracow Indological Studies* 4–5: 609–617.

———. 2004a. "The Structure and Function of the First Sarga of Māgha's *Śiśupālavadha.*" In *Essays in Indian Philosophy, Religion, and Literature,* ed. Piotr Balcerowicz, Marek Mejor, and Anna Trynkowska. Delhi: Motilal Banarsidass, pp. 479–487.

———. 2004b. *Struktura Opisów w "Zabiciu Śisiupali" Maghy.* Warszawa: Instytut Orientalistyczny Uniwersytet Warszawski.

———. 2007. "On Some Quotations of Māgha's Verses by Ludwik Sternbach: A Critical Review." *Rocznik Orientalistyczny* 60: 147–156.

Tubb, Gary. 2014a. "Baking Umā." In *Innovations and Turning Points: Towards a History of Kāvya Literature,* ed. Yigal Bronner, David Shulman, and Gary Tubb. New Delhi: Oxford University Press.

Tubb, Gary. 2014b. "*Kāvya* with Bells On: *Yamaka* in the *Śiśupālavadha.*" In *Innovations and Turning Points: Towards a History of Kāvya Literature,* ed. Yigal Bronner, David Shulman, and Gary Tubb. New Delhi: Oxford University Press, pp. 142–194.

Vātsyāyana. 1924. *Kāmasūtra.* Edited by Ramanand Sharma. Vārāṇasī: Kṛṣṇadās Akādamī.

Velankar, H. D. 1948–49. "Prosodial Practice of Sanskrit Poets." *Journal of the Bombay Branch of the Royal Asiatic Society* 24–25: 49–92

Viṣṇupurāṇa. 1997. Edited by M. M. Pathak. Vadodara: Oriental Institute.

Watson, Alex, Dominic Goodall, and S. L. P. Anjaneya Sarma. 2013. *An Enquiry into the Nature of Liberation: Bhaṭṭa Rāmakaṇṭha's Paramokṣanirāsakārikāvṛtti, a Commentary of Sadojyotiḥ's Refutation* of *Twenty Conceptions of the Liberated State (Mokṣa)*. Pondicherry: Institut Français de Pondichéry.

Zadoo, J. D. 1947. *A Critical Note on the* [sic] *Vallabhadeva's Commentary on the Shishupalvadham*. Kashmir Series of Texts and Studies No. 79. Srinagar: Normal Press.

Zumbroich, Thomas J. 2012. "From Mouth Fresheners to Erotic Perfumes: The Evolving Socio-cultural Significance of Nutmeg, Mace and Cloves in South Asia." *eJournal of Indian Medicine* 5: 37–97.

INDEX

ABOUT THE BOOK

Murty Classical Library of India volumes are designed by Rathna Ramanathan and Guglielmo Rossi. Informed by the history of the Indic book and drawing inspiration from polyphonic classical music, the series design is based on the idea of "unity in diversity," celebrating the individuality of each language while bringing them together within a cohesive visual identity.

The Sanskrit text of this book is set in the Murty Sanskrit typeface, commissioned by Harvard University Press and designed by John Hudson and Fiona Ross. The proportions and styling of the characters are in keeping with the typographic tradition established by the renowned Nirnaya Sagar Press, with a deliberate reduction of the typically high degree of stroke modulation. The result is a robust, modern typeface that includes Sanskrit-specific type forms and conjuncts.

The English text is set in Antwerp, designed by Henrik Kubel from A2-TYPE and chosen for its versatility and balance with the Indic typography. The design is a free-spirited amalgamation and interpretation of the archives of type at the Museum Plantin-Moretus in Antwerp.

All the fonts commissioned for the Murty Classical Library of India will be made available, free of charge, for non-commercial use. For more information about the typography and design of the series, please visit *http://www.hup.harvard.edu/mcli*.

Printed on acid-free paper by Maple Press, York, Pennsylvania.